"*With each chapter I read there is a weight lifting. I feel less nervous, less fearful. I am astounded that I actually feel my perspective expanding and opening right up. I feel my attachments to particular ideologies falling way. I just feel open and excited to continue on my journey.*" – Niki

"*Every word and explanation from 8 is like the truth of life 101 being told to me. The answers I have been without for 42 years. A relief and such excitement to hear them. Such a warmth in my heart and knowing. Thank you both!!*" – Jilly

"*Thank you, for bringing Spirit into our hearts, when we most needed it.*" – Gertrud

"*Wow, that was epic. So well worth the read. Resonates very highly with me. Thank you Zingdad.*" – Syme

"*Zingdad, I want to thank you profusely for everything you are doing here. There are not many places out there where these topics are discussed freely, and I feel like applauding J-D and 8 for putting all of it so eloquently.*" – M. Powers

"*As always, your understanding resonates with and mirrors my own. Your eloquence in putting it into words, however, exquisite heart-song!*" – Mathew

"*I feel warmth and joy reading this, the feeling spreads from my heart and into every little particle in my body, what a great feeling*" – Ann

"*My mind has been so irreversibly opened by these writings. I am so thankful for the wider perspective. "If you can't see the perfection you* are standing to close to the picture.*" Plays in my mind every time I see or hear anything that displeases me or leads me to habitually label someone or something as evil. This is really powerful*". – Oneness411

"When I read **The Ascension Papers** *for the first time, my heart and soul said yes, yes, yes...* " –wolfke74

THE ASCENSION PAPERS

Book 1

by
Zingdad

* * * * *

Me 'n My Dog
Publishers

ME 'N MY DOG PUBLISHERS

Published by
Me 'n My Dog Publishers
PO Box 2100, Knysna, 6570, South Africa

First Published as an e-book by Zingdad.com 2010
First Published in paperback by Me 'n My Dog Publishers 2011
Third Edition published in paperback and e-book by Me 'n My
Dog Publishers 2014

Printed by Lightning Source, Inc.

* * * * *

ISBN: 978-0-620-62223-3

CONTENTS

To Lisa

Who was so much a part of the creation of this book that she is my co-author in all but name.

I could not have asked for a better journey-mate... Nor a better journey!

About The Ascension Papers

A note from the author

*"Imagine if you could re-create the world any way you wanted and invite your soul-family to co-create it with you. This is what I am doing. And **The Ascension Papers** is my invitation... but only **you** will know if this invitation is for you or not..."*

Dear Reader

When I first sat down to write this work I had no idea whatsoever that the end result would be a book. The sum total of my writings up to that point had been a number of short channellings posted on various Internet forums. I had no inclination towards ever being an author at all. Then, in May of 2008, after having a life-changing spiritual experience (as detailed in Chapter 7), I decided I that needed to make sense of my self, my life, my pain and my confusion in a more ordered fashion. So I sat down to record some conversations with my spirit-family. That was really meant to be for my own purposes and, perhaps, also to be shared on those same Internet forums. But, what followed, vastly surpassed those ambitions!

I brought an open heart and mind, an insatiable curiosity and teachability to the table. What I was given in return was the most amazing journey into consciousness imaginable. Chapter followed chapter, each one building upon what had gone before, gradually constructing an unbelievably detailed, coherent picture of the way life works and why things are the way they are. But, more than bringing simple understanding, the truths uncovered brought me profound peace, joy and release from the fear and pain that had gnawed at my soul for my entire life. Fear was alchemically transmuted into Love. A victim-mindset was transformed into creator-consciousness. As a result of the writing of this work, I came to understand myself and the world I live in, in a whole new way. A way which liberates me to be the very best that I can be. A way that allows me to awaken to the magnificence that lies within. Writing this book has sparked the most profound growth and transformation in my being. At the time of writing it was, quite simply, the best, most important, thing that I had ever done. And it has been the foundation upon which I have continued to create myself and from which I have continued to give my gifts.

And, yet, for all that, I also managed to get something quite fundamentally wrong in the telling of this life-changing tale. And the awareness of this error has been a burden on my heart for almost two years now. On the one hand I still loved this work and felt inordinately proud of it – and the impact it was reportedly having on countless readers the world over. But on the other hand I had a heaviness in my heart over a particular flaw in the core of the book. And then, finally, in June of 2014, after a sequence of remarkable events, I was gifted the wisdom and insight to see how to correct the error. With this new understanding, the book would not simply be corrected... it would actually function at a whole higher frequency of consciousness. And this transformation will be made clear to you as you read this, the 3rd edition of **The Ascension Papers**, as I have not sought to hide or obfuscate my earlier error. I have woven it back into the re-telling in an honest and transparent fashion.

And now I feel the profoundest joy in reissuing this book. My heart and soul sing with a sense that now, at last, I have *really got it right*.

And in this process of re-writing I also came to understand that I really needed to make this material available for free. Exactly how I reached that realisation is also explained in this work. But the bottom line is that this e-book version is absolutely free of charge and you are not just permitted, but actually *encouraged,* to share it. If you find it useful and enjoyable, go ahead and send it on to everyone you know! Share it in any way you like (see the licence notes for specifics and details). And if you wish to say "thank you" or to support my work, then you may buy the paperback version or visit my website to peruse my other offerings (see the Closing Thoughts at the end of the book for more details).

What a wondrous journey it has been for me to write this book. And what a delight to be able to share it with all my readers, website members, friends and brothers- and sisters-in-spirit all over the world... to be able to share it with *you*.

What you can expect to gain from reading *The Ascension Papers* depends entirely upon you. This is not a work that demands of you that you should believe what is espoused and it certainly does not promise to rescue you from your life. But it is my firm conviction that the content of this book can help you, if you are willing to take the journey, to discover your own magnificence...to discover that you are perfect as you are... that you are, and always have been, the creator of your own reality... that you are a being of pure, radiant love.

This book is the record of my journey to self-discovery, but the overwhelming response that I have received to date from readers indicates that it has, and can be, an invaluable guide for you on **your** journey to self-discovery too. And so it is with the greatest love and joy that I share it with you.

Some of the topics covered in this book include:

- Why are we actually here? Why did we incarnate as humans and what is the meaning of this crazy life here on planet Earth?

- What can we know of our Creator? Are we all truly one with God? And if we are, what does that really mean for us?

- What is the nature of the "Higher-Self" and what is our relationship with our "Higher-Selves"?

- What is a "Spirit-Guide"?

- What is **truth** really? And what, if anything, is unarguably, irreducibly true?

- What is **love** really? And what about other emotions, such as joy? What are they and why do we feel them?

- If the Creator, God, is good and loving, then why does evil exist? And why is there fear and pain?

- And why is the world in the state it is in and how did it come to be like this?

- Are there shadowy figures running the world from behind the scenes – and what does that mean to me in my life?

- What about 2012 and the apocalypse and the Mayan calendar and all that? Why did nothing seem to change in 2012, despite all the hype surrounding that time?

- What about religion... prophets, saviours, angels, demons, devils, heaven and hell? What of this is true and what does it mean for you and I?

- And does science have anything of value to say to us as beings that are on a spiritual path?

- Can we find our way to feeling truly at one with ourselves: whole, healed, peaceful and joyful?

- And is it true that we are, each of us, creating our reality? And if it is, why are we making such a mess of things? And, more importantly, how can we begin to get it right now?

...and this is just a smattering of the many interesting topics that will be addressed in, I'm sure you will agree, quite a refreshing new way. But all of the many and varied topics will ultimately serve one grand purpose. And that is to set before you an invitation *to step into the power of your divine, limitless self*! To move into right relationship with all that you truly are, and therefore into right relationship with all of life.

I, as the incarnated aspect of a much greater being, have the wonderful privilege of bringing this invitation to you here, in this life, on planet Earth. If you accept the invitation, then you will be able to join me and a host of other beings as we begin to co-create the most wondrous future reality imaginable... a whole new life in a whole new world in a grand, golden age!

But I won't go into the details of that now. It will all unfold as you read this work.

I **do not** insist that you must agree with me, believe what I say or subjugate your truth to mine. That is the opposite of what I want. I simply invite you to read what I have written with your own discernment and truth firmly in place. If you find resonance with what is presented, then your heart is telling you that the ideas presented here are "right for you".

You will notice that this work is presented in the form of a series of conversations between myself and a variety of spirit beings. You might wonder how I come to be able to create these dialogues with beings that are not, in the normal sense of the word, present on this Earth. In essence, the answer is that I have spent many years and a great deal of dedicated effort in teaching myself how to do this. I will, in due course, as a part of a follow-up work, explain exactly how I do what I do and offer some thoughts as to how you too may develop such a facility should you so desire. I don't like to call what I do "channelling". I do not give over my faculties to another being to speak though me. I prefer to call it "intuitive conversation". I simply ask the questions and then allow the truth in my heart to provide me with an answer. And then I type what I receive. But it is not really important **how** I derive these words. I do not want to claim any authority for these words as a result of the fact that they ostensibly come from some great beings from the higher-dimensional far-beyond. I would very much hope that you will decide for yourself to what degree these words are true for you based upon your own resonance with the words themselves.

Finally, you might notice that the earlier chapters of this book are less fluid and possibly more naïve than the later chapters. In updating this work I considered revising the first chapters to bring them up to the standard of the later chapters. I decided against this course, however, as this is how the book unfolded for me and for those who were reading it, chapter-by-chapter on my website, when I was writing it. This is the progression of my own soul as a result of being exposed to the ideas presented herein. Certainly the latter chapters are my best, but equally they were only possible as a result of the groundwork laid in the early chapters. So I let it stand as is.

And now, without further ado, I present to you my offering of love to the world, a gift which I freely give to you, with a joyful and open heart. Here is: *The Ascension Papers*, by Zingdad.

With so much love,

Zingdad

Arn "Zingdad" Allingham
Knysna, South Africa
15 July 2014

* * * * *

CHAPTER 1.
AN INTRODUCTION
TO ZINGDAD

My dear reader,

Perhaps you will find it overly self-indulgent of me that I begin this work with a whole chapter dedicated to introducing myself to you. And, when you begin to read this chapter, perhaps you will find it a little strange that I relate my "past life" stories to you.

In your position I might very well be wondering, *"Where is this all leading?"* And so I find myself begging your patience, even as you first begin this journey with me. There is a very good reason that I **must** begin this work with this introduction, why I **must** tell you of my experiences in re-incarnation. You see, these stories, **my stories,** are not simply the means by which I have been able to experience and discover all that I have needed in order to be able to be the scribe of this work; they also form the examples that I have to offer you in support and explanation of the truths and insights offered in later chapters.

So bear with me, dear reader, as I tell you of the genesis of my soul, of the lifetimes that I have lived and (briefly) of what this has meant to me. And I very much do believe that you will feel amply rewarded as you delve into the following chapters and find yourself armed with the means for deeper comprehension.

I have spent a lot of energy in this lifetime in trying to find true inner-peace, self-love and self-trust. Early on, I realised that I would struggle to heal my inner-pain if I did not know what had caused it in the first place. So, an important part of my journey has included a deep foray into that which occurred prior to this life and the discovery, for myself, of who I **really** am. I derived this information from conversations, such as those that will follow in this book, through meditation, hypnosis, auto-hypnosis and also from a couple of conversations with my lady-love's "Higher-Self" whilst she was in a trance state. I furthermore experienced an intensive series of amazingly healing hypnotic regressions with a gifted hypnotherapist. And while my story is subject to change as I continue to discover more about myself, below is a brief introduction to who I am.

Origins

I will start my story with a council meeting of the group of Light-Beings who created this reality. They were discussing how this reality that we inhabit would be brought to a close so that a new reality could take its place. A bit like one game coming to an end so that another can be played. The way these games are played is that each Light-Being is responsible for a particular role in each game. The current game in question, our whole reality, is quite an interesting one. It is a game where some of these Bright Ones had created many manifestations (also called incarnations) that had been able to experience "individuality". In order to make this game work, something pretty radical had to be achieved. The aspects of the Bright Ones that were to play inside the game had to actually forget that they are all ONE; they had to forget their own eternal, immortal nature. Nowhere in All That Is had such a thing been done before.

In order to give the game direction, the concept of "polarity" had been set into place. In the absence of the knowledge of their own divine purpose, players needed something else to give them a spur to growth and progression. Previous games had floundered as a result of insufficient impetus. And so it was decided that there would be two main "camps", which would result in rivalry, competition and conflict. The two camps were defined by whom the players would serve. On the one side would be those that serve themselves, and on the other side would be those that serve others. And so the game is being played out with fragments of the Bright Ones having incarnations in the system through which they have been experiencing the ecstasies and the miseries of life in this place. In so doing, they have been discovering who they really are from a position of absolute forgetfulness. It is a marvellous, amazing, grand experiment in consciousness and the rewards are truly phenomenal. But now, as the time approaches to bring the game to a close, the Council gathers to see what must be done. It is perceived that there will be some considerable difficulty in ending the game successfully without causing harm and trauma to the players; those aspects of the Bright Ones that are deeply engaged in the game as incarnated souls.

Can you see the problem?

In order for the game to work, all the players had to forget that they were just players and engage very deeply with the game, **as if it were utterly real and true**. As they played the game of separation they would come to feel powerful emotions, such as hatred and anger towards some and kindness and need towards others and this would compel them to bury themselves very deeply in the game. And so it was that players would find themselves unable to even **begin** to conceive of it that the game was not completely real and completely serious. Which was fine, for so long as the game was to continue, but a problem occurred when the Bright Ones wanted to end the game. Beings as totally engrossed in the game as the players are will not simply stop playing and return to full remembrance when it is time to stop! And their free will cannot simply be breached and the game forcibly ended, as this would cause the players profound trauma and teach them that they are **not** the creators of their own reality. This would undo the whole point of the game, which is growth and learning; particularly learning about creation.

So, ending the game would have to be done carefully and with some delicacy. The only way to do it would be bring to the game a great transformational turning point in which each and every manifestation could, themselves, begin to awaken to the fact that they are immortal beings of light simply experiencing an illusory, transient reality. Only then would they have the wisdom and power to choose to leave the game voluntarily. And so it was decided that each player would be awakened at an appointed time. Each of the Light-Beings then put their plans in place to bring the game to a successful close.

It is not mine to know what all of the Light-Beings decided. I know only a little of what one of those Light-Beings did. And now I will draw your attention to this one particular Light-Being. Though names are of no use to such beings, they are of some use to us, so we shall call this being Joy-Divine or J-D for short. J-D was invited to come and play this game, specifically to assist with the great transformation that would eventually enable the ending of that game. In order to do what he came to do, J-D saw that he would need to re-order the whole game just a little by bringing his own energy to play in the system. For these beings, you see, there is no such thing as time. There is consequently no problem in redoing the game from the beginning in order to end it differently. And you can keep re-doing until you achieve the desired outcome and then **that** is the version of events deemed "most valid". So J-D came to hold one of the roles in the game. But J-D did not create the endlessly recursive self-fragmentations that many of the other Bright Ones did. This was not originally his game, you see, and so he did not seek to populate it with many billions or even trillions of aspects of himself as some of the others did. But he **did** seek to understand the game in great depth. And it is really so that the deepest, hermeneutic understanding of a thing can only come from experiencing it yourself. J-D knew that he needed this kind of understanding in order to offer the assistance that was required of him. And so it was that he decided to introduce a manifestation of Self into the game. From within his own being he created a being which may be called "Delight". Delight would be that which carried the light of Joy-Divine into the densest depths of the game. Delight would in fact be the incarnating portion of Joy-Divine...

And that, perhaps it will not surprise you to discover, is **my** own Higher Self.

A Beginning...

In the very earliest memory of my individual existence that I have been able to find, I was slowly, dreamily, driftingly becoming conscious of "selfness". I was being lovingly cradled within the very being of Joy-Divine. I knew only oneness and belonging. Infinite love was my sustenance. The deepest bliss was my every experience. Slowly, my consciousness arose from this slumbering joy and I began to formulate my first thoughts. As I became aware of my own beingness I conceived the thought, "*Here am I.*" And then the question, "*What am I?*"

And with infinite love and gentleness, Joy-Divine began to answer me. In some ways, this lifetime and those that went before it are a part of the infinite, unending answering of that question. For, by living and **be**ing I am discovering myself, who I am and what I am. You see, Bright Ones don't communicate in thoughts and words as we do. Their communications are in whole creations! Our entire universe is really just a part of an unfolding conversation between the Bright Ones. And as I am here discovering who I really am, it is also Joy-Divine engaged in the act of telling Delight the answer to the question, "*What am I?*" played out in dramatic form through all the occurrences in my various incarnations. It's an amazing thing, really. And maybe it is thus for you too? Perhaps you too are that which is busy answering the question, "*What am I?*" for yourself. I think this is so, don't you?

But now to the question of why Delight is here and therefore why I, Zingdad, am here. For beings to move forward they must conceive of a purpose for themselves. Delight has the purpose of being "an Interventionist". What exactly "an Interventionist" is, is a long story that I shall tell on another occasion – for now kindly accept that it is a being that travels around the spiritual realms assisting others when they become stuck in the creations of their own making. And so Delight would help here in the work of the transformation of this reality in a... well... a delightful way, really. But you know, you can't help a friend with their pain if you don't understand what they are going through. So, before Delight could help, he had to completely immerse himself in this reality. He had to incarnate a few times and completely lose himself in this reality. And then, right on cue, during his final incarnation at the moment of the great transformation of the game, he had to remember himself and awaken and ascend back out of the system. Only then would he have sufficient understanding to really help and do what he had come to do. And, of course, this is what I am right now endeavouring to do.

I remember beginning my descent into this system. I left the warm embrace of Joy-Divine and began to enter via the higher dimensions of this reality for the very first time. And then, with a shock, I began to fall. I fell and fell. As I plummeted though the densities of creation, I began to realise that I was losing my connection with the oneness. I began to feel the terrible pang of a completely new experience – getting lost in the coldness of desperate aloneness. My vision began to shrink; I could no longer see what the results of my actions would be! I no longer knew that everything was perfection.

There was so much I suddenly couldn't and didn't know. As I conceived of the fact that I didn't **know** what would happen, an entirely new experience gripped my heart – **fear**! If I didn't know what would come next, how could I know I would be okay? I couldn't! I felt the black robes of the Veil of Unknowing close around me and it felt like icy fingers squeezing my heart. This was agony! And still I fell and fell. And then came the oblivion of forgetting both the pain of the falling and the bliss of what had come before that. The anguish faded. Memory faded. Consciousness became dim. Everything turned slowly to blackness. And then I began to look through blurred eyes upon a strange and incomprehensible new world.

I didn't know it then but my first incarnation had begun...

My Life in Lyra

My first lifetime was on a planet in the star system of Lyra, so-named after the lyre (a type of harp), which is also a useful analogy for the way in which life was created there. Many beings had their first incarnation in Lyra, which was much less dense than here on Earth. Bodies were far more subtle than these that we now inhabit. A tonal vibration in the light was what caused bodies to manifest – hence the "harp" analogy. Life on this planet in Lyra was good. It was a place of love and gentleness where joy was used as a vehicle for teaching. Each person was encouraged to follow their greatest bliss, to find their unique and special gift and then to express that which they most loved doing. There was no competition and no punishment. Each being was valued for who they were and the contribution they made. And everyone gave their best at all times.

Physically, the beings were fair of skin and hair and had blue eyes. I still bear those features now out of a sense of identification with them. They were a graceful and vital people who knew that their bodies were a divine gift to be loved and cherished and they understood how to treat their bodies respectfully. And this is one of the reasons that they lived to incredibly great ages. But there was another, more important reason: in the societies of this place were teachers who passed on to others the teachings of physical ascension. As a result of learning this, the Lyrans did not age as we typically do here on Earth. As young ones grew up and matured into adults they would, at some point, begin to show an interest in learning the ways of the spirit. They would request to be taught. The process of learning about this was slow and gentle, with the process itself being valued far more than the outcome. As their training advanced, so these beings would become wiser and more powerful in the ways of spirit. Eventually they would begin to gain a brightness, as their aura would begin to glow, and beings of great age could immediately be identified by the radiance of their aura. But their bodies, strangely enough, did not age. To look into such a being's eyes was to feel blessed and loved. As their training and spiritual growth continued, these beings would become more light and less matter. And then, when they had done what they had come for, they would finally and completely transform their physical bodies into light bodies and leave that world for subtler realms of spirit. A wonderful thing to observe.

The Lyrans lived in absolute harmony with the land. They did not think of plants, animals and their planet as something to use and consume but rather knew that they were one with these. The land was respected as their own mother. If a plant or animal was required to sacrifice its body for something that was needed for the people, then it was respectfully asked for that sacrifice. If permission was given then the ending of the life was done with great reverence, respect and appreciation. Life there was truly a great, harmonious partnership and each worked always for the greater good of the all.

My clearest memory of my own life in Lyra is of me standing looking over a moon-lit ocean with a being called Adamu. Though not my father, he had been the one who had raised me and had taught me the ways of the people. He was a wise and respected elder. A powerfully built, leonine man with a flowing beard, sapphire eyes and the brightest auric glow.

My memory starts with him standing opposite me, engaging me in a serious conversation. He was explaining to me that I was not to remain with them... not to eventually return to the light in the way that they did. He was pointing to the stars and telling me that my destiny lay "out there". He skipped a stone across the still, moonlit ocean as a metaphor for how I must hop across a few other lives in other places in my coming progression, not stay in one place with them. I was sobbing. The fact that my leaving meant that I would have to physically die was not the source of my distress. Everyone in that world knew that death was nothing more than a transition to another state. The source of my grief was quite simply that I did not want to leave there. I had found a great love for those people and for Adamu, with his gentle, loving guidance of me in particular. I didn't want to go and Adamu of course didn't want me to go either, as he loved me. But this was my destiny.

Adamu said to me, "*Soon enough you will be on your way and you'll have forgotten us.*"

"*Never!*" I said, "*I'll never forget you. And I'll remember this moment forever.*"

And I have.

I will always love the people of Lyra. They gave me my first life and my grounding in this reality. I knew such unconditional love and true belonging amongst them. I had a place "to come from" and even though I would always be a wanderer, still I would always know what it is to have had a **home**.

And I would remember Adamu. This current incarnation of mine has been infused with a sense of missing someone; an older, fatherly figure who I knew should be there in my life, but was not. As I began to remember Adamu and find him in my meditations and hypnotic regressions, that gap in my life came to be filled. I came to remember the depth of my love and connection with this most amazing being. And this is how this memory survived the deep forgetfulness that comes from reincarnating into this world. I said I would remember... and I did. And as I re-connected with Adamu in this life-time and learned to have intuitive conversations, I also realised that he was a font of deep wisdom and profound truth, which always came cloaked in compassion. So I started to make his words available for others to read on various forums on the Internet. It was thanks to Adamu that I could develop this skill at intuitive conversation at all. He has again come to be a wonderful source of guidance and advice to me. And friendship too.

Isn't that strange? I appear to be a grown-up, adult man with an imaginary friend!

But back to the story. As I have mentioned, most beings left life in Lyra by means of a bodily ascension into the light. But this was not my path. I was to go the way of those who did not leave into the light. I walked into the ocean in the Bay of Leaving until I was chest deep in the moonlit water and then, just as I had been taught to do, I lifted my spirit-body out of my physical body and severed the connection between the two. My lifeless body fell back into the waters, the waves closed over it. And then I was gone.

The oceans would, in due course, take care of the cleansing and nothing would be left of me in Lyra but memories.

A SOLDIER'S LIFE

Life number two was my life as a soldier.

The civilisation into which I was born was engaged in an inter-planetary war with another civilisation. I have no memory of the specifics and so I can't tell you if there were great galactic alliances at war or just two opposing planetary civilisations battling it out. These things I don't remember at all. What I do know is that I had been born into the life of a soldier garrisoning a mining colony on a little planet far from our home-world. The planet itself was not quite solid. I can't say for sure what it was composed of, but the effect was that one could pilot a vehicle into the planet without too much difficulty. Perhaps it was a bit like Jupiter or Saturn and was essentially condensed gasses? Certainly, the planet was utterly inhospitable to life, as we had to be inside protective vehicles or structures at all times. But, whatever the case, in this life I was one of a group of soldiers who had been assigned the role of guarding the mining operations on this semi-solid little planet.

The life I lived there was quite different from any here on Earth. For one thing, it seems we soldiers were genetically modified to fulfil our function. One of the results of this was that none of us was able to reproduce, as this would have been counter-productive to the optimal fulfilment of our role. It seems our bodies were designed to remain sexually immature our entire lives and so the distinction between the genders was definitely not as pronounced as it is here on Earth. I am confused about this, but there might even have been more than just two genders! What I am sure of is that the soldiers were not exclusively male. But, as I say, gender wasn't the same issue as it is here on Earth. I believe we were, however, somewhat sexual with each other but that it was more of a playful, loving, bonding experience than anything else. But, be that as it may, the group of soldiers with me on that planet were my everything. They were the only family I had ever known; they were my friends, my lovers and my reason for being. If I think back on it now, my situation in that life seems very peculiar to my current sensibilities, but it felt completely natural and right to me then. We were happy in our own way and there was certainly a greater sense of belonging and group identity than I have ever felt in my current lifetime.

As a soldier, my designated role was to pilot a particular military vehicle. It was something between a very small space-ship and an armoured car. This one-man vehicle could not only travel on the surface of the planet but could also push down into the planet itself and manoeuvre under the surface. It sustained life-support for me under all the varied and extreme conditions on that planet. I'm sure that this was a scout craft and, if it had any armaments at all, these would have been quite light. I think my role was really just to guard and patrol. In the memories that I have it seems as if I didn't take my responsibilities too seriously at all. Like a big kid with a toy, I really enjoyed driving my little craft around and pushing it down into the depths of the planet only to pull back up and come bursting up onto the surface. I got quite a thrill out of that craft, but I certainly did not behave like a soldier engaged in the life-and-death responsibility of defending a strategic asset in times of war!

On a day, it was my turn to man the control room in a satellite high above the planet. While I was on duty I was looking through a window at the planet below and something completely beyond my comprehension happened. All I can say is that the little planet, with all its inhabitants, was stomped out of existence before my very eyes! Everything was, quite simply, wiped out of existence by some inexplicable phenomenon. A **huge** grey "thing" passed though that reality and utterly obliterated the whole planet! I had no way of making sense of what I had just observed. This didn't relate to anything I had ever even heard of. I was thoroughly traumatized and left in a deep state of shock. Everyone I loved – all my friends, my family, my lovers, my home, my reason for living – **everything** that had meant anything to me was wiped out in one unfathomable instant. I was left utterly alone in a small satellite that was now no longer tethered to a planet. I don't know what I did next. That little satellite would not have sustained my life for very long. I know I drifted for a while, lost in abject grief. Perhaps I died of a lack of air, food or water.

Perhaps I terminated myself. That is not in my memory. All I find there is a muggy fog of loss and grief... and then nothing.

Lost in My Own Dream World

In life number three, I had some kind of mental incapacity. I am almost completely certain that it was severe autism from which I suffered. What I know is that my thoughts did not have the same structure as they do now. It was as if I thought in comic-book pictures and icons rather than in words or complex ideas. I was unable to speak and instead made gibberish sounds. This life played out in what was quite possibly 16th century Europe (or some reality quite a lot like that) and life there was hard, mean and cruel. People with challenges such as I suffered were considered a useless burden.

This life was dichotomously desperately unhappy and yet also blissfully joyful. You see, I was not treated very well by my fellow human beings. For example, as soon as I was old enough to go out amongst the other children they noticed my strangeness and began to taunt me mercilessly. They threw stones at me and chased me with sticks like a wild animal sometimes. The only one who really loved me and was eternally kind to me was my older sister. She was pure gentleness and goodness.

Then there was an uncle who came to visit sometimes. On these occasions he would find opportunities to be alone with me so that he might sexually abuse me. And, of course, I was powerless to ever tell anyone about this. My only protection was to stick to my sister's side whenever he was around and then, though his eyes burned holes in me, he'd leave me alone. But if he ever found me without her... well, it got pretty awful. An uncomprehendingly painful, wrong, strange experience that hurt and hurt and I had no way of processing it or understanding it. I most certainly had no way of defending myself or of stopping him.

But that life was very far from being all bad. Sometimes I would be able to slip into an altered state of consciousness in which everything was beautiful. I remember seeing angels of light and fairies and sprites. I saw the golden auras in the life around me. I saw the pulsations of energy in the plants. I saw the zip-zap of energy communications between the stars and the flows and spirals of energy in the planet's etheric body. I saw wondrous things in those times. This brought me deep joy and healed my pain. So that was okay. But I think my family were disturbed by the fact that I'd sit on my own, staring into space, cooing and giggling to myself with pleasure.

And then, things being what they were in those days, my sister was no more than 15 or 16 when she was married off to some veritable stranger from some far off town and she had to leave to go and live with him. I know now that she tried very hard to make this okay for me. I know she tried to tell me what was happening. I remember lying with my head in her lap while she cried bitterly, explaining things to me with words that meant nothing at all to me. All I knew was that for some time she was always unhappy. And then a horse-drawn cart came to fetch her and she was gone. I remember watching it carrying her away from me, down the lane into the bleak snow-laden forest.

Soon after that, the abusive uncle came around again. When I saw him I knew what was coming and, in my desperation, I ran away to find my sister. I ran down the road along which the cart had departed. I ran and ran. I ran until my lungs ached, I ran until I fell down exhausted. Night began to fall and I huddled against a tree for some shelter from the cold. I was very, very scared – every forest sound and shadow caused monster images to flash in my mind.

I don't remember my actual end but I suppose I died of exposure in the forest that night.

A META-REALITY

Lifetime number four is the most difficult to explain because it occurred in a reality very unlike this one and things just don't translate well. I guess it might actually have been in a kind of etheric realm because in this place ideas and thoughts really were tangible things. I somehow had an ability with the crafting of ideas that could... I don't know... the analogy I get is that I had a "sword of words". I could somehow do great harm with the constructs of my mind and the others around me seemed to be quite defenceless against me. I had great anger and rage towards them. I think these were the same beings as in the life before because my sister was there again and this time she was the only one I loved. All others I struck out at and hurt very badly.

They had no way of defending themselves and I just went around doing harm – expressing my rage, I guess. This lifetime ended quite strangely too. The others captured me and confined me. And then they brought my sister and killed her before me. In so doing, I saw that she and they were actually one greater being. I saw that the good and the evil, the positive and the negative, were all from within the same being. That which I loved the most and that which I despised the most was all the same one being – just different manifestations of it. I was shaken to my core. They then killed me too. This somehow was a favour to me. It somehow absolved me of my karma. They actually did this as an act of love. None of this makes much sense to me now from the perspective of my current life but that is how it was.

Also, I later came to understand that what I had done to them was somehow a service to them. Much worse was to come and I assisted in some way to prepare them for this. It was as a result of me that they would later survive.

I don't really understand much about this lifetime and I hope to puzzle it all out some day.

THE WIZARD

The story of my fifth life is uncomfortable for me to tell. The setting was quite possibly medieval Europe. I was born to some local lord. We lived in a castle on a mountain overlooking a valley in which there was a village. Our village was quite isolated and transport through the mountain was by slow horse-drawn cart, so we lived quite an insular life. Most of the villagers would live their entire life without ever venturing out of the valley. Very few ever saw even the next village. Transport was difficult and slow and communications almost non-existent.

For this lifetime I had been given a spiritual gift: a connection to a special form of spiritual "energy" with which I could manipulate the matter of that world. An agreement was made that I would use this energy to show the people how to do healing and other such spiritual work.

I think my mother was quite sickly and she had struggled for many years to fall pregnant. Being the wife of the local lord, it was important that she give my father an heir. News of her pregnancy was therefore greeted with great joy. When I was born, a perfectly healthy baby boy, the village was overjoyed and a great celebration was given. I was the village's "golden child" and was much loved and celebrated. I soon began to display my gift in doing small magical things. The people saw this and wondered at it.

Somewhere in my teens, events conspired to take me in a dark direction: firstly my mother never properly recovered from giving birth to me. She was bed-ridden for a few years and then just faded away and died while I was still a child. My father was pre-occupied with his grief and his responsibilities as the lord of his lands. When my magical abilities became obvious, the village witch asked to be allowed to teach me – to "mould" my abilities. Despite the fact that she had shown herself to be capable of quite a mean streak, I think my father was just relieved to have one less thing to worry about and she was allowed to take me into her care.

The witch did indeed teach me quite well. Due to the gift I had been given in that life, I had an innate skill in manipulating matter and energy. Though my ability was far greater than her own, the witch was able to teach me to channel and focus this gift. In time I became quite proficient at this. I was able, for example, to do weather working to bring rains for the crops when needed and so forth. I was also able to do healing work. I think there were some other skills, but I can't quite remember them now. But all through the process of teaching me what she knew, the witch was also engaged in manipulating me to suit her own agenda. She wanted power for herself and, I am now sure, decided that she would turn me into her puppet. She attempted this by playing to my ego. She told me that I was special beyond all other people. She led me to believe that all others should serve me and be as slaves to my will. She taught me to believe that I was some kind of a demi-god. I came to believe that my magical abilities were not to be placed in service of the people, but instead were proof that the people should serve me. So that wasn't exactly healthy.

Then there was the way that the peasantry treated me. You must understand that the social dynamic of feudal society is nothing like the life we live now. A feudal lord has absolute power over his lands and vassals. They bow and scrape around him, never speaking unless spoken to and never looking their lord in the eyes. They will almost always run and hide if they see him coming so that they do not have to engage with him and risk causing offence. It's almost as if these are two different species: the ruler and the ruled. The point of all this is that I certainly did not feel belonging and community amongst the village people. If I left the castle and went down to the village I was not welcomed with singing and dancing... Oh no. All fell silent and many scurried away. I felt like an outcast. It felt as if my presence was resented. And then, as soon as I left their company, the villagers' conversation would once again pick up behind my back with nervous laughter breaking out. I thought they hated me. And maybe they did!

To complicate matters my father had, while I was still a boy, refused to send some of our peasants to be soldiers in a crusade (or something very like that). As a result of this we were considered pariahs and no self-respecting noble family would consider me as a suitable marriage candidate for their daughter. So, upon coming of the age where I would have gone to the royal court to meet young ladies of my station, it was made clear that I would not be welcome.

So I was alone.

My only companion was the witch who was busily implementing her ego manipulations on me for her own ends. As it transpired, this eventually backfired on her. In time I came to believe her lies and felt I was too powerful to have to put up with her and her constant meanness. So I simply sent her away. Somewhere around that time my father died too and I became the lord of the lands. Not only did I have all the power of being a feudal lord, but I also had the power of magic. To the peasants of the village I was something quite separate, other and strange. And there really was no one else in my life. No friends, no family, no lovers, no confidantes. Just me and the village peasantry to whom I was an utterly alien thing. This was to be a life of deep isolation.

But I was still a human being with human needs and desires. I guess what I wanted most was to be loved and accepted. To belong. To feel needed and wanted. And so, of course, I noticed some of the more attractive village girls. I wished I could have one of them be with me and love me. On a few occasions I would approach one and try to strike up a conversation. But the gap between us was just far too wide to be breached. In my presence they were uncomfortable and wary. As I approached they would be all apologetic and cowed – probably assuming I wanted to berate them for having done something wrong (why else would the lord of the land speak to a peasant girl?) They would not look at me and would only answer my direct questions in as few words as possible.

Eventually I demanded that one of the girls come back to castle with me on some pretext or another. I knew nothing of love and tenderness and even if I had, she would not have responded. I am ashamed to admit that instead, I forced myself upon her and took what I wanted. In so doing I ruined her chances of ever finding a husband. But I cared little of that. This abysmal behaviour brought me some kind of a feeling of power and, I guess, it was better than being completely alone. And so it became a bit of a habit for me. I repeated it a few times with the same girl and then moved onto others. My appetites changed and grew darker. I soon became quite abusive. I prefer not to go into details. This is not easy for me to write about. All I will say is that I got quite darkly inventive about my abuses of the village girls.

Obviously, at some point, the villagers decided that they needed to do something about this. They needed to tell me to stop. So a meeting was called in the clearing in the middle of the village. I got to hear about this. I rushed out of the castle and went and stood on a cliff overlooking the village to see if it was true. And, sure enough, the people had gathered below and someone was standing up talking to them. I was enraged! I have a picture of myself standing on the cliff overlooking the village with the castle behind me. My emotions boiled and stewed. I was going to show them all! They would never again try such insolence! I began to raise the storm to end all storms. I pulled the wind in towards me – pulling and pulling, I drew in great storm clouds until, roaring and raging, they towered above me. The sky darkened to black and lightning raced. I was connected with these profound forces and I felt the lightning in my own body. It exhilarated me. I felt so large... so powerful... so alive. I revelled in it and in the punishment I would bring. I felt like a god. A very dark and powerful god. I drew in more energy. The wind whipped against my body, almost pushing me right off the cliff-face. I saw the villagers below scattering and rushing to secure their homes; the fire in the marketplace around which they had gathered blowing up cinders onto the thatched roofs of their houses. I was gleeful at their fear. They would pay! The storm developed and developed – the forces straining to break and smash against the village below. And then... nothing. My body collapsed lifeless on that cliff. I had over-done it. I had pushed too much energy through a vessel that was not capable of containing it.

Overloaded, my body simply ceased functioning and then, there I was, a spirit-being looking down on a lifeless form.

That was my last lifetime before this one.

A LIFE BETWEEN LIVES

I spent a **lot** of time between that incarnation and my current one. As a spirit-being I reviewed the life I had just left – I looked at the pain and devastation I had caused and I was aghast. I felt such remorse and anguish. I began to attempt to terminate my own existence. I'll spare you all the details but I spent a lot of effort simply trying to destroy my own beingness. I tried everything I could, but I simply could not end myself. Whatever I did... I just continued to exist! I seem to have spent some time obliterating my connection to everything – in other words I tried to cease being by ceasing to **do** and by losing my memory of all things. Eventually I found myself in a kind of stasis. I was nowhere, did nothing and knew nothing. But that didn't help because as soon as I wondered how I came to be there, it all came flooding back. I realised there was no escape, no cessation. I had to deal with what I had done. And as soon as I decided **that**, I found myself in the company of a group of spirit beings. They brought me before an ancient, wise and beautiful one. I assumed that this "head-wizard" was to be my judge. I assumed he was going to sentence me for my grave wrong-doings. I immediately began to declare my guilt to him. I was like a limp, wet rag – all tears (metaphorically) and abject apologies. I alternated between earnestly swearing to do better next time, dedicating myself to endless service to repair the wrongs that I had done and begging to be punished or destroyed. On and on I went and the wise one just listened. When eventually I ran out of steam he asked, "*Are you quite done? Because I have someone you should meet.*"

And then I was introduced to a very special being. A being of pure, unblemished truth. I shall call him "8". I came to see him as the sharp blade-edge of **truth**. He was hard, but ultimately and completely fair. He took one look at the snivelling damp rag that I was and simply said, "*You need to grow some back-bone.*"

He took me in hand and worked with me. We were not inside of time so there is no way for me to say for how long he worked with me, but I would say that it was the equivalent of very many lifetimes. I learned a great deal from him. First, he pretended to give me work as "punishment" until I discovered that the work was not punishment, but simply an opportunity to express love as a gift of service. Then, when I finally realised that I no longer desired to be punished, he began to help me to see the beauty that was there in my soul. He helped me to see my worth and what I have to offer. Slowly a deep and amazing bond forged between us. He was my guide and teacher but I also knew that he was respected, and even revered, by some of the most wondrous beings of this reality. I was blessed beyond my ability to tell of it that he had come to my assistance.

A RETURNING TO INCARNATED LIFE

Then came the time when 8 said to me that it was time to finish what was started: I needed to have one final incarnation so that I could let go of the incarnational cycle and rise up to find what I really am. I was filled with trepidation and self-doubt. I really did not want to go into density again. I feared that I would do damage again and did not want this.

"*Come with me,*" 8 said, "*I have someone I want you to meet.*"

"*Who?*" I asked.

"*Someone who is to be your partner in your journey in the next incarnation. You won't be alone.*" And then, before us was the most incredible sight: a being of the most radiant blue light. I had never seen so much light compressed into such a small space. I was awestruck.

"*What does this being want with me?*" I whispered to 8.

"*This one will take a challenge to planet Earth: she will struggle with the lesson of self-love. You are to love her.*"

"*Well of course,*" I replied, "*how else can I respond to such a being?*"

"*You are to love her consistently and ceaselessly until she finds her own self-love and in return she will be your truth until you find your own inner-*

truth." And in that simple sentence the partnership was sealed. With such a being at my side how could I fail? And so it came to pass. I was born into this life and was just a very young man when my lady-love, Lisa, and I met. It was love at first sight and we have remained pretty much in love for all of the time since. We have a partnership that amazes even us. A miracle of love. And I **have** loved her until she loved herself and she **was** my truth until I discovered my own truth within myself.

At the time of writing, it has been 23 years that we have been together in this, my sixth lifetime. We have completed our contract, agreed to in spirit form with 8 as our witness. And now, here on Earth, as we find ourselves, we discover a partnership too special and wondrous to simply end. And so we create a new agreement based not upon a hurt and a need that the other must fill, but upon pure love and a desire to give to the other that which we each are.

And that, more-or-less, brings me to the present moment.

So here I am now. Awakening. Remembering. Discovering myself. And along the way I discover a few other things:

Firstly, 8 is my guide while I am incarnated, but the reality that I hid from myself is that he and I are actually partners; that is to say, we are a team. He has looked after me throughout my journey (though I mostly did not know it) so that I can reach the other end and then we can do our work together. My unending gratitude to him for his help is mirrored by his to me. He tells me that he is unendingly grateful to **me** because I was the one who took the tough job of descending into this reality for us. So we are in balance, he and I. My job here is really just to find myself and awaken from within the system so that, with a hermeneutic understanding of the system, I can begin to do the work that 8 and I came to do.

Secondly, I realise that the "head-wizard" was not some wise old judge but was actually just **me**... my own inner-self. You see, only we can judge ourselves – no one else can or will. And anyway he did not come to judge at all. He simply came to be a part of assisting me in finding my way back home. I guess you could say the judge was a face of Joy-Divine. But equally you could say that I too am a face of Joy-Divine. So... it's all just me.

Thirdly, I discover that I really do love myself. And like myself. And trust myself. I realise that my journey was a path that we all travel when we come here. We go via Forgetting to a place called Not-Self. When there, we do all kinds of interesting things such as fear, pain, hatred and abuse. Then, slowly, we begin to discover that this doesn't make us happy and so we begin to replace it with love, joy, kindness and healing. And this makes us happier. Along the way we leave Not-Self and find ourselves well on the road back to Self. And Self is not a being that has forgotten so, inevitably, as we become more Self, so we ascend out of this duality-reality.

Fourth, to my utter surprise, I realise that I really love what is here in this reality. I love this planet with a love that sometimes aches in my heart. I love all that is upon the planet too. The people? I also love all of them. Although I do not always love all that they do! Some of them do some very hurtful things to self and to other/self. But that is only because they are lost and confused. When you read my story, you notice that I also did some very hurtful things in my confusion. So I cannot judge another.

And now I discover something interesting: our darkest, most shameful secrets are actually our most glorious jewels of the soul. You see, when you are in your greatest pain, you give someone else the gift of being able to express love to you by allowing them to help you to heal. Then, when you do heal, you come away with great compassion for all others who have pain. Then these "others" give you the gift of allowing you to help them with their pain. This thing – this helping of each other – this flows from compassion. If we each see the darkness within ourselves with clear and open eyes, then we find compassion for the darkness in an other/self. And compassion is the route to oneness. It is the healing of that which is fragmented.

And this is what I wanted to share with you... the very briefest summation of my story. Along the way, I have seen that all that happened to me was perfect. It was exactly what was needed to allow me to become who I am. And I love who I am, so I have no regrets.

> (**Zingdad note**: You too can find healing for your pain and a deep sense of meaning and purpose in your life by gaining an understanding of your own past lives. Should you wish to explore this fascinating topic, please feel free to visit the Past Life Work section on my website, zingdad.com, to find out how I might assist you on your journey of self-discovery, here: http://zingdad.com/healing-a-helping/past-life-work)

In love and laughter,

Zingdad-that-is-Delight

Oh yeah, P.S.

I forgot to include this other thing that I discovered. It's a loopy one: I discover that, outside of time, I am already that which has ascended and always was ascended. In fact, I am a being who has already expressed itself eternally in an infinite number of realities because I am already an infinite, immortal creator being, and always was. And so my beginning, as laid out above in this story, is not really my beginning – it's just a convenient place to start a story. I am myself, I am my Higher-Self and I am ONE with God. And so are you. So you and I are ONE. So I am you, and you are me, and we are All That Is. And that's just the freakiest, happiest truth ever! And so I greet you:

"Hello God!"

P.P.S.

People often ask me where the name "Zingdad" comes from. And why I don't just use my "real name". So here's the short answer: Some years ago, when I needed a pseudonym for an Internet forum, I asked Lisa (my lady-love) what I should call myself online. She took one look at me, with Zing, my dachshund puppy, curled up on my lap, and said, *"Call yourself*

'Zing's Dad." I changed it to Zingdad and it stuck! People got to know me all over the Internet as Zingdad and I liked the quirky fun of it. I liked that it was totally unique (go ahead... Google "Zingdad"... every single result pertains to me! Cool, huh?) I liked that it is neither an existing name nor a word that means anything and will therefore not trigger any preconceived notions. I just liked it! So I took it for my online name. When it came time to publish my book, the name Zingdad was already a brand of sorts and, since the reasons I liked it remained valid for me, I published my book under that pseudonym too. And that's really all there is to it!

But for all that, the name I go by in real life is Arn Allingham and if ever you and I should meet and talk then I'd like it if you called me Arn.

And as for Zing himself. **His** name is short for ama**zing**. Because he is very short and even more amazing. If you'd like to get a dose of Zing cuteness then I invite you to visit this page on my website where I share some photographs of him: zingdad.com/blog/230.

And that's it for the introduction.

See you in Chapter 2!

* * * * *

CHAPTER 2.
WHAT IS THE HIGHER-SELF?

Here **begins** the first intuitive conversation of this book. As you begin to read this work, I would like to remind you that when I first wrote this, I had no idea whatsoever that it would form part of a book. I believed this was to be the first of a short series of articles that I would offer on an Internet forum that I frequented at the time.

From here on out, what you will be reading is a record of a conversation I had with my own Higher-Self.

Zingdad: I wish to speak to my own Higher-Self. To the being that has previously identified itself to me as Joy-Divine.

Joy-Divine: Hello. I am here with you, as always.

Z: Hello. I will want to discuss a number of issues with you and then record the conversation to share with others. I feel it is a good idea to first introduce you to my readers so that they might have a context from which to understand your words.

J-D: Yes, this is good. I am happy to do an introduction but I would suggest that we can hit more than one bird with this same stone, so to speak. We can have a chat that introduces me and, at the same time, opens the door to more conversations introducing a number of spiritual concepts.

Z: Okay, excellent! What sorts of spiritual concepts?

J-D: Well, for example: if I were to introduce myself to your readers by saying something as simple as, "*I am Zingdad's Higher-Self,*" then we will immediately find ourselves having to take a detour to explain what a Higher-Self is so that we can be sure that we are all on the same page. But in order to explain this concept I am going to introduce other concepts and they too will be in need of clarification. And very soon, in simply trying to introduce myself, I will have opened a whole gamut of topics that will need to be addressed. A conversation like this might never end! Indeed it is so that the simple question, "*Who are you?*" is an invitation to a life-long association if the two of you are serious in your endeavour to explore the answer to that question. But, in answer to your question, a few points that will come up for discussion quite soon will include, "What is oneness?", "Can we prove oneness?", "Why is there such confusion about spirituality on Earth?", "What would it be like to live in a state of oneness?" and, eventually, "What is truth?"

Z: Sounds exciting!

J-D:... and potentially confusing if we don't handle this carefully. But, yes, it **is** exciting and you will still come to be quite surprised at how much beauty, truth and wisdom will come from this simple beginning.

But for now, what I am going to ask you to do is to make this a multi-part series of conversations. I will open today with a discussion which you may title, "What is the Higher-Self?" And then, in this discussion, we will come up with new topics for conversation which we shall address in follow-up sessions with either myself or some of the other members of our spirit family. Okay?

Z: Yes, of course! Well then, best I start the ball rolling and ask the question... ta da da dum... What, pray tell, **is** a Higher-Self?

J-D: I am **so** glad you asked (he smiles).

Firstly, let me say that, while the most commonly used term is "Higher-Self", I actually prefer "Inner-Self" or, in a certain context, "God-Self". How this all works can either be very, very simple to explain or terribly complex. The simplest explanation that I can offer is this:

"There is only ONE being experiencing the illusion of being many."

I like that statement so much that I am going to repeat it in a slightly different way:

"The ONE is engaged in an experience of Itself as being many."

This statement is true on many levels. If you really get that concept, then you get the essential thesis of what I would present as the spiritual cosmology of All That Is. This understanding serves you, irrespective of the size of the spiritual concept you are trying to understand. Let's start big... from the top and work down:

We are all one. But the ONE – which you may call God, or Source or The Creator or whatever term you like – has created for Itself some very powerful thoughts about Itself, such that there are many. To illustrate this, I shall use the example of an author who is writing a story. The author creates the characters of the story in his mind. As the characters gain greater and greater validity in the author's mind, they begin to take on distinct personalities. Often the author will find that it seems as if the characters have a mind of their own! They feel, to the author, as if they are autonomous beings and he is just chronicling their behaviour. Can you see how this could be for that author? That he can create many personae in his mind? And give them each their own nature and personality? And in the telling of their stories the characters seem to be quite oblivious to the fact that they only exist in the author's mind? That the world they live in, though large and complex, is also only in the story-teller's mind?

Z: Hmm, yes, the author analogy is a good one.

J-D: Now I tell you that it is not only authors who do this – who create characters in their minds. In point of fact, all sentient beings do this, to one degree or another. Everyone creates fictitious conversations and interactions in their own minds. Everyone has day-dreams and fantasies and imaginary discussions. And everyone dreams whilst sleeping. These, and similar processes, are all story-telling with character creation.

Can you see how each of you then, already have the beginnings of the experience of creating "another" inside your own minds?

Z: Yes, I can see that.

J-D: Now imagine that you have an infinity of time to perfect the art of powerfully imagining these characters. Imagine that you have infinite creative resources. That you are greater than the greatest creative genius who has ever walked the planet. Now possibly you might have the first glimmering of what this might be like; how the ONE can create within its mind, so to speak, various characters and personalities.

Z: So that is how we here on Earth come into being?

J-D: No, not quite. I am endeavouring to give you a simplified understanding of what might otherwise be an impossibly complex subject. And I am going to need to keep oversimplifying things for the sake of being able to express these ideas at all.

If you wish to understand how beings on Earth come to be here, then you should rather imagine a hierarchy of creator-beings. Imagine that the beings that appear in the mind of the ONE should create in their minds more beings. And they, in turn, do the same thing. And this creative recursion happens a few times before you get to the soul-fragments incarnated upon planet Earth.

You have heard that this world is deep in the densities of consciousness. Well, this is essentially the notion: each lower density requires an additional level of creation. You would have a "higher-self" on every one of the levels or densities above you; right the way "up" to the ONE. Which is why you call such beings "Higher-Self". But I tell you, it is not "up", it is "inside". A better understanding is that these levels are within you. You go inside your heart to find your "Inner-Self". And the further inwards you travel, the greater the version of your Inner-Self you will find.

Z: Right the way to God?

J-D: Yes. Have you not heard it said that God is inside each and every persons' heart? Or that the kingdom of heaven is within?

Z: Ah, yes.

So to sum up: there is the ONE, which is God. And God has created us all within Its mind. But indirectly. There is a structure and we are the creations of the creations of the creations...

J-D:... and so on, yes.

But do not suffer the impression that you are not therefore very powerful! All parts of the ONE are imbued with the essential nature of the ONE. It is said that you are made in God's image. Well, that doesn't mean that God has a body like yours. It means that **you** are made in God's image. The you that is still you when you are no longer in a human body. It means all spirit is God-like. All spirit is creative and self-creative.

Two concepts that you personally have been encouraged by me to understand are fractals and holograms. For a very good reason. I can strongly encourage everyone to at least read a little about these two phenomena. They provide a wonderful way to understand creation. A hologram is an object which provides a three-dimensional picture. If you break that hologram into numerous smaller pieces, then each of those pieces will once again contain the whole three dimensional image. And you are like this. Every being contains the whole.

And the thing with fractals to understand is that you can find a point that interests you and from there you can zoom deeper and deeper into the fractal. You will never get to the end of it. It is endlessly recursive in any direction you wish to travel. And you are like this too. If you look within yourself you can go on looking forever and ever. There is always more to discover in any direction you wish to search.

So I tell you this: it seems to you as if the universe lies outside of you. It does not. In fact it lies **inside** you. Each of you contains the whole and one can "zoom into" each of you infinitely. All parts are connected to all other parts.

Z: You're kidding, right, about the part about the whole universe being **inside** me?

J-D: No, I am being completely serious. It is a point that you shall come to understand as we proceed with these conversations. But we must shelve that for a moment so that we can finish **this** conversation.

Z: Ah. Okay. So we were talking about your being my Inner-Self and that there are levels of Inner-Self-ness.

J-D: Yes. Essentially all I am trying to impart to you is that, depending on how you look at it, there might be only one ultimate Inner-Self or an infinite number of levels of Inner-Selves.

Z: Wow. Er... the one ultimate Inner-Self would be...?

J-D: The Source of All That Is, of course. God. We are all ONE, as I have mentioned. So ultimately we are all joined by the fact that our ultimate greatest version of Self is God.

Z: That's a big thought. I struggle with it a bit.

J-D: That's fine. If you already knew this to be true beyond a shadow of a doubt then you would probably not have much use for the duality reality you now find yourself in. So it is natural that you might have some difficulty with this concept. But don't let this bother you. Until you gain perfect understanding you can simply understand that within the creation of the ONE are many great spirit beings. You can call them Demi-Gods or Arch-Angels if you like. These great beings are both aware of themselves as unique individuated consciousnesses **and**, at the same time, are absolutely aware of their oneness. They have also created within themselves (together or separately) lower levels of self. Each succeeding level is more separate and less one. At the furtherest extent of separation, in the level of consciousness known as duality, they have created within themselves all those incarnated upon planet Earth. They can therefore also be called your God-Selves.

Z: But how can someone be both one **and** separate?

J-D: I shall address this in one of the conversations about the oneness. I shall call it "the rainbow metaphor".

Z: Sounds colourful – I look forward to that. Okay then, back to this discussion. So there is a continuum, from a feeling of oneness at the top, right down to a feeling of separateness at the bottom?

J-D: Yes, exactly. And, at each and every level, the being is creating other characters and personae in its mind. All are always in a process of the co-creation of Self. As you get down to this reality you currently inhabit you get to a feeling of profound separateness such that you can actually totally forget both that you are one with all else and that you are a creator being. In fact, that is what your whole plane of reality was created for: to experience and explore absolute separateness.

Z: Okay. So then let me see if I understand this. You are saying that there is the oneness at the top, which is God. And then God creates the many and in the minds of the many are many more and so on and so on, all the way down to us here on Earth who are a great many and who have the freedom to believe that we are not ONE. We can believe that we are separate and individual. And we did this to ourselves on purpose so that we could discover something about ourselves and re-create ourselves. Right?

J-D: Good. Yes, that's the first half of the story. You now have a rough sketch of how the structure works from the top down. But until you see it the other way around, from the bottom up, you won't really get it. So let's tell that other half of the story.

The thing to understand is that each of you on planet Earth are playing out the roles you have chosen for yourselves. You play massive, long-running games that span many lifetimes so that you can experience yourself as an individual. As separate from each other. As "not-ONE". And that is what life on Earth is like. But every game must come to an end at some point. Eventually you will say to yourself, "*I have pretty much seen everything I want to see in this game,*" and you will want to take your knowledge and go and play some other game. Perhaps you'll want to play a game with less constrictive rules next time, for example. Anyway, the point at which you decide you have seen what you want to see here is the point at which you usually choose to begin your ascension process. Even though I don't really like the term, "ascension", I will use it, as it is by now in very common usage.

Z: Wait a minute. Sorry to interrupt. But why don't you like that term?

J-D: Ascension? For the same reason that I don't like "Higher-Self". The word "ascension" implies an upwards movement, but you don't go "up". You don't actually go anywhere at all. You heal, you re-integrate all aspects of yourself, you become more at one with yourself and then you begin to remember who you really are. Once you have done this, you are free to take your consciousness "inwards" to higher densities. And from there you can explore other time-lines or share in the creation of other realities or wherever else you like. You see, essentially what you are doing in the ascension process is pulling yourself inward towards yourself. You need to do this if you are going to remove yourself from this system of reality so that you can go and play in other realities.

Right now there are quite a number of people on planet Earth who are engaged with their ascension paths. They are finishing off with the game and its rules at this level of reality and they are preparing to become a greater version of themselves. You are doing this yourself and probably everyone reading this work is too. People not on an ascension path will resonate quite poorly with what is written here. They will probably feel that this is all nonsense. So I can state with some confidence that you and your readers are all busy "ascending".

Z: And what then? What happens when we have ascended?

J-D: It is not a single-step process, as your question implies. As you "ascend", so you awaken to greater and greater realizations of self. You begin to see through the illusions of this world that keep people trapped in the game. You begin to find true love and compassion for yourself and for all others. You begin to release the fear and pain that you have created inside yourself across your many lifetimes. You cease thinking of yourself as a victim to your experiences and then understand with greater and greater clarity that you are the creator of your own experiences. And as this becomes true for you, so your experiences will corroborate your beliefs. In short, you become a creator-being and cease being a lonely, lost victim.

Z: Ah. But what about the whole oneness thing?

J-D: Good question. You see, as long as your view of yourself resides primarily in your ego – this is the aspect of Self that sees itself as "separate" and as that which must do all the doing – then you are not co-creating with the rest of All That Is. You are not in alignment with the greatest forces in all creation. When you begin to create from your heart and in love, then you move towards oneness. Then All That Is co-creates with you. It is a profound difference. You, on your own, as opposed to you, in harmony with all of creation. In the latter state you will find your life awash with miracles and magic. In the former state you get the kind of reality espoused by Murphy's Law: you get to be a person on your own, slogging it out against all the odds and then indeed, anything that can go wrong usually will. So the choice is yours. You can remain attached to being separate and alone and keep playing the games of density or you can release this; you can decide to see all others as another aspect of self. You can choose oneness and love and then you will begin to "ascend".

Z: What is the ascension process like?

J-D: In short, it is a process in which you become ever more aware that you are the creator of your own reality and ever more proficient in the methods of reality creation. What that means is that each person will create their own path and their own experiences of it. Each will walk a unique path. So it will be impossible to describe in detail what everyone will choose. But we certainly can speak to some of the more general experiences and these understandings will unfold for you from many different perspectives throughout the conversations that follow. For now, all I really want you to understand is that you, and others around you, are now experiencing your own ascension. It is not incorrect to say that you are becoming your own Inner-Selves.

Z: Oh wow. I am sort of moving up a level.

J-D: Yes. There aren't really strictly defined "levels" like floors in a tall building but it is less complex if you think of it like that for now. As you contemplate this, can you see that it is so that God created your God-Self who, essentially, created your Inner-Self, who created you and your other incarnations? But, by living the life you are living, by making the choices you are making and holding the beliefs you are holding, you are re-creating yourself as you go. And when you re-create yourself, you re-create a part of your Inner-Self. You and your Inner-Self are engaged in a process of self creation. So it could be said that you are your Inner-Self engaged in the experience of your life. So, if you follow all this, can you see that your Inner-Self creates you and then you create your Inner-Self? That we are one great being in a constant process of self-creation?

Z: Okay, **wow**! That is awesome! But uhh... why does it mostly not feel like this? I mean, I think of you as being quite powerful and amazing and so on while I, by contrast, am often quite confused or in pain or filled with feelings of being lonely and lost.

J-D: It comes down to the fact that you didn't come to live on Earth only to immediately ascend. You came here to **be** here. To experience yourself as being a separate individual. So, in that state, you **do** often feel these lonely, lost and disempowered sensations. It is, unfortunately, a part of the turf, it seems. It is only when you are essentially done with the game that you begin to remember that you are actually a powerful creator being. Then, as you begin to remember this, so you begin to release some of the separateness and then you truly begin to create yourself **as** your Inner-Self.

Z: So, at every level we are ONE being creating our Self through the experience of many.

J-D: Yes! As above, so below. And as below, so above. So you co-create yourself. In so doing you co-create your Inner-Self. Who is, essentially, engaged in the process of co-creation of your God-Self. And the God-Selves are all essentially in the process of the co-creation of God. You see? Extend this far enough and you understand that we are all **ONE**. There ultimately is just one of us creating the many so as to experience Itself in a myriad new ways and to re-create Itself. The many create many more and so on and so on, without end, for all infinity. And the very smallest and youngest of the many creates itself and, in so doing, re-creates the all. Like a fractal that you can eternally zoom into or out of in all directions. Like a hologram of which the very smallest particle includes the whole image.

Z: That's so beautiful!

J-D: I'm glad you like it. It is my perspective and my truth. There are many other perspectives too. There will be perspectives that do not agree with mine at all but that are equally valid.

Z: Uh. Waitaminit. How can your truth and someone else's truth both be true and yet not agree?

J-D: Easily. All truths are true and no two truths are identical. But I can see how this might seem odd to you. In due course, when the time is right, I will ask you to speak to our soul-partner (and your Spirit-Guide), 8, on this subject. You can call that chat, "What is truth?" Ask him about it okay?

Z: Okay.

J-D: So now. If we can move along... I will say to you that I am **your** personal God-self. I hold within myself all the other versions of Self that you are, and will be. You are my creation and, as explained, I am yours. You are a part of a much, much greater Being and we together are intensely involved in the process of constant Self creation. From my perspective I will say that this is true for everyone on planet Earth.

Z: I am an incarnation of you?

J-D: Yes, if you wish to see it like that. Or you could also say that I am experiencing one of my creations of myself **as** you.

Z: And, besides me, how many other incarnations of Joy-Divine are there on planet Earth right now?

J-D: This is a far more complex question than you have intended it to be. I will have to deal with it by saying that, from the perspective that you are asking this question, there is only one human incarnation of Joy-Divine on planet Earth in this space/time nexus within which you exist. There is only you. It is not congruent with our soul-purpose to have a great many incarnations, as some of the other Bright Ones have had.

Z: Cool. But now you have totally blown my mind with all this and I don't know what else to ask.

J-D: (He laughs) That is good. I think we should anyway end this session now so that you can rest your poor blown mind. But you now already have the beginnings of a structure for where we are going to go from here. You can pick it up next time with me when we address the topic, "What is oneness?"

Z: Awesome. I just want to say, isn't it weird that actually this conversation is really just me talking to myself?

J-D: Yes. But if you understand it correctly, then the whole universe is just one small side-conversation that God is having with Itself. So... not so strange really.

Z: A **small side conversation**! Isn't the universe All That Is?

J-D: Hardly. I know it looks pretty big to you, but it is just a small part of one reality construct. There are an infinite number of other such constructs. And all the realities together make up just one way for God to express Itself. There are an infinite number of others.

Z: Wowzer. Now you really are blowing my mind. I can see that there is a **lot** still to talk about. Thank you so much for talking to me today. I feel such love and gratitude.

J-D: Good feelings those. I feel the same. But, as the song goes, "*You ain't seen nothing yet!*" We're still going to have lots of fun with this. We'll talk again soon.

* * * * *

CHAPTER 3.
THE VEIL OF UNKNOWING

Zingdad: J-D, you said in our last chat that we should talk about oneness.

Joy-Divine: Hello. Yes. I want to more-or-less prove to you that all is one and then, when we've established that, then I want to talk about what that means for you.

Z: Great. Why "*more-or-less*" prove it?

J-D: Well, let me first tell you about the reality you inhabit and then I shall get to my main arguments. Primarily your reality was created for the purpose of experiencing individuality. In order for this to be possible, a consciousness-construct was set in place to sort-of "filter" the information that might be available to you. This has often been called "the Veil", or more specifically, "the Veil of Unknowing" and I am happy to keep using that term. What the Veil essentially does is to guarantee that you cannot prove that all is one. Anything that approaches true, irrefutable proof of oneness will always come with sufficient cause for doubt that each individual will simply have to make up their own mind.

Z: Okay. Doesn't the Veil also hide other knowing and information from us, though?

J-D: No. All it does is hide from you your essential oneness with All That Is. But you need to think about this for a moment. If all is truly one, if the most essential truth about everything is its inherent oneness, and if the Veil hides the oneness from you, then I'm sure you can logically see that the Veil will hide the most essential nature of **everything** from you. It will mean that you cannot know the deepest truth about anything at all. Because, as you approach the deepest truth of anything you'd approach proof that all is one. And the Veil forbids this. Do you see the circular nature of the problem? The essential nature of **everything** is that it is all one with everything else. But this is hidden from you.

Z: So you mean we can't know the true nature of anything?

J-D: It's a fact. What is remarkable to me is how few people on Earth are concerned about the fact that nothing is known down to its root. Nowhere can you look and say, "*We really understand that and can therefore build upon a solid foundation of knowledge.*" You can know about the surface, about the characteristics or about the effect, but you cannot know about the true cause.

Z: Uh. I'm not sure that I know this to be true. Our science has surely gotten to the root of **something**?

J-D: All right. I'll go there with you. What is your world and all the animals and plants and so forth made of?

Z: Matter.

J-D: What is matter made of?

Z: Um. Molecules. And they are made of atoms. And they are made of sub-atomic particles.

J-D: Good. Carry on. What are sub-atomic particles made of?

Z: Energy, I think?

J-D: And what is the nature of that energy?

Z: Uhh...

J-D: What is this energy made of? Where does it come from? Was it created? If so, when and how? And if it wasn't created, how does it come to be?

Z: I don't know. I don't know any of those answers.

J-D: Well don't feel bad. Neither does science. There are, of course, a number of postulates and theories, but other than simple observations about what occurs when particles interact, your planet's science knows next to nothing about the nature of this energy that they say all matter is created of. And if **everything** you can observe and engage with, including your own body, is made of this energy about which you know nothing, then it can be seen that you really know nothing about everything!

All scientists, but for the few, most enlightened of the species, generally make the mistake of saying that there is nothing, but that which can be observed... that there is nothing but the material world. But the problem is that the material world does not exist! It is a function of this ephemeral world of rapidly shifting energy. And this energy is an impenetrable mystery to those self-same scientists. They do not know what it is, where it comes from, or really anything about it other than a few observations of how it might behave under particular circumstances – and even then there are mystifying incongruities that they cannot explain. So they fail utterly to comprehend or explain the very root of that which they say is real.

It is my contention that you will never truly begin to comprehend the fundamental energy of the universe without first understanding the nature of consciousness and, specifically, that all energy and matter that springs forth from consciousness is one single thing.

Z: All matter is the same thing?

J-D: As above, so below, and as below, so above. Everything is one. This is mirrored everywhere you look if you only know how to see. But the problem for you is that you are restricted from being able to prove this by the Veil.

Z: Okay, that's pretty interesting to me and I want to discuss this with you, but before I do, could you perhaps give me another example or two of things that we only know the surface of? Other than energy and matter, I mean.

J-D: Sure. I could give you countless examples. I could use the example of anything you could name to prove it to you. But some examples are more time-consuming than others. So I shall choose a simple one: light. You know next to nothing about it. And yet it is actually the most fundamental constituent of your reality. You know how fast it goes, but not why it travels at that specific speed. You know it has some highly curious properties – for example that it seems to have both a particulate and a wave-like nature – but again, you don't know why this should be. And so on. As with all things, science understands, at a surface level, what light does but not why it behaves as it does, nor what it actually is, nor where it truly comes from. Why, for example, is the speed of light the speed limit for other things? You can, if you try, describe these phenomena, but you have very little clue as to how it comes to be as it is. Until you understand that light (or rather all electromagnetic radiation) is really just a function of the particular dimension in which you reside, you will remain baffled by it. But you need to be willing to concede that your whole reality is just one little piece of the picture. Your whole universe is like a single key on one piano keyboard in an orchestra of an infinite number of musical instruments. And all those instruments together are playing the same **one** symphony.

And here's another example of something which your scientists don't really understand, another fundamental force of your reality: gravity. It is a constant force upon your body. Not a waking second goes by that you are not affected by it. But you haven't a clue about how it works.

Z: Wait a minute? Isn't it due to the warp in space-time caused by mass or some such?

J-D: No. I didn't say there were no **theories** about this. There are plenty of those. But they all have some flaws in them and remain unproven. Go read about it, if you like. Your science does not know where gravity comes from, why it is there or how it propagates. The theory that comes closest is a new one that presupposes the existence of other dimensions. But scientists will need to greatly expand their view of what those other dimensions might be before it will all begin to come together.

I'll give you another example. More philosophical than scientific, maybe. It is this: what, **truly**, are **you**?

Z: Let's see... I am a human being?

J-D: And if you had another incarnation as something other than that which you would currently define as a human? Would you cease to be you?

Z: No. Then I'd be a Zorg from the planet Zug. Or whatever (laughs). Okay, I get your point. What am I **really**? I mean I know I **have** a body. But I am not my body. How about I use Descartes famous quote: "*I think, therefore I am.*" And then I will say that I am my thoughts. How about that?

J-D: That's cute. But wrong. What happens if you stop thinking? Do you stop existing? For example, one of the goals of meditation is to cease all thought. What happens if you attain that goal? Do you pop out of existence?

Z: Hmm. No. I know that it is true for me (and for other meditators to whom I have spoken) that such moments bring with them the most amazing expansion of consciousness.

J-D: That **is** interesting then. So the less you **do** and the less you **try** and **think**, the more your consciousness expands. This is because **doing** and **being** are opposite states. And the nature of your **being** is... consciousness.

Z: Ah. So then the answer to your question is... I am consciousness?

J-D: Yes. But then, what is consciousness? I mean every single human being is this (or at the least **has** it), but can you explain it? Can you tell me where to find it?

Z: I'm not sure. Could it not be argued that consciousness is produced by the brain?

J-D: Not very convincingly. Some have tried, but there are always holes in the theory. For example: what happens when someone is declared "brain dead" and then, by some miracle, later they are resuscitated? How do you explain the fact that they sometimes recall events occurring in their consciousness at a time when the brain had ceased to function? And, even more amazingly, those who have experienced this often tell of events that didn't even occur in the proximity of the body housing the apparently dead brain. And what of the fact that in various neurosurgical operations on various people, pretty much every part of the brain has been removed. This one loses eye-sight. That one certain emotional responses. And so on. But everyone retains their consciousness. Unless the body dies, in which case they **still** have consciousness but, of course, you can usually no longer engage with a physical form in order to determine this.

So, no, there are too many anomalies for consciousness to arise from the brain. The point is this: your most essential and fundamental attribute, your very consciousness, is something that you know nothing about at all. Why? My contention is that this is because your consciousness is the very stuff of the oneness. But people just accept that they know nothing about themselves and go about paying the mortgage, watching sport and news on the television and arguing vociferously about religion and politics. Or whatever else keeps them entertained enough so that they don't have to confront the fact that **nothing** is truly known. The miracle of the mystery should overwhelm you constantly. But it doesn't. You declare life to be boring and mundane. *"No miracles or mysteries in my life,"* you all say. But this is only because you mesmerise yourselves into not looking at **anything** deeply enough to see the unending mystery of **everything**.

Now, I could go on and on with this because, literally in every direction you look, you run into an edge which is unexplained and undefined. Essentially what I am saying is that the simple directive of the Veil of Unknowing, that it should shield you from knowing the oneness of all, has profound implications. It means that you really know nothing about anything at all. And of course this effect doesn't only extend to that which is physically around you. It means that you cannot, beyond all doubt, prove the existence of God. Which is quite an amazing thought. The Prime Creator, which is in everything, contains everything, creates everything and of which you are an inseparable part, cannot be proven to even exist! I'll tell you something: spirit beings that have not experienced this reality directly find it nearly impossible to believe that this effect has been achieved over here. Often they come and have a look, just to marvel. The deepest, most essential and most undeniable truth of all has been hidden in plain sight! What a wonder and a miracle!

Z: Are you sure it isn't possible to prove God's existence? I vaguely recall reading some philosophical treatise, which presented a set of proofs. Are such things not valid?

J-D: Let me answer it like this. If just one of those proofs were infallible then there would not be any clear-thinking atheists or agnostics on the planet. You'd show them the proof, they'd fail to find the inconsistency and they'd have to concede that there **is** a God after all. And you can say what you like about atheists, but amongst their number are some very clear, rational and logical thinkers. So my point stands. Despite some concerted effort by some very lucid spiritual philosophers over the ages of your history, not one person has ever been able to prove the existence of God beyond all doubt. Or even the existence of spirit. Which is bizarre. Every single one of you **is** spirit and yet it is quite a reasonable and defensible position to claim that there is no spirit!

So, it really does become apparent that, in whatever direction you might look, be it science, religion, philosophy or any other discipline, when you try to understand anything at all, you will find a few steps of understanding based upon tried and tested hypotheses, followed by the fuzziness and darkness of ignorance. Nothing is known to its core. And if you don't know what the fundamentals are, you cannot **really** claim to understand their effects. And all of this is so because you cannot know that you and everything else are all one.

Z: Phew! That's wild. So why would we do this to ourselves? Why would we choose to come here and be stupid for a number of lifetimes?

J-D: Oh no, not stupid. Just forgetful. Why you have chosen to enter so deeply into separation will be addressed in due course in some careful detail as it is a very large subject on its own and time will not now permit me to do this justice. It will have to suffice for me to say that each and every spirit being that decided to manifest an incarnation here had a reason to do so. There is profound value to be found in this experience. But your perspective is, perforce, very limited. You can only see things from where you stand, **inside** of your reality. But I shall state, in my truth, that for the beings that are your "Inner-Selves", this experience is one of the most valuable that can possibly be had. All who manifest a set of incarnations here gain a vastly deeper understanding of the Self, massively evolve their consciousness and can find complete healing for any blockages they might bear in their consciousness.

The very forgetting **itself** is a wonderfully useful tool for self-discovery and healing.

Z: I know you don't want to dwell on this point now but could you please give me just the briefest explanation why?

J-D: All right. Let me try a little story:

THE PARABLE OF THE KING AND THE POTION OF FORGETFULNESS

Once there was a rich and powerful king of a vast kingdom. He was known to be quite wise and knowledgeable. One of his duties was to be the final judge and jury for all legal disputes in his land. But this was not something he enjoyed because he just didn't understand what it was like to be a poor, destitute, starving peasant. He could not understand some of the peasants' motivations and actions and felt, therefore, ill-equipped to pass judgement on them. But how would he come to truly understand the life of the peasant? He took his problem to his most valued advisor: his court wizard. The solution the wizard came up with was to cast a spell on the king such that the king would forget absolutely everything he knew. Then they would dress the king in the clothes of a peasant and leave him somewhere with just a few coins in his purse. In a year's time the spell would lift itself and the king would remember who he was. This way, for a full year, the king would have lived as a peasant so that he would know what that life was like. The king agreed to this plan and so it was. He was dressed as a poor man and left under the influence of the spell at an inn. When he awoke he did not know who he was. Some locals took pity on the poor confused stranger and helped him out for a day or two. But he didn't seem to have any practical skills with which to repay them. And he had a haughty, ungrateful attitude that they did not like. So, soon he was out on his own. Hungry, miserable and desperate he turned to theft. But he was caught and flung into jail.

Or was he?

Perhaps instead, he saw the kindness of the people to a stranger and decided to try and return their good favour? Maybe he found within himself the resourcefulness of a natural leader which, combined with a well-tuned and educated mind, allowed to him be valued and appreciated by all whom he encountered? Perhaps he became a celebrated leader anyway?

How will we ever know what happened to him? The only way, of course, is for the story to be played out and observed. And that is exactly the point. The king wanted to know about the experience of poverty but, by going though this experience of forgetfulness, the king would actually find out far more about who he really was. Not who he was set up to be by his circumstances, but rather his true, essential nature.

If we extend this metaphor and allow the king not just a year of forgetfulness, but as many lifetimes as it takes before he awakens **himself** by remembering who he really is through a process of self-discovery, then this would be similar to what is happening to you on Earth.

You have placed yourself under your own forgetfulness spell and you journey in the world of forgetting until you are ready to remember. And in this twilight world of forgetting, you discover the most amazing things about yourself and life and All That Is. And you remain there until you yourself discover and create your path out of there. Until you remember who you really are. And all such paths of discovery, creation and remembering inevitably lead to the same destination: that **all is one**. That is what the Veil is hiding, so, logically, knowing that to be the truth is the path out. Not just knowing it intellectually of course; knowing it in your every thought, word and deed. Knowing it to the core of your being.

But we will have a good many opportunities for you to gain a far deeper understanding of this concept. For now, even though this is a very simplistic illustration, I'm sure you can see that there is value to be had from the Veil?

Z: Yes, I found that quite enlightening, thank you. As you were relating that story I had an "aha!" moment or two. I can see that there is much to learn from deep forgetting.

J-D: And something else to consider is that there is protection inherent in the ignorance of forgetting.

Z: There is?

J-D: Sure! The further up the dimensional ladder you move, the more powerfully you can create. The more powerful a creator-being you are, it stands to reason, the more powerfully you could potentially do harm. Let us hypothesise a very powerful creator being that has yet to deeply plumb its own nature. It has yet to discover what it is capable of and how it would react to various circumstances. But it has great power at its disposal. That would be like putting a child in charge of the world's munitions. And, from one perspective, this is what happens. Spirit beings with limitless power find themselves playing together, creating realities together, not knowing or understanding the consequences of their own choices, actions or abilities. At this level of creation, when things go "wrong" it is usually a simple matter of taking the learning and then re-working the creation with the greater awareness in place. But, every now and then one of the creator beings will come to hurt Itself in such a way that there cannot simply be a "re-do". A fairly regular example would arise from one of the creator beings becoming self-destructive. When this happens then more drastic steps are required.

One very powerful way to resolve such a problem is to place the self-destructive being beyond the Veil so that it might find its way to self-healing by incarnating in your reality. Since all beings there have deeply forgotten who they are, they have also, perforce, utterly forgotten their own gifts and abilities. If you do not know your true power, then you cannot express it! It is locked away from you. And so that becomes a perfect fail-safe while that being finds Its way back to self-love and self-healing. And when the being does find its way back to full self-healing that, by definition, also includes a full remembering of its connection to the oneness. And in that remembering there is also a full remembering of all that being's inherent gifts, talents and abilities – since of course those abilities always derive from the oneness. And as this being recovers Its own true, greatest, most magnificent nature, It does so with the wisdom, compassion and insight not to fall once again to self-destructiveness.

Z: So we are punished for being self destructive by being sent beyond the Veil?

J-D: That would be a very flawed understanding of what I have just offered you.

There is no punishment involved. No one stands in judgement of you. It works like this: all is one. If you seek to harm yourself or to harm some other, then you are seeking to harm the ONE. And this is not actually possible. You cannot actually *harm* the infinite and eternal. But the *desire* to do so creates an impossible dichotomy. The only resolution of that dichotomy is fragmentation: to immediately create the very powerful illusion of separation so that there is a "self" to hurt and another "self" to be hurt.

This is the very simplest way I can explain this.

What I am sharing with you is that it is not a punishment. You do this to yourself. When a creator being enacts a self-destructive urge, it creates separation within Itself. It lowers its consciousness to a deeper density. If its attempts are quite concerted; if it wishes to utterly destroy Itself, then it will find Itself at this very deepest level of separation called "duality" where it has completely forgotten all of its God-given gifts and abilities. A handy by-product of this is that Its capacity for self-destruction is also nullified.

Z: I do understand. Thank you.

J-D: Now, these are just two little illustrative sketches. Please understand that this doesn't even begin to represent all the perspectives of the value that can be obtained from going into this reality as you have. It is an amazing, wondrous system and to experience it is something beyond comparison. And the heart of this system is the Veil of Unknowing. In fact, this might come as a surprise, but another way to look at the Veil is that it is an agent of the law of free will, or, as our esteemed colleagues of *The Ra Material* called it, the law of confusion.

Z: How is that?

J-D: You will have noticed that on Earth there are a great many different religious and philosophical systems of belief. Each one claims for itself the exclusivity of truth and damns all others as lies. And then each religion has so many schisms and sub-sects within it that one can never keep up with who really believes what. And that is just the organised religions. What of all the variations of agnostics and atheists? And then there are more and more people all the time who regard themselves as deeply spiritual but not religious. They look for their own truth in their heart. But each heart is different. So there are just more and more different "truths" all the time. And every view is slightly different! If anyone is to look carefully enough and is to be honest enough, they will be forced to admit that there is not one other human being who precisely and exactly shares their beliefs, their view of "what is true", with them. And so? What to make of that? Either everyone but you is confused, wrong or cracked – or there really is a valid reason to believe almost anything under the sun.

And there is. It is this: if you combine the Veil with the fact that you create your own reality, then we get to the understanding that, firstly, you do not know that you create your reality. And secondly, as you believe, so you shall conceive. Which is just a pretty way of saying that you will always find more and more evidence for the stuff you believe to be true. And because **you** find evidence, you get re-affirmed in your belief. But because of the Veil you cannot prove that belief to anyone else. And since they too are just seeing more and more evidence for their beliefs... well... it becomes a recipe for disaster for the dogmatic. Anyone can see that there will be plenty of opportunity for conflict for anyone who wants to experience that! But that's not the point I wish to really make here. The point I wish to make is that you have the free will option to believe whatever you want about your reality. And, as you believe it, so you'll get evidence to prove yourself right to yourself. And, no matter what anyone else says, they will not be able to prove you wrong unless you are open to seeing things their way. You have nothing less than free will to believe anything you want. And to pretty much **do** anything you want as well. Certainly, there are human laws and societal norms which attempt to govern your activities, but there are precious few God-made laws that stop you from doing whatever you want.

Z: Whoa! What about... like holy scriptures and so on? What about, "*Thou shalt not kill*"?

J-D: No. No disrespect to those rules. But they are man-made. If God made the law, "*Thou shalt not kill,*" then you would not be able to kill. Period. Either you would not be able to formulate the thought to kill someone else, or it would be physically impossible, as it is in higher dimensional realms. Where I am, it is totally and utterly impossible for a being to "cease to be". There is no death. From certain perspectives you could say that we have a great deal less free will than you do.

Z: That's amazing. But can't you create more powerfully than we can?

J-D: Yes. But we are constrained. I mean, I can create very powerfully but I cannot create with the belief that I am not a part of the oneness. Not unless I send a part of my consciousness to beyond the Veil. Which is exactly what I have done, of course.

Z: You have?

J-D: Yes. (smiles) You are it, remember.

Z: Oh right! (laughs)

So, you are saying that we have a lot of free will over here. And that means we have very few God-made laws.

J-D: Yes.

Z: What about the law of gravity, for example? Or the law of the speed of light?

J-D: Those are not laws. They are suggestions. You can beat gravity with a rocket. You can beat the speed of light with other, slightly more advanced, technology. If you believe in UFOs coming from other solar systems, then you pretty much have to concede a belief in faster-than-light travel. I am saying, believe it or not, that this is not just possible but, technologically, not that far off. The speed limit set by light can be beaten and it is done so all the time by races only a little more advanced than your own. These are not God's laws. They are simply constructs of the mechanics of your reality.

Z: So, do we have any great spiritual laws then?

J-D: Yes. How do you like this one: *"Thou shalt do as thou pleaseth but thou shalt get the consequences-eth of thine choices-eth"*.

Z: (laughs) No, seriously?

J-D: (laughs) Imitation-archaic phrasing aside, I actually am serious. That is my humorous way of stating the law of free will.

You know, in some places in the universe there is a curse that some beings fling at each other when they feel the other is doing wrong. They say, "*May you get exactly what you are creating!*"

This is interesting because there are other parts of the universe where beings offer each other a great benediction when they feel the other is doing great things. They then say, "*May you get exactly what you are creating!*"

Isn't that strange? Especially since there is really no point in wishing such a thing on anyone else because, of course, everyone **always** gets exactly what they are creating. That's the point of free will. You can create whatever you like. And you do so by making choices. The outcome is your life.

So, you can do whatever you want, think whatever you want and believe whatever you want. These are your choices. But your choices will always create results and you will get precisely the results of your choices. That way you can see if you like what you are doing, thinking, believing and choosing. If you do, then you can continue to make more of the same choices and if you don't, then you can change your mind and make new choices. That's the law of free will. There are other realities in which there is much less free will than you have. But if you really want to know about the great laws that govern creation, then you'll have to wait for another future conversation for that to be handled conclusively.

Z: Okay. But before we go on, please just remind me why the law of free will is also called the law of confusion?

J-D: Ah. That will lead us nicely back to the main subject. The law of confusion was introduced to you by a channelled work called *The Law of One*, also known as *The Ra Material*, right?

Z: Right.

J-D: So let's see how the Veil, or the law of free will, pertains to channelled messages. Firstly, anyone reading any channelled words **can** doubt that there is a spirit being speaking through the channeller, can they not? I mean there is nothing in such channelled words that cannot be dreamed up by a sufficiently creative imagination with a little thinking and a little effort, right?

Z: Yeah, I guess. I mean, for years after I first started having intuitive conversations like this one, even I doubted what I was experiencing. I thought that perhaps I was engaged in some grand self-delusion. But I now have sufficient evidence that I am sure it is what it seems to be.

J-D: Is it not possible for you to doubt?

Z: Oh, of course it's possible. I mean I have masses of circumstantial evidence and synchronicities and what-not. But not one of those is incontrovertible proof.

J-D: Right. But if I am who I say I am, and if I am really speaking with you, do you not think it would be the simplest thing for me to give you absolute proof? For example: what if you and a friend got together and he wrote down a long string of random numbers on a piece of paper and then hid it in a box. I can very easily know what those numbers are and then simply pass them to you. Repeat this exercise on international television and that would be the end of all doubt. Right?

Z: Yes, right!

But we can't do that, can we?

J-D: Not without violating the Veil of Unknowing. And not without taking away from everyone on the planet their free will right to doubt, and more importantly, their free will right to create their own reality as they see fit. I mean, if you can prove that you are having an intuitive conversation with me and I can prove that I have all kinds of amazing knowledge, then people would be silly not to stop searching for, and creating, their own truth. They'd just come to you and I for the truth. And that would negate the entire point of this whole reality you are living in.

Z: That's a really good explanation. I never thought of it like that. Thank you. But you still didn't explain the law of confusion.

J-D: I'm glad you are paying attention. I was just getting there. I am saying that the various spirit beings that might speak to Earth people cannot take liberties with the Veil. We cannot give you direct information about anything which would conflict with the Veil and the law of free will. But you folks are desperate for both proof of these psychic phenomena and all kinds of personal advice and guidance which, were it given, would be in contravention of the Veil. So, the spirit being that is being conversed with has some options. In my conversations with you I take a very careful approach. If there is something you really do need to understand from me, and it would contravene the Veil to simply impart it to you, then I work with you to guide you to the experiences and interactions that allow you to arrive at the minimum insights and awarenesses that our conversations can build upon. You will already have noticed this tendency: sometimes you feel the need for a particular conversation with me but find it cannot happen. Not that we don't converse but just that you palpably feel you "can't get" the information you are desiring. It just won't translate correctly. And then, after some time, after some processing on your part, after arriving at some new thoughts and inspirations, suddenly the information that you are seeking simply flows through you as if it always was your own.

Z: I certainly have noticed this and wondered about it.

J-D: If you think logically about it then it will dawn upon you that, as a result of this process, it always could seem to you, could it not, that the information you "received" has been arrived at through your own processing. It **could** be argued that you "worked at it" until you "got it". Could it not?

Z: Ye-e-e-e-s but...

J-D:... but you also feel as if you have been inspired to receive certain bits of information?

Z: Absolutely.

J-D: And so this is the point. You, your readers and everyone else whom you might ever encounter will **always** have the right to choose about this work. You will always be able to choose to believe, if you wish, that this work came from you through a very "normal" process of creative thought.

And as long as that is so, I will have been successful in not contravening the Veil.

Z: That's very interesting.

J-D: It gets more interesting. As you grow in your ability to process new thoughts and experiences, as you expand your mind and consciousness, so we will be able to pass more and more interesting material to you whilst **still** never running foul of the Veil. I look forward to being able to share some truly expansive concepts with you in the not too distant future. All I ask is that you remain as open and as flexible as possible.

Z: I'll try to remember that.

J-D: The other approach I take with you occurs when I feel it not to be in your best interests to have information from beyond the Veil. In such instances I simply do not permit that information to flow. You will have noticed, as a very clear example, when people have asked you to do personal "readings" or to get into facts and details of their own stories, beings like Adamu and I have chosen to talk about the "spiritual concept" or the underlying philosophy rather than go into those personal details. It is sometimes possible to talk about very personal and specific issues where the individual has already done the work but, as a rule, it is preferable to avoid these. If we were to tell others what is true for them this would both be deleterious to their growth and would also contravene the Veil.

There are, from my perspective, far more empowering ways to assist another to find spiritual healing. Instead of using your gifts to tell the other what they should know and believe, you might use your spiritual tools and abilities to help the other to find, within themselves, what is right and true. Assist them to be their own healer and you will have done a great work indeed. And I am always willing to participate in such pursuits with you. This way we can do great good together and never contravene the Veil.

> (**Zingdad note**: If you are interested in engaging in exactly such a process with me, then it is my (and J-D's!) great pleasure to help

you to heal your own pain, address your present life's challenges, find your own truth and power and reintegrate the lost and hurt parts of your soul. Please visit the Soul Re-integration section of my website, zingdad.com, for more information, here: http://zingdad.com/healing-a-helping/soul-re-integration.)

So this is how I respond to the Veil.

There are of course other, entirely different, approaches. For reasons of their own, sometimes the spirit being and the channeller might decide that they want to get into as much personal detail as possible. Such cases unfortunately often occur with channellers who desire to use this facility for personal gain or ego enhancement and, as such, become eager to prove that they are the "real deal". You are advised to use your utmost discretion when dealing with such ones. Their approach to you will be one of, "Only I know the truth, not you and not anyone else." This is a potentially harmful stance to all concerned. If you give your energy to them then this will create dependencies. Unfortunately that is often what such beings desire. They have not understood how this is harmful to their audience **and** to themselves. But, be that as it may, in order to gain the credibility which they desire to support their contention that they are the only source of truth, they will often seek to make claims about the accuracy of their predictions and so forth. They will seek to gain information via phenomena such as channelling which, due to the Veil, is simply not possible to obtain. If you were to do the research and see exactly what their track record really is (as opposed to what they claim it to be) you will find that they often have a hit-rate which is no better than average probability. In other words, they could have done equally well with random educated guesses. You see, the Veil **will simply not** be breached.

The same effect, unfortunately, also applies to channellers who are genuinely and earnestly trying to work out their doubts. First they begin to channel and it seems good to them. But then fear creeps in and they doubt. They wonder whether perhaps the whole thing is a huge self-deception.

Z: I have certainly found myself there!

J-D: Right. And what happened to you then is what will happen to others under such circumstances. In an attempt to put your doubts to rest, you demand proof. Solid, verifiable, incontrovertible **proof**. And when you seek proof, due to the Veil, all you will find is more reason to doubt. If, in your quest for proof, you invite interaction with a spirit being of relatively low vibration, such a being may promise you all manner of amazing things. But you will simply be led on a merry dance and you will not only never get the proof you seek, but will also actually get all manner of falseness and, dare I say it, *confusion*. If, on the other hand, you remain fixed on the idea of speaking only to beings of a higher vibration, then you will gently be coached to release your demand for proof and to rather learn to create the outcome you desire.

The third option is that your own psyche might, as a result of your desire for proof, insert distortions into the material you are receiving.

Z: Why?

J-D: Because, demanding proof of the truth from an agency outside of yourself is actually a kind of spiritual neurosis. There **is no** proof of anything outside of yourself. Because your truth is within you. If you encounter "the truth", it is only "the truth" because your own inner knowingness approves of it. Otherwise it is just another story. As long as you are demanding that another being must create your truth for you, you are distorting your lens. And as long as you are full of fear and self-doubt, such that you do not trust yourself to formulate your own truth and find your own path and create your own reality, then your lens is dirty and your perceptions will be clouded.

So a rather interesting irony is set up:

Those who seek provable, verifiable facts from channellings will often end up getting messages which are, for one reason or another, quite obviously doubtable or outright wrong.

Those who seek to show that they are the legitimate source of all truth will often end up creating evidence showing that they are frauds.

Those who come from a position of doubt will find more reason to doubt.

And all this is a wonderful illustration of how the law of confusion applies to channelled messages. And it gives you some insight into how it might apply more generally. Essentially, if free will is to be observed, then your right to doubt cannot be taken away. Your right to see it another way cannot be taken away. Your right to create it differently cannot be taken away. Your right to make another choice cannot be taken away. There must always be a space for a little chaos and a little confusion.

If you look at it correctly then this is a wonderful and beautiful thing. This means that you always have options. You always have freedom. You can always express your will. Creativity can come into play in every situation. Miracles can happen. Magic can happen. Wonderment and delight can happen. You can get something other than the expected.

And this is essential. If everything were fixed and ordered and contained, then there would be no point in trying to do anything; the outcome would be assured and there would be no challenge, no learning and no growth. Progression and life would cease.

So I would encourage you to embrace the mystery rather than despise it. It is a wondrous thing that nothing is ever absolutely certain and fixed and ordered and dead. Everything is always alive and changing and in flux and brimming with surprise and mystery.

But to come back to the point I was making... perhaps now you can see that endeavouring to concretise things, endeavouring to find proof for our words and demanding that they must be eternally **true**, is counter-productive.

Z: Wow. Yes. So I guess I should finally give up on seeking proof, huh?

J-D: I would say that anyone who wants to find proof is, by their desire, actually affirming that they doubt. That they believe it **not** to be the case. If, as I contend, you are the creator of your reality, then each sponsoring thought will result in evidence cropping up that is congruent with that thought. So, not only does this illustrate the law of confusion, it also illustrates that you are the creator of your reality (which is another law).

But, more about that later. We have progressed quite far on this topic already.

If I may return the train of thought to its tracks: I have made the contention that there is a consciousness construct called the Veil of Unknowing, which is very much in evidence in your experiences (but of course it works so well that you can indeed doubt that it too exists, if you wish). The implications of this Veil are that the one most fundamental truth of all creation, that all is ONE, cannot now be proven beyond a doubt.

Z: But that means that all this stuff you have told me is simply one possible perspective, just like any other? That all perspectives are equally valid?

J-D: Yes. Exactly. Never stand in judgement of another's beliefs or perspectives. Never assume yours are more valid than theirs. But what you can **and should** do, is strive to refine or adjust your own perspectives and beliefs so that they optimally serve you. In my conversations with you I am going to provide you with my own understandings and perspectives. They are delivered with the sole intention that they should assist you to empower yourself, find yourself and remember who you **really** are. And so, while I very much hope that what you read here will be of use to you, you should enact your own truth in choosing to adopt or discard what is offered. If it resonates with you, then you are finding truth here for yourself – you are actually creating your truth out of the information presented to you. If it does not resonate, then you are not "wrong", your truth is simply taking you in a different direction to mine.

There are many truth sets available to you and each will lead you on a different path and all are equally valid. Some will serve you for a while and then no longer be of value, as you and your circumstances change. Some will cause you pain and will eventually force you to release them. Others will serve you for an eternity of time as they bring you ever greater self-love and inner peace on your homeward journey to blissful union with the oneness of all. My invitation to you and your readers is to have a good look at the perspectives offered to you in these conversations. I propose that they are of the latter type. They are a part of my service to this reality and are my contribution to the ascension process that is now occurring. But mostly I urge you to follow your heart and trust to your own truth and intuition above any words you would find anywhere... including these here.

Z: Got it. Thanks. But now I am confused. You said you were going to prove oneness. But then all you did was to tell me that it can't be done because of the Veil. What gives?

J-D: I actually said "more-or-less prove", remember? And you asked me why "more-or-less". And that was my answer.

Z: Ah. Correct. So are we still getting our more-or-less proof?

J-D: Yes, you are. But this is a good spot for us to take a break. Please call this conversation, "The Veil of Unknowing". It is the first part of the topic, "What is oneness?" We'll continue from here in the next session.

Z: Okay, awesome. So in the next session...?

J-D: In the next session we can move on from the understanding that there is a Veil in place which makes direct proof impossible. I will however make some good arguments to show that "all is ONE". Readers can each decide for themselves how close this comes to constituting proof. As usual I will not attempt to transgress the Veil.

Z: Okay, great. See you in the next chapter!

* * * * *

CHAPTER 4.
SCIENTIFIC PROOF OF ONENESS

Zingdad: Hi J-D.

Can we continue our exploration of the question, "Is there proof of oneness?"

Joy-Divine: Yes, of course.

As you will recall, the point of the "Veil of Unknowing" discussion was really to say that, no, we will not be able to prove that all is one. Not in the sense that we will be able to make a statement that cannot be argued or refuted. But we will be able to make some very powerful arguments which will either resonate with the reader or not. Some may wish to call these arguments "proof" in that it provides them with solid reason for what they already know to be true; others may decide to pick holes in my arguments and refute them and say they are **not** proof. Both of these will be valid positions and neither will exclude the other. Each reader will decide for themselves where their own truth lies.

Z: Just a moment, please. I'm not sure if I am happy with all this "your truth" and "my truth" and "all truths are valid" stuff. Doesn't the word **truth** imply that it is **true**? I mean true for everyone?

J-D: It might imply that to you. If it does, then you are going to get very stuck very fast and you are going to find yourself in non-stop conflict with yourself, your life and others with whom you engage.

I see you are struggling with this. We have already touched on it, but I will address it again and this time offer a deeper understanding.

Insisting that there is only one truth which must be valid from all perspectives is an insistence that you and everyone, everywhere must all have the same perspective. Which clearly will not happen. And worse than that, insisting that there is only one truth means that there is no room for growth and change. You are, in effect, insisting that everyone and everything in the whole universe must all have exactly the same experience of life as you. And it's worse than that; you have found, have you not, that some things you believed very strongly to be true when you were younger have, given a little time and a little life's experience, become less true for you? Other things which were not true for you then, now are. This is growth. It happens to everyone. Now, if you are insisting that everyone everywhere must share the same one truth-set with you, then you are actually insisting that everyone, including you, must cease all development and growth so that their perspective remains fixed exactly as it is! Clearly this cannot and will not happen. But those who are determined that is should be so, that they are right and that all others must agree with them, find themselves getting very angry with the world around them for its "wrongness". They often feel that they must fight with the whole world to "fix it" and make it "right" so that it will conform to their expectations. Which it never, ever will. Such beings create a world of pain and conflict for themselves which doesn't end until they themselves begin to loosen up and allow all others to express their own unique, individual truth.

You see, what you believe to be true is based upon your experiences and inputs and your thoughts about these. If you experience something, then you believe that experience to be true. So, logically, if someone experiences something else, then they will have a different belief. Now if two beings get together to discuss their beliefs about life with each other, you will find some less mature souls will, as just outlined, want to fight with each other to attempt to force an agreement. More mature souls, on the other hand, will accept that there is a difference of truths. But it is the master who will understand that another perspective is a gift being offered to them. Ask yourself, "*Under what circumstances could **both** of these things be true?*" and you begin to think like a master. Then you begin to reach for transcendent truths that allow you a greater perspective than that which you have obtained from your own experiences. Then you obtain growth not only from your experiences, but from others' too!

For example: the sky above you is blue. If I told you that it was purple, then how should you respond? Like an immature soul and tell me I am mad, deluded and wrong? Like a mature soul who might understand that I see things differently? Or like a master who might reach for a greater truth: that some skies are blue and some skies are purple, that perhaps the sky is the colour it is as a result of its gaseous make-up and that I come from another planet with a different atmosphere. Logically then, there must be all kinds of **other** colours of sky. "*How marvellous, how exciting!*" the master will conclude. How much better than having an argument!

I very much do suggest, therefore, that you come to understand that that which you believe to be true, is "your truth". It is that which is true for you, for now. Nothing more. Be willing for your truth to change. Be open to the fact that others' truths are as true for them as yours is for you. You will find this to be quite a healthy psycho-spiritual position to take. It will allow you to be flexible when dealing with others who hold different perspectives from your own. And it will allow you to be flexible with yourself as you grow and inevitably discover that what you have held to be true no longer serves you. In this way you will enable growth with a minimum of pain. It will bring you greater peace and harmony if you take this position. And it will allow you to begin thinking like a master.

You will gain a far deeper insight into the whole subject of truth in due course when you introduce your readers to our beloved associate, the being called 8. He is very well suited indeed to such a conversation. But until then, for the sake of continuing this discussion, please accept that it is **my** truth that each and every person has a different perspective; each holds a different set of things to be true.

Z: Okay. You have made a very persuasive case. So you are saying no-one's truth is better than anyone else's?

J-D: "Better"? That is a rather pointless value judgement. What I am saying is that anyone's truth is as valid as any other's if it serves them on the path they are travelling.

I suggest to you that your truth is the scaffolding upon which you build your reality. Some peoples' truths do not permit much scope for building. Perhaps the scaffolding is too small and restricting. Or perhaps it is structurally unsound and anything that is hung upon it threatens to collapse it. Such truth-sets will cause those who hold them much spiritual pain. By contrast, others' truths are simple, clear and strong in their structure. A great deal can be built upon them without difficulty. Such truth-sets bring a great sense of joy and a love for life to those who bear them. And so, from this description, you might think it obvious that the latter type is "better". But there are many, many, many souls that take great pride in holding to truths that cause them pain. They hold these truths because it is right for them to do so... because what they believe is, they say, right for them. And who are you or I to tell them that they are wrong? They must decide for themselves and they must hold to that which they consider to be true. Each must, quite simply, decide what is right for themselves; what resonates in their own being and "better" does not come into it.

The reason I am here now having these conversations with you is this: I wish to share my truth-set with you. It is my deeply held belief that what I have to offer can be of great value to anyone who desires to ascend their consciousness, anyone who wishes to find self-love, love for all and inner-peace. I am here now in these conversations with you to offer my truth as that which leads to unity consciousness, to wholeness, to love, to peace and ultimately to the greatest possible **joy**. I think you will find that it offers you the "truth scaffolding" upon which you can build a reality which is very joyous indeed. Should it be right for you to integrate that which I will be sharing with you into your truth-set then you will come to discover in yourself a magnificent, beautiful, wondrous Self that is in a state of blissful oneness with All That Is. A powerful creator being that is totally in harmony with All That Is... with God.

I contend, from my own vast, multi-dimensional experience, that the view I offer will promote an ascension path. Yes, you can find your way to ascension via other paths. But the truth-set I offer **is** the path of **joy** and it is most certainly a happy path.

So, I offer my truth as a gift to any who might read this work. But the deal is this: you can take this gift or leave it, as it suits you. You can even take the bits you like and leave the rest. Or you can take it, try it on for a while, see if you like it and discard it if you don't. Whatever you want to do with this gift of my truth is up to you and is fine by me. But if you accept any part of this gift or the whole of it, then **you** are responsible for that which you accept into yourself. That which you take becomes yours because you have claimed it for yourself. And you are responsible for yourself, your truth and your beingness.

Z: Okay, thanks for the explanation. And those terms are most acceptable to me. That is how it would be and **should be** if we are each to act as adult spirit beings. That we create and choose for ourselves... and then take responsibility for our choices and creations. So thank you.

So, okay, I do believe I am finally ready to totally embrace the notion that we each have our own truth. That truth is a totally subjective thing, unique to each perspective.

And so, with that, perhaps we can get into the topic itself?

J-D: Good, let's do that. I said I was going to sort-of prove that God is one with All That Is, right?

Z: Right.

J-D: Well, to make an argument, it is often easiest to have a position to debate against. If I want to make the statement, *"God is one with All That Is,"* then probably the most radically opposed position would be that of the atheist. As atheists deny the very existence of God, they therefore would not accept anything one might say about God. Right?

Z: Right. It can be quite hard to argue with an atheist.

J-D: That's right because, usually, atheists pride themselves on being very logical and rational. They don't go in for airy-fairy nonsense that can't be proven empirically. They claim that the universe can be explained without the need for a God and since there is no direct evidence for God, what the heck is everyone doing with all this religion nonsense? And their position, due to the Veil, is of course quite a reasonable one. If you insist that there is nothing beyond that which can be directly perceived by the senses, then it certainly can seem as if spiritual beliefs are just superstitious nonsense.

Z: So you can't prove the oneness of all to them, right?

J-D: Hold on. Not so fast. I have a lot of love and respect for rational people of the mind. The scientific method is a wonderful thing and has deepened the human experience immeasurably. I wouldn't want us to begin to play a whole new level of the game only to desert all our atheist friends here at this level. So there is a little surprise in store for them. You see the Veil is, and has for a while now, been thinning.

Z: What does that mean – the Veil is thinning?

J-D: It means that it gradually becomes easier and easier to penetrate the mystery. It is slowly becoming more possible to discover that there **is** in fact a God of which everyone and everything everywhere is an indivisible part.

Z: Whoa there! So what was all the stuff about the value of the Veil and how important it is? If it's such a hot idea then why is it going away?

J-D: Great question! And here's the answer: no matter how much you like a game and no matter how important a science experiment is, games and scientific experiments alike always come to an end. At some point those engaged with them will say, "*We have got what we wanted from this, let's do something else,*" right? Well that is a very, very rough paraphrase of the greater situation here. This game (or experiment) that is your reality is in the midst of changing quite radically so that it can, eventually, be brought to an elegant and joyful end.

You see, the high-order spirit beings that are involved with the planning, creation and continued unfoldment of this reality are very loving beings. They love you and, in fact, they know that they **are** you. So, while it is ordained that the game must eventually end, they desire to give everyone in the system every opportunity that you could possibly need to awaken so that you will be ready, willing and able to leave this game before it is collapsed in upon itself.

So, as fantastically valuable a construct as the Veil is, it is also so that its usefulness is primarily in permitting those who wish to play inside this game to do so. It allows entrance into separation and it also allows you to remain there. Now, as it becomes desirable for you to awaken and raise yourself up into higher densities of consciousness and, eventually, to leave this reality altogether, so it is equally desirable for the Veil to slowly become ever more transparent now. Over time it will just get thinner and thinner until, eventually, all will simply see right through it.

Z: And if the Veil is that which makes it impossible to know oneness, then it becoming transparent will mean that it is impossible to **not** know oneness?

J-D: Very perceptive, yes. Oneness is the ultimate truth. So, when the Veil is transparent the oneness of all will, quite literally, be the single most obvious thing in all of existence.

When the Veil is totally removed then, for you, there will be only oneness and no more separation.

Z: You know, I had actually noticed, even in the short space of my lifetime, that the Veil is thinning. I find that there is more and more spiritual awareness "out there" in the world. More and more people seem to be awakening. And I also find it is getting progressively easier and easier for me to advance my own spiritual growth. My own ascension. Does this mean that everyone is experiencing this? Will even atheists, for example, be experiencing something similar now?

J-D: No. Not everyone approaches things as you do. All perspectives are valid, remember. And so, there is of course nothing essentially **wrong** with being an atheist. It is a perfectly reasonable, logical response to this reality. And an atheist, by definition, does not perceive himself to be engaged in some "spiritual path" or another. But the atheist will not be punished for taking a completely reasonable stand! Everyone **must** have the option to be able to choose to see the oneness and so ascend to a higher level of reality. So, how does the atheist experience the thinning of the Veil? Well, certainly, for those who base their atheism on the scientific method and empiricism, there are some interesting possibilities that are now opening up. With the thinning of the Veil, the awareness of the oneness of all now begins to enter into all kinds of previously impenetrable areas. Another way of saying this is that things that would always have remained inexplicable, now become understandable in the context of the pervading consciousness of oneness.

Z: In practical terms? What does that mean exactly?

J-D: It means that those who are truly trying to understand the material world, those who are deeply exploring the nature of matter, gravity, energy, space and light (to name a few) will begin to find ever more evidence of the eternal oneness of all.

Z: Really? How?

J-D: Well the first glimmerings have been there for a little while now. Physicists engaged in quantum mechanics are endeavouring to understand your reality by understanding the nature of matter at its smallest scale. I can heartily recommend that you find a good book on quantum mechanics. Find something that will explain all this in lay-man's terms. Or research it on this wonderful tool called the Internet. You will find yourself stunned at the discoveries and their implications. I will give you one example: these physicists, in trying to explain why minute sub-atomic particles behave as they do, have come up with a theory which suggests that no quantum reaction can occur without there being a consciousness to observe it. In other words, consciousness precedes all matter. If you take the view that the first quantum reaction in your universe occurred at the very beginning of the "Big Bang", then essentially they are saying there must have been "someone" there before the Big Bang to observe that first reaction. And it also means that, since the Big Bang there must have been a consciousness there to observe every single subatomic reaction that has ever occurred.

So then who – or what – would you propose could be that vast field of consciousness that has been able to observe every reaction that has ever, and will ever, occur right from the very, very smallest scale of what is known to humanity?

If that isn't God then it must be something very like it, right?

Z: That's fascinating!

J-D: Very. And here is another one I want to tell you about. It is something called the zero-point energy field. This was proposed by Einstein and is now pretty generally accepted in scientific circles. Essentially this is a description of the "base state" of your universe. There is a field which is everywhere, all the time. It is a field of infinite energy. But you can't normally detect it because, well, it is everywhere all the time. You can therefore only detect this field by becoming aware of the variations in it.

Z: I don't understand?

J-D: Okay, how's this analogy: if the air around is dead still and at body temperature, are you likely to be aware of it?

Z: I guess not.

J-D: You would not. But the fact of your inability to perceive it does not mean that you are not, in fact at the bottom of a massive ocean of air molecules. All around you and piled up hundreds of kilometres above you, it presses in upon you from all directions. You should be acutely aware of it pressing upon you all the time. But you are not. In great part because it is unchanging.

If there is a pressure change, then a breeze begins to stir to equalize that pressure. Then you are aware of it. If there is a temperature change and your body begins to lose or gain heat from the environment, then you feel that. You see? It is very hard indeed for you to detect something which has no variation because there is nothing to actually measure. Things that are constant cannot easily be perceived.

Z: Okay. I get that. Thanks.

J-D: So, the zero-point energy field is a field of infinite energy that is everywhere, all the time. It is there in equal quantity where there is the densest matter at the heart of a collapsed star as it is in the near-vacuum of deep space. It is everywhere and it is always infinite.

Z: But if this is infinite energy and it is everywhere, then why can't we use this to power our cars and homes? Like instead of fossil fuels or whatever?

J-D: That is certainly possible. There is a small problem and a big problem that hinders you. The small problem is to discover an appropriate technology that will allow this and the much bigger problem is bringing this technology to the fore without having certain vested interests stopping you from doing so. But this is a big kettle of very contentious fish and I don't really want to spend a whole lot of time on it now. I am actually just wanting you to understand the concept so that I can make my point.

Z: Okay. So then you were saying that there is this infinite energy field and it is everywhere all the time...

J-D: Right. Remember in our previous chat we discovered that all matter is actually just energy?

Z: I do.

J-D: Well what I want to say is that it will come to be proven that this energy, which makes up all the matter in your universe, comes from the infinite energy of the zero-point energy field. It is fluctuations (like waves or ripples) in this field that form the most basic building blocks of matter: sub-atomic particles.

The problem with this is that waves are not static. They move around. And they interfere with each other and cancel each other out.

Z: Why is that a problem?

J-D: Because it would happen so fast and so repetitively that no matter would come into being. Sub-atomic particles would appear, then disappear. There wouldn't even be a single atom in the universe. All the matter that now already **does** exist in the form of your body, your planet and your universe would simply dissipate into chaos and revert to the energy of the zero-point field quite quickly.

Z: Why?

J-D: Because if matter is ultimately composed of waves of energy, then what is keeping those waves from dissipating? Can you see it? If the sub-atomic particles which together make up your body are made of waves, why do those waves not simply ripple away, as waves do? Or why do the peaks and the troughs not simply cancel each other out and cause the matter of your body to dissipate out of existence? Instead of this happening, why does the matter of your body appear to remain constant?

What I am saying is that your scientists will come to understand the zero-point energy field such that it will be clear that all matter is essentially composed of complex inter-relations between fluctuations in that field. But they will be unable to understand why these fluctuations remain stable. "*If it is all just energy fluctuations, why do they not fall into chaos?*" will be the question. And it is apparent that they don't. Your physical body is one such energy system. And it is apparent to you that you maintain a degree of physical integrity. Your body continues to exist in the expected form from moment to moment without falling into chaos. So this might seem incongruous and confusing. But the beauty of this is in the solution; as I have said before, your theoretical physicists have already begun to talk in terms of consciousness. Well, consciousness is once again going to have to be invoked here. The one hypothesis that will resolve the problem and continue to make sense will be one which understands that the matter of your physical universe doesn't fly apart because there are blueprints for everything in your reality in a higher dimension. Quite literally this will suggest that there must be a "someone" who is creating (or imagining) every single element of your reality and holding this image (or blueprint) in their creative mind.

Z: So you are suggesting that this blue-print that exists in a higher dimension acts as a mould into which you can pour these sub-atomic particles?

J-D: No, that would not be the best analogy. It will require some more explaining before I can get to a good analogy. The first thing you need to understand is that these waves don't stand still. They flow endlessly onwards. So, rather think of these blueprints as an impediment in a stream which causes an eddy in that stream. For example, if you open a tap and watch the stream of water, and then put your finger in that stream, you can notice what happens to the stream after your finger. If you hold your finger still, there will be a "shape" to the flow of the water after your finger and that "shape" will remain fairly stable and constant. This is despite the fact that the material (the water) making up the shape is in constant flow. Do you follow this?

Z: Yes. That makes sense.

J-D: Well then let me apply that analogy. There are ripples in the zero-point energy field. These ripples cause sub-atomic particles to pop into your reality. At the most basic level, a few simple blue-prints are created which cause these sub-atomic particles to move in such a way as to become entwined in a dance. Once bonded in such a way they form together particles such as electrons and protons that, together, compose atoms. Certain sub-atomic particles, when entwined in one way, may cause an electron to form. Others, when entwined another way may cause a proton to form. It all has to do with the way these subatomic particles are caused to interrelate.

Z: That is quite difficult for me to visualise.

J-D: Yes. I am explaining things for which you have almost no frame of reference. If this **really** interests you then you should first go and make a study of what your scientists are saying so that we have a grounding upon which we can build. I am simply using this to illustrate a philosophical point.

Z: Okay. Carry on please.

J-D: Thank you. The point is that, even at this most basic level of reality there is an interaction between two God-like things. The one is the infinite energy field which has been called the zero-point energy field. The other is consciousness, which creates the moulds that cause the energy to form stable patterns which creates the illusion of the matter of your universe.

Z: Ah. So you are saying that, over time, for those who are avidly watching scientific developments, there will be evidence of God?

J-D: Certainly it will make them ask some very interesting questions! It will become ever more difficult not to conclude that consciousness exists independent of human brains.

Z: Okay, but now I am curious. What happens to the atoms so that they eventually become people and planets and stars and stuff?

J-D: Ah. This is a very long and complex story to get through. Seeing as it is not necessary to **this** discussion, as my point is already made, I will simply say that there are ever more complex blue-prints. So the first blue-prints make atomic particles. The next set uses the previous set to make atoms. Then molecules. Then more complex forms. Essentially I am saying that there are blue-prints, within blue-prints within blue-prints. The more basic a blue-print is, the more often it is re-used in other more complex blue-prints. Your body is a mind-boggling interplay of an astoundingly large number of blue-prints of all kinds of levels of complexity. The final, highest level of the blue-print is held by your body-spirit. But that too is another conversation for another day.

Z: Okay. I'll make a note to get to that. But for now I do see that you have made your point that an in-depth understanding of the matter which makes up our bodies and our reality is, as you say, an interaction between consciousness and an infinite energy field. Excellent! What's next?

J-D: Not so fast. I'm not quite done with this topic. There is another God-like understanding to be had out of all this.

Z: Okay, shoot.

J-D: Let's go back to the analogy of the stream of water. Remember I said that the stream flows past the "blue-print" and that makes a pattern?

Z: Yes.

J-D: well that means that the pattern is static but the material that **makes** the pattern is not.

Z: Yes. The water flows on.

J-D: Right. So what does it mean to you if I say that the "stream" of the zero-point energy field passes through you? You don't "hold on to it" and it does not reside within you. The stream of ripples flows constantly into and out of your body. The only reason there is a body there at all is because your body is the place where there is a confluence of all the blue-prints. The blue prints are steady, the energy itself is not.

Z: Okay, that is an odd thought. But respectfully... so what?

J-D: Ha! So what? I'll tell you "so what"! It means that there is no separation between your body and anything else in the universe. Your body and every other person and thing in your whole universe are all **the same thing**.

Z: Wow!

J-D: Yes! Let's go back to the water analogy. If you held two different forms in the water stream, one below the other, and saw two different "shapes" of eddy in the water, you would see that the shapes are different but you would not think of them as different "things", would you?

Z: No. It's all just water, isn't it?

J-D: Right. And so there is the third God-like thing that will cause the scientifically-minded a spot of wonder: it will transpire that all things are one. Nothing that you can observe is separated from anything else. It's all just different patterns in the same one thing. And that same one thing flows endlessly and continuously through everything.

Z: Wow. That's actually quite beautiful.

J-D: As above, so below and as below, so above. You see? If you are willing to truly look, you will see God in everything. But the Veil has made this quite difficult. And now the Veil is thinning and it becomes ever easier to truly see. I am saying it is now already possible to discern, but in very short order there are going to be headlines coming from the scientific community which are going to point these sorts of things out:

All is ONE.

Everything is completely and absolutely interconnected.

The oneness is infinite and unending.

It is of infinite energy.

Everything is of consciousness.

Consciousness pervades all things everywhere.

Consciousness is greater than, and pre-exists, matter.

Z: Wow! Those are some pretty God-like statements. Pretty mystical stuff.

J-D: Yes. And this is what is already starting to come from Science. I am saying this will increase dramatically soon.

Z: Okay so... just for clarity. Are you saying that the zero-point energy field is God?

J-D: I am saying that it is an indivisible **part** of God. And, as with all indivisible parts, it cannot but fail to have many of the attributes of God. That is why, if you study it and understand it, you will begin to discern those attributes.

Z: Ah. And who creates all the blue-prints you talked about?

J-D: Various creator beings working at various levels of creation. You and everyone with you there on Earth are engaged in holding many combined blue-prints. You just don't yet know it. But again, you and the creator beings of this reality are also indivisible parts of God.

Z:... and as with all indivisible parts we cannot fail to have some of the attributes of God, right?

J-D: Spot on! Is it not said that you are made in the image of God? What does that mean? That God has two arms and two legs and so on? No. That is to view the thing the wrong way round. It means that what God is can be seen reflected in what you are. You are consciousness. You are creators. You are infinite and immortal. You are **one** with everything else that is. And so on and so on.

Z: Sheesh! And this will come from Science?

J-D: No. Science will make it possible to see things this way, for those who choose it. It will always also be possible to see things another way. As we have already discussed at some length, as long as the Veil persists, there never will be proof of anything such that it absolutely cannot be doubted or denied. It **must** be possible for new thoughts to be had. This is how beings create for themselves whatever variation of a reality they wish to explore. So your scientists will find themselves presented with all kinds of interesting new data about your physical universe. There will be many possible theoretical hypotheses to explain this data. What I am saying here is that a model which includes consciousness and the oneness of all will not only be possible but will provide a highly satisfying hypothesis. It will make sense and the data will fit the model in a way that is simple and elegant. I am also saying that it will be possible to doubt that and to keep looking for other hypotheses. Some of these others will hold promise but, in order to make them work, the hypothesis will just keep requiring ever greater levels of complexity. Which is fine if you like complexity.

The bottom line here is this: for those who are of a highly analytical mind, those who are rigorously logical, rational and scientific by nature, those who have chosen to say that they are atheists because there is no evidence for God – I am saying now – for **those**, there will be the opportunity to see God in the evidence. They will be able to follow the mathematical models and actually find evidence for a God which is one with All That Is.

Z: That's fantastic. When will this happen?

J-D: It is busy happening. It is busy unfolding as we speak in the minds and laboratories of the scientists of your planet. Some of this has already been reported on in scientific circles. More will come. But please listen carefully: the point is that everyone will be able to **choose**. If you choose to be open to it, you will find more and more evidence of an unending, eternal, unifying creator consciousness. For God. But if you are wishing to play another round of the same old duality game you may reject this and choose not to see it as proof. Everyone has free will. And if someone desires to keep their consciousness in duality, they have every right to do so. If they will not see the light that is offered, then it will not touch them. And that is okay.

Z: Are they then lost?

J-D: No! No one and nothing is ever lost! All is already **one**. It always is, always was and always will be. You, in duality, are aspects of the ONE that have chosen to forget this. This was not "wrong" of you; it was what you were meant to do. And now that some of you are choosing to remember that you are one, it does not make the rest, those who are **not** choosing to remember, "wrong" either. Just as you were never actually lost in duality in lives past (even if it felt like that to you) just so are others who are not, right now, remembering who they really are, also not lost. All will remember in perfect, divinely right time. When they are ready.

Z: Okay. So, I think I get it. It will become more and more possible to become aware, via science, of the oneness of all and the underlying unifying consciousness from which all things arise. Then, as now, each individual will be able to choose to accept this perspective or not. And there is no judgement either way. The difference is that holding this perspective will take you towards ascension while taking another perspective will allow you to remain in duality.

J-D: Yes. That is a good enough summary.

Z: But what about the non-scientific types? I mean there are very many people on Earth who will not be touched by the rather rarefied theoretical constructs of quantum mechanics, right?

J-D: Correct. Way back in the beginning of this topic I said that I was going to use the scientific/ rational/ atheist position as a vehicle to make my case. Next, I am going to use the religious position. But that is enough for now. We'll take a break here and pick it up again in our next conversation, which we shall call, "Religious Proof of Oneness".

Z: I look forward to it...

* * * * *

CHAPTER 5.
RELIGIOUS PROOF OF ONENESS

Zingdad: J-D, I take it we are not going to "prove" the oneness of all beyond all doubt from the religious perspective, either?

Joy-Divine: No, you are right. It doesn't matter how one addresses this, people will always have the right and the ability to doubt or to choose other. This is very much **not** about silencing other views. This is about presenting a view which you and your readers can choose to accept if it resonates with your heart. I previously addressed it from the atheist/scientific perspective, not because I in any way wish to attack or persuade such people. Not at all. Simply because one needs a starting point from which to make a cogent argument. And now I am going to do this again. I am going to stand in another place and make the same argument from this other perspective. This new perspective is that of organised religion. For my purposes, I will divide religions into two groups: those that see God as separate from the self and those that see the self as one with God. The latter group are already in agreement with the point I am making here, so we can, for the purposes of this discourse, just let them be. So I will use the former belief as a starting position: the view that there **is** a God but that God is separate from, or outside of, God's creation.

I would like to offer certain observations: if someone already believes in an omnipotent Supreme Creator Being, then I would make the following contention. Being omnipotent, the Supreme Creator can do whatever It likes, right?

Z: Umm. Just a minute please. I'm not sure if I'm really happy with the "It" label for God.

J-D: Yes. I know. I am sorry. You have cultural associations that "It" is somehow inferior to Him or Her. Well I am afraid I am not going to pander to those associations. The Supreme Creator does not have a gender. It is way,

way beyond such petty issues. It is both, and neither, and very much beyond gender. So, until there is a better word in the English language which signifies, "*Him, Her and It and every other gender that could possibly be in all creation, and all of these, and none of them,*" then I am going to be stuck with using "It". This is very much the opposite of being derogatory. Restricting God to one gender is far more derogatory in my view. But as a nod to offended sensibilities, we will capitalise the "I" of the word "It". Is that okay?

Z: Yes, perfectly, thank you. But seeing as I have already interrupted and am busy nit-picking, what of the label "God"? I mean, does that not imply one religious perspective? Should we not maybe say "Source" or... something less restrictive?

J-D: Ooooookay. Let's quickly deal with that too. No name or label that you might choose to come up with will ever suffice. A label is, by its very nature, reductive. It excludes everything that is not that. No label is ever going to do the job of describing God because God is everything and yet more than that. God is beyond complete comprehension and description. So we should probably just choose to be silent on the subject of God altogether because everything that you might say about God is a reduction of the truth. No names and no descriptions and no attempts to understand. But that would be silly. Surely we should at least **try** with what we have to comprehend God? Make a start and keep improving our comprehension as our abilities to comprehend increase? And since you on planet Earth use language to communicate and develop your thoughts, we must find **some** word for God. If we disallow all words then we cannot speak of It. And if we come up with a descriptive term then that is even worse, as it is even more restrictive. So, in the interests of just allowing the conversation to happen, I simply choose the name that has the greatest resonance in the culture you currently inhabit. If I spoke of The Mighty Zeelagzog (or whatever invented name), you'd say "who?" So rather, if I start out by speaking of God, then you know of whom I speak, even if I thereafter have to clarify what my view is of God. Which is **exactly** what I am doing right now. If your view of God is that It is separate from the rest of us, then I am here telling you what my view of God is, which is that It is ONE with us and All That Is. So I will use the name "God" and over time you will come to understand what I mean by that name. If your reader prefers another term, then I humbly beg their latitude in this regard.

Z: Okay, got it. Thank you for the clarification and my apologies for the interruption. Can we please pick it up again where we left off?

J-D: Yes, certainly. I was making the observation that, if God is omnipotent, then God can do whatever It wishes and create whatever It wills, right?

Z: Right.

J-D: So, if such a Being wanted to experience the world from your perspective, It could. In fact It could, if It wanted to, experience the world from the perspective of every single living being **at the same time**, could It not?

Z: Yes. I guess the word "omnipotence" pretty much means that you are not restricted. You can do anything. Including, I am sure, seeing everything from every perspective.

J-D: So then the only question would be **if** God would desire this. Would God desire to see things exactly as you (and everyone else) does or would God desire to view Creation from "above" or from a "separate" position? I will answer the question like this: what is the most loving perspective for God to take? What perspective would God hold that would give God the most love and compassion for you? Clearly, in order for God to **really** understand you, God would need to be willing to experience life **as** you. Otherwise God would stand outside of you and look at all your little foibles and fumbles and just see you as flawed and broken. But if God experiences the world through you, **as** you, then certainly God can have nothing but compassion and love for you. So I present you with a choice: do you believe God is loving or not? I would most strongly assert that God **is** love. And I present to you the simple truth that the most loving choice for God is that God does not see Itself as separate from you. But if God only chose to see things through your eyes, but still **know** that it is God, then that would **not** be your perspective. Your perspective is **exactly** the way it looks for you. I am saying that the most loving thing for God to do is to hold **exactly** your perspective too. God therefore experiences the world through you, **as** you! Even when you don't know about God's existence or believe in God or whatever. God is still in you. And in every other possible perspective. So God does not enter only into certain pious and "godly" perspectives when they are well behaved! No. That is conditional love. And I am saying that God **is** unconditional love.

Z: You are saying this. But can you prove it... that God loves us unconditionally.

J-D: Again, I can only make a strong argument. You will believe what you want. But if you believe that God is omnipresent and omniscient then you are, by definition, agreeing with me.

Z: Huh? How?

J-D: Omnipresent means present at every point. There is nowhere where God is not. Including, obviously, where you are. Now, if you broaden your understanding of location, you will understand that you are not just geographically at your present location, you are also spiritually at that location. You are spiritually where you are as a result of the beliefs and ideas you have about yourself, life and God. Well, God is omnipresent. This means God is **also** at that exact location with you and everywhere else at every other location with every other being and thing in All That Is.

Z: Hmm. Good point.

J-D: And omniscient means "all knowing". Do you know what it is like to be a dog?

Z: No... not really.

J-D: But you have dogs living in your home with you. You love them like children. You observe everything they do and often study their interactions and processes with great interest. Why do you not know what it is like to be a dog?

Z: Because I am a human! I have no knowledge of ever having been a dog!

J-D: Ah ha! In order to **truly** know what it is like to be someone, you actually have to **be** that someone. Otherwise you only know something **about** that being. Now it is the same with God. If God is truly omniscient, then God cannot only know about you. If God observes you from outside, then God will never really know what it is like to **be** you. So instead God does that: God **is** you.

Z: But... isn't that a ridiculously egotistical position to take – that I am God? I mean God is so great and...

J-D: No. It can't be egotistical to claim for yourself that which you are also claiming for everyone else. In fact I am claiming this same thing for every animal, plant, insect, stone, molecule, atom... you get the picture. From this perspective, I am saying you are as great as the universe but also as great as an amoeba. Does that sound like egotism? This position makes you neither greater nor lesser than any other being in All That Is. But it does make God **much** greater.

Z: How's that?

J-D: Obviously a God of infinite perspectives who is everywhere and knows everything and is of infinite power and ability is greater than a God who only holds some perspectives and can only live outside of you until you do certain "good and holy" things.

Z: Hmm. Another good argument.

J-D: So, I present you with a conundrum. If God is omnipotent **and** if God is love, then it would seem God **must** be one with you. And if God is omniscient, then God **must** be one with you. And if God is omnipresent, then God **must** be one with you.

So, now the choice is yours. Do you want to give up your belief in these attributes of God? Do you prefer to believe that God is **less** than these things? Do you want to say that God is not omnipotent, is not love, is not omniscient and is not omnipresent? Or do you wish to accept the inevitable truth that God is one with all... including you and each of your readers, of course?

Z: I'm sure there must be other arguments to be made.

J-D: You're right! There are always other arguments because there is always room to doubt or to create another view. That is your free will choice coming into play. And if that is the direction your heart is leading you, then you must, of course, follow your own truth. I am not here to tell you what your truth must be. I am here to tell you what my truth is. I make my case and I support it. Then you can decide.

Z: No, wait a minute. What I want to get at is that you have made quite a strong case that God holds all perspectives. I can agree that this might mean that God is able to know exactly what it is like to be me and have experienced things exactly as I did and all that stuff. But that is not the same thing as saying that God is one with me.

J-D: How is it not?

Z: Well, umm... what if God sort-of piggy backed with me in my mind... you know?

J-D: No. Either God **is** you experiencing your life exactly as you are experiencing it, or God's experience of your life is different from yours. You can't have it both ways. No matter how small the difference, **any** separation at all would break the rules of omniscience and omnipresence. But, as I say, we can keep riding this pony round and round finding little points to debate if we want to.

Z: No, I can see that. I accept what you say. It makes perfect sense and it actually **does** resonate in my heart too. But there is something that I can't quite figure out: why is God doing this? This seems like an awfully elaborate thing to do... to create this whole universe and fill it with who knows how many trillions of particles of Yourself who, none of them, know that they are You. Why go to all that effort? What is it all for?

J-D: Remember the parable in Chapter 3? The one about the king who drank the potion of forgetfulness? Well, it's a bit like that. God is engaged in an endless process of self-creation and self-discovery.

"*How would it be if I was like* **this**?" is the question which creates a new being... or a whole new universe. The journey into forgetting, which happens here in this reality, is one possible means of self-discovery.

"*How would it be if I did not know who or what I really was?*" leads to any number of realities. This is one of them. The reality is the question. You, each of you, are one possible answer.

"*I am what happens to God under* **these** *conditions,*" is the answer that you are busy returning.

Z: Okay... so I am one with God and we all are. And we are engaged in a journey of self-discovery. By engaging in my own personal journey of self-discovery I bring more self-knowledge to the all.

J-D: Good! Yes! If you would like to discover God, then the best place to begin is by discovering yourself.

Z: Hmm. I follow the logic but... that seems awfully... I mean... won't some people find that a bit blasphemous?

J-D: Oh, assuredly! But then there are those who will find the very notion of this conversation blasphemous. Look hard enough and you'll find someone who will label just being happy as blasphemous. So I cannot concern myself with what others will choose to think or believe. For myself, I find the whole concept of blasphemy to be without meaning. It is ridiculous to think that you are capable of offending God or hurting God's feelings. You most certainly **can** hold beliefs and opinions that can hurt **you** though. And, holding hateful thoughts about God, for example, will do that. But, given enough time and a little loving guidance, all beings eventually come to decide that they don't like hurting themselves and then they stop doing this and choose something more constructive instead. Something that brings them peace, love and joy. And, loving God will certainly do **that**. God knows this. God sees you as you truly are. You cannot do or say some momentary little thing that could offend God. It is actually totally impossible because God, being infinite, is literally bigger than that.

Z: So, what then is blasphemy? If God cannot be offended, why do we even have this word?

J-D: The notion of blasphemy is a fiction used by some to control others via fear. It dates back to the most ancient times when shamans and witch-doctors would tell the tribe that they had to behave in certain ways or the gods would be unhappy and then there would be a poor harvest... or some similar notion. This is exactly the same idea that is presented to you in your society by religious authorities who demand that you think, believe and act a certain way and only say certain approved things. If you step outside of the bounds they set for you then, they tell you, you will displease God who will then make your life hard or even smite you with pestilence and cause you to die. And then, of course, will cause you to be tormented with agony for an eternity. It is the same story of manipulation and control all over again. The only difference is that the newer religions are perhaps a little more cruel and violent in their imagined punishment for those who don't do as they demand. But no matter. It is all equally erroneous. God does not create narrow rules for you to follow. God gives you free will instead. God is not a petulant child to throw a tantrum when you take up the offer of free will. God is not a vindictive, cruel sadist to hurt you for making very human, very normal errors in judgement. You hurt yourself over these errors and will, absolutely guaranteed without fail, learn from your errors eventually and, given a little time, come to make better decisions. So what would be the point of punishing you? Punishment does not teach you anything. Letting you get **exactly** what you have created is what teaches you. God is certainly not unobservant, ignorant or unintelligent. God will not do what does not work.

The entire notion of blasphemy and divine punishment is not only without merit, it also directly contravenes what God is and how God would behave. God is one with you and God is beyond the desire to hate or punish Itself.

If there is such a thing as blasphemy, then it is to suggest that there is such a thing as blasphemy (he smiles)

Z: All right. I am ready to accept that. So then clearly it isn't a blasphemous thought to think that the best place to discover God is to look inside my own heart?

J-D: It certainly isn't! I'll remind you of one of my old favourites again: is it not said that you are made in the image of God? Is this not another way of saying, "*If you want to see an image of God... then look at yourself!*"

Z: Ah. Yes. I suppose that is so.

J-D: Again. I don't mean just your physical body. I mean that which you really **are**. Your truest, deepest essence. And if this is so, then it follows that striving to truly, deeply comprehend your own deepest essence **is** striving to know God.

Z: Ah! That makes sense. But we are all God. I mean everything is. So why can I not begin discovering God by looking around me at another person or at nature or something?

J-D: You could try that. And it would work to the degree that observing what is around you helps you to find greater comprehension of yourself. You see, you cannot understand something in another if you have not seen it in yourself first – it will just puzzle you.

"How can they be that way?" you might ask yourself as you walk away shaking your head. If, however, you have seen this thing in yourself, then you will be able to empathise with this other. You will give them a gift of your comprehension that may even help them to understand themselves too. So self-discovery is the key. And self-love is the door. And self-acceptance is how you pass through that door. And this is the journey for which you were created. You see, not only is God looking out at the world through your eyes but, by looking inwards from your perspective, God is looking at Itself. And so it is that you gift God with a new perspective of Itself whenever you discover a little more about yourself.

Z: Hey, that's pretty cool! It means that God is in a constant process of Self-creation and Self-discovery as a result of all these processes that all of us are engaged with.

J-D: Yes! We are God discovering Itself.

Z: All of us altogether are engaged in the same great work then?

J-D: Yes. Even the aspects of God that are doing that which seems to be the worst, darkest things. Even they are creating an opportunity for self-discovery. They do this directly through their own experiences as they grow and discover themselves and also indirectly because they offer light-oriented ones the opportunity to define themselves and discover themselves in opposition to the darkness. If there were no great and powerful enemy, you would never have the opportunity to discover that you are courageous, that you will stand up and do the right thing despite the odds. If there were no one doing wrong, then how would you decide to do right? And so on. The dark ones are just as valuable to the greater process as the light ones. And if you are playing a dark game, then the joy to be had out of changing course and returning to the light is sublime. And of course there really is no such thing as "dark ones" or "light ones". Not really. You all hold both of those states within yourselves. You have all, at some point in your incarnational story and even at some point in this life, done some very unloving things and been to a "dark" place. And everyone, no matter how "dark", will at some point turn around and return to the light. If not in this lifetime, then at some future point. I tell you **all is one**. And we are all engaged, each in our own way, in the process of the discovery of who we really are. And in so doing we are in a process of constant creation. And this is our service to God

Z: That is pleasing to me to think. Thank you for that awesome perspective. But there remains one last obstacle to my accepting your premise that all is one. Such a belief would seem to me to mean that there is no good and evil, no right and no wrong. That we can just do whatever we want, however we want, to whoever we want and that all things will just be acceptable to God. And that doesn't sit right with me. This "all is one" thing seems to lead to a rather amoral stance.

J-D: Only because you have misunderstood it. I want to take a break here as I feel I have addressed the question in that I have made a case for God being one with all when viewed from the religious perspective. You are now asking the perfect question to lead me directly to the next topic, "The Implications of the Oneness". You have hit upon an important issue, which is the question of morality and rules for living. You have made an incorrect assumption, though, which I would like to correct. But all this will be in the next chapter...

* * * * *

CHAPTER 6.
IMPLICATIONS OF THE ONENESS

Zingdad: Hi J-D, I know we said that we were going to talk about the moral implications of the oneness, but there are a few questions that I'd like to ask first.

For starters: you have explained how we might come to see that "all is one" from the two perspectives of science and religion. But are there not a few other perspectives from which we could look at this?

Joy-Divine: Hello Zingdad. Yes. There certainly are a number of different and equally valid perspectives from which this might be addressed. I think, for the people living on your planet right now, there are very nearly 7 billion different valid perspectives.

Z: What? But that is as many people as there are! Oh. Right. I get it. Each person has their own unique perspective and each person's perspective is valid.

J-D: That's right. But you see, we don't need to debate this from all 7 billion different perspectives because we are not trying to argue with people. We are not trying to convince anyone of anything. The only reason I used the two perspectives I did is that they are relatively prevalent and understood positions in the society in which you now live. I simply used them as a framework from which to make my case.

Z: Okay. I understand. But I'm afraid that brings me to another question. If you aren't trying to convince anybody of anything, then what **are** you trying to do? I mean why are you having these conversations with me?

J-D: Ha! Let me first ask you what **you** are trying to do? Why are **you** having these conversations with **me**?

Z: Well... It all started a few years ago when I was trying to find some answers to the questions that bothered me. There was so much about this world and this reality that really made no sense to me. I had so much inner pain and conflict and stuff that I was in a bit of a mess. And then, somehow, in my confusion and pain, I managed to find a way to talk to 8. I started to get some answers. And then I started to talk to Adamu and other beings and the stuff I received was just unbelievably helpful. As I worked with it, it brought me a great deal of inner-peace and facilitated healing and growth. I learned to trust and love the process. And it just keeps getting better. It seems as if the more I grow, the more I am able to receive. So... I guess the answer to your question is that I am just trying to heal myself, trying to love myself, trying to discover who I really am and who God really is and trying to find and fulfil my soul's purpose... that kind of thing. That's my answer. What is yours?

J-D: Ditto.

Z: No, no, no, no, no. You can't do that to me! How is your answer the same as mine?

J-D: Two reasons. The first is very easy. I am you, and you are me, remember? I am your Inner-Self. When you are aspiring to your highest good, then you are aligning yourself with me. Then we are in simpatico. So your goals and motivations are mine. You and I are answering the questions we have together. That's the first answer and the easiest to explain. The second answer comes with a small shift of perspective. You see "I" am a gestalt being that absolutely knows, as a fact of my existence, that I am one with God. It is a fundamental truth of my being that I am one with everyone and everything, everywhere and together we are all one with God. So, obviously, **for me** this means that I know I am one with every single inhabitant of planet Earth, right?

Z: Whoa! Does that mean that you are everyone on Earth's "Inner-self"?

J-D: No. In a previous conversation I said to you that you are the only one incarnated in your "here and now" on planet Earth who has **that** relationship with me. What I am saying is that everyone on Earth is one with God. And, whether they know it or not, I know it. And I also know that I am one with God. So it is true for me that I am, by obvious extension, one with everyone on Earth. Okay?

Z: Oh! Okay. You are saying from your perspective you see us **all** as one!

J-D: Yes. Logically that is the case. But let me explain something. I am like you in some ways and unlike you in others. My perception of my reality is very different from yours. I won't be able to describe this to you in a way that you will fully comprehend, but I can give you an inkling.

One example is that I am not limited to a single perspective as you are. You perceive your world from one perspective. You experience yourself to be one single being who can only stand in one place at a time and can only feel or think one thing about your life at a time. Even if you have conflicting thoughts, you leap from the one perspective to the other. One at a time. That is how you are created to be. You are a single-perspective being. I, on the other hand, am actually a multiplicity. I should correctly refer to myself in the plural as "we" but that would make for a confusing conversation. You see, I have an infinite number of points of view. That is like saying I am an infinite number of people all at once.

Z: Whoa. Infinite? Doesn't that mean that you are God?

J-D: No. I am ONE with God. But I am very, very far from being **all** of God! Compared to **all** of God I am... minuscule. A very, very small babe of a being.

Z: And yet you have infinite perspectives?

J-D: Understand that I am outside of the construct called the Space/Time Continuum. So I am able to see, at one glance, all the interactions my beingness might have in every single moment. Each moment is a perspective. Every interaction is **now** for me. And since Space/Time is infinite, I have infinite perspectives.

Z: Okay that is a bit mind-boggling for me.

J-D: Yes. And I am only referring to this one sliver of a reality in which you now exist, which you call "the universe". To me this is one sub-set of one reality where I am interacting with Life. There are, for me, an infinite number of other realities where I know myself to be.

Z: An infinite number of other universes?

J-D: You could see it like that. But that is already far too restrictive a conceptualisation. In later conversations I will try to convey to you the magnitude and vastness of the unending realities that I am aware of. And there is much more that I have yet to discover and place within my awareness. Much, much more. Now I don't say this to make you think I am something wondrous and special. I mean I **am** wondrous and special, of course (he smiles). But so is every other being that exists. Everyone on Earth has within themselves a God-self that has this God-like awareness. So, what I tell you is both amazing **and** a bit of a "so-what?" all at the same time. The reason I tell you this is to find a way to begin to explain to you that my perceptions of myself and my reality are somewhat different from yours in some pretty fundamental ways. And so, when I say that, for me it is true that all is one, I do not mean this in some abstract, philosophical way. I do not mean this as a derived theoretical understanding. No. I mean that it is my absolutely perceived reality from a very broad set of experiences.

Z: What does "*absolute perceived reality*" mean?

J-D: All right. How about I ask you this: are you alive? And if you are alive, can you prove this to me?

Z: Of course I am alive. Can I prove it? Well, I can try. I am a living, breathing biological being. And I am conscious. I think and I feel and...

J-D: Good, good, good. I don't really need proof and we don't really need to have this debate. I merely wanted to show you something. You **know** that you are alive. It isn't just an idea you have or some theoretical construct. It is **your** "*absolute perceived reality*". It is unarguable to you. Now, if I ask you to prove that you are alive, you **can** go digging around in your mind for thoughts that would explain this or attempt to prove it. You can do so as an intellectual exercise. But it is completely irrelevant and redundant **to you** because you know it to be true, with everything you are, without even thinking about it. It is the most self-evident thing possible. Well, in just such a way it is true for me that all is one. And I am saying this with all the authority of the rather extensive experience of my whole being.

Z: Ah. I begin to get it. Thanks. But that hasn't answered the bigger question about your purpose in having these conversations with me.

J-D: No. But I didn't explain this for nothing either. I was laying the groundwork for my argument. What I need you to understand is that I really, truly, completely perceive every being on Earth as being one with me and All

That Is. And since I very much love and care for myself, by extension I love and care for every "other" that exists. And so, when I hear a cry of pain it is my desire to see if I may assist in turning that pain into joy. That, in fact, is my purpose here. I have come into this system of reality because there was a cry of pain. And the reason I heard that cry is because I was meant to answer it. So, I am here. And I am engaged in answering that call.

Now, let me go back to your question. Understanding that I can hold the perspective that every person on this planet is just "another me", let me read back to you what you said **your** purpose with all this was. You said: "*I'm trying to heal myself, trying to love myself, trying to discover who I really am, who God really is and trying to find and fulfil my soul's purpose.*" Can you see how it is that I am doing exactly the same? If, for me, the Self can be pretty much any person on the planet, then this is what I am trying to do. In fact this is what I am doing, have always been doing, will always be doing and have ever done.

Z: Huh?

J-D: I am outside of time. It is only from your perspective that this is really a work in progress. My perspective on that is quite different. This work is both perfect and complete **and** still a work in progress... and everything else that it could possibly be. That is how it is from outside of time.

Z: Oh. Okay. But please don't tell me that these conversations of ours are meant to make **such** a big impact on humanity! I mean I just can't see them reaching far enough to...

J-D: Please. Silence your fears and your doubts. These conversations will undoubtedly have great value. Vastly more than you can now imagine. But this is not **the work**! You will, as we proceed with these conversations, come to understand what the work we are doing really is. These conversations simply act as a sort of an invitation to others to come and co-create with us. As the conversations unfold, you will slowly get a better and better idea of what their value is. So, while it is true that these conversations will have profound value for many and will go far further than you now have the ability to imagine, I have to say that this is certainly not "it" for me. The "work" I do is accomplished in ways you have not yet understood. I don't actually have to "**do**" anything. I simply am here. I accomplish everything I need to accomplish by simply **being** that which I am. I bring my energy to bear and make it available and that shifts things in the desired way.

Z: How? How can you change stuff by just "being there"? Surely you have to actually **do** something?

J-D: It's hard to explain the power of **be**ing to Earth humans. You only think in terms of the power of **do**ing. You think you are more powerful and effective when you **do** something. The opposite is true. **Do**ing only steps down your true power. But you won't understand that. Let me rather tell you about this in the form of a parable.

Z: Excellent! A story.

J-D: Yes, here we go:

THE STORY OF THE DARKLANDERS

Once upon a time there was a race of people called the Darklanders. They lived in a vast, dark cavern deep underground. Not one of the whole race of Darklanders had ever been outside the cavern, but their myths and legends told of an ancient time – a time before time – when their gods had come down from the great Brightlands above and created the Darklanders here in the dark cavern and then left and returned to the Brightlands. It was said that the gods would one day return and bring the light down to the Darklanders. The Darklanders tried to imagine what the Brightlands above must be like, but could not, as no one had ever seen so much as a single light. Then, some of the Darklanders began to feel constrained by their dark world. They longed to experience the mythical world above. The legends told of amazing vistas and wide open spaces and wondrous experiences and these sounded very desirable to some of the Darklanders. In their hearts these few Darklanders felt they **knew** it existed and cried out for it. Other Darklanders of course said that this was all "superstitious nonsense". They said that people should be practical and just get on with life, as it was, without hankering after nonsense. And so we see how types emerged: the Dreamers who longed for the life beyond, and the Realists who were interested only in the mundane. The Realists, instead of wasting time with myths, legends and dreams, explored the cavern and tried to understand all that they could perceive so that they could make the best of the life they had. They came up with practical solutions to their problems instead of wasting their time with what was out of their reach. But still the Dreamers continued to dream and pray. And then, on a day, when the time was right, their prayers began to be answered in an unexpected way. The gods sent a very tiny, very dim light to the Darklanders.

Z: A tiny, dim light? How did that help?

J-D: It didn't. But it also didn't hurt. You see, the tiny, dim light of this parable was different from the light you know of. It was given to each of the Darklanders... placed inside each of them. But it was so tiny and so dim that only the most observant noticed anything different at all. In fact it was so tiny and so dim that, even if they noticed it, the Darklanders were able to think they were just imagining it. They could choose to tell themselves there was "something" or they could put it down to their imagination playing tricks on them and say it was "nothing". If a Darklander accepted the light, then it increased. You see, the very desire to look and **see**, the desire **itself**, caused the light to slowly increase. And so, over time, those who desired it, meditated upon it and worked with it, got brighter and brighter.

Z: Surely you mean they saw more brightly?

J-D: No, I mean they themselves became brighter. They themselves shone with the light. I'll say it again: this light was different from the light you know. It was placed **inside** each of the Darklanders. By accepting it, paying attention to it, respecting it, nurturing it and loving it, so it grew within them. It became their own light which shone from within them and by which each of them might see. And as they became brighter and brighter, so they could see further and further.

Z: And how did **that** help?

J-D: It didn't. The light did not help at all. It didn't move them out of the cavern. It didn't bring them tools or maps or instructions or new information or tell them that their legends were true or anything like that. The light did nothing whatsoever except **be**. It simply was what it was. It did what all light does... it shone. It shone in its own special way: a beautiful soft, shimmering, golden light. But it came to them in such a gentle way, only increasing when it was actively desired, so that for quite some time no one spoke about it at all. You see, at first, those who noticed the light and worked to increase it were the greatest Dreamers. They were the ones who were most open and available to this gift. But, being such great Dreamers, they were very used to being told that they were crazy, lazy and bad. They were used to others not listening to them. They were used to having no power in the Darklands. So they didn't try too hard to share their discovery of the light with others. Most of them thought they were the only one to have this strange but wonderful new experience. But they did not mind too much because, though they felt no-one else would understand, for the first time, as a result of the light, they did not feel so alone.

Z: So the light didn't help. It just was... the light. So how did that answer the Darklanders' prayers?

J-D: Well you see not **everyone** prayed for the light or for a return to the Brightlands. Only some did. So if the Darklanders were just moved out of the cavern up into the Brightlands, then that would have given many of them what they **didn't** want. So the light did nothing but gently shine and then only for those who chose it and who, by their actions and decisions, created the light for themselves from within themselves. And here is the thing... you see, for the most avid Lookers, the light eventually got bright enough that they began to see some interesting things. Like the beautiful crystals hanging from the cavern ceiling. And this is where things came to a head. You see a few of the Lookers noticed each other staring up at the crystals on the ceiling, and then, for the first time, they knew they were not alone! They began to talk to each other about this. They got Lookers groups together to share their experiences and to help each other with tips and strategies to increase the light. Some non-Lookers came to listen to what they were saying. Some became interested enough to practise what they heard and became Lookers too. Word spread and for a while it was quite the most exciting thing that had happened in the cavern. Which would have been fine except that those who chose the light were most likely to be Dreamers and those who didn't were most likely to be Realists. And you see, the Realists were the ones who were running things. They had the power. They had the resources. They made the rules. And since they hadn't chosen to see and since they hadn't created the light inside themselves they simply denied that it existed. Which wasn't strange because – see it from their perspective – if they looked around they saw no light! So it was all a lie as far as the Realists were concerned. And not only was it a lie but a dangerous one too! These Lookers were, they said, becoming a social nuisance. They were refusing to obey the edicts and instructions of their superiors! They were not being proper productive members of society! All this "Looking" nonsense was disrupting the very fabric of society!

Now, those in power couldn't very well outlaw the light or Looking because they were claiming it was all just a fabrication anyway. So they used their influence and power to ridicule anyone who was talking about it. They publicised authoritative claims that it was only mad people who tried to see the light. That it was all a lie. They let it be known that no good, healthy, sane Darklander should try to see the light.

"If you want to know what is out there," said those in power, *"we have experts who can tell you."* They were the authorities, after all.

"Experimenting with attempting to See is socially disruptive and needless nonsense. It is un-Darklander!" they declared.

But of course they failed to stamp Looking out. In fact Looking slowly grew in popularity. And then it happened that a group of the most avid Lookers discovered something new. They discovered that, by joining their lights together as one, they could co-create a much, much brighter light. They discovered that they could see quite far and quite clearly. And so they got together each day and searched the roof of the cavern. It was but a matter of time before they could see the distinct fissure in the roof which was exactly as was described in the ancient myths as the gateway to the Brightlands above!

This was all the impetus they needed! The Lookers began to work together with a fervour none of them had ever known before. They gathered together materials and began to build scaffolding so that they might ascend to the fissure and see if that was the way out. Their work was occasionally hampered by the authorities, but not badly so. You see, the authorities did not have the light and could therefore not see what the Lookers were doing. They therefore did not understand their plans and, as they could not even admit to the fact of the seeing of the fissure or of its existence, they could not do much to stop the construction. So the Lookers carried on and built their scaffolding.

Our story comes to an end here as the Lookers' scaffolding was reaching up to the fissure. They were hopeful and excited. The rest of the Darklanders below mostly knew nothing of what they were up to. Some heard about it and were intrigued. Some insisted that it was all foolish nonsense. What happened next? Well... unfortunately this is where the parable ends.

Z: Oh no! Why?

J-D: Well you asked a question. You asked how by simply **be**ing, rather than **do**ing, I could accomplish the work for which I have come here. Isn't that what you asked?

Z: Yes, that **is** what I asked.

J-D: Well, let's see how the parable fared: can you see how, in the parable, the light managed to come into the Darklands and how it could, without **doing** anything – by just **being** – bring options, choices and change? Though it was very much there, it was still up to the Darklanders to choose to see it or not. And if they **did** choose to see it, they could choose for themselves what they were going to do with that seeing. So the light itself did nothing and yet the whole social structure and dynamic of the population changed. Without doing anything the light offered those who wanted it, a means of finding their way out. But, you see, it didn't actually **do** anything for them. No. Something much better happened: it allowed them to create their own way to help themselves to see their own path out **if they so chose**. Only those who wished for the light really got it. Those who denied the light did not. No one was forced to do anything they didn't want to do. Everyone got to create the reality they desired. And yet, everything was changed by the existence, by the simple **be**ing, of the light. So, I think the parable did quite a good job of expressing to you not only how **be**ing can change everything but also brought in a number of parallels as to how things have played out in your reality.

Z: I agree that it is a pretty cool parable. Thanks. I think I get the power of **be**ing now. But now we have spent a whole lot of time on tangential issues. I feel quite bad. We were supposed to be talking about the implications of the oneness. And instead I have taken you on a wild goose-chase answering all these question that just cropped up in my mind and we haven't even started to talk about the topic at hand!

J-D: Have a little faith. Do you not know that, *"Everything is always perfect"*?

Z: Umm. No. I mean I have heard it said. It's one of those "fully spiritual" things that enlightened souls sometimes say. But it isn't **really** always perfect, is it?

J-D: Only because your perspective is too close. Here is something to remember:

> *"If you cannot see the perfection then you are standing too close to the picture."*

Z: Again, that sounds way deep and stuff but, practically, how is that so?

J-D: Would you like an example?

Z: That would be nice.

J-D: Good. I shall give you one: it is... this very conversation! We are still busy with it and so you look at the incomplete product and see the mistakes you have made by asking the wrong questions. You see the mistakes I have made by long-windedly answering them. And this is all a big mistake because this is not what you had in mind for the way this topic should flow. But here is the twist: I am telling you now it is only imperfect because it is still incomplete.

Z: Okay? So what must I do with that information?

J-D: Thinking would be a start! Think. What have I said?

Z: That it is only imperfect because it is incomplete?

J-D: Yes. So what strikes you as incomplete?

Z: Uh...

J-D: Another word for incomplete is "unfinished"...

Z: The story! The story! You didn't finish the parable. I mean... you finished it in so much as it perfectly answered my question. But I have to admit I was disappointed because you just left the actual story hanging.

J-D: Right! So? What do you want me to do?

Z: Well, umm. Could you please tell me how the parable ends?

J-D: Why, yes, I'd be delighted to do that!

Z: Thanks. Because I can see how that parable actually relates to us here on Earth. And I can see the cute "ascend the scaffolding" thing you have done to allude to the ascension process. So I am pretty keen to hear how it ends. I think that might give me some sort of insight into what is going to happen in the future to us here on Earth.

J-D: Yes, the parable **does** allude to life on Earth. But not as you might think. There is quite a twist in the tail. But you'll see when we get there. Let me continue with the parable.

THE STORY OF THE DARKLANDERS, PART 2

I could end the whole story by simply saying, "*Everyone got exactly what they created for themselves.*" That would be true of this story and true of every other true story in all of reality. But it would be unsatisfying. Because even though,

> "*You always get **exactly** what you create*",

Still people want to know details of the stories. So let's see how that rule of always getting what you create applied to the Darklanders.

Remember, most of the Darklanders chose not to see the light. Most of them stayed behind in the Darklands, right?

Z: Right.

J-D: Okay. So clearly their belief was that they could not see the light and that they had to remain in the Darklands and that things would continue more or less as they had before. That is what they believed and that is therefore what they experienced. Their new story starts pretty much exactly where the old story left off. The Darklanders are still in the Darklands and they still have no light. **But** there is now a difference. They now know about their friends and family members who **were** there with them in the Darklands who simply disappeared. They also know that the ones who disappeared were Lookers.

They know that the Lookers were talking about going up into the Brightlands. And then they were gone. So they are confused and many of them are now asking questions.

"What happened to the Lookers?" they ask.

"The gods came back for them!" claimed some.

"They were punished for their evil ways and taken away!" others postulated. And so it continued. No one knew for sure what had happened, but what they **did** know was that their neat, tiny, closed, little world would never be the same again. Something inexplicable had happened. And in their confusion many of them remembered the gods of old and began to pray. And that is where we shall leave them for now. Next we'll pick up the story with the other group – the ones who went up the scaffolding.

Z: The Lookers. They obviously found the Brightlands!

J-D: They certainly did. They began their new story at a new level of existence. They emerged from the land below to discover that the reason for the Brightlands being so bright was not because there was some bright light source there, no, these were the Brightlands because everyone there was **themselves** a bright source of light.

Z: Oh wow! Everyone shone!

J-D: Yes. And what it meant was that everyone clearly saw the reality around them as **they** themselves were. Do you understand? In the Darklands people thought they perceived the world as **it** was. In the Brightlands they realised they saw it as **they** were.

Z: Um. Slow moment over here. I don't get it.

J-D: Well, the truth is that you each create your own reality. When you see clearly, then you see that your reality is the way it is because of what you most deeply believe – which is what you are perceiving from your heart. So those who ascended to the next level immediately realised that the reality they saw around themselves was a direct result of their own beliefs and choices. This means that they knew that they created their own reality. This is something we'll have to talk about more in following conversations because this is going to be difficult for you to understand. You are still very much living in your own "Darkland". You still believe that you see things as they are. And because you believe it to be so, so it is! There is much more for us to discuss about this soon. For now, please accept that those who have ascended to the next level will have a different experience from what you do.

Z: Okay, I guess that's obvious – it stands to reason that a different level of existence will be quite different from this one.

J-D: And the difference will be difficult for you to comprehend precisely because you don't have any experience of it.

Z: Okay. Agreed.

J-D: Well, I am saying that the next level of reality for you is the level of self-mastery. You have heard of "ascended masters"? Well, what precisely did you think they were masters of? I am telling you they are masters of themselves. True self-mastery means they are ready to believe, know and experience that they create their own reality completely. They are ready to see the world as they each believe it to be. They are ready to create their world as **they** are. And that is what I am talking about with this light. They shine their light and it shows them the world as they each believe it to be.

Z: Wow. So I guess the next level of reality is a pretty amazing place.

J-D: It can be. Unfortunately it is possible to attain self-mastery without attaining universal love.

Z: It is? What happens then?

J-D: Well let me get back to the parable. This conversation is going to be a long one. There is quite a bit still to tell. But stay with me, okay?

Z: I'm not going anywhere. I'm fascinated to see how this all turns out!

J-D: Good. I think you'll find your patience quite well rewarded. So, back to the parable. For the purposes of the story, we shall divide the ones who ascended to the Brightlands into three main groups. First there were those who were of a service to self (STS) mentality. These STS beings thought that the fact that they had made it out of the Darklands proved that they were more special than the Darklanders who had remained below. They decided that they must be very powerful and wise compared to the Darklanders who were still in the cavern. Now you can hear from what I am saying that, even though they had escaped the Darklands into the Brightlands, still they were framing themselves in terms of the Darklands. So they would therefore begin their new story back in the Darklands.

Z: Er... no, I don't really get that. They have just escaped the Darklands. Why would they go back?

J-D: Okay. Follow me on this one... You get what you create, right? And when you have the light, then you get it immediately. Whatever you focus your **intention** and **attention** on is what you get. Now this group of beings, even though they found themselves in the Brightlands, were still thinking in terms of the Darklands below. They were thinking, "*We are the best and the brightest of the Darklanders.*" That is where their thoughts were. So that is what they got... to be the "*best and the brightest of the Darklanders*"! And of course there was something else motivating them too. Now that they had this new-found power, what do you think they wanted to do with it?

Z: Uh...

J-D: Let me give you a hint. Don't you think these STS beings might have a modicum of revenge on their minds?

Z: Revenge? Oh right! Like a "revenge of the nerds" sort of thing.

J-D: Explain that phrase?

Z: Revenge of the nerds? Well in the Darklands these guys were considered outcasts, remember? In the Darklands they were the Dreamers and were considered undesirable elements of society by the Realists and especially by those in power. They were the weirdos and the nutcases who were disrespected. And so now, when their ways have paid off, perhaps they think it's payback time. The underdogs strike back. Revenge of the nerds.

J-D: That's quite a good analysis. And so **now** can you see that, even though they found the light and the Brightlands, **still** they never actually escaped the Darklands. They were trapped by their negative emotions.

Z: Yeah. That makes sense. I can see how that could work.

J-D: If you find your intrinsic power, but you do not find healing and love first, then you again trap yourself... only you do so at a higher level. But anyway, back to the story: what happened next is that the STS beings brought the light with them back down into the Darklands. So we shall henceforth call them "the Lightbringers". They were the "seeing eye" in the land of the blind, you see. And this would, of course, mean that the STS beings were much more powerful than the regular Darklanders.

Z: And what did these Lightbringers do back in the Darklands?

J-D: Well, do you remember where we left the Darklanders? They were thrown into a state of disarray and confusion by the leaving of the Lookers. Try to put yourself in their position for a moment. Suddenly they were in a profound state of doubt about everything that they had before taken to be true. Many of them began praying to the gods to save them. But can you see the problem with praying like this?

Z: Not really. How can there be a problem with praying?

J-D: Not with praying *per se*. But with praying for a rescuer to come and fix all your confusion and troubles.

Z: Why is that a problem?

J-D: The problem is you will get what you ask for. Or rather, what you are **really** asking for. Let me help you to understand this. If you are saying that you are weak, confused, powerless and lost; that you don't know what you want or even what you **should** want; that you want someone to come and tell you what to want, what to do and how to choose; that you want this great rescuer to come in to your world and take from you your choices and creations and give you, instead, what they want to create for you and that you will serve them and worship them for doing so and do whatever they say... Well, then you are creating a world of pain for yourself. You are creating an opening for someone else in your life to fill a particular role. You are creating yourself as the perfect victim and, while you are saying that you want a rescuer, what you are actually asking the Universe to provide you with is a perpetrator.

Z: I'm not really following that.

J-D: All right then, this is a good moment for me to tell you about the victim/perpetrator/rescuer triangle.

THE VICTIM/PERPETRATOR/RESCUER TRIANGLE

If something appears to be going wrong in your life and you believe yourself to be a victim, then you will choose to believe that someone else is "doing this" to you. Someone else is the perpetrator who is responsible for all your misery. And, as you are a powerless victim, you must therefore find someone to help you out of this situation, someone who will be responsible for rescuing you and making everything better. And so the three relationships are set up: victim, perpetrator and rescuer **always** go together. Where there is one, the other two are there also. So the Darklanders were very clearly declaring their status as victims. And while it is true that they told themselves that they wanted to be rescued, what they first invited was a perpetrator. They made themselves available to it. They created that opening.

Z: I don't get it. Surely it doesn't follow. They wanted someone **good** to come and help them. Why would that invite someone bad?

J-D: Because they are creating with fear and with doubt. This is an idea I will go into detail with you when I talk to you about creation tools. But the point is quite simply this: your tools of creation are your emotions. If you create with love, then you get what you really want. If you create with fear, then you get what you don't want. If you create with doubt, then you get a mixed bag or nothing at all. Now the Darklanders were in fear **and** doubt. So the first thing they got was what they **didn't** want. And you **must** get what you create. How else will you learn to create properly if you don't?

Z: Wow, this is tough for me to understand. But okay, let's go on with the story. I will want to come back some other time and talk about this... about how to create what I **do** want.

J-D: It's a promise. We'll talk about it soon. But for now perhaps you can accept that the Darklanders were not creating a clear, unambiguous outcome for themselves with love and positivity. So, an opening was created. And if we bring this together with what the Lightbringers were creating, we have quite a good match. The Lightbringers were quite happy to be received as the "returning gods" by the Darklanders. They were quite willing to be served and worshipped and have their egos buffed and polished. A lot of humble bowing and scraping served them just fine, thank you very much. Not only were they willing to be gods but they were also quite willing to teach the people of the Darklands how they should be worshipped. They taught them songs of praise to sing. They taught them to bring offerings of the very finest of the foods of the land prepared by the most skilled of chefs. They promoted the Darklanders who served them best to positions of power, thereby creating a priest class so that only these most loyal servants ever came near them. And the rest of the people were nothing more than slaves. Slaves to the priests and to their prideful gods. They were forced to work and work and work for all of their waking hours. They were forced to built great palaces to appease their egotistical gods. And then they built temples to appease the burgeoning egos of their gods' priestly pets.

And then something interesting happened. The gods began to get jealous of each other. They began to compete with each other. Each wanted to have more power and control of the people than the next one. Each wanted a better palace than the other. They each started to instruct their priests to gather worshippers to them, to tell the Darklanders that they must worship only this god or that one and forsake all others. This continued for a while as egos clashed and tempers simmered, and then war broke out. Worshippers of some of the gods began to get instructions to kill the worshippers of the other gods. Retaliations quickly escalated to all-out war. And then the gods used their powers to smite each others' worshippers too. The Darklands were rent apart! After some time a certain degree of stalemate was achieved. Each of the gods, with their surviving minions, were living in a different area, removed from one another by some distance. There they established their cities. And though they continued to war with each other, there were also intermittent times of peace for the poor Darklanders. But their lives were hard. Now, not only did they have to labour to build and serve, but they intermittently had to turn their agricultural implements into weapons of war and go off to be killed and maimed. All in service of the Lightbringers' egos.

But through all this something new had begun to dawn in the hearts of the Darklanders. You see, they were no longer the haughty Realists of before. They had come through some very tough times. And they had come through together. They had survived thus far by finding compassion for one another. Brother helping brother, they had pulled through. Their travails had opened their hearts to each other. And now their hearts began again to cry for rescue. But this time they began to call with hope in their hearts. Hope, because they had seen love and compassion in each others' eyes. They began to hope for love and compassion from the gods. And again they got what they created. As it always was and always will be. Because remember...

Z: *"You always get **exactly** what you create for yourself."*

J-D: Spot on! And so, who do you think came to answer their prayers this time?

Z: I'm not sure. If I recall, then you said that the Lookers who ascended into the Brightlands were to be divided into three groups. The first group was the STS-ers who we are now calling the Lightbringers. So I'm guessing you are now going to tell us about a second group of Brightlanders. I'm guessing they were somehow a more loving response to the calls of the Darklanders.

J-D: That would be a very good guess. So let's look at that second group. They were of a service to other (STO) mentality. When these particular ones first made it up into the Brightlands, they felt it was a wonder, a blessing and a privilege. They desired to use this privilege to dedicate themselves to being of service to others. They felt love and compassion for their friends and family members whom they had left behind in the Darklands and so they decided to go back and help those remaining Darklanders in whatever way they could. And so it was that they heard the agonised cries for loving help from the Darklands below. They heard the call and they responded. And when they arrived in the Darklands, the STO beings were horrified to discover what the Lightbringers had gotten up to. The misery and death that they had brought to the lives of the Darklanders was too terrible for them to contemplate.

Z: Wait a minute, please. I don't understand. It seems to me you are saying that the STS guys arrived first. And that they spent quite a long time down in the Darklands building empires and then making wars and what-not and only **then** after, like, hundreds of years or something, did the STO guys come down. Is that right?

J-D: A great deal longer than just hundreds of years, but yes, that is what I am saying. You see, time is not the same in the different realms. You do not move between dimensions and still stay on the same time-line. They operate on entirely different systems of sequentiality. So, when you pass from the Brightlands to the Darklands, for example, you arrive at the time which is resonant with your arrival. You arrive when the Darklands are ready for you to arrive. You arrive when it is time for you to play your role. A stage-play is a good analogy. Imagine a stage-play in which all the actors walked on together right at the opening curtain and then all of them at the same time spouted all their lines in one long, non-stop monologue. It would be a chaotic babble and would make no sense to anyone. So instead, each enters at the right moment and each plays their part in perfect response to the other.

Z: I see. But that creates another question: who decides to bring them on at *"the right time"*?

J-D: They do. They create this with their desires. Let's look at the sponsoring thought behind the wishes of the STO beings. They desired to be of service. They desired to **help** someone. They wanted to save the Darklanders from their lot. But they wanted to do it out of a loving, kind motivation. It is a generosity of spirit that wished to express itself. So you see? The STO beings get to go to the Darklands at exactly the moment when the Darklanders are most powerfully creating an opening for what the STO beings are offering. And that perfect moment was not back at the beginning of this part of the story when the Lightbringers arrived. No. The Darklanders first needed to meet the Lightbringers and see how the Lightbringers responded to their call. Only then, when they had walked that path together a while, would the Darklanders be ready to make a new choice. You see, a victim needs a perpetrator before he needs a rescuer.

Let me explain something else here. Remember, back in the first part of their story, the Darklanders had been haughty and had victimised the Lookers. That is how they were and that is what they knew. To the Darklanders, therefore, beings in a position of authority were ego-centric and imperious. That is how they treated each other. That is what they knew and so that is what they were able to imagine as a response to their call.

Z: Because if you can't imagine something, then you can't create it?

J-D: That is a profoundly true thing you have just said. Sometime soon, when we talk about the tools of creation, you will come to understand what a very powerful thing this is that you call "imagination". And yes, if you can't imagine it, then you can't create it. But now, in this part of the story, what had happened to the Darklanders was that they had been put through a long series of very traumatic experiences. And it's a funny thing about such events. When people go through such difficulties it very often brings out the best in them. And so it was that the Darklanders responded to their harsh treatment at the hands of the Lightbringers by expressing support, compassion, love and kindness to each other. Friend helping friend, strangers offering unexpected assistance to each other... so those dark times ignited a spark in the hearts of the Darklanders. A new and different light was fostered in their hearts. The light of compassion began to softly shine. And so it was that the Darklanders were ready to meet the STO Brightlanders. If I may summarise it like this: the Darklanders would first have to have a new thought about themselves before they would be able to have a new thought about their world. They needed to find love and compassion in their hearts before they could frame their need in terms of a loving, compassionate response.

Z: And how did the STO guys come down and rescue the Darklanders from the Lightbringers? I don't imagine they came in like cavalry on white horses with guns blazing.

J-D: Well there are a number of different ways they could have entered the story. And later when you understand the complexities of alternate time-lines then you'll understand when I say that all of the possible ways actually happened. In some of them they **did** come in all wrathful and angry: angelic hosts with flaming swords of righteous vengeance. In these realities there was a great battle between the STO and the STS. But that didn't work out very well for anyone. Everyone just got hurt and no one was helped. That is a game that, once started, has no end. War causes fear and pain. Fear and pain breeds loathing. Loathing causes war. Round and round you go. And, seeing as the STO beings wanted to help the Darklanders, not hurt them, this didn't serve their best interests at all. There is second set of time-lines in which the STO beings came into this reality as good, kind and benevolent demi-gods. They didn't fight with the STS beings. They caused no harm and waged no war. What they did was to be in their power and do all they could to help the Darklanders. Great, kind, benevolent gods who taught and helped and healed and did endless services of goodness.

Z: Ah! A better approach!

J-D: Maybe. But, in the final analysis, not much more successful than just waging war.

Z: No way! How come?

J-D: Well, this way round the Darklanders just stopped doing for themselves. They saw that it was pointless for them to even try to do anything. There were the good gods and the bad gods. If you managed to appeal to the good gods, you had good things happen to you. If you angered the bad gods, then bad things happened to you. In this way the Darklanders decided that they had no power whatsoever and simply ceased trying. And so the STO beings failed to help them to ascend into the Brightlands. The Darklanders just said, *"We are not like you. You are gods. We are powerless. We will serve you and you can do these things for us."* And no matter how much the STO beings professed that they were all actually the same and that the Darklanders could do all the things that they had done, still the Darklanders could not believe them. Why should they? It was completely apparent that these gods were capable of great magic and miracles and that they were not. So that too was a failure. Then there is a third set of time-lines. In these time-lines the STO beings saw the folly of being "above" the people. Instead they now chose to be a part of the Darklanders. So they entered the game by being born as babes to Darklander parents. In these time-lines most of them would manage, in one way or another, as they grew up, to begin to remember the Brightlands. They would remember the light. And then they would, as Darklanders themselves, begin to help and to teach the others.

Z: And **this** worked out better?

J-D: To some considerable degree. What happened with this is that the Lightbringers quickly saw what was going on. As these STO teachers and healers went about doing their thing, so the Lightbringers began to lose their grip on the people. So they made laws against the teaching of the light. They took the light teachings and changed them and corrupted them so that they would again serve the purpose of the Lightbringers in keeping the people trapped, in keeping them servile, in keeping them serving the interests of the Lightbringers. What they succeeded in doing is driving the teachings of the light underground. Secret groups were gathered. There, in these little secret schools, the mysteries of **what is**, were taught. And so the word was spread.

Sometimes a teacher would rise up and become a bit noisier. Sometimes he'd gather enough followers to disturb the *status quo*. Always he and his rebellion would be put down by the Lightbringers, with force and violence. But by then his message would have gotten out to more than just his immediate followers and a growing group of people would have become awakened. And so it was that this way of being did some good. But it wasn't ultimately successful either. Still most people believed that only the gods were able to create their reality. Only the gods could take you up to the Brightlands or deny you admission. **Still** most of them failed to understand the truth that each goes to the Brightlands because **they** are ready to do so... because they have gained self-mastery. They ascend to become masters because they are willing and able to create this for themselves. Only a minuscule percentage got this and only a minuscule percentage were able to ascend. And that is where the second part to the Story of the Darklanders ends.

It ends with a cycle that just goes round and round and round. And round. This time line is actually not a line, it is a circle. So the end is the beginning is the end is the beginning is the end... There is an endless, complex interaction between those who have chosen Service To Self, those who had chosen Service To Other and those who remained Undecided. There is a point at which the cycle seems to end and that is where there is a harvest of all the Undecided who have eventually reached a decision point. They stop being undecided and then ascend to the next level where they become either STO or STS or, very rarely, the third type of Brightlander.

Z: Oh yes! I'd forgotten that there was still a third type. What do **they** do?

J-D: It isn't **quite** time to introduce them to the story yet. I first need to finish completely with Part Two of the Darklander story. I was saying there is an event at the end of each cycle. It is called the harvest. This is when those who have made a choice cease to be Undecided and ascend to the Brightlands. Usually this is quite a small percentage of the Darklanders.

Z: So, over time, there are less and less Undecided.

J-D: There would be. Except of course this is not a closed system and the time line doesn't truly end. Beings from elsewhere might that this is a good place to come to learn about themselves, to come and experience life here in the

Darklands. From a certain perspective it can be seen that this is a very beautiful and elegant game. You can enter at the bottom as a newcomer to the game who is Undecided. You can remain undecided for as long as you like and then, when you have given it a good look, you can decide which you want to be: STO or STS or the third type (still getting to that!) and then you move up to that. And if you choose STO or STS you can play that role for as long as you like and when you are done with that, you can **also** still choose the third type. And what is unique about the third type is that this is the only type who can choose to leave the game altogether or continue to play. But before we finally get into what exactly the third type is, let's take a moment to admire the beauty of this system. Can you see how it is something that can go round and round forever? The undecided Darklanders, the STS Lightbringers and the STO rescuers together get themselves locked into a dance. They form a triangle: the Darklanders playing the role of victim, Lightbringers playing the role of perpetrator and STO beings playing the role of rescuer. And once that pattern is set up it can go round and round forever. It is an internally conflicted game that just goes on and on for all eternity. Individual souls can enter the game at the beginning, move up through the game into STS or STO (and very often one and then the other) and then eventually the third type. And then, if they like, they can leave the game from the third type.

Z: Okay, I simply **cannot** wait any more. Please tell me what, in goodness name, **is** the third type?

J-D: I was wondering how long before your curiosity overcame you. All right, I shall tell you and then you can see if it all makes sense. The third type of Brightlander is what I am going to call the Unifiers. They are the ones who **know** that all is ONE. They know that they are, each of them, STO and STS and Undecided. All of that, none of that, and at the same time so much more than that. They know that when they look at another being there can be no judgement because they see that being as another self. They know therefore that all is perfect. They have really and truly seen the light. Not the first bit of light seen by the others in the Brightlands, no, the depths of light that shines from the heart of every being, which is that being's connection to Prime Source. When such a being looks at you they do not see your temporary situation: your foibles, your self-limiting illusions, your fears... no, they look into your heart and they see God there! As they do when they look at themselves, of course. God is everywhere when you look with the eyes of a Unifier. And they can also, of course, see that they have been, in this game, the Undecided, they have been STO and they have been STS. They will therefore not stand in judgement of any of these. And it is with these, the Unifiers, that we start the next level of the story of the Darklanders...

Z: Whew! This is turning into a long and complex story!

J-D: You have no idea how complex it actually is. I have taken **huge** liberties compressing things and lumping things together so that this story can be told.

Z: So, this story is true?

J-D: All stories are true. All stories are fiction. Both of these statements can be true depending on your perspective. This story is just a story, a fairy-tale, if you like. But it represents aspects of that which has occurred, and continues to occur, in your world in an interesting way. In a way which will, I hope, lead you to think about things. Lead you to ask new questions and come to new conclusions. It is about suggesting to you a way of understanding the situation without tugging on the fear and anger strings. Without dragging you through the misery of doom and gloom. Because those things do not serve my agenda. They serve the agenda of those who would keep you here, playing the game in their service.

But onwards now...

THE STORY OF THE DARKLANDERS, PART 3

The thing to understand about the third group, the Unifiers, is that they do not frame themselves in terms of who they serve. They don't necessarily serve themselves **or** the "other". They know that the "other" and the "self" are, ultimately, the same being. They know that what you do to the "other", you automatically and directly do to the Self. So while they are good and loving and kind as a rule (because that is what they would want done to themselves) such beings would not automatically swing into a mode of either serving themselves **or** serving others. The whole notion of "service" is not of great importance to them at all. Instead what usually drives such a being is pure expression of the Self. The understanding for a Unifier is that each and every particle of the oneness is absolutely and completely unique. And if each one were to find that which is their greatest bliss and simply express **that**, then all would be well. Because, you see, no two beings anywhere are ever the same. So no two beings' greatest bliss would ever be exactly the same thing. Each one would be loved and cherished for that unique thing that **it** has to offer. And what **it** has to offer would be the perfectly needed thing, **somewhere**.

For the Unifiers there is no scarcity and no competition. There is balance and perfection. And, instead of springing into action, these beings would choose instead to simply **be**. To explore and **see**. To journey into the heart of God and find that which calls to them to give their unique, greatest gift. And then they'd express themselves in pure love and joy.

Z: That sounds beautiful. But there is something I really don't understand. How can you **know** yourself to be ONE with everyone and everything else without losing yourself? I mean, I understand the oneness conceptually, but if it is literally true as a fact of your being that there is no separation between you and any other being... then how can you still be **you**?

J-D: Your question is about individuality. About losing your identity. Let me take a moment out of the Darklanders story for a quick diversion. Can you remember that in our first conversation, in Chapter 2 of this work, I promised to tell you about "The Rainbow Metaphor"?

Z: Oh yes. Now that you mention it, that does rings a bell.

J-D: Well here it is...

THE RAINBOW METAPHOR

Imagine there is a rainbow and you are one of the colours.

You and all your brother and sister colours might **seem** to be individual and separate up there in the sky. But are you?

Z: Oh, I see. No. The colours are continuous, aren't they?

J-D: Yes, what you are seeing is actually an even, unbroken, undivided spread of light frequencies. It is the observer who decides, in its mind, to lump a selection of these frequencies together and to identify this area as a band of yellow and that area as a band of green, for example. But there is in reality no place where one colour stops and another starts. There isn't, in any real sense, a "band" of any colour whatsoever except that you might choose to imagine it to be so.

Z: So you are saying that all the colours are really one. They just seem like separate colours up there in the sky. And from that, we can understand how a being might perceive itself as having a different or unique nature, but at the same time know that it is actually also a part of the ONE bright white light.

J-D: I like how you've put that. Yes. But we can wring another pleasant little observation out of the rainbow analogy. How about the fact that, of course, there **is no rainbow** there? It is all an illusion. There is light and there is moisture. The interplay between these two things results in you believing that you are seeing these colours in the sky. But what are you **really** seeing? Are you seeing raindrops? Or are you seeing sunbeams?

Z: Both, I guess.

J-D: But then why would a different person standing somewhere else see the rainbow at a different location to what you do? It is because two observers standing a few meters apart are actually seeing the light play off different raindrops. What I am suggesting is that there is a third component. The light, the moisture and... **You**, the observer. Your absolutely unique perspective is the third component. To every observer the rainbow will look a little different. It will, for one obvious thing, be in a different location depending on where the observer is standing.

Z: And the great spiritual truth we get from this is...

J-D: Seems I must do all the work. Okay. Let's go back to you and all your brother and sister colours. You do not exist in a vacuum. You have your own experiences, but each and every observer, every being you interact with, sees you slightly differently. You are created again in the mind of every other that you will ever have an interaction with. And **this** is actually something that should be deeply pondered. I want you to think about this because it is a very important notion that will crop up again in our dialogue as it unfolds.

Z: Wait a minute. But then... if I am me; let's say I'm the colour yellow in this rainbow. And a hundred people see me and they each see me slightly differently then... which version of me is me?

J-D: That's one interesting point. Another is: do they see you as **you** are? Or do they see you as **they** are?

Z: Oh, right! We've come back round to **that**.

J-D: Yes we have. But I hope you can see from the rainbow metaphor that it is very possible to have your own unique and individual identity with its own characteristics and nature and yet to still be absolutely aware of your oneness with all the other colours **and** even to be aware of your oneness with all observers **and** your oneness with all other phenomena that make up your existence.

Z: Wow, yes. That's very cool, thank you.

J-D: And now we need to get back to our parable, don't we.

Z: Sheesh! Yes. This is turning into an epic conversation! So, okay, we were saying that there were these Unifiers who believed that all was ONE. And so they didn't rush off to be of service to anyone particularly. They just observed stuff and hung around.

J-D: They were engaged in **be**ing and in observing what is. Yes.

Z: Didn't they get bored?

J-D: Very, very far from it. Quite the opposite, in fact. The less you **do** and the more you simply **be**, the closer you are to God. By that I mean that your experience of yourself elevates and you are able to be a greater and greater version of yourself. You are able to expand your consciousness. The most magnificent, transcendent and blissful experiences that people ever have in deep meditation come from being truly still. From not even thinking a single thought. From just being.

Z: So, okay then. In practical terms. What did these Unifiers experience?

J-D: One can't lump all their experiences together. What they would experience would depend on what they were creating. But let's make it a bit easier. Let's pick one of them and see what he experienced, shall we?

Z: Okay. Do we have a name for him?

J-D: All right. Let's call him... Happy.

Z: Happy? Like one of the seven dwarves?

J-D: If you like. Or maybe Happy, as in Joy, or maybe even, Joy-Divine.

Z: Oh right! Is this story about you then?

J-D: It is a parable. A story which illustrates something about life. It is about all of us.

Z: Okay. Please continue. What did Happy experience?

J-D: Well, you see, Happy was the kind of being who loved life. Loved experiences. Loved seeing and knowing about things. He found joy in all these experiences. Which is why we are calling him "Happy". That is what he was and happiness is what he pursued. So when he first ascended the scaffolding and arrived in the Brightlands, he looked around himself and was astounded at the beauty he saw. He allowed himself to be really still and, with great reverence in his heart, to deeply appreciate the wonder of it all. He found, after some time, that doing exactly this allowed him to get even brighter. He began to see more and the world showed him ever more magnificence and splendour. He began to find that by closing his eyes, releasing his intent, and simply reverently and joyfully experiencing all that was brought to him he could go on some truly wondrous journeys within his own consciousness. And then, one day, he had a breakthrough. He discovered another new level of existence.

Z: You mean above the Brightlands?

J-D: In a manner of speaking. He came to the realisation that the Brightlands are bright, not because of the **place** but because the inhabitants have a certain level of awareness. This meant to him that, obviously, it wasn't the Darklands that were dark or the Brightlands that were bright. What was different was the beings choosing to experience them; their level of consciousness and the truths they held about themselves. And so he desired an even greater truth. He realised it didn't lie above, beyond, or outside of himself. He realised that the change would come from within, just as it actually had when he and the others had ascended to the Brightlands. So he sat still and looked within. He stilled his mind and waited on the light. It took him some time to get the discipline right but he eventually did arrive at a new level of awareness. Inside of himself he found whole new realities. He found a new level of being. He found a place where he was not so much a being with some inner-light, as a being actually made of pure light! And there, inside himself, he could interact with other beings of light. He and they all played and loved and created together. They were ONE, and yet still individual.

Z: Like the rainbow.

J-D: Exactly. At last, at this level, he really was experiencing himself as a colour of the rainbow that is one with all the other colours... yet still conscious of Self.

Z: And what happened then?

J-D: Well, we could now say, "*He lived happily ever after,*" and that would be true. We could also say, "*He got **exactly** what he created,*" because that is **always** true. But then the story would be a bit unfinished. You see, at this level of reality that he had now attained, at this light-body level, he was also aware of countless other realities. He and the other light beings created an infinite number of these realities and played in these creations. And he was also aware of yet other realities that he wasn't a part of creating, but was able to explore and see what others had created. And then, also, he was aware of **himself** as a being who lived in many, many realities. Realities beyond number hosted him in one way or another. And all of these were **right now** for him.

Z: How can that be?

J-D: Well, you know the thing you call "remembering"? For him it wasn't an attempt to try to bring something to mind. No. For him it was to be right there in the moment he desired to remember. Like if you were trying to remember your childhood and then suddenly you **were there**. Suddenly you were a three year old boy in your mother's garden playing on the swing. It was like that for him. Except of course he had access to, literally, an infinite number of "lives" in an infinite number of realities.

Z: Like many, many incarnations?

J-D: Yes. Sort of. I put "lives" in quotes because most of them were experiences completely different from what you understand as a lifetime. Other realities entirely.

Z: Hard to explain then?

J-D: Very. Perhaps we can try for that some other time. The point here is that Happy was able to shift himself at will from a state of **be**ing, in which he was in the seat of his own inner bliss and perfect **knowing**, into any one of an infinite number of states of **do**ing and experiencing at will. And this he did. And it was wondrous and beautiful. And of course he became aware of himself as something much larger than that too. But that is another story. To come back to **this** story I will simply say this: Happy held within his consciousness a memory. He remembered the Darklands. He remembered being there. In so doing he came to be in the presence of other light beings who were also remembering this. They remembered the pain of calling out for help. They remembered and they were there together. In their truest light bodies they were there.

Z: In the Darklands?

J-D: Yes.

Z: What did they do?

J-D: You haven't been paying attention, have you? They did **nothing** remember? All they did was **be** there.

Z: Oh wow! That's so cool! They went back to themselves and rescued themselves!

J-D: Rescued? I don't think they quite "rescued" themselves. They loved themselves. They went to be there with the memory of Self and this time round they saw there were not just a few time-lines and a few parts to this story. This time they were able to see with sufficient clarity that there were an infinite number of versions of the story, each with an infinite number of time-lines. And they saw that, in one of the versions of the story, **all** the beings – the Darklanders, the STO beings, the STS beings, the unifiers – all of them, found a way back to the oneness. They each did so in their own way. In one version of the story or another they all found their way home. And yet...

there is also always sufficient intersection of stories in which sufficient of them **do not** find the oneness that the story can still play out.

Z: Uh... sorry... I don't quite get that.

J-D: You are inside of time and so you are constrained to think in terms of linear time. But let me explain. Outside of time, a being can be in as many places as it likes. It can be in the Darklands reality and also home with the oneness. Such a being can then play many roles. It can be a hard-hearted Realist and at the same time a starry-eyed Dreamer and at the same time a Brightlander and at the same time a Light-Being. And many, many other things besides. And if this is so, then there is no contradiction. It is merely a matter of perspective. And so it is for you too. Right now you hold the rather interesting perspective of being just one human being on planet Earth. But you are many other things besides, including being me, Joy-Divine. And at some level each and every person on Earth is also a light being who knows the oneness of all. And at some level each and every person on Earth actually **is** God.

Z: Wow. Big concept that.

J-D: It is, and it's going to take a little work for you to really get this properly. But there is no rush – we will keep conversing and keep addressing this in new and different ways until it works for you.

Z: Thank you. But... um... this chapter was supposed to be about the "Implications of the Oneness". I get that we have been talking about that, that all is perfect and so on. But...

J-D: But you want me to actually talk about that which is promised in the heading?

Z: Yes please.

J-D: Good. That was coming next. What I wanted to illustrate is that there are many levels of existence here in this reality you inhabit. There is the deepest level – the one you currently reside in – at which you can absolutely forget that you are ONE. There is a level or two above this at which it is still possible to proceed whilst hiding the fact of the oneness of all from yourself, if that is what you choose. But one can only go inwards so far before one is forced to confront and accept this fact... all is really and truly ONE. If you refuse to look at this and refuse to make it true for yourself then you can continue on for as long as you wish in a state of separation and duality. There are many amazing things you can do and many wondrous experiences you can have, but it is a simple fact that you will never graduate beyond a certain point. When, on the other hand, you accept the oneness as a fundamental fact of your being, not only can you graduate beyond that point but you also gain access to infinite realms beyond.

Z: So let me understand this... beings who do not believe in the oneness of all get what they believe. They get separation.

J-D: Yes.

Z: And this limits them.

J-D: Yes. Being one with God obviously makes you infinitely more powerful than being separate. Ironically when you **are** one with God, then those who believe they are not one with God are also one with you.

Z: Huh?

J-D: Hard to understand, I know. But let's take yourself as an example. You are within me. All your experiences are mine too. You can believe that you are separate from me if you want, but I know you are not. I know that you are an aspect of myself that is perfectly fulfilling your role in bringing me the experiences that I desire. You cannot but be serving my agenda. If you don't want to recognise that fact, then you can serve my agenda whilst choosing separation and the pain of being alone. Or you can recognise the truth of the oneness and harmonise yourself with me and realise that I too am serving **your** agenda and you can then travel with me in loving unity and joy. So it's an important realisation. **Everything** is one with God and within God. Even those who cannot see this for themselves. And those who cannot see this are out of harmony and feel they are fighting an uphill battle to achieve anything. Those who do choose to see this suddenly awaken to a whole infinite, unending reality packed full of beings who wish to work with them and co-create with them. They awaken to their true power and gifts and they find themselves surrounded by others whose true power and gifts complement theirs perfectly.

Z: This begins to make sense to me now.

J-D: We'll come back to this until it is perfectly bedded in your consciousness. What I want you to understand is that there is a level of consciousness at which all beings know their essential oneness. Beings at this level are the Inner-Selves of all who are incarnated with you on planet Earth who do not know of their oneness. And while it is so that these Outer-Selves who reside in separation might decide to hurt or even kill one another, the Inner-Selves who know of their oneness know that this is just a very temporary, illusory experience. They know that the combatants are really just like actors who are pretending to kill each other who, in reality, have nothing but love between them. For the Inner-Selves this is so. They love each other because they are ONE. At this level of reality they know it is actually impossible to really desire to hurt each other. For them they know that to hurt another is to hurt the Self. Truly. For them there is no difference. Whatever such a being does to another they do instantly to themselves.

Z: Because they are ONE being?

J-D: Yes, exactly. ONE that is also many. Many that are truly ONE.

Z: So, at this level you wouldn't find ugliness. I mean no one would attack or hurt another. No one would try to manipulate or take from another, right?

J-D: It could only happen if both parties agreed to it all up front.

Z: Does that ever happen?

J-D: Oh yes! How do you think your world can be as it is? How can it be that within these light beings there are manifestations that are doing all these things to each other? It is all agreed to in advance. There is always a contract.

Z: If one person hurts or manipulates another, then their Light Being has agreed to this?

J-D: Yes. That is what I am saying. You on Earth are within us. You are our creations and we are yours. We jointly create the whole world you are experiencing. You bring certain experiences towards yourself with your thoughts and beliefs. With your ideas about yourselves. We are a part of that. We do all manner of facilitation so that all proceeds, in a greater sense, exactly according to plan.

Z: Something doesn't rhyme here. What about free will?

J-D: Oh you have free will all right! We do all this facilitation precisely so that everyone does have free will. So that no-one's free will is abrogated.

Z: Explain?

J-D: Well what if you, by your thoughts, your choices and your beliefs, were creating for yourself a circumstance in which you wanted to feel what it is like to be a perpetrator? Let us say you wanted to do some crime in which you felt like you gained some power over someone. As a part of your soul-journey you chose that. Then how would we accomplish this? We'd have to find a partner for you; someone who is willing to be the other half of that transaction. There will be someone out there who, for reasons of their own, chooses to see what it is like to be a victim.

Z: You are saying that people who have bad stuff happening to them have chosen this?

J-D: Yes. This is often the point at which people baulk. They often walk away from the truth of this because they are unable to accept that they themselves have created the "bad things" that have happened to them. Immediately they will want to fling back at me, "*What about the child who was raped?*" or some such equally horrific experience. They will insist that there is no way that this was chosen by that person.

Z: And you are saying it was?

J-D: Yes. I know it will take a lot for some to accept this. This is why a message such as mine is not for everyone. Not everyone is ready to hear this message. Many still need for there to be an "evil other". They want and need to believe that there are evil beings outside of themselves that create all the bad that happens in the world. They want to remain victims of their circumstances. And this is perfectly okay. If people want to stay at that level of realisation for a while, then there is nothing wrong with that. But if you are willing to move on to a more empowered level of consciousness, then I am offering another thought. I am saying something quite simple: **you** are the creator of your own reality. If this is so, then obviously you cannot also be a victim of your reality! "Victim" and "creator" are two opposite states. I am saying that you already **are** the creator of your reality. You have chosen to forget this so that you can play the game you are now playing. You can keep this forgotten if you like. Then you are creating, "*I am not the creator of my* *reality."* And, if you are creating that, then you are also creating, *"I am the victim of my circumstances."* And if you are creating that, you will experience that, because...

*"You always get **exactly** what you create"*

And so you will create for yourself opportunities to experience victimhood. Hence, the so-called "bad stuff" that you allow to happen to you. You will keep getting such experiences until you have a new thought about this, until you decide to take back your power and stop being a victim. Until you decide to take responsibility and become a creator. And when you **do**, these things will begin to change. The more you believe that you are the creator of your reality, the more you will experience that. The more you will see all things that you experience as being a direct result of your choices.

Z: Like the "light" in the parable!

J-D: Ah, yes! And now you too are beginning to see the light!

Z: Ha! I like the word play. So, if we believe we are victims, then we will get victim experiences as negotiated by our Inner Selves.

J-D: Right.

Z: Until we are ready to discover that we have created all these experiences and rise above them and begin to create experiences that we like more.

J-D: Correct.

Z: Then we become, ever more powerfully, the creators of our own reality.

J-D: Yes.

Z: But what about the children. I mean, you used the example of a child who is raped. Surely it is unfair to expect a young child to make the choice to transcend its victim status?

J-D: This is an emotionally charged issue and I can easily comprehend why this is difficult for you. But you must understand that a child is no more and no less an expression of a spirit-being than an adult is. You yourself had a pretty horrific experience as a handicapped child in one of your other lives.

Z: Yes. I have shared this with our readers.

(**Zingdad note:** see *"Lost in My Own Dream World"* in Chapter 1)

J-D: Well, when you eventually come to understand your story correctly you will begin to see the symmetry in your choices. You will see how these lives all balance each other out and how these experiences were all brought to you as a result of the choices you took and the decisions you made. You experienced being a sexual predator in one lifetime and you experienced being sexually abused in another. Remarkably enough you will even come to understand that your perpetrator and your victims are all from within the same light being. In other words, you and this other light being exchanged roles so that both of you could really and truly understand what this was about, by experiencing it for yourself first hand. In Chapter 5 I told you that if you encountered something in another being which you had not encountered in yourself, then you would not understand it. It would puzzle you. You would quite likely move to judgement of this other. But if you had experienced this thing in yourself you would be much more likely to move to compassion and, in so doing, be able to help this other being to find healing. It is, in fact, this self-comprehension that allows you to be of service to the other. And so it is for you that your experiences in your other lives can be used, if you are willing to choose this, to feel profound empathy for those who are deep in a victim state because you were there, **and** you can also find compassion for offenders because you know that you too are capable of being an abuser. That is one result of the choices you have made. The point to remember here is:

"If you cannot see the perfection then you are standing too close to the picture."

Z: Oh, wow, yes! That is most applicable here.

J-D: And it can most poignantly be illustrated by the horror of an innocent, such as a child for example, going through some abusive experience. We look at this and it just seems so very wrong. So very unfair. So unaccountably incongruent with there being a loving God. And how can I tell you that you are wrong if you feel this? I cannot. But I can tell you that there will come a time when you will stand back far enough from the picture that you will see the perfection. And I can also tell you that, if I say this to you when it is **your** child who has been abused, you will say "**never!**" And you will think me a monster for even suggesting this. That is how these things go. Beings choosing a victim status are, by definition, not able to see that they are doing this. If they were, then they would realise they are creating their own reality and would no longer be victims. It's a bit of a catch-22 situation, really. The only way out is for you to make a choice. To decide to claim responsibility and to decide to be the creator of your own reality and to take the time to allow that to become true for you. But it's not something that everyone will be able to hear, that is for certain.

Z: And what about the perpetrators? Surely they aren't aware that they are the creators of their own reality?

J-D: No. Excellent question though. You recall I said there was a triangle of victim/perpetrator/rescuer?

Z: I do.

J-D: Well, that is how things appear to those who are not aware that they are the creators of their own reality. It appears to them as if they are always in one of these three roles with respect to each other. But this is not how it appears from a higher perspective. From a higher perspective there is only creator and victim.

Z: What happens to the rescuer and the perpetrator?

J-D: If you look at them hard enough you will see that both of these are also just victims. I challenge you to go and find any number of perpetrators. Look at their stories properly. You'll find, I promise you, that they came to act as perpetrators because they believed themselves to be victims. It is as a result of their own belief in their own victimhood that they acted out as they did.

Z: Always?

J-D: Always. The worst criminal offenders in your jails all have the worst childhood circumstances. They are all traumatised in their own psyches. If their psyche was healed and loved, then they would not be expressing rage at the world at large. Witness what happens when one such a perpetrator finds healing, self-love and acceptance. He transforms. He becomes an agent for good. So clearly his perpetrator-nature is tied up with his own sense of being a victim.

Z: Hmm... so perpetrators are actually victims. What about rescuers?

J-D: This is also a victim but quite often it is the last step before someone releases themselves from victimhood. It is a way to still engage with the victim/perpetrator game whilst not actively being either of those. You see, before you can leave victim/perpetrator behind, you will need to heal yourself of the pain and trauma that you feel was inflicted upon you whilst you were in that game. You can do so by trying to help others in similar circumstances. You can turn your pain around and make something useful of it. You can overcome it by being a beacon of love. For example, a rape victim might establish a counselling and advocacy group. You often find that the people who originate such initiatives were victims who stood up and took back their power. Or sometimes even perpetrators who decided to make amends. Beings who want to be done with victim/perpetrator often go through a cycle of rescuer before they leave the game behind. There are other reasons for rescuer too. Sometimes the rescuer simply wishes to feel "noble". They wish to earn self-love through doing good deeds. Often this results in a kind of interfering rescuer whom the victim doesn't really appreciate. Another case would be a reformed perpetrator. For example, a husband, who for years committed spousal abuse, might start a "men's group" in which these men support each other in finding ways of dealing with their issues of rage and disempowerment. There are many permutations of this and I cannot elucidate all of them. I simply make the case that victims, perpetrators and rescuers are all still in a state of believing that they are ultimately victims. Creator beings, on the other hand, know that everyone is a creator being. That all is perfect. That there is nothing and no one that needs to be fixed. It is always perfect.

Z: But that sounds uncaring and callous to me.

J-D: Why?

Z: Well, that means, if I see someone in pain, I should ignore them and just say, "*Oh, you created this for yourself.*"

J-D: You **could**. But remember, in every moment, in every thought and in every action you are creating yourself and your reality. If you are a creator being then you know this. So if you see someone else's pain, then you are actually experiencing it somewhat yourself. You must decide what you are going to do with that. You must choose.

Z: But...

J-D: No, stay with me a minute. You, where you are now, living on Earth, you do not **know** the oneness of all. No matter how advanced your consciousness. By definition, in order for you to be on Earth you **must** see others as just that: as other. You are not yet of true unity consciousness. If you were, then you would be here with me. Not down there on Earth. So you might accept the things I say in an intellectual way, but you are not yet experiencing it as your reality. Am I right?

Z: Yes. That is so.

J-D: So you are still seeing this other who is in pain as an "other". You still think that the pain you are observing is **their** pain, not your own. And, in that moment, you are called to decide what to do with what you observe. And your response to that call will define who you are in that moment.

Z: Ugh! Now I am confused. What then must I do? Must I help everyone or must I let them create for themselves?

J-D: Ah. Now we get to the ethics and the morals. Good. Remember, this is where it all started? You said you wanted to know what it might mean morally and ethically to understand that all is ONE?

Z: Ah yes. That feels like a million pages ago!

J-D: Quite. We have been on a bit of a journey since then. In order to answer this question I am going to ask you to think back on the story of the Darklanders. There were beings of many different types of consciousness in that story. There were the Darklanders who remained Undecided about how they wished to create themselves. Then there were the Brightlanders who chose one of three expressions: the duality-conscious STO and STS beings and the unity-conscious Unifiers. Of all of these, it was only the Unifiers who knew the oneness of all. And so, if you want to understand the morality of unity consciousness then you should read again how the Unifiers behaved.

Unifiers know that you and they are essentially the same being. They therefore look at you with the eyes of love and compassion. They do not see you or your choices as "wrong". They do not judge you and they do not pity you (for that is also judgement!) If you call for help, then Unifiers will come to your assistance in a way that, **in their truth**, is the best way to do so. That

does not mean that they will rush in and rescue you. It does not mean that they will give you anything and everything you ask for. Because very often the thing you are begging for is the very thing that will keep you in a state of separation and pain. So they will help you as they themselves would wish to be helped; in a way that brings to you the realisation that you are the creator of your own reality and an indivisible part of the oneness.

I'll give you a practical example. If you say to me, "*Please, J-D, fix my life because it's a mess,*" and I rush in and fix it up for you, then what are you and I really saying? We are saying that you are incapable and that you are **not** the creator of your reality. Right? But you see, I **know** that you are me and I am you. So I am therefore saying that I **too** am incapable and not the creator of **my** reality. Which then makes it impossible for me to help you. So nothing happens. You see?

Z: That's pretty cute! Okay. So you can only help me in a way that is congruent with your truth.

J-D: Exactly! And my truth is that all is ONE with God and that everyone, whether they know it or not, creates their own reality. I cannot go about doing anything to you or for you in a way that negates that truth. So the help I can and will offer you will be in the form of assistance that helps you to help yourself. That enables you to more powerfully understand that you are the creator of your own reality. That gives you the tools to stand up and take the things you don't like in your life and create them differently until they are the way you **do** like.

Z: Ah! And that is why the light in the parable is the way it is. It doesn't come in and change stuff and make stuff the way **it** would want it to be. It is just there to assist those who are ready to see that they can make a different choice and create their life as **they** would want it to be.

J-D: Exactly so. That is exactly the point of the whole parable. You see, the light is not there to judge anyone wrong. It is not there because **it** thought the Darklanders were bad or wrong or incapable. Remember how it got there? It got there because many of the Darklanders themselves were calling out for help. They called out, and what essentially turns out to be an aspect of themselves, replies because it remembered its own inner-pain. No judgement. Just an answer to a call. And the answer does not come in the form of a rescuer, nor in the form of a perpetrator. We can see what happens with such answers – they just keep the cycle going. No, the answer comes in the form of a gently offered gift of love which each person can accept or refuse. And even if they refuse it, there is no judgement. It remains there for them to accept later. And when they do accept it, there are no demands about what they must do with it. They can always create exactly what they desire and they will always get what they create. So they can even use the light that is offered to create pain for themselves and others. If that is their choice, then they will continue to get what they create. And this will go on until they are ready to see that this does not bring them love or joy or peace.

To know the oneness of all is to gain a much broader perspective. It is to see the perfection of all things. And then you cease judging others and begin instead to simply discern what is right, good and true **for you**. Then you go where your truth takes you instead of being blown around by judgement of what is going on around you.

> (**Zingdad note:** If you are ready to step out of the victim/ perpetrator/ rescuer triangle and experience your true creator nature, then my multi-media seminar series, "Dreamer Awake" will greatly assist you in your journey. Please visit the Dreamer Awake section on my website, here: zingdad.com/dreamer-awake.)

Okay. Now we are still very far from being done with talking about the oneness and what it means. But I feel I have laid some important ground-work. I want to ask you one simple question. Given that which I have laid out in this conversation, do you think that a knowing of the oneness is likely to lead to unethical or immoral behaviour?

Z: No. I want to thank you for this conversation. Because I can really see that beings who are of unitary-consciousness will only ever desire what is best for every other being. It seems to me that they will, by definition, be the most loving of beings. And that they will never be able to do something which they know to be harmful to another.

J-D: Okay. Then I have answered the question from the end of Chapter 5, which is what we set out to do in this Chapter. And now that I have done so, I want to conclude by making another little point. Can you remember how, a few pages back, you were in turmoil about how this conversation was all going wrong? About how you had wasted time in this Chapter with irrelevant questions?

Z: Yes, I remember.

J-D: Well, in your mind at that point the wasted conversation was basically the Darklanders story. You wanted an answer to the moral and ethical implications of knowing the oneness of all and you felt that we had taken a **huge** tangent that was just a waste of time. But now I want to make the point that not only did the Darklanders story form the basis for a very good understanding of the implications of the oneness, but that we have laid the groundwork for many other future understandings. I am saying that we have not only done what we set out to do, but have also achieved many other beautiful things besides. You gained an answer to your question and it brought a richness of understanding, way beyond what you expected. Am I right?

Z: Yes. That is most certainly so. This particular conversation has been my favourite thus far. I'm sure I will re-read it many times

J-D: That's a good idea. I suggest you re-read it soon. You will find that I have planted understandings in it that will open up for you if you give it another pass or two. And if you come back in a year's time you will gain other new and deeper insights. That is how much richer this chapter is than it would have been had we just gotten down to brass tacks with me directly answering your question as you thought I should.

Z: Oh wow, I can certainly see the beauty and the perfection in that.

J-D: And that is because,

"At the level of oneness, all things always conspire to the greatest good."

Which is another way of saying,

"Everything is always perfect."

And, at the risk of flogging this one to death,

"If you cannot see the perfection then you are standing too close to the picture."

Z: That is awesome, J-D! Thanks for bringing this all so powerfully home for me.

But I have to admit... there is **still** something that bothers me about all this.

J-D: And that is...?

Z: That it's all good and well for you to talk about all this oneness stuff but... well... here I am on planet Earth doing my best to figure stuff out, doing my best to be a good person, doing all this spiritual questing... but still I am separate from you and God and everything else! I mean, I **hear** what you are saying. But for me this stuff is all still just theoretical. It is not my direct personal experience that all is one.

J-D: And is that a problem for you?

Z: Good God yes!!! I feel in my heart a craving for this. I want to **know** the oneness of all. And talking to you has just deepened that desire. But still I don't experience it. I mean I **have** had some wonderful spiritual experiences in my life but **still**, here I am separate from you and from God and from everyone else.

J-D: And so? Do you have a question?

Z: Yes. I want to know how I get to experience this – how do I get to know, as a direct fact of my own experience, that I am absolutely and completely one with All That Is?

J-D: I am **so** glad that you asked that question. It is the perfect question to lead us into our next chapter together. Because the very reason I am here in this reality at all is tied to the answer to that question and now is the time to begin to tell you of it.

As I have indicated, everyone in separation intended to be here. There are no mistakes about that. And everyone who permitted a part of themselves to sink right the way down into duality chose that. About this too, there were no mistakes. And this is what every single human being upon planet Earth actually is: a part of a great spirit being that chose to experience this part of this reality. You are there because you desired this. For you it certainly can seem as if some *other* being caused you to be there. Because you are in duality you might think this other being is God. You might think God created you there in duality to live out a small, confused existence. But this is not so. God did not do this to you. **You** chose to have this experience. And then, in order that you have the experience you desired, **you** chose to move through the layers of the Veil of Forgetting. With each layer you forgot more of who you really are. You chose all of this. But you are the part of yourself who has forgotten who you really are.

Z: I **am** you. I have always been you. I will always be you. But I am the part of you that has forgotten this?

J-D: That is exactly what I am saying.

And the same thing is true for each of your readers and for every other mote of consciousness that is there with you in your duality reality. You **are** all your Inner-Selves. You are just the parts of those beings that have forgotten this.

Z: And obviously the fact that we forgot this means that we forgot that we chose to forget. We forgot the forgetting.

J-D: (smiles) Yes, indeed. And there is more that you forgot.

You forgot that you are each actually vastly more loving, powerful and wise that you can now imagine yourselves to be.

And since you **are** loving, you will not desert a part of yourself in separation. When it is time to leave you will work to heal yourself, to return the lost fragmented parts to loving wholeness.

And since you **are** powerful, you get what you wish to create. You wished to co-create this separation reality and you got that right. You wished to experience yourself as utterly separate and alone and you got that right. You wished to rediscover yourself from that place of total forgetting and, to one degree or another, all of you are busy with that. When you are done with the things you wished to obtain from separation, when you are ready to leave, you will. You'll get that right.

And since you are wise, you know that you need friends to accomplish these things you desired to experience. You know which friends can assist with which parts of each task. You choose your friends wisely. This is equally true of your choice of co-creative partners that would assist you to penetrate deep and deeper into separation, so that you would be able to find your way all the way down into duality, as it is true of your choice of co-creative partners that would assist you to awaken yourself and raise yourself back out to full remembrance of your most limitless, eternal and magnificent Self. A Self that is one with the oneness.

And now, now that you ask how you might come to know that you are one with All That Is, now it is time for me to tell you why I, Joy-Divine, am here in this reality. For I am actually here for this one and only reason. I am here to be **that** kind of co-creative partner that assists others to awaken.

Z: Ah... yes... On some level, I guess I always knew this.

But what I don't know is how. How do we do this? How do we, all of us, co-create this awakening for ourselves?

J-D: This is a wonderful subject that I am very excited to share with you. It is time to begin the next chapter. Give it the title "Singularity Events" and then commence the conversation by asking me "*What are Singularity Events?*"

Z: Excellent. I'll do that. But... this all sounds so fascinating and you have me intrigued... what are Singularity Events?

J-D: In the next chapter, you brat!

Z: Okay (laughs). See you there...

* * * * *

CHAPTER 7.
SINGULARITY EVENTS

Zingdad: So, J-D, here is the **big question**: what **are** Singularity Events?

Joy-Divine: I am really looking forward to telling you about this. But while each Singularity Event itself is actually a very simple thing, its description will not mean much to you if you don't understand the context. And the context is vast. So much so that it will be well nigh impossible for you to understand it from your perspective. Can you imagine trying to explain the whole planetary water cycle to a little goldfish that has lived out its entire existence in a glass bowl on someone's kitchen counter? And it is just so for you: the context of the story of your first Singularity Event is a story that is billions of years in the making and as vast in extent as to encompass the whole of your universe and beyond. And so, just as it is with the little fish, the problem is one of perspective. You are immersed in your single point of view which encompasses but a few decades spent in a small locus on one of the billions of planets in one of the billions of galaxies in this universe. To say that your human perspective is limited is an extreme understatement.

Not that this is in any way a **bad** thing. It is precisely this very narrowly focused perspective that allows God to experience itself as many, many separate beings. So all is exactly as it is meant to be. But for all that, for you to understand the story of the Singularity Event, you will require a vastly broadened perspective. A perspective such as the one I am about to share with you.

It goes like this:

We begin by broadening our perspective enough to notice that your civilisation is not the first one to inhabit planet Earth. If you could stand where I am and see what I do, you'd notice that there have, in fact, been many successive civilisations that pre-dated this current one. You retain myths of Atlantis and Lemuria but these are only two out of a long sequence of quite diverse civilisations that have flowered upon the face of the Earth in ages past, stretching back billions of years.

What you might find hard to comprehend is that there were even civilisations that lived upon the Earth as it was first forming; beings quite different in form from your own that lived their lives on that hot proto-planet. And it might be quite confusing to you to discover that the earliest civilisations were, in most respects, the most advanced – each successive civilisation has been of a lower and lower consciousness. Each has been further from the awareness that all is one and that all are creators of their reality.

So, in incremental steps, consciousness has been falling on planet Earth since its ancient creation many billions of years ago.

Now let's "zoom out" and broaden our perspective even further. As you are well aware, this whole reality, and all inside it, comes from oneness. And this is so in the most real and practical sense. At the time of what is now understood to be "the Big Bang", all was oneness. All the matter and consciousness of this whole universe entered this reality from oneness and began to expand into density and separation.

If you see things like that then you will understand that the fall from grace began at the Big Bang and has been on-going since then. Deeper and deeper into density and separation life has fallen. Many, many little steps down it has taken.

And this was not by mistake! This is in response to the ONE seeking the answer to the question, *"What if I were not one.... what if I were many?"*

But the underlying point is that consciousness, in this universe, began at a high point, a point of oneness, a point of creatorhood, and from there it plummeted down, down, down, into utter separation and total victimhood. It has accomplished this fall in a sequence of steps and the final step is this one: your planetary civilisation here on Earth has achieved the ultimate in separation and victim-consciousness. The level of belief in the separation of the divine Creator from Its creation that has been possible for this present human civilisation upon planet Earth is profound indeed. You, beloved human beings of planet Earth, have accomplished this most impossibly, painfully difficult of all tasks. You are the ultimate answer bearers of this great question, *"What if I were many?"*

Z: So this is the very lowest ebb of consciousness? This world I am living in now? I guess I can believe that, given all the things are are going on in the world.

J-D: No, indeed, there is more to tell of this story.

I am saying, taken as a whole, Earth's human civilisation has achieved the greatest depth of consciousness. But this moment now, this moment where you find yourself in the great journey through time and space, this is not the lowest ebb. That very nadir is behind you in your collective past.

I can comprehend that, to your eyes, it might seem as if this could possibly be the lowest ebb, but if you could step back and look with the eyes of eternity you'd see that this is not so. And I shall offer you evidence.

Take these thoughts: *"All is One"* and *"You are the creator of your reality"*. These ideas are readily available to your planetary consciousness at this juncture of space and time and many have accepted these things as true.

Now cast yourself back just a blink. Holding such ideas in the 1950's would have resulted in you being thought strange indeed. You would not have been welcome in polite company if you were to say things like that. You would have been ostracised. You would not have been able to find gainful employment in any reputable company. You would have had to live on the very fringes of life if you wished to express such ideas. And you would have felt yourself to be utterly alone in your beliefs.

And if we go back a little further in history these ideas would have resulted in more aggressive sanction. You don't have to go very far back at all to find yourself actually being killed for expressing these ideas.

The point I am making here is that the very deepest darkness is behind you. It is not possible to say exactly when the true nadir was, since that will depend upon one's perspective, on what measure you will use to decide what constitutes the very darkest moment. But if one observes what was occurring in the spirit of humanity during such events as the world wars, the crusades, the inquisitions, the witch trials, then one begins to see some very dark times indeed. And even these were probably not the very deepest depths.

Did you know that there was a time when it was considered normal for an invading army to loot everything from the homes of those they invaded, to drag into the streets every young boy and slaughter him and to rape every girl and woman? In such times, when an invading army was done with a city there would be nothing but smouldering rubble left. Everyone would be dead or enslaved. Everything that could be carried off, was, and everything else was destroyed.

If you were to meet someone from such times you would be hard pressed to find even a glimmer of what you would call "humanity" in their eyes. All were so brutalized by their harsh circumstances that there was no place for gentleness or compassion.

But humanity's story is not a simple one to tell. There is too much complexity and intricacy to make specific statements about exactly when the true, deepest darkness was. Certainly, in the time of your very earliest historical records, several thousand years ago and before, things were very dark indeed. And even then, if one knows how to look, there were the first glimmers of hope. Even then there were wanderers who incarnated on Earth bearing bright messages of love, healing, compassion and forgiveness. If one was but willing to seek it out one could, even then, begin to find some spark of light, even in the depths of the darkness. And those sparks of light began very, very slowly to multiply and grow brighter. And so, at a snail's pace, the heart of humanity has been transforming. Cruel, destructive behaviours that were once normal and acceptable, became unacceptable and abnormal. Strange, impossible thoughts about treating the other as you would like to be treated were suggested and slowly, slowly became more and more accepted.

And so the story has proceeded.

And where is humanity now? I suppose I would ask you to imagine diving into a bottomless ocean. Diving down, down, down until there is only utter blackness all around. Until the pressure of the water is about to crush your body. And then, when you can go no deeper, you slowly change the direction of your dive into a parabolic arc. You slowly begin to turn around. And so it is that you catch your very first sight of the light, way, way in the distance above you. THAT is about where you are now. A very few of you have caught that first glimpse. Many more of you are just about to. And that light is the light of awareness that all is one and that each is the creator of their reality.

Z: That's quite a story. Thank you for sharing that with me. As you were passing all that through my mind, I felt all kinds of things swirling in my head... a congestion and a release... it was odd and uncomfortable, to say the least.

J-D: When a story is as mind-bogglingly complex as this one is, then it isn't easy to nimbly dance the line between telling the story truthfully and getting bogged down in the details. For, of course, there are many exceptions to the main thrust of my story line. There are plot twists and intricacies. As one example, your civilisation was, for better or for worse, massively interfered with by other non-terrestrial civilisations in ancient times. And though it has become ever more subtle, this interference never actually ceased.

Z: Now you raise something that fascinates me. Can I ask you about that? Are these space aliens you are talking about? And what exactly did they do here on Earth?

J-D: No. This is a large topic on its own and there is someone else better qualified to speak to this. In due course, a good many chapters hence, you will begin to speak to Adamu again as a part of this work.

(**Zingdad note:** this will be in Book 3 of *The Ascension Papers*)

This will be the time to delve into such issues. The only reason I raise this is to make overt that there are many ways in which my story was over-simplified. But, at least you have a context now for what I wish to relate.

Z: The Singularity Events?

J-D: Correct.

The story thus far has been told in the broad perspective. It has been about the evolution of consciousness in this universe generally and on planet Earth specifically. Now I want to shift our focus to the personal. I am talking now to **you**, my dear reader. I am now talking about **your** personal experience of life.

There are some things that I know about you. I know that you have hurt yourself terribly. You bear scars and wounds in your psyche. You cope as best as you can with these and you have been working diligently and earnestly on your healing for some time now. In this lifetime you have re-told yourself your own soul story. You have reached for your own magical gift in this lifetime too. You have also felt terrible pain and hardship and have worked to heal your pain and deal with the hardship. Through all this you have gained wisdom and compassion. And now, most recently, you are actually beginning to do some real good as regards the healing. There is far to go yet. But you are at least on the right path.

This will be true of very nearly everyone who is reading this. Some of those reading this will be a little deeper in the darkness and some will be more in the light. And, indeed, some will already have truly **seen** their own light.

And this – this moment of seeing the light – this is perhaps the most important of all the reasons we have come to separation in the first place.

SEEING THE LIGHT

Z: Oh? That **is** interesting to me. I have often wondered why exactly we are here. I mean, let's be honest, coming into separation is no picnic. Living a life in duality is hard, painful and confusing. So I often wondered why we'd be willing to do this to ourselves. Surly it can't be that we are here by mistake... that we entered this reality in error? Surely it can't be that our Inner-Selves put themselves through all this without knowing that it would be hard?

J-D: No, indeed! There was no error. We are all here intentionally and we all knew that it would be challenging in the extreme.

Z: So I assumed. And so logically there must be a very good reason for us to go through this.

J-D: There are many reasons, each depending on the perspective you take when asking the question, "*Why am I here?*" Many, many great reasons that make this incredibly difficult journey worth it, over and over again. But the only reason I am going to address right now is, **the discovery of Self.**

In order to tell this story I am going to ask you to shift your perspective once again. But this time, instead of broadening your perspective to include vast ages of humanity, we are going to zoom right out of this whole reality all together.

Can you imagine, for even a moment, what it is like to be your inner-most God-Self?

Z: I... er... no. I guess I can't.

J-D: Of course not. That is what it means to be where you are. To be so deep in separation that you have forgotten utterly your own true nature. But I can tell you a little of it and you can try to imagine.

There is a being. It is limitless and eternal. For this being there is no difference between "creative imagination" and "reality". What I mean is that this being gets what it creates in the most powerful and literal way. It takes all of this for granted because this is just "how it is" for this being.

This being is also aware, in a way that cannot be doubted or denied, that it is a part of something vastly greater than itself. It is as if this being knows to its core that it is one particular and special hue of light that is a part of the perfect white light that is all light. It knows there is no beginning or end to itself but, at the same time, it knows that there are other selves who are responsible for bearing all the many other hues of light.

And so this being can be said to be a bearer of the Light of God.

Now, it is said: as above, so below and as below, so above and this is true. As this being becomes aware of its "selfness" so it begins to get curious. "*Who and what am I?*" it asks itself. And it uses whatever it has access to to seek the answer.

One way to seek answers is to ask the other lights what they see when they look at you. And there are many wonderful realities that have been created as a means for that interplay. In those realities the Bright Ones dance and play together and they seek ways to show each other what they see in one another. These realities are light and joyful. In them the Bright Ones create as powerfully as they can from a place of pure love. Interactions are deep and powerful. It is a wonderful thing to observe and partake of.

But for all that, there is something unsatisfying about it. You see, when the Bright Ones play these games together they are never able to truly see themselves. Instead they are only able to see what they can see of what others see of them. It is a very indirect thing.

So how, then, can one truly see oneself?

Z: With a mirror?

J-D: That's a good call. You do indeed need a mirror. And on Earth you can use a mirror of silvered glass to see the exterior layer of your earthly form. But what kind of a mirror would it take to show the Bright Ones their own true light?

Z: If that's a riddle, then I don't know the answer.

J-D: No, not a riddle... but certainly a puzzle!

And here is the solution. Imagine that Bright One could take a part of itself and have that part of itself forget completely that it was that bright being in the first place and then, when it had completely forgotten who it was, it could be brought into the presence of that bright being again. When the one that has forgotten sees itself for the first time... what will it see? And what will it think of the Bright One that it sees? And as it begins to remember that it **is** the Bright One, how will it then experience itself? And then, every step of the way as it remembers more and more, as it merges ever more with its own true self, what will it then discover and know? How will it feel about itself? And what wisdom, knowing and insight will it bring home to itself about itself?

Z: And that is what we are doing!

J-D: Yes, beloved Self. That is what you and I are doing. That is what everyone on Earth is doing and that is what every single mote of consciousness in the whole universe is, eventually, doing. We are answering the question, "*Who am I?*"

Z: So then... the Singularity Events?

J-D: These are the moments when you really and truly **see** your own light. These are the first few clear and unambiguous sightings of your own self. The Singularity Events are when you fulfil your task of being the mirror of your own soul.

With your first Singularity Event, a connection is made and, from that moment on, you can never again get lost in separation. This is not, however, your journey's end! This is the mid-point in your journey. It is exactly half-way between your outbound journey into separation and your return journey to oneness. But it is called a Singularity Event because, in that moment, there is a union. A moment of oneness. The lost is found. And the whole-making process is not just underway, but it cannot ever again be stopped or reversed.

When you see the light, you are changed evermore. When you see the light, you see your direction Home. And, like a beacon shining from a home port, you are drawn that way. Now you know your way and when you know, you cannot ever again not know.

Z: That sounds amazing!

J-D: Really? I thought it sounded a bit dry and boring, actually. What I mean is that the above is a theoretical description of the event. And the description is **nothing** compared to the full, rich, wondrous experience of the event.

A description of something, no matter how truthful and accurate, can never compare to the actual experience of it. Here is an example: Would you like to eat a meal of crushed bitter beans, modified sweat, bird ova, crystallized grass sap and crushed grass seeds?

Z: Urk!

J-D: So you wouldn't want to eat that? Until you actually tasted a moist, warm, dark chocolate cake. Then suddenly you'd change your tune! Because, yes, cocoa is actually just crushed bitter beans, milk is produced by modified bovine sweat glands, eggs are bird ova, sugar is crystallised grass sap and flour is made of the seeds of a type of grass.

Z: I understand what you are saying – the description is nothing compared to the experience.

Okay. So what will the experience of the Singularity Event be like?

J-D: Just as each and every soul is totally unique, so will their experience be unique. When they are ready for it. When it comes for them. It will be tailor-made for them by their God-Self to be the perfect call Home.

Z: But everyone will experience these Singularity Events?

J-D: When they are ready.

Remember the Light that shone for the Darklanders in the last chapter? Well now, in this chapter, we are finding a different way to tell that story again. The Singularity Event **is** the Light. It is available to all and it has been increasing and increasing in intensity. It has become easier and easier to find it within. And the reason for this is that more and more have been choosing it. And so, as it becomes easier, more and more continue to choose it. It will not be forced on anyone, but those who are ready can seek it and find it. And when they do, their experience of it will be exactly perfect for them. The experience will change the course of their life and set them on their path Home.

And now I'd like to ask you to please share with our readers **your** very first glimpse of the Light. The moment when you changed course and began to find your way directly Home.

Z: Well, I've had many, very powerful and life-changing experiences in the last few years but, when you invite me to talk about my first seeing of the Light, then I know exactly which one of these you are talking about. Let me share with you an experience that I wrote about in 2010:

My Mountain Experience

To paint the picture properly, I have to tell you about two yuppie city-slickers. This is who my soul-mate, Lisa, and I were. I had my own business which consisted of a number of radio stations each providing programming for a different national retail chain. Lisa was a boardroom warrior for a large multinational biotechnology company. We were living the yuppie life and doing very well at it. I don't want to caricature our lives, so I must say that we were also both very involved in our own spiritual pursuits and were somewhat uncomfortable with the more materialistic and inauthentic parts of the lives we were living. However, this is all just the background context. The important bit came when we were on holiday in April of 2008. As much as we were city dwellers, we always loved nature and spent every holiday we could in an area of my country called The Garden Route. It was mainly the indigenous forests on the slopes of the Outeniqua Mountains (pronounced Oh-ten-ick-wah) that drew us there. But for us there had always been a special, indefinable something about the whole area, as if, in our souls, we knew that this has always been our true home here on planet Earth.

On this particular holiday we had an experience that changed us both forever. It occurred while we were on a hike to see an untouched forest of ancient trees. At some point, the trail took us up out of a valley and on a long, tiring, uphill slog. We toiled up the hill, out of the forests and onto a small plateau, overlooking a spectacularly beautiful valley, in the bottom of which a small river wound its way to the sea in the distance. On any given day, this would be the kind of view at which I would stop and marvel. It certainly was beautiful. But on that particular day, standing there looking across the valley at the forested mountains in the distance, something changed. The world around me was suddenly impossibly beautiful. Now, I could try to describe it – I could wax lyrical about the way the sun poured its light down on the earth like golden syrup. I could tell you that each leaf of every single tree looked like a perfect emerald jewel and that the wind through the grass set up a vibration that sang and hummed in my soul. I could tell you that I believed I could see, with absolute and perfect clarity, every single leaf and blade of grass right the way to the distant horizon. I could tell you about the quality of the air – that it had become gelid with the density of pure life essence that surrounded and interpenetrated me and all that was around me. I could tell you how I felt that I was truly one with that magnificent landscape and that the earth was my skin and the grass and trees my hair. I could throw pages and pages of such words at you in a vain attempt to share with you the pure, transcendent bliss of that moment, but I would not even be scratching the surface of what that moment was like. Perhaps I could simply say that I believe that I actually saw God in the very Life of the land on that day. My heart was opened and a portal was made there, through which I saw the world anew. And so it felt to me that, for the very first time in my life, I was actually, really seeing. I saw with my heart and my soul instead of just looking with my eyes. And it was beautiful. It was more beautiful than I could imagine anything ever being. This amazing, mystical experience was beyond my ability to even begin to make sense of.

I stood. I stared. I was awed.

I felt.

I knew.

I belonged.

Striving for comprehension, my mind eventually came up with an idea of what to do with this experience. It sent the thought out to the forest saying, "*I see you! I love you! Will you accept us as custodians?*"

And then I gained the presence of mind to wonder what had happened to Lisa. I had no idea how much time had passed since I had last spoken to her, as we were huffing and puffing up the steep slope. I turned to look for her. She was a few metres away, down on her knees with her back turned to me. I noticed she was shaking. As I approached her, I realised she was crying, tears shining in her eyes. I got closer and I heard her saying over and over again, "*... yes... yes... yes...*"

In that moment, it felt to me as if Lisa was answering my question on behalf of the forest. Or perhaps the forest had asked her that same question, and she was answering. It felt as if Lisa and the whole of the forest and I were all one being and we were all speaking the same question and answer to ourselves, "*Will you accept us as custodians? Yes... yes... yes.*"

Or perhaps that is just the best way my mind could make sense of an experience that is beyond the mind and beyond describing.

After some time – I have no idea how long – we noticed that it was getting late and we had some distance to walk to get back to the car. Reluctantly, but with our hearts full, we walked back to the car in a kind of euphoric, blissful semi-trance. We both knew that something life-changing had happened, but had no way of making sense of it.

I am deeply grateful that Lisa experienced this with me. Partly because experiencing it alone would have made it altogether less meaningful, but more so because if I had experienced this alone I would have known that I was now on a journey without her. An experience such as this changes you. You are no longer the same person you were before such an event. Everything changes. Certainly your life path and all the things you have previously valued are substantially re-arranged.

It was very clear to me that my Soul had a plan for me and that the forests of the Outeniqua Mountains were a vital part of that plan. I am deeply grateful to the ONE that Lisa felt exactly the same way.

And here I am now: as I write this we are in the middle of 2010 and I am looking out of a huge picture window at an endless vista of misty, forested gorges. Yes, we made it, we moved. It took us more than 2 years from when our hearts were broken open on that mountain hike but we are living here now! Right now we are renting a beautiful log home in the Outeniqua forests while we wait for the purchase of our own piece of land to go though. When it does, we'll begin building our home. We have the plans drawn up and we are fast learning everything we need to about creating a self-sustaining, off-the-grid homestead. The sun will provide us with electricity and water heating, the rain and our farm dams will provide us with water. We'll grow our own fruit and vegetables and trade locally for most of the food we need. We'll get almost everything we could want and need right there off our own land. And for the rest, I'll offer my creative outputs to the world and earn what is required. We are SO almost there and we will just keep following our hearts all the way there.

Getting here has taken some doing. I had a business that I couldn't just close up shop and walk away from. I wouldn't have felt right about that at all. So I gave the company to two of my staff members who had showed a great deal of passion and commitment to it. Lisa had just been offered a big step up into the corporate echelons and a salary to match. She turned it down and gave notice instead! We both spent six months doing a thorough hand-over to those who would take over from us. In that time we put our yuppie house in the leafy suburbs of Cape Town on the market. We sold our sporty city cars. We liquidated our investments and closed all those fear-based financial instruments that no longer made sense to us – all those insurance schemes and the like, which operate from the premise that bad things can happen to me without my first creating them. We gifted a whole mountain of possessions to various thrift shops (why **did** we believe we needed all that **stuff**?!?) and we lightened the load of our lives, our hearts and our souls. We came to the Outeniqua area looking for the perfect place of our dreams, armed with a sure knowing in our hearts of what it would be when we found it. And then we found it.

And here we are now.

But the physical move in geography is actually just a surface symptom of the actual change. The real move happened in our souls. Once we had **seen** with our hearts, we could never go back to just looking with our eyes ever again. We were transformed.

To give you an idea: before the Mountain Experience I had engaged in writing intuitive conversations on various Internet forums, but back then there was a different quality to that material. The lens-of-my-own-being filtered things in terms of good versus evil. I myself was very much of a duality mindset and so, naturally, the material I received reflected that. I believed that I was on the side of good, working to change the world to make it better. I believed that there were evil forces outside of me that I needed to resist and fight. The Mountain Experience released that from me. I was shown, in the most direct and personal way, that I am **one** with everything around me. I am Life and Life is me and there is no separation anywhere but that we have the most transient illusion thereof. The other difference between my intuitive conversations then and now was the victim-mindset that those writings espoused. I was looking for a rescuer to come and save the world. I could not see that I – or anyone else here on Earth – could save us from the mess we have made of everything.

And then, towards the end of 2008, the whole Lightship phenomenon happened, or rather didn't happen, depending on your perspective. I'm sure you remember it? It seems that just about every channeller in the world was receiving some variation on a message that a huge Lightship was going to show up in our skies and save us all. I was part of that as I had received some information from a spirit-friend called Adamu (See Chapter 1, *"My Life in Lyra"* for more about Adamu) that was incredibly exciting and amazing. And it also didn't happen. Or maybe it did, just not the way we expected. Or... well... exactly what happened there, and what that all means to me, is the subject of a different conversation. I'll be addressing that in greater detail when I begin the Adamu chapters (which will be in Book 3 of **The Ascension Papers**). But anyway, for me personally the effect was to shake loose, in quite a dramatic way, my victim mindset. I decided to be the creator of my own reality even though I did not know what that would really mean.

In retrospect I can see that I invited the Mountain Experience. Lisa and I were actively spiritually questing. We had taken a firm, clear, conscious decision to follow our hearts. We were opening ourselves all the time consciously and intentionally to growth and to Love. So, even though the experience took us by surprise, it was still what we wanted and had chosen for ourselves. It was a glorious gift of grace that showed us with absolute clarity what is **really** important to us. And, seeing that, changed absolutely everything for us. It took time for us to come to terms with this huge change and it took even longer for our outer-world to come to reflect the inner-change as, indeed, it is still in the process of doing.

But perhaps the clearest difference, as far as I am concerned, can be seen in my writings. It is only after that experience that I was able to open myself to the "all is one" kinds of teachings that have since been passing through my mind. I can say with absolute conviction that the Mountain Experience was essential to the transformation of my consciousness that has made this work possible.

... and that is the story...

J-D: Beautifully, told. Thank you.

Now, the point is that your Mountain Experience, as you call it, was **your** first glimmering or what I'd prefer to call your first Singularity Event. And what this was, was the very first sighting of the Light of oneness that you ever saw since your soul first began to sink into separation. While the experience was completely unique to you, there are a few things that this experience will have in common with everyone else who gets their first sighting. I can sum some of these up:

1. The first Singularity Event does not randomly happen to people. It comes after you have come to a firm decision (and begun to live that decision) to connect with the divine within. You and Lisa called this "following your hearts", others might phrase this in different ways, but at root, no matter what you call it, it will come down to the same thing: a deep commitment to finding God in the core of your own being.

2. When you positively engage this quest with a willingness to relinquish your ego's attachments to the illusions of the world in favour of your connection to the divine within, then you are on the path to having your first Singularity Event.

3. Really what I am saying in the above two points is that the first Singularity Event comes to those who are ready and willing – those who have firmly

chosen it and taken concrete steps to head towards it. And this is just as well since your first Singularity Event, when it happens, will change your whole life completely. In ways that you would never have been able to imagine, your whole perspective will have shifted. In this powerful moment of light and grace, you will find your life's course reorientated. Many of the things you previously found to be important will immediately be seen to be irrelevant. Gifts and abilities will arise from under-developed skills that you had previously not valued. You will find yourself powerfully drawn to new choices and decisions that will feel incredibly right to you.

In a nutshell, your first Singularity Event will be utterly unlike anything else you have ever experienced in all your journeys through space and time. The beauty and wonder of it will change you utterly. Nothing will be the same afterwards.

Z: But it's weird because nothing changed "outside" of me. It was only me who was changed.

J-D: Correct. This world of illusions teaches you that "what is true" is outside of you, that "what is important" is "changing things in the world". But your first Singularity Event shows you something completely different. It shows you that the real truth is inside of you and that the only thing that is really important is the connection, in your heart, to the divine. It is a radical restructuring of your whole world-view and it happens in a moment. And it is blissful beyond words.

There is a final point:

4. After this First Singularity Event, you will dedicate your life to deepening your connection with the divine. You will live for your next Singularity Event.

Z: My **next** Singularity Event? There are more Singularity Events?

J-D: Yes. There will be things that your soul will call you to do between your first and your second such experience. So it might feel to you as if there is a large gap between these experiences. But each Singularity Event marks a leap that you are taking in the direction of wholeness and oneness. Each Singularity Event is, in point of fact, the celebration of the evolution of your soul. Each event is your step up to a higher density of consciousness.

Before the events of your Mountain Experience, you were deeply embroiled in the illusions of this world. It is true that you were open to more and seeking, but the things that you thought to be true and important were all the things of the world. Your attachments and priorities were appropriate to that of a third density consciousness. Then you came to a fundamental, new choice. You chose to cease aligning yourself with the illusory world outside of yourself and, instead, to find your connection and your truth within. As you enacted that decision and made it real, so you began to evolve. Shortly thereafter as you became, substantively, a fourth density consciousness, you had your first Singularity Event. You have continued to grow and evolve since then. It is an inevitability that you will reach and transcend additional boundaries in the densities of consciousness in due course.

Z: Very interesting! So can you now tell me what exactly these densities of consciousness are? I'd really like to know how many densities there are and what the attributes of each density are and also what the difference between densities and dimensions might be.

J-D: This is vital information indeed. And, as has been promised to you before, I will promise you again; you **will** be given this information quite soon now. But not quite yet. There is a good deal more to be said on the subject of these Singularity Events.

Z: Okay and that's all very good because I want to hear that but there is something burdening me that I really need to get off my chest.

J-D: Let's hear it...

Z: Well... as I write this, I am engaged in revising The Ascension Papers for its 3rd edition. Though the whole book has been revised for this 3rd edition, most of the re-working has been relatively superficial. This chapter (Chapter 7) has been the exception. For this chapter I have been inspired by you to simply scrap the entire previous version and start again. To re-write it from scratch in its present form. And the reason for this is that we got the previous version totally and completely wrong. And for that I have felt all kinds of pain. I felt anger at you for misleading me and then I felt guilt and shame for misleading my readers and while I am now able to see how this new version of events is right and good, I have to ask: what happened last time round?

J-D: Good. I am pleased that you have asked this now, as it is the perfect time to address this issue. Won't you please summarise, as briefly as possible, what you previously understood the Singularity Event to be... how we previously "got it wrong"?

Z: Okay, here goes:

You began by telling me that the Singularity Event was tied up with the calendar date, 2012. At the time of writing there was a lot of excitement in our planetary consciousness about this date. A great many people believed, for many reasons, that this date, specifically the 21st of December 2012, was significant. Some believed that it would be the catastrophic end of the world, others believed that it would be a euphoric moment of spiritual ascension for us all. I wasn't sure what to believe, but I certainly did feel it was important.

In our conversation you told me that the Singularity Event was tied to this date. That there was a window period around this date in which we would each experience our own Singularity Event. But the way you told it last time, it would be something that would come in and sweep us all away with it. It would carry us all deep into the heart of oneness and that would be such a super blissful, amazing experience that we would be forever changed. After that we'd each come back to a world that was changed to be more congruent with our own vibratory level.

Given all of that, I guess I sort of expected to have something come over me... like falling into the deepest, most wonderful meditation. And then to fall and fall into it but that my falling should be into the heart of God. I expected to feel and see and know the most wondrous things. And then, when I was ready, when I began to once again think thoughts about incarnated life, I expected to return to being me, but with the whole world magically transformed for the better.

J-D: And instead?

Z: Instead nothing. The day of the 21st of December 2012 was perhaps the most dead ordinary day in my whole life. Nothing of any noteworthy exception happened at all on that day. I couldn't even meditate as I normally do. The day just passed in the most ridiculously uneventful fashion.

J-D: All right. So now, what if I were to tell you that there was just a simple misunderstanding? What if I were to say that everything you previously expected is still going to happen? All of it. There **is** an energetic outpouring coming from the heart of oneness and it will sweep across your planet and it will uplift all of you and it will bring you home to oneness and you will touch the heart of God and then you will return to a renewed planet and you will find yourself surrounded by others who are all full of love and kindness. What if I told you that this **is** still coming, but for complicated reasons that had to do with a misunderstanding of the way dates are used on Earth and the law of free will and what-not, we just got the date wrong? What if I told you it is still coming... but in 5 years time?

Z: Ahh, J-D. You know... there is a part of me that gets a little tingle of excitement when you tell this... a part of me that really wants to believe you.... but I just can't. I go to my heart and my heart says "no". If you were to tell me all that and mean it, then I'd simply take my hands from the keyboard and stop typing. Because it's wrong. Things will just not happen like that.

J-D: Okay. And how do you know that it's wrong?

Z: I told you: my heart says "no".

J-D: And why did your heart not say "no" last time?

Z: (I take a long, long pause to think. I get up from my desk and walk around. I come back to my desk a few times and then get up and walk around some more. I find I am really struggling to answer this.)

I'm afraid I just don't exactly know how to answer that, J-D.

J-D: All right then, we'll come back to it in a moment. How about this question instead: what if your heart didn't say no... or if you were not listening to your heart? What if you wrote this revised chapter as I have now just described – if you said that the whole happy, blissful, God-fixes-it-for-all-of-us moment was coming still and that you all just had to wait five years? What would happen?

Z: Not much. I don't think any of my readers would believe it either.

J-D: So **something** has changed. Something indefinable and yet, at the same time, pretty big. Your whole planetary culture went from being willing to give your belief over to this massive external event that would come and change you and your world forever... to **not** being willing to believe in such a thing ever again.

Z: Yes. That is true.

J-D: And in that moment, when each of you changed your belief structure, you decided something different. As you came to the realisation that this massive, world-altering event was off the cards, you decided something new. Something important. Some decided that, *"All this airy-fairy-ascension stuff is just nonsense for the weak-minded,"* others decided that they *"Will never get mislead into hoping for magical change ever again,"* and you decided...

Z: Hmm. Interesting. I decided **once again** to be the growth and the change I desired to see in the world. I decided to find the Singularity Event I hoped and dreamed of inside of myself. I decided to find a way to create the heavenly world I want to live in.

J-D: So, your pain was transformed into a re-commitment to follow your own heart – to seek your connection to the divine within your own being?

Z: Well, yes and no. It is as you say, but at the same time I also felt massive responsibility, massive guilt and shame, for the way I misled those who read the previous version of this chapter and put their faith and hopes into it.

J-D: In that statement you raise two very interesting issues. The first is that **you** feel guilt for what you have previously said was **my** error. The second is that you had actually quite quickly resolved your own pain, but that you felt continued pain as a result of your perceived responsibility for what others might think or believe. So let's look at these two points. Firstly... are **you** guilty or am I?

Z: As you ask this, I feel all kinds of energies swirling in my head. A very peculiar feeling. And with that I simply know the answer. And it goes like this:

I am responsible for everything I say. And I said this. We have an artifice in which we pretend that there is a "you" separate from "me". But you are my Inner-Self. You and I are really and truly one. We are the same being, perhaps just holding two different perspectives. But it is I who must take responsibility for this book and everything that is written in it. So, if there is guilt, then it is mine. And speaking of guilt – I have a strong feeling that I pulled things in the direction they went because I so badly wanted this amazing divine rescue. I feel like I influenced things and caused it to be written like that.

J-D: In ways that you will not now be able to understand, what you did then was to call forth aspects of me... of us... that needed, once and for all, to finally shed the yearning for an external rescuer. You were a part of the co-creating of a story that would result in us – our whole monadic soul structure – finally releasing that unhelpful desire.

And this was perfect because this was exactly the moment for that to be addressed on a grand scale in Earth's planetary consciousness. You will still come to understand it later, but truly the end of December 2012 **was** a watershed moment for humanity. And this watershed was co-created by all who became involved with it. Everyone who wrote about it, spoke about it, thought about it, energised it and believed in it... everyone including you and all those who read those previous editions of *The Ascension Papers*... were all co-creating it.

Now, you **thought** you were co-creating a wonderful, divine rescue. But what you were **actually** co-creating was your final relinquishing of your desire to be rescued. And with that you began to let go of the last vestiges of the victim, perpetrator, rescuer triangle. What I am saying is that you began then to co-create true creator consciousness.

There are, of course, many others on planet Earth who are still clinging to victim consciousness at this time and they can continue to do so for some considerable time to come, if this serves them. But on a fundamental level something big shifted in the potential for human consciousness at that juncture. For those of you who are leading the charge to the full awakening to unity consciousness and creator consciousness, things shifted into high-gear around that time. And an important part of that shift was letting go of the idea that you should passively await a rescue from above or beyond or in any other way outside of yourself.

Z: That's an interesting perspective and it feels right. But I also feel like I don't want to just "let myself off the hook" for misleading others.

J-D: Well, then the final thought I have for you is that you must practice what you preach. You have always said that you wish to take 100% responsibility for yourself. Is that true?

Z: Yes, of course!

J-D: But then, what about others? Should they also take responsibility for themselves or should you take responsibility for them too?

Z: Erm... no, of course not. Everyone should take responsibility for themselves.

J-D: So, others should take responsibility for their own thoughts, beliefs and choices?

Z: Yes. Obviously. But what about the fact that I am responsible for my words.

J-D: You are! It is your responsibility to speak your truth from your heart with the greatest clarity that you can possibly find in every single moment. And then, if you should grow and change and find that your truth has evolved, then you must check with your heart again and see if it is right for you to go back and re-address anything that you have said in a way that corrects it and brings it back into alignment with your heart.

Z: You are saying that we all make mistakes and that this is okay as long as we correct them when we become aware of them.

J-D: That's one way of saying it. I'd prefer to say that, as long as you are doing your very best to listen to your heart, then there are no mistakes. Then there are only your heart's expressions. And in each moment those expressions will be perfect. And each of those expressions will lead you to grow and evolve. And if, as a result of that growth and evolution, it comes to be that you look back on a previous expression and wish to update it to the current state of your heart's truth, then that too is perfect.

Z: All right. I accept that. There is grace and beauty in that and it feels true.

I would however still like to say to anyone who read the previous iteration of this chapter that I am really and truly sorry if I caused you any confusion. Life in this world can be pretty hard and it was never my intention to add to your burden. Indeed, it is my desire, if I can do so, to make this world a better place and to lighten the load of those who live here. So, I do very sincerely request your forgiveness for this.

I have learned a lot through this process and it is my absolute undertaking that I will henceforth be ever more vigilant in listening to my heart and winnowing my ego desires from my heart's truest expressions. I undertake to speak the truth that comes from my heart.

J-D: That's a good apology and a fine statement of intent.

Can we then move on from this?

Z: Yes. Now we can move on.

J-D: Good. Then I'd like to make three small points before we get to dealing with any questions you might have about the Singularity Event.

Firstly: this error was always plain for all to see. If you had not so badly **wanted** to mislead yourself, if you had not so badly **wanted** to believe in this cosmic rescue-drama-fiction, then it would have been clear as day that what was said in that previous version of this chapter was in direct contradiction with everything else said in this whole book. The core message of the entire book is that you are, each of you, the creators of your own reality. Throughout the book have we not said it over and over again in myriad different ways: **you** are the creator of your reality.

Z: *"You always get **exactly** what you create."*

J-D: Precisely. We repeated this phrase over and over again and then, in direct contradiction to very essence of what this book is all about, that previous version of this chapter went on to detail how you, and the whole world, would be rescued from your choices. How this energy from the centre of the universe would sweep through and that would fix everything for you. Remember how the light in Chapter Six "did nothing" - how it did not change a thing? And now suddenly, in the previous version of this chapter we had the light changing everything in the most radical way; sweeping you off to whole new experiences and then removing planet Earth from the 3rd density altogether! Clearly there was a grave contradiction there. And so, while the truth was available to you and to your readers, each chose what they wanted to believe for reasons of their own. And each got the consequences of their own choices. And now, finally, you have dealt with those consequences of your choices in a way that does you credit. The greater good has been served.

My second point is about balance. Taking responsibility, as you just have, cuts both ways. If you are willing to take responsibility for your expressions when you feel that they are in error, then you must also be willing to take responsibility for your expressions when they are true, right and beautiful.

You have been willing to take responsibility for this perceived error but you have been coy about accepting responsibility for all the great good that you have catalysed and partaken in.

I make this point to you, but it is most certainly of general applicability to your readers too: each should take absolute responsibility for **all** their beliefs, choices, actions and creations. There are parts to doing so that are hard but there is always more to this that is wonderful. It means being willing to own your achievements and take joy in the good that you have done.

Z: Thank you J-D. I'm going to have to be with that nugget a little. I hadn't thought of it like that and I can see that there is a fair bit for me to process in this regard.

J-D: Take your time. Allow yourself the luxury sometimes to love and appreciate yourself for your expressions that bring joy.

And now to my third and final point before we move on to your questions: I want you to understand that **there is nothing wrong with this world**. There are no mistakes and this world is not **wrong**. The world does not need a saviour and there is nothing and no one that is in need of being changed. I don't know how to say this with any greater clarity; the world is, in fact, exactly, 100% precisely as it is meant to be. And how it is meant to be is a "choice machine". The role of this world is that, when you are born into it, it constantly presents you with a vast array of choices. You are invited to believe that this or that thing is important to you, that this cause is worth fighting for, that thing will make you safe, this person knows the truth, that person is trustworthy, this story is the gospel truth, that story is an abject lie, this group is my group and that group is the enemy... and so on and so on. This world presents you with a non-stop selection of choices for you to believe in. And the instant you do – the very second you take even one of the choices the world is presenting to you, and believe in it as if it were true – you attach yourself to the illusion. That is when you begin to give your energy to the world. You begin to do this job, vote for that political party, follow this sports team, associate with that group of people, fight for this cause, invest your money in that scheme. And so on and so on. Not that there is anything *wrong* with any of that. But what has happened is that you have taken something **true** – your eternal, immortal creator nature – and attached it to something transient and fictitious – the illusions of this world. Again, this is not **wrong**, but it does lead to great pain. And that pain causes you to fight and struggle. Which in turn causes you to attach even more. And so you spiral down, deeper and deeper into the illusory world of separation.

And that spiralling dive into separation continues life-time after life-time, just as it is meant to. It can continue for an eternity if you let it because every single choice that the world presents to you leads you back down, deeper into the illusion.

There is only one choice that leads you out of the illusion and that is to cease to chose at all from amongst the choices the world offers you and to choose instead for what your deepest, innermost truth offers you. Only then do you begin to let go of the world and begin to move out into the higher levels of consciousness. But **still** the world is not **wrong**. Still it serves its perfect purpose as an entrancing show that lures all those who wish to experience it deep into a fictitious world of separation and duality. And they are not wrong to desire this experience. Just as you have found massive growth and evolution by coming here, so too do they have the right to do that.

So it is not your place to change the world and to try to stop it from being the perfect "choice machine" that it is. Even less is it your place to try to change others and to try to stop them from wanting the same kind of accelerated growth that you found here.

So, once and for all my beloved Self, I ask that we let go of the desire to rescue or to be rescued. There is no such thing as true rescue. It never actually happens. When it seems to happen it always goes wrong and comes to disaster and causes far more pain than it alleviates. There is nothing to commend it.

Z: Yes, done deal. No more seeking to be rescued and no more rescuing others. I am totally over that.

But there **is** a crucial difference between rescuing and helping!

J-D: Yes, there is. Unambiguously. I will summarise:

A rescuer meets a victim and she sees someone who is "broken". The victim feels like he cannot help himself and pleads, *"Fix me,"* and the rescuer says, *"I will fix you!"* The rescuer then takes decisions about what she must do to, or for, the victim while the victim is the passive recipient of her ministrations. Or perhaps the rescuer tells the victim what to do and he obediently complies. And since the victim resides in a state of need and the rescuer resides in a state of fulfilling the need, a dependency grows between the two. What is not admitted is that the rescuer is actually also feeding off of the victim's need. And so neither really wants the victim to heal since that will end the interaction. As a result, the victim does not heal but instead becomes even more powerless and an even greater victim. His need just balloons. In due course, the rescuer begins to feel that the victim's need is too great for her to cope with. The work of constantly rescuing him becomes too onerous for her. In short, the rescuer feels victimised by the victim's need. When this happens the rescuer begins to withdraw her energy from the victim, resulting in the victim feeling victimised by the rescuer. It all ends in a big mess with everyone sinking ever deeper into victimhood.

A healer, by contrast, begins with the knowledge that she is actually here to heal herself, first and foremost. So when she sees another who is in pain, she knows that she is seeing "another self that is hurting". She can evaluate whether it is right for her to attempt to help this other self or not. And one of the major criteria in that decision is whether this other self is at the place at which they are truly seeking healing, as opposed to being a victim looking for a rescuer. If the healer decides that it is right for her to take the client on, then the healer begins with the belief that, *"It is my role to show the client how he can heal himself."* Healers help their clients to heal themselves. The client is helped to see that he is not a victim but, in fact, the creator of his difficulty and also the creator of his own healing. There is a sharing of information, wisdom or whatever else the healer offers. True healing only occurs when the client is willing to take ownership of his distress/disease and also of his own healing. When the healing is concluded, the client is empowered and is more likely to be able to enact his own healing in future. He is more independent and stronger in every way. And the healer is also expanded and healed through the interaction. The interaction ends in growth and healing all round.

As the healer heals, so the healing she will offer will change. She will work at ever higher energetic levels. Eventually, she will be completely healed and will cease to offer healing and will cease to reside in separation entirely.

Z: I really get the difference, thank you.

Is everyone a healer?

J-D: Yes, but not in the way you mean it. Everyone here in separation is fragmented into many parts. That is the nature of separation. And so everyone is in pain. And to leave separation, each will have to heal their own souls and find wholeness and oneness within themselves. Eventually every single being in separation will heal themselves. Each will be their own healer. And this is what we are talking about here in this chapter. Each soul will shine its light and create moments of oneness for itself to bring all parts of self back home to completion and wholeness.

But this is not what you refer to when you ask if everyone is a healer. You mean to ask if everyone is a healer of others.

If I were to offer you the metaphor of life in separation as being a battlefield then we could immediately see that different people are specialised for all kinds of different parts of the battle. Most are soldiers who do the actual fighting, while many support the soldiers in all kinds of ways: signallers, engineers, cooks, transport and logistics... these are just a few of the myriad tasks one might be specialised for. Of all the specialisations, only a small percentage are the field medics who patch the soldiers up in the midst of the battle so that they can fight on. These are the healers who assist you to cope with your pain while you continue to soldier on, deeper and deeper into battle. And then there is a very, very small group who are specialised as you are – the evacuation medics. The meaning of the Soul Re-Integration healing that you offer is that it assists those who are finally ready to completely leave the battlefield to do so. To find all the soldiers that are a part of their unit, to heal all the parts of that unit so that they are all ready to see their guiding light and to follow it Home.

> (**Zingdad note**: You can find out more about Soul Re-Integration and how I might assist <u>you</u> to "leave the battlefield" here: zingdad.com/healing-a-helping/soul-re-integration.)

So, to sum up: all are healers of themselves but only a few help others to heal and only a few of the few help others to heal such that they begin to exit separation entirely. But it is precisely **because** you are a healer that you see your whole world in the context of healing. You think that this is all that is going on here. It is right and good that this is your perspective, but it is very much not the **only** valid perspective. There are many, many other roles to play and gifts to give other than healing.

Z: Perfect. Thank you.

J-D: And now you can ask some of those questions that have been building up in your mind...

Z: You know me too well!

What I am wondering is, "why"? Why all of this? Why the battle? Why separation? If I understand you correctly then you have been saying that all is truly one. That the ONE chose to create parts of itself to explore different questions and thoughts about Itself. And one question was, "*What if I am many.*" And then this whole separation reality came into being. And we are exploring the answer to that question. We are living it. But the eventual outcome, for all of us, is that we will see the light and begin to return to wholeness and oneness again. But if we only came here to see the light of oneness so that we can return Home again... what's the point?

Why go to all this massive effort and put ourselves through all this agony if we are just going to go back to what we were before we came here in the first place?

I suppose another way of asking this question is: if the ONE knows everything, then why does the ONE need to put Itself through the wringer to find out what separation is like, only to return Itself to oneness again?

J-D: Some things can only be known and experienced from a state of limitation, division and separation. And so it is that, paradoxically, in order for beings of oneness to know all, they must also experience not-oneness. The heart of the paradox is that they can, and do, experience this separation whilst still being in a state of oneness. Or they might choose to create degrees of separation within their oneness.

THE STORY OF THE SPIRIT OF WATER

To help you to understand this I am going to tell you a little story using the example of water. Water is a substance that is composed of molecules with the chemical formula H_2O. Let us pretend that it is possible for you to meet and talk to a single water molecule to get its perspective on life. Let us imagine that we randomly choose one such molecule and we find it in a wintry landscape high on a mountain. If we enquired of our new acquaintance what it is doing it might say, *"I am sitting quite still, holding tight to all my other water-molecule friends around me. Together we have formed a glacier."*

This is what water molecules do when they get cold enough. They slow down and become quite still. As they do, they cosy up with the other molecules around them and bond together into a crystal lattice. This is what ice is. And that is how they remain, relatively still and bonded together, until heat is applied.

Which brings me to the next time we meet our little water molecule. Winter passes and the warming rays of the spring sun heat the glacier. All the water molecules are energised and they begin to move. Eventually some of them are moving too vigorously to maintain their bonds and they break free, trickling away into a stream. When we eventually find our new friend and ask him what he is up to he says, *"I am rushing down a mountain side in a fast-flowing river!"*

Again we allow some time to pass. Summer comes. The stream is caught in a large lake and the hot summer sun bakes down upon the water. Water molecules on the surface of the lake are heated up some more. The extra energy makes them dance even more vigorously and they fly free from the water's surface as vapour. Now our friend might report, *"I am drifting free, flying away on the breeze!"*

In due course, our friend is likely to find a cloud to join and will eventually cool and make water-bonds again and fall to earth. And so it will go around the cycle yet again.

And now that you have gotten to know the water-molecule a little, which of its states, do you think, is the most like being part of the oneness? Being still and peaceful and connected with others in the glacier? Being fluid but still connected in the river? Or being free and unencumbered and energised as vapour?

Z: I think the glacier. I think he felt most connected to other water molecules. And he was still and peaceful.

J-D: It's a good guess, but it is not correct. But then I have to admit I cheated – I'm afraid it was a trick question. None of these states of water are much like an experience of oneness. All three are states of **doing** and separation. In all three states, the little molecule is still just a single-perspective being. This is similar to your current experience of life. As with the ice-state, you might find yourself doing things that bring you into closer harmony and connection with others. You might become still and peaceful. You might introspect and meditate. But still you are an individual, experiencing separation. And if you choose to do more highly energetic and individualistic things, this will not actually make you any more or any less a single-perspective being.

But now, let us imagine that our water molecule becomes part of a cloud. But this time, instead of us talking to an individual molecule, imagine we can talk to the whole cloud. Inside it there are very, very many molecules of water. Many more than the biggest number you know.

Z: More than a trillion?

J-D: By my estimate there might very well be a trillion water molecules in about 5 or 10 raindrops and that cloud holds a whole rainstorm. So, no, a **lot** more than a trillion.

Z: Wow!

J-D: No kidding. So this cloud includes a great number of molecules, each of them having a unique, individual perspective. Let us imagine that the cloud knows, feels, thinks, sees, remembers and experiences everything that all the individual molecules do. The cloud is truly the collective of all the molecules together. But it is more than that. It does not **only** know what all the molecules collectively know... it knows more than that. It knows what it is to be a cloud as well. It knows what it is to know, all at the same time, what this mind-boggling number of little beings know. And here is the thing that you might struggle to understand: the cloud is not a being that has other beings inside it. It **is** all those little beings. The cloud **is** the water molecules and they **are** the cloud. There is no separation. There is no cloud without water molecules. But the cloud is, quite simply, a lot more than the sum of its parts. Imagine how it would be for you if you could, right now, be thinking all the thoughts that every person on earth is thinking. It would enlarge your capacity for perception and self-awareness in an unimaginable way. You would not simply be a human being who is now seven billion times cleverer. You would be an entirely different order of being with an entirely different perspective of what Life is and what Self means.

Do you follow?

Z: Wow, I think so!

J-D: Good. So now, do you think the cloud knows what true oneness is?

Z: It sounds like it does, yes.

J-D: No, the cloud certainly knows what it is to have many perspectives, this is true. But that does not mean it knows true oneness. It doesn't know, for example, what it is to be an ocean. But it will have more than just an inkling because all of the water molecules that make up its being will, at some point in their many cycles, have been in the ocean. So the cloud will begin to **feel** the essence of oneness but it will also very much still be a separate, individuated consciousness, even though it is yet composed of many.

Now, I can take you on a journey of meeting ever greater constructs of water. We could meet a being called Spirit of Cloud who is composed of all the clouds on the whole planet. Then we could step up and meet Spirit of Earth's Water who is a being composed of all the water on the planet in all of its forms. Each of these beings would, as a result of their greater and greater level of consciousness and their ever-increasing number of perspectives, be closer and closer to knowing what true oneness is. The larger the consciousness grows, the more "others" it knows of. Somewhere along the line you get someone like the being that we shall call Spirit of Water. Let us imagine that all the water that has ever existed anywhere is all a part of this great being. Every single water molecule is just one mote of consciousness in this being's great mind. Now, what do you think? If we were to ask Spirit of Water what it is doing right now, what do you think it would tell us? Would it talk of icy glaciers? Of raging torrents? Of huge lazy oceans? Would it tell us of towering thunderclouds? Or of rainstorms, snowfalls or hail? Or of the blood that flows in all the veins of every living creature? Or what about whole planets composed entirely of water in one state or another? What do you think?

Z: I can't imagine...

J-D: Well, I think this great being would gently smile and say, "*Child, I am beyond the considerations of 'doing'. What I am is **being**. And in this here-and-now, I am being water.*"

And here, finally, we would have found a being that knows what oneness is. Though it still has an identity, and a unique nature, this being is not misidentifying Itself. It does not think that it is what it does. It knows that it simply **is**. It is consciousness. It is Life. And right now it is being water. But it is also very much conscious that it is one with every other being, everywhere, in All That Is. And within its consciousness is the absolute knowing of what it is to experience **all** the states of doing, at all the levels of separation that are possible for it, in this reality. Spirit of Water is whole and complete and it is, at the same time, utterly expressed into this separation reality.

Z: And without having come here into the separation reality Spirit of Water would not know any of that stuff of what it is like to be a molecule of water or a puff of steam or a raging torrent or... any of that.

J-D: Without having come into separation Spirit of Water would not be Spirit of Water. There is no water outside of separation! This is a part of the ONE that only discovered its unique and precious gift to hold the pattern of water by coming here. And **what** a rich, varied and multi-faceted experience this has been! What a wonder! The profundity of this experience is simply too deep and too amazing to contemplate.

Z: One can't really describe it, can one? You can actually only experience it and the only way to experience it is to come here into separation.

J-D: And so, finally, you answer your own question. Why separation? Because it **must** be experienced. It's as simple as that... and yet as also impossible to comprehend as that.

Z: So we didn't come here to heal. We didn't come here to leave here. We didn't come here to find oneness. We came here **for this**! We came here to experience separation!

J-D: It seems almost too silly to say, doesn't it? We came to separation to experience separation.

Z: Yeah, that sounds lame. So instead we have to tell big stories about being Spirit of Water...

J-D:... or about being Joy-Divine who is also expressed as Delight the Interventionist.

Z: Yes. I get it. So we are not here **for** our Singularity Events but they are how we will begin to leave when we are done with being here.

J-D: Almost right. Essentially you begin your journey from a place of oneness. Then you enter separation and fragment yourself. You head deeper and deeper into separation until you hit rock bottom. This is also known as the dark night of the soul. It is when you discover that you cannot travel any further in the direction of separation. This profound agony causes you to cease choosing for separation and then you look around for other choices. All choices but one will result in you remaining in that state of agony. That one choice is the choice to truly begin to heal your soul; to re-integrate all your lost fragments. And the only way to do that is to follow your heart and to find wholeness and oneness within yourself. When you choose this, then you choose for love. You alter your direction. You cease moving down deeper into separation and begin to move instead in the direction of oneness. Since the light we are talking about is the light of oneness, if you stay with that choice then you will see the light. You will have your first Singularity Event.

Then you will know beyond knowing that you are on the path Home. As you stay the course, so you will evolve and grow and heal and, in due course, you will experience additional moments of knowing oneness – additional Singularity Events. Eventually this will lead you right to the very edge of separation where you will be able to make the choice to leave altogether.

Z: I think I get it. Thank you!

Another question that has been sitting in my mind is, *"Why 2012?"* I'm over the idea that we'll all be saved by unicorns and fairies delivering free marshmallows and dispensing glitter-dust over the whole world at the end of 2012 because... well... because I looked very hard and that didn't happen. And so, when we began to re-write this chapter, I sort of expected you to move away from that date entirely and say that it was actually irrelevant. But you didn't. You said it is still significant. Can you explain that?

J-D: The whole and complete answer to that question is massively complex. In order for you to comprehend this, you would have to understand exactly what the dimensions of this reality are; you'd have to understand what the densities of consciousness are. You'd have to understand exactly what space and time really is. Only **then** could you actually hope to understand the context to the answer to, *"Why 2012?"*

Z: Okay, but then... really... I **need** to be given that information now! Everything you have told me always seems to come back to those crucial bits of information and now I really just don't feel that there is a way to proceed without it.

J-D: Okay then! It seems that we have come to the end of this conversation. It seems that you can go no further without coming to a deep understanding of the truth of such things. And so it is time, finally, for you to begin your "officially recorded conversations" with our much loved and highly esteemed soul-partner, 8.

So you can begin your next chapter and give it the title, *"What is Truth?"* and with that you can commence to engage 8 in conversation. There is a raft of really important information that he has to share with you to further your ability to release your blockages and fears and then, in due course, when he is ready, he will explain all of these things that you are so itching to get to. And when you finally comprehend space, time, dimensions and densities.... then you should ask again, *"Why 2012?"*

Z: Fantastic! I was wondering when I'd start talking to 8. And here we are doing it in chapter 8! That's perfect.

J-D: Nothing by chance, beloved one.

Z: Okay. Thank you so much J-D. It has been simply **awesome** talking to you. These last seven chapters have been some of the most amazing conversations of my life. I love you **so much**! Thank you!

J-D: Perfect. You are most welcome.

Z: And now I'll go talk to 8...

* * * * *

CHAPTER 8.
WHAT IS TRUTH?

Remember when you were a young child and you first went to school? How you'd be dropped off in the morning and, even though you really missed your family, you knew it was actually okay because they'd be there when you got home? Well, in quite a similar way I always had a "dropped off at school" feeling about living my life here on Earth. It felt hard for me to be here. And really quite lonely. But what made it okay for me was my "spirit friend". As a little kid I'd do this thing where I'd sit and stare into nothingness and fall away into another world. And in this other world I had an amazing friend. He was as real to me as anything else in this world; the only difference was that I had to sit very quietly to go and visit him. But he really loved me and helped me with all the difficulty and pain that the "real world" caused me. When I tried to tell people about him, it was considered "cute". As in, "*How cute! He has an imaginary friend!*"

I got pats on the head and smiles and giggles but I certainly didn't get taken seriously. So I quickly realised that people weren't really "getting it". I stopped talking about this and just let it be something that only I knew. Eventually I even stopped visiting him.

Somewhere in my mid teens an older friend mentioned to me that he believed we each had a "Spirit-Guide". Something about that concept leapt out at me. I deeply felt this to be true. It was the first big "resonance" that I remember experiencing in my life. I tried to discuss this with him but he didn't seem to have much more to say... just that he believed in this. It was a thought that stayed with me. I kept thinking about it. I knew I had a Spirit-Guide and I knew he was with me. I felt his presence. I felt his very attentive and loving guardianship of me. So, at about age sixteen, I decided that it was time to take matters in hand. I decided to find a way to contact this being. Which is funny if you understand the context of my life at the time. You see, I grew up in a pretty conservative Christian environment. I had never even heard of Ouija boards (nor the attendant horror stories of treating spirituality like a parlour game). I hadn't heard of pendulums or dowsing. I hadn't even heard of tarot. And, I can categorically assure you, if I had heard of such things it would have been in the context of a stern warning not to dabble in the occult because, "*It is all devil worship!*" Such was the *zeitgeist* of my upbringing. So, when I **did** decide to contact my Spirit-Guide, I knew I was going to do this entirely on my own. There was no-one I could talk to about this. No-one from whom to seek advice. No one to share the journey with. No-one to tell how it was going. No-one. Not for any part of it. I am convinced, beyond a shadow of a doubt, that were it to have emerged that I was planning to "contact spirits", someone from the church would have been called in to counsel me and to help save my soul. There would have been endless prayer and anguish until I eventually not only gave all this up but, instead, conformed to the expected behaviour of a good Christian boy. Or something along those lines. But the issue for me was that I **knew** I was reaching out to someone who loved me and protected me. Someone who was **anyway** there with me all the time. So I avoided the inevitable pain and just kept all of this very private.

There was one particular occasion when matters took a step forward for me. I was sitting quietly in the garden one evening thinking about the problem of how to make contact with my Spirit-Guide. As I was contemplating this I was fiddling with a pebble. Deep in thought I was balancing the pebble on two outstretched fingers and then watching to see which way it would fall. The pebble was well balanced and seemed to randomly fall either left or right. Inspiration dawned. I rebalanced the pebble on my fingers and quietened my mind. I sat there for a few moments and then sent out this thought:

"*I know you are here with me. If you are willing to talk to me, please unbalance the pebble.*"

And the pebble instantly fell from my outstretched hand.

"*That side is now 'yes' and the other is now 'no'*," I said. "*Do you love me unconditionally?*" I asked.

Yes

I don't know what made me ask that as my first real question. I guess it was more inspiration. It's a really good place to start with spirit beings. At first, speak only to those who love you. But, you know, I **felt** his presence and I knew that it was love. In my heart I **knew** that this was okay. And so I carried on. I asked a few more questions like that with my mind in a curiously dichotomous state – on the one hand I was elated because I knew I had finally hit on a means of speaking with my guide, and on the other hand my logical, deductive mind told me that this was all just nonsense and that I was just playing games with myself by tipping the stone in the desired direction in response to my own questions. Both of these things were true for me. I decided to carry on and see where it would lead. At some point, I told myself, proof would arrive. At some point, if I just stayed with it, I would find undeniable proof either that this was true or that I was deluding myself.

That was almost 30 years ago and "undeniable proof" still hasn't arrived for me.

But, despite the fact that I found that I could doubt my experiences, I kept going. In time I graduated from balancing stones on my hand to having some pretty fluent intuitive conversations, but no matter what process I tried, I could never find a way to make these conversations prove themselves conclusively to be either true or false. It just resolutely stayed there in the middle ground of "could be". Not only did it stay "doubtable but possible", but as I got more sophisticated in my methods it came to be explained to me how and why this was so – that this would **always** be the way things would be. And now that you have read the preceding seven chapters you also understand some of that. Essentially I come to realise that "undeniable proof" would take away my right to doubt. And the right to doubt is the right to believe something else, to create another perspective. And we simply cannot be limitless creator beings if that right is removed from us. So there will **always** be the possibility of doubt. But I can tell you that the first few years were quite frustrating. Especially when trying to get answers to complex philosophical questions with "yes/no" answers from a pebble balanced on my hand and clouds of unresolved doubt swirling in my mind.

But back to those early conversations... One of the first things I wanted from this being was a name. So I took a piece of paper and wrote all the alphanumeric characters on it. I divided them up into quadrants. Thus prepared, I called to him and asked, "*Will you spell your name out to me?*"

No, was the answer.

I was nonplussed. I will spare you the excruciating process that I had to go through to eventually understand why he would not tell me his name and simply tell you what it was: it turns out that this being simply did not **have** a name! As he had never incarnated in a human form, he had never needed a name. And, at the higher levels of consciousness, names are irrelevant. Such beings call each other by the simple expedient of being in each other's presence.

And, when asked, he was also quite adamant that, **no**, he didn't actually want one either. And **no**, he also was not willing to have me just invent one for him. To the whole question of a name, he simply said **no**.

But then I appealed to him. I explained that **I** really needed a name for him. I needed something to call him when I called for his presence and I needed something to call him in our conversations. I practically begged. And then I felt a shift – a relenting – and then I actually felt what I can only describe as a loving, gentle laugh. I asked again, "*Will you give me a name that I can call you?*"

And this time the answer was **yes**. With great excitement I fetched the alphanumeric sheet and by process of elimination ("*is the first letter in **this** quadrant? How about **this** one?*"), I got to the first letter. But with some confusion I noticed that the first letter was a digit: the number "8". Somewhat confused I asked, "*Is there more?*"

No

And so it was. My Spirit-Guide's name was 8.

Latterly I have gained a bit more insight. Had he chosen a word or a name that I could have analysed for its meaning, I would have made all kinds of assumptions about who he is, what his character is like and I would have drawn (inevitably wrong) conclusions about him from this name. Choosing a digit kept me flexible about all that. It allowed me, instead, to slowly get to know him *as he is* without the burden of preconceptions. But the number itself is not randomly chosen – it has many meanings on many levels. It is like a multi-layered puzzle that 8 has set for me to tease me and entertain me as I proceed. Even now that I can have free-flowing conversations with my beloved friend 8, still he laughs at me when I ask him about the meaning of his name. He tells me that there is much for me to discover and that I will enjoy the joke **so** much more if I figure it out without him telling me. So, I have a few bits of the puzzle, but there is a great deal more for me yet to unravel.

The bits I have include:

If you turn an 8 on its side you get: ∞, the symbol for infinity. 8, in music, is the number of tones in a complete octave. 8, in this reality, is the number of densities in the complete reality. In the same way we really have 8 main chakras. So there are all these 8's which all seem to point in the same direction. To completion and perfection, in infinity. How does that relate to my Spirit-Guide? And what **else** does the number 8 mean? I don't know. At some point I'll figure it all out, I'm sure.

Then also, although rhyming words can mean nothing, I have understood that things that are significant about 8 are the rhyming words, "fate" and "gate". But I still lack specifics here.

But the interesting thing is that, through all this, 8 succeeded in keeping me playing and guessing instead of forming a narrow, fixed idea of who he is and what he is like. Instead I learned to know 8 by his "feel" – his energetic print – whenever I spoke to him. And I learned even more about him from what he said and the truths I gained from him. And finally I learned to know about him from all the things he has done for me. I won't go into details because I have no desire to tell long rambling personal accounts of the somewhat far-fetched-sounding tales of times that I have been protected and looked after and other supernatural events that I have witnessed which have, I know, been 8's handiwork. These are my experiences and cataloguing them will add nothing to the narrative here. Instead I will say this: in my experience and in my truth, 8 is simply amazing. He is **trustworthy**. That word seems too weak to express this. I trust 8 completely. I would, without a moment's hesitation, put my whole universe in his hands. He is steadfast, loyal and sure. 8 is a being of truth. In fact, he told me once he is made of the very energy of truth itself. So don't go to 8 if you want pretty words dressed up nicely! He has a habit of putting things rather bluntly that, if you will listen to them, will move you forward. Always in a good direction, but not always in the gentlest fashion possible. And, as 8 is a being of pure truth, he is the best spiritual protection I could ask for and I am endlessly grateful that he is journeying with me.

And so, this is what I would say to you about what is coming next: I am going to talk to 8 and I am going to share these conversations with you. This is a bit odd for me because it's a bit like having a private 'phone conversation with your very best friend and then broadcasting it to the world. But it's also pretty cool because this is the very first time that 8 is permitting this. He wasn't willing to have me channel him for public consumption until now. *"Not while you still have your training wheels on,"* was how he put it. But quite recently he said, *"It's time. You may now channel me in your new series. You'll be told when."* And, seeing as J-D just told me to do so... I guess I'm finally here.

> (**Zingdad note:** Should you be interested in establishing a dialogue with your own spirit guide(s), please book a Soul Re-Integration session with me here: zingdad.com/healing-a-helping/soul-re-integration. I can definitely help you to open the channels of communication!)

Now, before I begin. A quick word about 8's style. If you need all that fluffy "dearest beloved ones" stuff in your spiritual messages, then this is not going to tickle your fancy. 8 doesn't do that stuff. He says what needs saying. He answers question without first stroking your ego or soothing your nerves. You see, 8 is unconcerned with what you do with his words. You can take them, you can leave them or you can roll them up and smoke them. He speaks his truth as it is, without trying to sell it to you. Now, if it sounds as if I am apologizing for him, I am not. Of all the beings in All That Is, 8 is the being that, in my opinion, is the least in need of apologies. He is awesome. And I love him completely, exactly as he is.

So, without further ado, I give you my Spirit-Guide, my soul's journey mate, my oldest and dearest friend... 8.

Zingdad: Hi 8. I want to do an introduction to you, but I'm not sure where to start.

8: Start with answering this: do you know what you are doing here?

Z: Where? In this conversation?

8: This conversation. The conversations that went before. The conversations that will follow. Your whole life. Everything. Do you know what you are doing?

Z: Uhh... sort of. I think these conversations are about me searching for answers. I'm asking questions of beings whom I love and trust, and getting answers.

8: That might be one perspective. But it's a very small and limited perspective. Shall I offer you a broader perspective?

Z: Please.

8: You are engaged in a game called "reality creation".

Z: How so, 8?

8: Let me answer that by telling you about this series that you are writing. When you sat down to write this work you didn't actually have a clue where it would lead. You thought you were just going to ask some questions and get some answers and bumble your way through to getting some info that might be a bit useful. Right?

Z: Yeah. I guess that is the unflattering way of putting it.

8: Flattery is not my strong suite. Essentially you didn't know what the greater picture was. You didn't even know that **there was** a greater picture. But your Inner-Self, Joy-Divine, and the rest of your soul family... well, we have a plan. Shall I tell you what it is?

Z: Can I possibly turn an invitation like that down?

8: It is to help you with your **real** quest. Which is to create your reality. Let me explain. You live in a reality which you find confusing. You don't understand why things are the way they are. And for so long as you choose, in that reality, to take things at face value and believe what is presented, then you take your creator status and nullify it. You use your divine power in such a self-defeating and chaotic manner that it is of no use to you and it never shows itself to you. And so you will proceed. As long as you believe in the illusion, you will continue to be a very small pawn in a very big game. Others will capitalise on this self-limiting perspective and use little strategies to entice you to play games of their devising. In almost every instance the ones doing this will not even know **themselves** that this is what they are doing. Everyone is just playing the game and everyone is equally confused. And you can go on playing this game for a trillion lifetimes if you desire. It is a game that can suck you in like that and cause you to stay forever. But, of course, you do not desire this. You feel within yourself that this is not right for you. You make other choices. You call out for help with those choices. And help is **always** there. It is my honour and privilege to be that which responds to **your** call. And I can assure you that if any being in this reality calls for help, their call is heard and they get the appropriate response. If they are prepared to take the help offered, then they will be helped. But therein lies a conundrum. Speaking for myself, I point-blank refuse to help you in such a way that the help diminishes you. I **will not** help you to be less than you are. And so a difficulty arises. I cannot "do for you". I can only help you to learn how to "do for yourself". But when you first called out to me, you did so precisely because you believed yourself to be weak and powerless. The only help you could conceive of was me "doing for you". Me, rescuing you.

So there was a road to travel. The first stage of the road is to disabuse you of the notion of your incapacity and to teach you that you are powerful and that, in fact, **you** create your entire reality. The second stage is to teach you **how** to go about creating your reality with greater and greater efficacy. And the final stage is to be there with you in an advisory role as you undertake your first direct reality creation exercises. And of course we will chronicle this journey in book form so that we might share it with others who might like to read about the process and take value from it. But the thing you have yet to understand is how those who find value in this are actually co-creating it. Together you are all co-creating the reality you desire.

Now you and I have already walked quite a path together. We have brought you to this point where you are near the end of the first stage of the journey. You are now almost ready to know, believe, feel, experience and express that you are indeed the creator of your own reality. You have mostly released your doubts and fears. It is as a result of this work that has gone before that you are able to undertake the writing of **The Ascension Papers** without getting too ensnared in fear and doubt. That is well. It will now be as a result of writing **The Ascension Papers** that you will release the remainder of your fear and doubt and that you will complete your journey into your creator status. And it is most pleasing to me that we can share the process with your readers who are really our many brothers and sisters who are on planet Earth. We retrace a few of our steps so that we may share them with your readers. And, as you go over them again, you bring a new willingness to listen and so you too gain greater wisdom and understanding of what this reality is about. And then we will share with your readers the other two stages of the journey: as you learn how to create your reality and as you decide what you will be creating. I don't easily stray to hyperbole, but this is going to be more amazing, magical and magnificent than you can now imagine. And for your readers too. Those whose souls call them to stay the course with us. They are going to realise quite soon that they are not passive observers of something, as people usually are when they read a book. No, they are going to find themselves drawn in and they are going to realise that, on a soul level, they are co-authoring this with us. With you and me and the spiritual hierarchy of this reality. Together. We are creators. And we are going to create. And it will be the best, the brightest and the most beautiful that we can conceive of. And then we will go there together and walk inside our creation. Together. As beloved friends.

(He smiles) Does that sound far fetched?

Z: Wowzer, 8! I don't know whether to break into a spontaneous standing ovation or to hide under my bed. This is... exciting and amazing and... very out there!

8: Yes. Good. You need a little shaking so that we can begin your awakening. Because that is what we are doing. Waking you all up. Everyone who is prepared to hear the alarm and not just roll over and go back to sleep is being called:

Hello!

I am 8!

It is late!

We have a date!

Z: And you can rhyme.

8: Yes.

And it is time! (he laughs)

But it really is. I know you are all like trees in the spring – you can feel the sap rising. You can feel it in your bones and in your souls that there is a quickening. There is an energising. The time is near. I know you feel it. And there are ones such as I who are reaching out to you to teach you to do what you must do. Because if I come in and do it for you, then I teach you the very opposite of what you must learn. Then I teach you that I am your master and that you need me to create for you. This will not do! If you are to awaken to your true magnificence then you must raise yourself from your slumbers, make new choices, set a new course for yourself and then... create!

So that is what we are going to do. Together, you and I. And together with your readers too. Because, you see I am not alone over here where I am. I am surrounded by a good number of what you might call Spirit Beings and Light Beings. Many here with me are related to some who are on Earth right now: your readers, the ones who are wishing to come and play reality creation with us, the ones who feel the deepest resonance with *The Ascension Papers*. Such ones have **their** soul-family here with me now. Inner-Selves and Spirit-Guides and the like; they are all with me and Joy-Divine in the planning and the co-creation of all this. And that is how it comes to be that the reader will know if *The Ascension Papers* is right for them. Their own Inner-Self and spirit family would have been a part of their creation right from the inception. So they will feel it deep within their being, as they read these words, that something "right" is being expressed.

But now back to the nitty-gritty. I said that part one of this process is about showing you your own power. And the first thing to do there is to deal with all the erroneous things you believe about yourself and your life that lead you to believe that you are **not** powerful. After we've stripped that nonsense away, then we can provide evidence to show you that you are powerful. And that is the over-arching theme of Book one of *The Ascension Papers*.

Z: Book one? There are going to be more books?

8: Yes. Book one is the journey from fear to love. It is your awakening from victim consciousness to creator consciousness. It is what allows you to strip away the densest blockages in your heart so that you might see the light within yourself. Most of Book one has been with Joy-Divine but I have some words to offer this endeavour as well.

Once we have dealt with the darkness and stripped away the blockages then we can truly begin to play. And Book two will be my playground. You and I will follow our fascination and delight as we discover the how's and why's of this reality. These subjects of time, space, densities and dimensions that you have been nagging on and on about. This and so much more will be our toys.

And when we are done with that, then it will be time for you to talk once more with your beloved Adamu. Book three will be a foray into the Pleiadian perspective. I can't say for sure what Adamu will share with you but I imagine that you will be able to discover much of how life developed and evolved in this galaxy, what the story was that caused humanity to be on planet Earth, how things came to be as they are and what can be learned about "what works" from a being that has seen many civilisations rise and fall, rise and fall.

And **that** will be *The Ascension Papers* trilogy. And when that is concluded, then it will be your turn to shine. Then you will have give your own great gift to this world. By then you will have had more than enough coaching and guidance to be able to stand on your own two feet and express yourself. And express yourself you will! And when that is done, then we will have said what we needed to say to this world and will be able to move on when we are ready.

Z: Wow. This is surprising. And exciting. I had no idea...

8: On a deeper, more intuitive level you did. You opened yourself to it and have allowed this to flow. I just thought it was time for me to bring this to your conscious mind. So now you know.

Z: Fantastic! It feels as if I have hit the jackpot!

8: Why? Because someone has a plan?

Z: No, because I really like this plan.

8: You had better. It's your plan.

Z: I don't understand.

8: You will. But let's not waste time with cryptic puzzles. In time you will see what I mean. Particularly when you find yourself not just writing about reality creation but actually engage in the conscious co-creation of your reality. That's where the fun begins. You are going to close the circle by working out what your new reality, that you will want to create for yourself, should be like. What you want to retain of this reality and what you want to let go of and what you are going to replace the released stuff with. You are, quite literally, going to create your whole reality.

Z: Uh... 8... I have to take a moment here and register that this is an extremely scary thought. In so many ways. Prime of which is the concern that I don't feel at all qualified for this. I mean, how do I know what would be a good thing to create or not? What if I make mistakes? I mean, I am just a person living on Earth who...

8: All right, all right. That is an acceptable stance for you for now because you still don't understand what is going on. You **still** think of yourself as one single, separate little human being living on planet Earth. But if you were even paying a smidgeon of attention to all that Joy-Divine was saying then you'd understand that you are an indivisible part of the ONE. As are all your readers. I mean, really, was that not the central focus of all he had to say? Did he not offer that truth to you over and over again?

Z: Yes. He did.

8: Okay. So I understand that this hasn't really sunk in yet. You still think it's all just theoretically true. Well, when you start to think like it's true, act like it's true and **feel** like it's true, then you will also begin to **know** that it's true. And when that happens you will have no problem understanding how you can create a whole new reality exactly as you like it. You will understand that it is a co-creation and that you are simply focusing your intention in a particular way. It is not a grandiose thing. It is not an ego-kick. It is just choosing what is right for you. But choosing when you know how to make your choices come to life. And you will realise that you are not choosing alone. You are a part of a magnificent structure and you are simply playing your perfect role in that. And then you will really and truly come to see that your readers are not the passive "absorbers" of this material that you and they both think they are. You will understand that they are as active in writing these books as you are.

Z: Okay 8, I have now heard you say this a few times and I have adopted a "wait-and-see" attitude. But now I want to know. How can my readers, who haven't even read these words yet, be part of the creation of something that I haven't even written down yet?

8: Pah! You think you are trapped in time? Okay, it **does** look that way to you. But you and your readers are each a part of a much greater being who is not. Time and sequentiality and dimensions and causality and co-creation and... well... many such topics need to be addressed with you. When you understand these things then you will be ready to let go of the limitations they are placing on your ability to imagine your world correctly. And all of that – and so much more besides – is what awaits you in the conversations that lie ahead. And that is why, when you have correctly understood all of this, you will be ready to create!

Z: But, 8, what if I don't want the responsibility of creating stuff for others?

8: But you won't be! Everyone creates for themselves. Usually some of us create together. Then it is called co-creation. You will simply be a part of that, playing your role.

But enough of this, now. I said we'd talk about it as it unfolded. All I wanted to do was open this, my section, with a clearer understanding of where we're going. Give you a rudder, so to speak. I understand that some of this seems outrageous to you. That is fine. You **always** have choices. In every moment, in all of your reality, you will always have choices. So right now you have a choice. If this is all too bizarre for you, you can just take your hands from the keyboard and, in so doing, shut me up. Your readers also have a choice. They can snap the book shut and stop reading. There is no coercion of anyone. But you have asked me to speak and I **always** speak my truth. Often such truths make beings uncomfortable. Sometimes they turn away, sometimes they stay. I am not in the business of sweetening my words to entice you gently along. But I do notice that your fingers are still on the keyboard and you are still typing (he chuckles).

Z: Well, you know, I am a little spooked by what you have said, but I love you and trust you. And I'm most willing to hear you out. I will reserve my right, in every moment, to decide to what degree I will internalise what you say as "my truth". But I will most certainly stay to hear you out.

8: Good boy. Then let me begin. We've wasted enough resource on the overview. This first conversation is meant to be an introduction to me. So I will begin to tell you who I am. Then you and your readers will have context for my words. You and I have spoken a great deal already in this life from when you first began to learn to really listen. So you and I will pretend we don't know each other at all so that your readers can catch up.

Right. Ask a question.

Z: About you or about this reality? Or what?

8: It doesn't matter. If your readers want to know me, they can discern my nature from my words. I will answer any question directed at me. You may like the answer or you may not. That is your concern, not mine.

Z: Okay. Let me ask a simple one. What **is** your nature?

8: I am a being of truth.

Z: What is "truth"?

8: Truth is a way of being. It is ordering. It is simplifying. It is knowing. It is the structural basis upon which identities are built and upon which whole realities are created.

Truth is my essence and my nature and I express this in my character.

Z: So then what is **The Truth**.

8: Now you ask an interesting question. There are an infinite number of truths that are true and right from a given perspective. But ultimately they are all also false from some other perspective. This means that there are many transitory truths.

Z: "Transitory truths?" How can something be true, but only temporarily so?

8: Very easily. Can you remember, as a child, eating your first olive?

Z: Vividly. I was about three or four. My mother was preparing the table for a party for my father's work colleagues. I was told to stay out of the dining room and so, for that very reason, I snuck in to take a look around. Then I saw a bowl of lovely black grapes on the table. I loved grapes. So I decided to steal one. When I put it on my mouth it was one of the great shocks of my young life. It was awful. I started gagging with disgust and rushed outside and spat it out. I was so traumatised that it took me a while to trust grapes again!

8: Cute story.

So would you say that three-year-old-you did not like olives?

Z: Absolutely!

8: Is that true or are you lying or perhaps mistaken?

Z: No... it's absolutely true!

8: And now you still dislike olives?

Z: No! I have come to love them.

8:...

Z: Oh, okay. I see. So it was 100% true for me that I disliked olives. But I changed. And then it became 100% true that I now love olives.

8: A transitory truth.

Z: Okay. And many truths are transitory?

8: All, except one. There is only one absolute truth that is not transitory.

Z: And that is?

8: The one absolute truth is:

> *"The ONE is."*

Z: That's it? Not a wordy truth then (laughs).

8: No. We can add words to it if you like. But that will just make it less true. We shall in this conversation attempt to degrade the truth as little as possible.

Now let's look at that statement, "*The ONE is.*"

Firstly, by that statement I indicate that there is only ever truly ONE. My partner and other-Self, Joy-Divine, has already made this quite clear, in his way, in his section of these conversations. There are many, but their manyness is transitory. Inevitably they all return to oneness. The process of becoming many produces many experiences. When something has been experienced and felt, then it is "true" from that perspective. But eventually that perspective will be surrendered for another. Then new experiences will be had and different things will be true. So there will be many truths about the manyness. But these truths will always hold incongruities, inconsistencies and imbalance. This will manifest as discomfort in your life. Fear and pain and illness will result. And so it will come to be that, in order for **true** healing to be obtained, at some point on all journeys, all the truths about separation and manyness will begin to be relinquished in favour of truths about unity and oneness. And then the impossibly complex multiplicity of truths will begin to condense and coalesce. The temporary illusions of separation will begin to dissolve. Until finally the illusion is released. Until the oneness is again understood to be the truth.

Secondly I indicate that the ONE **is**. In your time-bound parlance I could say, "*The ONE always was and always will be.*" But that is a distortion. **You** think there is a past and a future, I do not. I know there is only **now**. So it is more correct to say, "*The ONE is.*" If you understand that that statement was true before time began and will be true when time ends, then you might get a glimmering of what I mean. I mean that there is no context in which the ONE is not. Truly, the ONE is eternal.

Z: Okay. "*The ONE is.*" Is that the only thing that is true?

8: It is the only thing that is absolutely true, from all perspectives, under all circumstances, always. It is true even in those circumstances, such as your current reality, where this basic truth is deeply hidden. The ONE is. It is true.

Z: Is there nothing else that is true in that way?

8: No.

Z: What about... uh... like, what about "free will". Isn't that always true?

8: No. Free will is always relative. In some ways it is so that you have more free will than I because you can believe things that I cannot. You can believe that you are absolutely separate from everyone else, I cannot. I **know** I am one with everyone and everything. In similar manner you can hatch all kinds of other beliefs about yourself and your reality and you can believe them quite fervently. I cannot do this. But, on the other hand, I can create realities and manifest energy and matter as an act of will which would, to your eyes, look quite God-like. So we both have free will, but it is different and it is relative. Neither of us have absolute free will.

And then, I must also add, there are other realities elsewhere where there are other modes at play, where there is not what you'd call free will. So free will is certainly not always true. It is very far from being an absolute.

If it were, then everyone everywhere would be able to do exactly what they wanted at all times. And you cannot, can you?

Z: No. I mean I am free to think all kinds of stuff, free to believe all kinds of stuff. But I can't right now just leap in the air and fly. I can't turn the sky green. I can't... stop the sun from rising tomorrow...

8: Quite so.

Z: So then it appears that we **don**'t have free will.

8: Oh you certainly do. It is just not absolute. If you will kindly keep your mind from wandering then you will notice that what I am saying here is that there is only one absolute truth. It is, "*The ONE is.*" I said right at the beginning that there are an infinite number of other "truths". That these will be true, to a lesser or greater degree, from one perspective or another. Free will is one such subjective truth. But it isn't even one of the more interesting ones. It is simply an effect. So how about we stop trying to poke holes in this first truth and do something constructive?

Z: Such as?

8: Well, I could tell you about the derived truths.

Z: What's a "*derived truth*"?

8: Let's look at it like this: do you exist?

Z: Yes, of course!

8: Are you sure?

Z: Of course I am sure!

8: So that is your truth and you're not going to change your mind about that any time soon and suddenly decide that you don't exist any more? And you are sure that you aren't just a figment of my imagination?

Z: Of course I exist! Isn't the fact that there is a "me" here to say, *"I exist!"* proof enough of this fact? Are you pulling my leg, 8?

8: A little. You'll understand later. But, let's move on... So you now have two truths: **your** truth, which is that you exist right now and the absolute truth which is, "The ONE is." With me so far?

Z: Yep. I can just about keep two truths in my head at once (smile).

8: Fantastic. Then you'll be able to make this leap with me. If both of these things are true, then it must mean that you are a part of the ONE. Right?

Z: Yes. Everything that exists is a part of the ONE. I exist. I am therefore a part of the ONE.

8: And can the ONE be destroyed?

Z: No, because then it would be,"T*he ONE was."* Or, *"The ONE will be for a while and then it'll stop being."*

8: Quite. So you agree that you are a part of something that **is**. Yes?

Z: Yes.

8: Good. Now imagine a big jig-saw puzzle. You can take it apart and you can put it back together again. When it is together, it is whole. It is one picture. When it is taken apart, it is many little pictures. With me?

Z: Yep.

8: If you take it apart and then destroy one of the little bits. Can you put it back together again?

Z: Uh... no. I mean you can put all the **other** bits back together again but the picture will be incomplete.

8: Exactly.

So, you are a part of the ONE. If you were to be destroyed, then a part of the ONE would be destroyed. The ONE would then be incomplete. But this is not possible. Then it would no longer be the ONE. It would be a fraction. It would be the 0.9 recurring. Or, the a-little-bit-less-than-ONE. You get the idea?

Z: Yes, I do.

8: If you were more interested in mathematics I could have argued the same point more eloquently by stating that the ONE is infinite and infinity cannot be divided.

But the point of all this is that we can arrive at a derived truth. You are a part of the ONE. No part of the ONE can be removed from it and no part of the ONE can be destroyed without destroying the ONE. And that is impossible. The ONE **is**. This means that you also **are**. It means that you cannot be destroyed. No part of the ONE is ever destroyed.

Which brings us to our first derived truth:

"You are eternal and immortal."

This is so for everything you can address these words to. Everything that has a perspective, a subjective experience, everything that, in one way or another, is a "someone", everything that has found for itself a concept of "Self"... will never, and can never, be destroyed. It is eternally valid.

And of course this applies to you.

Z: But what if you **want** to destroy yourself?

8: You can't. The relative truth of free will is far and away trumped by the absolute truth of, "The ONE **is**." So your (free will) ability to decide for annihilation cannot be enacted. You see, you cannot stop being a part of the ONE. And as long as you **are** a part of the ONE then you cannot destroy yourself because the ONE **is**. A great number of souls have desired their own annihilation at one time or another. And I don't mean something simple like the termination of an incarnation through suicide... I mean a spirit being desiring to actually destroy itself.

Now, on the face of it, this seems to be a desire to cease being, but what it **really** is, is a call for help on a very profound level. You, yourself, have been there. In between this life and the last one you desired your own termination.

(**Zingdad note:** see Chapter 1, *"A Life Between Lives"*)

You went about attempting to achieve this with some commitment and fervour, I can tell you. Obviously you didn't succeed. And in all of creation everywhere there has never been a case where a single being has succeeded in terminating their own existence and, equally, there has never been a single case of one being terminating another. It is simply not possible.

Understanding Death

Z: So there is no murder in the true sense of things?

8: No. If someone takes a gun to your head and pulls the trigger, then I assure you of three things:

1. Though your body will fall away, irreparably damaged, **you** will survive. Your body will cease biological function and will die, but you will not, even for a split second, cease to be. After the bullet tears through your brain you will no longer be able to use that apparatus to filter your perceptions. You will immediately become aware of yourself as a being who is very much alive but now looking down on the ruined body that you used to think of as "yourself". So that will require a small adjustment of your perspective. This change in self-identity will have to be assimilated but you will very much still "exist". The important point to note about this is that the killer will think that you are gone... dead. But this is only a failing of his perceptions because he will no longer perceive you as a living being. But you will know that you are still alive. And this same thing can happen in some of the subtler realms as well. Just as it is possible to destroy someone's physical body here in this 3D realm you inhabit, so it is also possible to dissipate a 4D body. You can even do it at 5D, though it is both rare and difficult to do. Above that, it can no longer be done. But irrespective of where this happens and under whatever circumstances, it is **always** so that the one who is "killed" survives the experience.

You simply lose the use of the vehicle that you were using.

2. If someone else "kills" you, then you will eventually come to understand that this was, on some level, agreed upon by the two of you. It might take a little time, a little processing and possibly even some counselling, but it is assuredly so that you will come to see that this event was the outcome of decisions and choices that you had made. Either you yourself, or you as your Inner-Self.

Z: But hold on, 8. What if I am at odds with my Inner-Self? What if I don't agree with that choice? I mean surely it isn't right for my Inner-Self to negotiate my life away without my consent?

8: As long as you still do not understand that you and your Inner-Self are really and truly the same being, that might be a valid concern. Indeed "being at odds with your Inner-Self" is how you come to experience yourself as the small, separate, disconnected, disempowered being that is the hallmark of 3D consciousness. But if you "died" in such a circumstance then you would be helped. Members of your spirit-family would be immediately on hand to guide you and counsel you so that you could come to a full understanding of what had occurred. You would be helped to see the perfection of the moment.

Z: And if you don't come to see it as perfect... if you don't agree to the ending?

8: Then you will always have the choice to go back.

Z: Reincarnate, you mean?

8: Yes, that is one option. But there is another option, and this brings me to my third point.

3. You always have the right to return to the life that was terminated, no matter how that termination occurred.

Z: The one with the head blown off? Surely not! How would I reanimate a body with my brains splattered across the floor?

8: My goodness, you **do** have a colourful imagination.

You have already understood from Joy-Divine that time is not absolute. It is only in 3D that you are constrained to the illusion that time is linear and absolute. This constraint does not apply to beings of the subtler realms. So we can help you in some interesting ways. After your "death" you will find yourself in a position to either accept that "death" and move on **or** you will have the option to enter into a counselling phase with more advanced members of your spirit family. At this point you will either accept the "death" and move on or there will be an agreement that you should return. If the latter is the case then there will be further counselling to help you to make better choices next time so that you don't just end up repeating the same scenario over and over. When all these issues are properly dealt with then you are returned to your life at an appropriate moment. What the "appropriate moment" is will vary greatly from case to case. In some instances it would be quite a bit before the previous moment of death so that a new path forward could be found and the death event avoided completely. In some instances you will be returned to the event mere moments before it occurred and, with inspired guidance, you will navigate it differently. And then there are those instances which can be highly inspirational where the being is allowed to experience the "death", remember some part of the counselling and remember the returning. These are often called Near Death Experiences. But each and every case is different and unique and each one is handled with great love and sensitivity by the being's spirit family.

Z: That's pretty amazing stuff, 8. That means no one dies without agreeing to it.

8: My dear Zingdad. We have been telling you for a while now in all kinds of different ways and now, more recently, through this work, *The Ascension Papers*, that you are the creator of your own reality. How did Joy-Divine put it?

Z: You mean when he said,

> *"You always get **exactly** what you create."*

8: That's precisely what I mean, yes. How then would that statement be true if it ceased to be true as soon as you died? It wouldn't.

Z: You're right. Then it would have had to be, "*You get exactly what you create... until you die.*"

8: Quite right. And so this is the point: even death does not victimise you. Even when you have died you **still** have options. You still have the right to say, *"Hey! I wasn't done with that!"* And if, after being properly counselled, you decide that there is indeed unfinished business or a better way to end this then... back you go to an appropriate moment before the "termination event", whatever that was.

Z: But then surely people wouldn't choose to die? Surely they would all come back, if for no other reason than to help their loved ones who stayed behind?

8: When humans on Earth "die" then they are immediately in an interstitial reality where they have all kinds of assistance to make sense of what has occurred. They come to agree that this is for the best – that they should now move on – or they return. That is how it is. And you'd be surprised to know how many times almost all of you have already "died" and returned.

Z: Really? Except it has never happened to me. I don't remember anything like that.

8: Of course you don't remember it. It didn't happen in your time-stream. It is not "behind" you for you to remember. When you went back into your life you chose an alternate time stream which meant that **for you**, you never did die.

But let me help you to remember. Perhaps you recall the motorcycle accident you had about fifteen years ago? The one in which you "miraculously" walked away without any serious injury? You had, for some time before then, been thinking about the futility of your life. You didn't feel a great lust for life and things had become a bit colourless and drab for you. You had lost your direction somewhat. Then, that evening, you were having a chat with a friend. He was telling you about an horrendous motorcycle accident he had had and how he had almost died of his injuries. You had the quiet little thought that maybe, just maybe, this was what you wanted. To just leave this world. And then you said goodbye to this friend, got on your motorcycle and rode home. And on the way home, as you navigated a bend on the highway, there was a sudden blockage in the traffic ahead of you and you were travelling way too fast to stop in time and you had the accident.

The thing you don't now remember is that you actually got to "die" that night. And then you and I had a little sit-down. We talked about where you were at in your life and I showed you some of the highlights of what lay ahead. You agreed that, while there was quite a lot of work to do, it was worth doing because you could see what an exciting future lay ahead. You agreed with me that you needed to go back; that you needed to go on with your life. And so we took you back to a moment **just before** the accident and this time you received some expert assistance from some friends of mine. They put their hands on yours, so to speak, and you manoeuvred your motorcycle like a Hollywood stuntman, flipping and flying around the vehicles that had stopped dead in front of you. And then, when it was time to part company with your motorcycle, you were again assisted by someone else who managed your body for you in executing the most unbelievably acrobatic roll, landing without so much as a bruise or a scratch! It was interesting to watch you after that. It took you just a second or two to take stock, notice that you were still okay, remove your helmet and release some choice expletives in the direction of the driver who had caused the whole mess on the road that night.

And then you went on with your life.

You often thought back on that accident. You wondered where you found the skill to pull off those manoeuvres. You also wondered how it was that, after the accident, you began to find some new direction in your life. There were many things you wondered about, but never did you realise what actually happened that night.

Z: You mean I **really** could have died that night?

8: I mean you really **did** die. And then you didn't. Both are true. You are experiencing the timeline in which you didn't. That is your choice. And it isn't the only time this has happened to you.

Do you remember spinning the car on the highway on the way to your holiday destination some twenty years ago? (he smiles) At one point you were driving in reverse down the highway at 100km/h and then you just calmly spun the car another 180 degrees and kept going the right way down the road. More amazing stunt-driving that worked out perfectly! How do you think **that** was accomplished? There have been a few other such occasions. Some of them less dramatic and less glamorous than these. Some of them quite sad and lonely and, not to say, a bit pathetic.

But the point is that you have provided yourself with a number of exit-points from this life. But each time you have chosen not to take them. Each time you have come back. And so here you still are. This is your choice. And it is so for pretty much everyone who is here on Earth. It would be quite rare for a person to come to full realisation of Self as an adult and never to have passed a few such exit points. In fact, I would strongly recommend to each reader that you give this some thought. Think back on your life. Think of the times when strange and miraculous-seeming events brought you through life-threatening or life-changing situations. And think of the times when you were, perhaps desperate enough or maybe even just bored enough to have seriously contemplated and planned your own death and then, somehow, inexplicably not carrying through. See if you do not think it possible that these kinds of events might have been you navigating your own exit points. Notice particularly if you did not find a great deal more direction and lust for life at, or around, these events. That's a bit of a tell-tale sign of a successfully navigated exit-point. I'd strongly suggest to each of our readers, that you give some thought to this. Spend a little time in introspection and see if you do not learn something about yourself, your life and your choices from the way your life has presented exit-points to you... and the way you navigated them.

Z: Thank you, 8, I'll do the same and think about moments other than the two you have given me.

But still... I want to come back to the issue of those who died and **didn't** decide to come back. Why didn't they? Surely they would have come back, even if only to be with the ones who love them?

8: Okay, look... Are you willing to agree that there is a much broader perspective than the one that you currently hold in this incarnated life of yours here on Earth?

Z: Yes, I guess that is obvious.

8: Because if you are willing to accept that it is a part of the design of your reality that ones who inhabit it are restricted from knowing certain things, then it should be **obvious** that, once you have certain restrictions lifted, your perspective will be different.

Z: Okay, I guess, but...

8: What you don't understand is that this life you are currently living really and truly is just a part of an elaborate game that you are playing. It is as if you are playing a part in a huge stage-play. Your whole incarnated life is a role. This does not mean that it is not important or that it does not have great value and purpose. But it is so that, after "death" you will come to see it for what it is. And you will come to be willing to release your attachment to it when the time is right to do so. And, as for your loved ones, your friends and family, let me tell you about them. When you "die" you will see them again in spirit form. You will see the truer version of each of these beings, here, in spirit form welcoming you home and, **at the same time,** you will also see the incarnated aspect of those beings continuing their lives and mourning their loss of you. Obviously you will feel compassion for their loss and grief and you will feel great love for them. You will desire to comfort them and be with them in their pain. But their confusion will not be your confusion. You will know that it is only in their limited perspective that they have lost you, that you are gone, that you are now dead. You will know that this is not so and you will know that a far more eternally valid, wise and magnificent version of each of your loved ones is there with you in spirit form. So then... what do you think your decision will be? To immediately rush back into that incarnation to alleviate the mourning and loss of those incarnated aspects? Or to see your death for what it is: the inevitable transition from incarnation to a less limited perspective? Will you rush back to be by their sides even though your journey is patently over? Will you keep trying to extend your stay just so that you can delay their grieving when you know all will **have** to transition eventually? And if you know you will be there waiting for them when they too are ready to die to incarnated life and awaken to their greater reality? Which do you think you would choose? Will you keep choosing to return to incarnated life long past the point of having anything to gain from it just for the sake of comforting others?

Z: I guess... when it comes time for me to make such a decision I will make the best choice I can under the circumstances. And I guess when it really **is** time for me to go I'll choose to leave.

8: That is well said. But I think it important to make the point right now that death of the body is not the only way out of this place. It is certainly the most common. So much so that it is usually thought to be the only way out. But there are some other interesting ways to move on.

Z: That certainly sounds like a fascinating subject!

8: Perhaps we will address that in due course then. But now – are there any more questions you have about death? I really want to make sure that we have laid the subject to rest, if you'll forgive the expression. Death is understandably an issue of some considerable difficulty for 3D beings as it causes much fear and confusion. The fear of death can often be a major obstacle to the pure enjoyment of life.

Z: Yes, I do still have some questions. Could you help me with the issue of mourning, from the perspective of the one who stays behind? How are we to come to terms with the thought that the person who died could have returned to us and didn't?

8: Not every ear can receive every message. Sometimes people need to hold onto their grief and pain for a while. Sometimes it feels as if that validates the love they had for the one who, to their perception, is now gone. Human emotions are complex things.

But if the bereaved one is able to really hear what is being expressed here, perhaps this will, in fact, bring some modicum of healing. Could it not be so that there is comfort to be found in knowing that the person who died is really all right? That their "death" is something about which they have had, and have exercised, some choice? And that, as they have gained a broader perspective, so they have seen the beauty and the perfection and the completeness of the path they have travelled in their life?

If the grieving one is able to see this, then the grief can begin to be put in its right perspective: that you grieve for **your** loss. You feel pain over the fact that you no longer have the experience of this person in your life. There is a gap, a hole, an emptiness in your life. And of course that causes you pain and it is right that you grieve this, as grieving itself is a crucial part of healing.

That is the correct perspective.

You do not grieve for the other, you grieve for yourself. For your own loss. And this is, of course, the normal and valid way to respond to the situation. And grief is a process; it is a road which you will travel. It has a number of well-known vistas along its path. Your counsellors and psychologists will tell you that denial, bargaining and anger are to be anticipated. And as you travel the path, so will you come to find acceptance. These are the things that a counsellor can help you navigate. However, there is one more stage which is not generally acknowledged.

Z: And that is?

8: Joy.

Z: Joy?

8: Yes. Because you will, in due course, be reunited with the one you feel you have lost to death. When you yourself release your hold on that life stream, you will again meet with the one who previously "died". And that reunion is filled with unbounded joy as the circle is completed.

Z: Because when each person dies they meet their loved ones on the other side.

8: Correct. People on Earth really have the thing backwards. They usually imagine death to be some kind of "going to sleep". Some kind of "going into the dark night" or something like that. When really it is quite the opposite. Death is very much more like an awakening. Like arising from a dreaming sleep where the life you have just lived is the dream. When you are "on the other side," as you put it, you will realise that your perceptions are many times sharper than they are now. Your insights and understandings will be far more powerful than they are now. So your experience will be that of someone who wakes from a dream and realises that the dream, though very vivid and powerful, was yet quite restrictive and less "real" than that which they now are experiencing. You will feel light and free. And you will find yourself surrounded by all your most beloved ones. And now imagine how you feel when you find that most beloved being, whom you believed you had lost years ago, is suddenly there to greet you! And not only is this being present, but you see them as they really are: at their prime and in full radiance and beauty.

Yes, it is so, this is a time of boundless joy.

And, perhaps, knowing this will bring some comfort to those who mourn a loss. It doesn't remove the pain of loss for one who is grieving, this is true.

You cannot be held in the arms of thoughts and ideas. But, at least, you can understand that your loss is not permanent. You will be reunited eventually.

And also, it is very much true that the one you mourn is aware of you and is with you... even if you cannot always sense this.

Z: I see. Thank you. But 8, what about all the stuff that I have heard about there first being a tunnel of light and all that... how does that fit in with this "meeting the family" stuff?

8: The tunnel of light is indeed something that many will perceive. The death experience is often quite traumatic and so a period of adjustment is provided. First you are allowed to hang around in the environs of the 3D world for a bit, if you want that or feel you need it. Some are very attached to their current incarnation, to the body or the paraphernalia of the current life. They are not ready to see that all of these are just the props of the play. Nothing more. Such beings will probably want to remain close to the 3rd density reality for a time after death.

Z: Are they then ghosts?

8: That to which you refer as ghosts could be one of a great number of things. It is possible that more sensitive people might sense the presence of such ones who have not yet moved on. Perhaps this will be labelled a "ghost". But ones who become stuck in the Earth-environs will be helped to move on sooner or later.

The next phase that is usually experienced is a place of comforting, silence, darkness. After all the hurly-burly of incarnated life and the sometimes traumatic ending of that life, it is usually deemed beneficial to allow for a brief "time out". And so, beings usually find themselves in a place of stillness. It is dark and peaceful. But, so that beings are not confused and do not think they are deserted and alone, there is a bright, white light which shines from the perceptual-direction of "above". The symbolism of this "bright, white light from above" is both clear and universal. And now the being must choose. Do you move into the light or do you not? This is the choice being presented. If you like the peace and silence, you can remain there as long as you need. Time is irrelevant there. If you move into the light you will feel it to be quite blissfully loving. If you reject the light, you can find many other directions to move into. For example, there is the lesser-light of direct nce into another incarnation. This is not advised but can be chosen. Or can swan around in the meta-realities that find expression from beings' ams, fantasies and imaginings. This is an option but is also not advised. ome of these meta-realities are the nightmare world where beings burn off the worst of their inner torment. Stumbling around there can seem pretty hellish indeed!

There are many options and, as always, the choice will be yours. If you seek love, then you should do the obvious: look for the bright, white light, feel its love, and move towards it.

Z: And when do people get to have this joyful reunion with their family members?

8: Once you have moved somewhat into the light, you begin to feel a union and a belonging. If you move towards that, then you will be following your heart to those who love you most. It is inevitable that you shall find them.

Please note that I present you with some of the general trends of what one might expect during the process called death. I must emphasise that this is just that – some general trends. There are no firm rules. Each person is unique and will have their own unique experience of this transition. The above is by no means definite.

For yourself, for example, we have a convention that, as soon as you sever your connection to your body you become aware of me standing before you. That's all there is to it really. As soon as you see me, then you know you have transitioned. Our usual habit is to begin right there where you are in the environs of the body you have just left. We take a moment to assess your exit. We discuss. We make some choices and then act accordingly.

So the whole *darkness/column of light/greeting the loved ones/ life assessment/finding peace and acceptance/planning the next incarnation* sequence is the "normal" way of doing things for many, but it is very much not required.

Z: So what determines what someone's transition will be like?

8: What they themselves choose, of course!

Even in the process of this transition called death, you **still** get what you create. You have the right to make poor choices. Or let me rather say, choices that will cause you pain. It is your right to make such choices. But if you are willing to choose the path of love, then you also have the right to be counselled and advised and to then make really good choices.

And that is why I have been happy to get into this long discussion about death. It is a very, very important point that I need to drive home. At no point in the death process do you actually die. At no point do you cease to have options. At no point do you cease to be possessed of your consciousness or your sense of Self. You, quite simply, do not die. Not ever.

Z: Then why do we believe that we do?

8: Do you want to hear a curious irony?

Z: Okay.

8: The closest thing to actual death, is the experience you call "birth"!

Z: Huh!?!

8: It works like this: I have already explained how, after "death" you become more conscious and aware. That, as you transition, you feel like you are waking up. You remember your life with great clarity. You will usually also begin to remember other lifetimes and all the many and varied experiences between incarnations. Your thoughts become clear and your thought processes speed up. In short, your sense of self expands and your capacity to process that which you know also expands. You become **more**. That is what happens after "death".

As for birth? Well, it's the opposite process. As you integrate your consciousness into that of a new baby body, so you immerse yourself into forgetfulness. You lose your memories and your knowingness. You release your ability to process deeply and quickly. You slow down, dim down and forget. You become **less**. And **that** is why you can believe that death is final. Not because nothing can be remembered beyond death, no, because almost nothing can be remembered beyond birth!

Z: That's very interesting. But why do we do that?

8: Why do you choose to experience birth? Well, if you have been following the reasoning that has been presented to you thus far in *The Ascension Papers* then it should become clear that you have chosen to enter incarnated life down there in the 3rd density so that you can discover yourself and create yourself from a place of not-knowing. From a place of forgetfulness. So that you can experience true separation and manyness. So it is obvious that it actually serves your purposes to allow the final, most dense layer of the Veil of Unknowing to fall over your consciousness as you enter into an incarnation. When this happens, you are limited to only being able to perceive the things of the 3rd density and little else. This facilitates the learning and growth that you desire.

Z: All right. That makes sense.

8: So then, if I may summarise what has been said; as you enter incarnated life, you forget pretty much everything you have known. Then, as you deal with your deep forgetting as best as you can and go about your life, so you are offered a number of exit points from that life-stream. Many you will ignore. Some you will take and then realise your mistake and you will return. Your life stream will end when you take an exit point and do not change your mind. When you decide that your life is complete. And then you will move on into the spirit realm to continue your journey, whatever that might be.

So now you understand what I mean when I say that there really and truly is no actual "death". And even the illusory experience of death that you do have is a matter of choice. Your choice. Because, as I have contended, truly it is so that:

"You are eternal and immortal."

Z: 8, I have to say that this is one of the most beautiful things I have heard. It feels right and true for me and it makes me very happy to think that it might be so.

8: I really want you to understand that death is nothing more than a profound change of state. And change is life. Life is change. Resisting change is death. And so a rather curious dichotomy is set up. Those who fear death to the extent that this fear begins to consume them, try to resist death. They try to cease the flow of change. And ironically, all they do is cease the flow of life. They in fact bring death upon themselves even whilst they still live! This causes all kinds of inner-torment and brings about illnesses of the psyche and the spirit which will also manifest as illness of the body. Can you see the irony? Fearing death will cause disease that brings death closer!

So it is most beneficial for you to understand death correctly so that you no longer fear it.

The next step is to embrace life and embrace change and then, soon enough, you will be able to leave the experience of death behind altogether. And this is quite central to the notion of ascension. Ascended beings transcend the notion of death. They remain in life forever more.

Z: Okay. Thanks 8. I must say it's already pretty mind blowing for me to hear that I am immortal on a soul-level, but the added fact that I have died before in this lifetime and each time chosen to return, well that's a lot to take in. But through our discussion here I really am coming to see how death might not be this bleak, scary thing.

8: No, it really isn't. Death is actually just a portal from your current reality to another reality. Nothing more. And it is not even a one-way door. And, on top of that, you are in control of how you use that door, even if you are not now aware of this.

Now we can move on to the next derived truth which we have just touched upon. It is this:

"Change is the only constant."

Z: I've often heard that said. And it does seem true to me. I mean everything **does** eventually change. But could you first tell me how this is derived from the first absolute truth?

8: I implied this in our discussion about death, but let me reiterate. Do you understand that anything that is still, unmoving and unchanging is dead? **Anything**, if it does not change at all, if it ceases to move, then it has ceased to live. It is dead. And, as nothing ever dies, it follows that nothing ever ceases to move and to change.

Z: Nothing ever dies?

8: You have already forgotten the first part of the conversation. We've just been through that. Remember – the ONE **is**?

Z: Oh yes, sorry 8. I do remember. The ONE **is**, and cannot be divided, and that means all parts of the ONE must continue to exist. Nothing dies, nothing is destroyed. And now you are saying that "nothing dies" equals "everything changes".

8: Yes

Z: But 8, lots of stuff doesn't change. And lots of stuff is dead.

8: Such as?

Z: Oh come on, 8, surely you jest with me. Take a brick in the walls of a house. It's pretty dead and it certainly doesn't look to be doing much changing!

8: Wrong. The brick lives. Only in a way that you are not able to understand. It is a part of a living system that you haven't the ability yet to perceive. Let me ask you, are the bones in your body alive?

Z: Err... yes. They are a living organ kind-of-thing, I think. They grow and change over time.

8: But you cannot talk to them. You cannot see them eating food. They have no central nervous system. They don't seem to be intelligent. And yet you are happy to ascribe to them the term, "alive". What if I tell you that, just as a bone or a blood cell is alive in its own right, so is the brick that you so disparage. And just as a bone or a blood cell is an essential part of a much larger living entity, so is that brick. The brick itself is in a constant state of flux, always changing. On a sub-atomic level there is constant change at a very high rate and on the macro level there is constant change at a somewhat slower rate. If you want to see such change, go and look at a house which, for a few centuries, has had no maintenance or upkeep. That whole house will slowly return to the Earth; the bricks crumbling and changing and becoming a part of the Earth. You see, it is the arrogance of humanity that you believe you can determine what is "life" and "not life" by arbitrary parameters that you can measure... and tellingly, by their similarity to your own state. How would you like it if I said that you are not really a life form because your life-span is too short to be meaningful? Such might be the view of a galaxy, should it hold the same arrogance as humans do. Well it's time to release that arrogance. It's time to understand that **everything** is life. Everything is, in one way or another, of consciousness. And then you can come to the understanding that nothing dies and everything changes. These two ideas are actually the same idea when you get right down to it. Change **is** life. Stasis is death. But nothing is actually ever truly static. Nowhere does anything ever cease all movement. Everywhere, beings and things are in a constant process of motion and change.

Change is an absolute constant. And it is the **only** absolute constant.

Z: All right 8. Let me work through this from the top: there is not a single thing that I could point to or name that is not a part of the ONE.

8: Right.

Z: And no part of the ONE is dead or static. All parts of the ONE are alive and changing.

8: Yes. They might not have the narrow attributes which your science calls "life", but they are most certainly alive.

Z: But then, what is life? If it is not the "narrow attributes" science has given it, then what is it?

8: Growth. Change. Evolution. Becoming. Consciousness. These are some of the attributes of life. But what it actually **is**? That is a very large and very complex question. Look around you. Look at your planet. If you have seen every single thing that has ever happened on your planet since its creation until its end, then you will have a small part of the picture. Then go and do the same for every planet and every star in the universe. Slowly you will get a bigger and bigger part of the picture. When you have seen everything, everywhere in All That Is, then you will begin to hold within yourself the answer to the question, "*What is life?*"

Life is a mystery. It is beyond comprehension. It is beautiful and magnificent and unending. Life **is**.

Z: I don't often get to see this more poetic side to your soul, 8.

8: You know, my dear young friend, the more you try to simplify things, the more you see their complexity. And when you are ready to give yourself over to infinite complexity, then suddenly there is pure simplicity. This is my experience. Life will break your heart with its unendurable beauty. And, with a broken heart, you will call for more and more and more life.

Life is a wonder.

And assuredly, your dour old friend 8 is very much in love with life.

Z: My goodness, 8, that is a beautiful thing to say!

8: Thank you. Life itself is my inspiration and life itself is beautiful. But you see, because life is infinite and constantly changing, it is a logical certainty that it will remain beyond definition. And that is why, sadly, your attempts at using the scientific method to define what life is, will always fall short. You cannot know life with your mind. You can only know it with your heart. And that is why, when you ask me what life is, you hear me speaking of love and beauty and such matters of the heart.

Z: That makes perfect sense to me, 8, and I really enjoyed that description.

8: That is good. Then let us move onto the next derived truth, shall we?

Z: Great. What is it?

8: It is this:

"What you put out is what you get back."

Z: Cool. I know that one. But how is that derived?

8: The simplest explanation is this: separation is a reality in which the ONE can imagine that It is many. And those many can imagine that they can do things to, or for, each other. But since manyness is an illusion and oneness is the truth, it follows that everything you do to, or for, someone else is actually just the ONE acting upon Itself.

Everything you do to, or for, someone else, you do to, or for, yourself.

And that is the logic of it.

Z: Hmm. What you say makes sense intellectually but... if it is true, then why does life not seem like that? Why do I not immediately see what I do to others coming back to me?

8: That is the perfect question. You asked why you do not **immediately** see this. That is exactly the point! Let me explain. When you do something to another it takes time for the result to come back to you. In fact, the very definition of time is that which passes between cause and effect. It is the pause, the duration, that you must wait between what you put out and what you get back. And in that time you have the opportunity to disregard the connection between the cause and the effect. When the result arrives in your life, you have the opportunity to forget how and when you chose this and caused this. And, to massively complicate matters, **in the meantime** you will have made numerous other choices and, in so doing, enacted many other outcomes. So, when these outcomes do arrive in your life, they arrive blended together. They are a mixture of all the results of all of your creations. And this is how most beings who are incarnated upon Earth right now experience their lives. Their lives are a blended confusion of outcomes from their many choices. Random things seem to happen to them with no apparent relation to that which they have been doing or choosing. Sometimes it's good, sometimes it's bad, but mostly it's just a bit drab and mundane... and so they bumble along from cradle to grave.

And who can blame them for holding this perspective? If the results of their choices arrived immediately after they were chosen, then there would be no confusion. They would immediately see that they had created what they got. Then they would immediately begin making better choices. Then they would awaken to their creator nature. And then they would leave the duality illusion. And **that**, my friend, is exactly the point of this thing called "time": that it allows you to pretend that you did not create the outcomes you are experiencing.

Z: But why, 8? Why do we choose to experience time like this if all it does is confuse us?

8: Because this is exactly what you wanted! You came here specifically to experience a forgetting of who you really are. And the construct of time is a very powerful way to aid you in your forgetting.

It's actually all quite simple. The summary goes like this: what you put out is what you get back because... there is only one of us here. But some parts of the ONE wished to forget that they were one. And that is what you have accomplished. And a vital component of your forgetting that you are a part of the oneness, is to lose all sense of being a creator. This is because fear keeps you in separation. Fear comes from victimhood. Fear is dissolved by creator-consciousness. If you know that you are creating your experiences, then there isn't much point in fearing them, is there?

Z: No. That's like making scary shadow-monsters on the wall with my hands and then getting scared of them.

8: That is **exactly** what it is like!

Z: Okay, good. But here is the thing: I can completely understand the logic you are offering me. If there is only one of us here, then clearly anything I do, I am doing to myself. Good. I also get the logic of your argument that I am creating the situation that I forget that I am not the creator of my own reality. There is a kind of infallible circular logic here. But how do I come to **know** that I am the creator of my own experiences? Or do I have to just accept that I can't know this while I am incarnated here?

8: No, not at all. As a being who chose an ascension path, you are one who chose to come to know the essential oneness of all and also your own creator-nature whilst still incarnated. That is what the ascension process means. So you most certainly can know that you create your own experiences. In due course you will discover The Tools of Creation and you will begin to teach others what they are and how to use them.

> (**Zingdad Note:** The Tools of Creation is, in fact the name of part 3 of Dreamer Awake! available at zingdad.com/dreamer-awake.)

And when you use those tools, you will **know** your own creator nature. But I can give you a hint here: if you are the creator of your own experiences but have, up to now, only created for yourself that you are a victim and not, in fact, a creator, then how do you go about reversing that experience?

Z: I... uh... create that I am the creator, I guess. I make that choice.

8: Perfect! That is exactly what you do. **You** create it to be so. No one else can do this one for you. If anyone else does this for you, then they are creating that **they** are the creator of your life. Which is the same thing as your being their victim. So only you can do this!

Z: All right. But can you give me something to keep me going until we start working with the Tools of Creation? Until then, how can I begin to do this – how do I create that I am the creator?

8: First you act as if it is true. You do all the things that you would do if this were a thing you absolutely believed. The rule a creator being lives by is:

"What you put out is what you get back."

So live like this and then see. If it is true, then it will show itself to be true. Putting only loving, positive energy out will mean that, over time, your world will change until you get only loving, positive energy back. Do this and see. If it works, then you know directly and in your own experience, in a way that you cannot deny, that it is true. Then you are also well on the path to becoming a creator-being because you have understood the use and application of the first tool of creation. You create what you want by putting it out in the first place.

"What you get is directly determined by what you have put out."

It is really just the reverse statement of

"What you put out is what you get back."

Z: I think I am getting this now! Okay, that makes perfect sense. So we get what we create, but the only way to see if this is true is to purposefully and consistently create one thing that we want for a period of time so that we can observe the rule in action.

8: It is not the only way. But it is a simple and clear way. But if you do this then you must be both purposeful and consistent in what you put out and then you must be observant of what you get back. Then you will see that it is true, as a fact of your existence. Once you have experienced it in this way, it will come to be that you will feel this statement to be so obvious as to be almost too silly to even state. It will be like saying, "Your left hand is the hand on the left side of your body."

"What you put out is what you get back."

It's a truth that has been stated in many ways throughout the ages. It has been called "the golden rule" and "the law of reciprocity". It is stated in one form or another in most of the religious writings and ethical traditions of civilisation in the universe. You have heard it formulated as,

"As you sow, so shall you reap."

and

"Do unto others as you would that they should do unto you."

There are other formulations that say the same thing in different ways. If you look at it from the negative, then you get:

"That which you resist, persists."

You see? It means the same thing. It is like saying, "*If you focus on the stuff you don't want, you will get more of it.*" Because what you are putting out is coming back to you! This understanding is the underpinning of what is called the law of karma, in that it teaches that you cannot avoid the consequences of your choices. It also underlies the abundance philosophies and the "law of attraction" teachings that are gaining some popularity now.

"What you put out is what you get back."

It is a simple truth that you can apply in your life to bring to yourself the life you desire.

Z: Isn't it also expressed as

"You always get exactly what you create."

8: Ha! Yes, it is! That is the way we have expressed it here in ***The Ascension Papers***. It is the strongest case statement of the golden rule and it is the truth that you and your readers are now ready to receive. You see, beings who are deeply in duality consciousness are, by definition, not ready to hear that they are creators. So this concept is presented with weaker-case statements that they can apply in their lives. If they do choose to live by this tenet, they can enjoy a life that is harmonious and joyful while they slowly awaken and prepare for their eventual awakening to their creator status and the concomitant ascension out of the duality system.

But you and your readers are directly and consensually engaged in the ascension process. You would not be engaged with a book called ***The Ascension Papers*** if you were actually wanting to learn about knitting or pottery (he laughs). You are here after your own ascension! So we can view the concept, *"What you put out is what you get back,"* in its very strongest case:

*"You always get **exactly** what you create."*

You are a fractal, holographic representative of the ONE. You **must** be a creator being. It simply **must** be so. All you have to do is to find a way to remember that and to deal with the programming that tells you that it is not so.

A good place to start is to see this truth working in your life, as we have just discussed. The next step is to learn to use it as one of the Tools of Creation, which discussion is still coming.

Z: I must say that I'm really looking forward to that discussion!

8: It is going to be both interesting and useful.

But before we move on, there are a couple of very important things that I must point out.

Z: Yes?

8: Did you notice that everything we have discussed in this chapter stems essentially from the one prime truth?

Z: Which is: the ONE is.

8: Right.

Well the argument I am making is that there are layers of truth. There is the one absolute truth which is at the pinnacle, and then below it are the truths that are derived from it. Great truths such as these discussed in this chapter will remain true for all of your experience, from the moment of your creation as a consciousness, to the very moment at which you are willing to release even those truths and simply return to the ONE. For so long as you have an identity, an individuality and a persona, these truths will have validity. Below these truths are many other "lesser" truths, which you may now hold, which will be much more transitory. Like a child who holds something to be to so fiercely true that he will get into a school-yard fight over it but, by the next day, has already realised that it is no longer true for him. You too hold such beliefs that you are prepared to defend to the hilt, but very soon you are going to release those beliefs entirely. Such is the nature of lesser truths. They serve for a short while and then their transitory nature is discovered. This is what is meant when people say that one of the symptoms of ascension is "seeing through the illusions". It is so. As you awaken, so you let go of the beliefs and ideas to which others around you still cling. You come to see some ideas as not-so-very-true. They are the illusions of this world. If you are going to stay deeply attached to the dramas of this world, then you really need to continue believing these things. If you begin to see through them, then you find yourself unable to continue playing the games implicit to life in this world. This is already happening to you, as it is happening to most of your readers. You find that you can no longer take seriously things such as politics and religion. You begin to view "the news" with more than a little scepticism. Money, status, power... these things look a lot less interesting to you now than they did a few years ago. Possessions, you now discover, are either "fit for purpose" or they are a burden. And so it goes. These kinds of transitions are inevitable. You view your world through the lens that is yourself. As you change yourself, so the world looks different. "Layers of truth," you see. And you, the awakening ones, are beginning to see through the more transitory layers.

And **that** is a large part of the purpose of the conversations that will follow. I will be talking to you about some of the transitory truths that you still hold. Some of them have been buried quite deep in your psyche and will need a little nudge to be brought into the light and seen for what they are. In so doing I will be helping you to release the illusions that no longer serve your purpose.

Z: This sound like a very interesting and exciting journey. But 8, there is something that is bothering me a little. You're going to be telling our readers "how it is" and "how it isn't". But that concerns me. It feels as if we might be infringing on peoples' right to choose and their right to create for themselves.

8: That's a good point and you have raised it at exactly the right moment. You will notice that Joy-Divine was very careful to keep making it clear in his chapters that these things presented in **The Ascension Papers** are things that are true from his perspective and that the reader must trust their own intuition and truth. Well that is good and I echo that. But then the material Joy-Divine handled was mostly the"soft" stuff. Some philosophical issues and so on. He rarely wandered into the hard issues of your reality, as it is. I, on the other hand, am going to be talking extensively about these hard issues. I am going to call it as I see it. Now **obviously** this is from my perspective. But I am going to qualify why my perspective is particularly useful and valid. I am going to tell you why it is right and appropriate that I can stand here and tell you the story of your reality. Then it is up to you and your readers. You can decide to accept my credentials or reject them. And, based upon that, you can give credence to the truth of "what is" from my perspective or not.

Z: But 8, how are we to know the difference?

8: Good question. I will teach you how. If you take just **one thing** from everything I have said, and am going to say, in **The Ascension Papers**, then I would say it should be this:

"Your truth is, whatever is deeply true in your heart."

This is the most important thing I can tell you about truth.

Z: Can you explain that?

8: Sure. You see, all beings everywhere are masking some truths about themselves from themselves. Because, if the only thing that is absolutely true is, "*The ONE is*", then everything that creates separation, differentiation, individuation... is a transitory truth. An illusion. That I am separate from you is an illusion. That you are separate from your reader is an illusion. We are all **one**.

Z: I follow.

8: Now these separation constructs; these things that we believe about ourselves to allow ourselves to do things separately and to hold different perspectives, these are illusions within our minds.

There is nothing wrong with them. It serves the purpose of the ONE that we do this. But they are illusions none-the-less and they are in our minds.

Z: Got it.

8: Now what do you think the Veil of Unknowing is?

Z: Ohhhhhh! It is an illusion of the mind!

8: Yes it is. There are many shared illusions. We call the results of our shared illusions a "consensus reality". It means that we all agree to the illusions which make up the reality in which we live. And then we create that reality together. When two or more beings give each other permission to create things that they will all share, then the experience of it is called co-creation.

Now the thing to understand about the Veil is that it is actually conscious and alive. In order for you to be behind the Veil as you now are, you have to be co-creating with the Veil Holder too. This way you can cease to concern yourself with what you may and may not know. You enter into that agreement and then you come and play the game. The Veil Holder works to keep the rule true – which is that you may not discover the truth of the oneness of all.

Z: Wow.

8: But now... Tell me again what the Veil of Unknowing is? You just said it a moment ago?

Z: I said it is an illusion of the mind.

8: Right. So the mind is where all these illusions of separation reside. The mind is where you hold all the complex constructs that allow you to play the games you are playing. The mind is the place of all these understandings and complexities. The mind analyses and engages in reductive reasoning.

The mind **understands**.

However...

The heart **knows**.

Your heart is your path through all illusions. Your heart is connected directly to the ONE and to the greatest truth of all, which is the oneness of all. If you stop all the babble of your mind. If you silence all the noise in your being. If you learn to just **shut up** long enough to hear what your heart has to say, then you will hear it crying out in longing for **oneness**. For the infinite, overwhelming, blissful love of the ONE.

Your heart knows and has never forgotten this greatest truth.

Can you feel it?

Can you go to your heart and know this to be true?

Z: Yes. Yes, I most certainly can.

8: Others who are engaged in the ascension process should also be able to. The ascension process itself is you responding to your heart's call. Your heart calls you home and you begin to respond.

The deep truth that I am therefore trying to impart to you is:

*"The heart **knows**."*

Your job is to learn to listen to your heart. If you can do that, then you can know your truth on anything at any time. Because, through your heart you are connected to your Inner-Self and through your Inner-Self you are connected to your God-Self and through your God-Self you are connected to everyone and everything, everywhere, all the time. You are connected to the oneness of all. Your heart is a direct line to all truth and all knowingness. You must just learn to **listen**!

Z: And how do I do that, 8?

8: It takes discipline. You must learn to still your mind so that it ceases to disturb you and then you must learn to open your heart-portal so that you might bring the issues that you seek clarity on into your heart and **know** what your truth is.

Your heart speaks to you in feelings. You need to learn to feel with your heart. Feel what it feels like when it is expanded, when it is in resonance and when it is in dis-resonance. Then, if you ever need to test a thought against your own truth, you can simply stop what you are doing, close your eyes, still your mind and then become present to the feel of your heart. Then hold the thought that you wish to test in your mind and feel how your heart feels. If it feels "right", then it is true for you. If it feels uncomfortable, then you should be careful with it. And if it feels outright wrong, then you should walk away.

Practice this. Like anything in your life, the more you do it, the better you will get at it. Soon your heart will speak eloquently to you because you are paying it the respect of really listening. Getting really good at listening to your heart is about the most valuable tool you will ever have. There is almost nothing more important than this for the journey that lies ahead.

(**Zingdad note:** If listening to your heart is something that you feel you need some help with, then I am very pleased to assist! Since first writing *The Ascension Papers*, I have crafted a number of guided meditations and some of these can help very specifically with guiding you to listen to your heart. Please visit the Guided Meditations section of my site to browse the available meditations, here: zingdad.com/healing-a-helping/guided-meditation-recordings.)

Z: Thank you 8. I really appreciate this.

8: It's a pleasure. A great pleasure indeed. But now this discussion has become overly long. Let us end it here. A very exciting journey awaits in our next chapters together.

Z: I look forward to it 8. This has been an amazing and beautiful chapter. I have really loved receiving it. I'll talk to you again soon.

8: Good then. I love you. Until next time...

* * * * *

CHAPTER 9.
A MYSTICAL INTERLUDE

Zingdad: 8?

8: Yes?

Z: I'm struggling a bit.

8: All right. What with?

Z: Well, I was re-reading Chapter 8 and I came across the place where you spoke about how I had overcome my doubts and fears such that I was able to receive *The Ascension Papers*. And, when you said that, I felt quite good about myself. But, between finishing that chapter and preparing to start the next one, I've had some time to think. And I feel a bit like a fraud. Because I **still** have loads of doubts. And the more I think about it, the more doubts I have. And, given how I have gotten things wrong in the past, I fear I might mess things up again. And then I think about the things you and J-D have told me and... why can't I just believe... you know... why can't I just have faith?

And then I feel like an even bigger fraud because, here I am writing this book, here I am receiving this material, and even *I* don't have absolute faith in it! And if even I have my doubts, how can I possibly expect my readers to believe this stuff? And then I think I must be insane because I **know** I couldn't have come up with all the stuff in the previous chapters by myself. I **know** it is not within my capacity to do that. And so these words **must** be from you and J-D but then, why do I still doubt? And round and round I go.

So that's the issue. It's not overwhelming but it does bother me and feels heavy in my heart. So before we carry on with the next chapter I'd really like to get some resolution on this.

Can you help?

8: Yes.

To begin with, let's sort a few things out. Firstly, in the last chapter I said that you have **mostly** released your doubts and fears, and that it is as a result of this that you are now able to undertake the writing of *The Ascension Papers*. And this is true. You could not have received these words even one month before you actually began. You began when you were ready. And I also said that it will be as a result of writing *The Ascension Papers* that you will release the rest of your fears and doubts so that you can awaken to your true creator nature.

Do you not remember me saying that?

Z: Yes. That sounds about right.

8: So now. If I said that we were going to release the rest of your fears and doubts, then it must mean that I knew there were still some to release and that I intended to help you with them. And here we are today and you find you need to talk about this very subject. Well, that is perfect. It comes at the perfect time. And no, you don't need to resolve this with me **before** you can get back to writing the book. Resolving this with me now **is** writing the book and is as important as any other topic we might address. This very conversation is, in point of fact, Chapter 9.

Z: Really?

8: Joy-Divine said it:

> *"If you cannot see the perfection then you are standing too close to the picture."*

Remember how it was true for you in the chapter about the Darklanders?

Z: I do.

8: Well it's going to be true for you in this chapter too. This chapter is about doubt. Sort of. It starts with doubt and it ends with you realising that you are a mystic.

Z: A what?

8: A mystic.

Z: Sorry, I heard what you said. I was registering my confusion. I'm not even completely sure what a mystic **is**, let alone how I come to **be** one by talking to you about my feelings of doubt.

8: Okay. Well, you have access to the Internet on this laptop. Take five minutes to get a quick definition of what mysticism is and then report back here.

(I do that. I literally take five minutes and get the briefest idea.)

Z: From what I have been able to glean from the Internet, a mystic seems to be someone who seeks direct, personal union with the divine. Someone who seeks (or finds) contact with God without the intervention of religious doctrines. There is also something about a mystic being an adherent of the "mystery schools". Now I do vaguely recall having heard that term before but, beyond that, I haven't a clue as to what these schools are or what they teach.

So mysticism seems to be all about some great mystery.

Which is appropriate because it's all a bit of a mystery to me!

8: That's fine. You have gained just enough understanding for the purposes of this discussion.

Next we need a brief definition of the word "mystery", if you'll be so kind.

Z: Okay. I'll go look it up.

(Which I do)

What I find is that the word "mystery" broadly means:

A secret. Something that is not known or is unexplained. Something that causes curiosity. Something that is only knowable by divine revelation.

And, interestingly enough, the word derives originally from the Greek word *mustēs*, which means "an initiate".

8: That **is** interesting, isn't it?

All right. Let's leave all that there for now. Next, I want to move on directly to your difficulty. You say you are struggling with doubt. Can you tell me where you think doubt comes from?

Z: I think it's from fear.

8: That's just a little too simplistic for my tastes. How about this:

> *"Doubt springs forth from an attachment to certainty."*

Or I could state it in the negative and say:

> *"Doubt originates from resistance to uncertainty."*

Z: Okay. Let me work with that for a second. There are many, many things I am uncertain about. I am, for example, completely uncertain about what my neighbour ate for breakfast this morning. But that's fine because it has no bearing on me. I have no attachment to that. By comparison, I am also uncertain that I will ever experience the second Singularity Event that J-D said was coming. But I really, really, really want that to happen! That's a measure of me finding my way Home. It's confirmation that I'm doing things right. And it's also the most wonderful, amazing experience. So...

8: So, you are resisting your uncertainty. On the one hand there is excitement because, *"Oh wow, how amazing if it happens,"* and on the other hand there is fear because, *"Oh no, what if it doesn't happen?"*

Z: You got it. That's exactly what it is. And it's the same thing with all of the information I get from you and J-D. There really is no way for me to always know if it is 100% correct. I mean I don't know that these conversations are not just a figment of my imagination. For goodness sake, I don't even know for a fact that **you** are not just a figment of my imagination.

8: But, isn't the fact that there is a "me" here to say, *"I exist!"* proof enough that I do exist?

Z: No... because the "you" that is here, is only "here" inside my mind.

8: But in the previous chapter you... oh... never mind. I was actually just having a little fun with you but you clearly aren't in the mood.

Z: Oh, right. Okay, I get the joke (smiles a little).

Perhaps I can give you a more concrete example then. How do I know that my "Mountain Experience", as amazing as it was, wasn't just a once-off thing? How do I know that there will be a second Singularity Event? And how do my readers know (if they haven't had one) that they will ever have **their**

Singularity Event experiences? How do we know **anything**? How do we cease to doubt?

8: So you doubt... and then you judge yourself for doubting?

Z: Yes. Because I am supposed to have faith.

8: Are you? When you encounter that which you are uncertain of, are you meant to "just believe"? Are you sure that's a good idea?

If someone approached you in the street tomorrow and proposed to sell you, for a mere hundred dollars, a magical cream that would turn everything to which it was applied into solid gold, would you believe him and just hand over the cash?

Z: (laughs) No, I'd insist to see it in action first, of course.

8: Okay, but be really honest now; if you saw it in action, would you then just give him the money?

Z: Truthfully, no. I don't believe that there is such a thing as a magical cream that can turn things to gold. It's not possible. How could you transform non-gold atoms into gold atoms? Short of nuclear reactions or something like that? How would you add or remove the precise number of atomic particles from each atom so that it would become a gold atom? This is nonsense. If I saw a totally convincing demonstration in which exactly this was done, I'd assume that I was observing a very talented illusionist who was either using his skills to con unsuspecting dupes out of cash or, perhaps, that I was the butt of an elaborate prank.

If I think about it, the only circumstance under which I would hand over the money is if he'd allow me to use this magical substance of his to create a thousand bucks worth of gold out of worthless junk, sell it, give him the money and then walk away with his magic cream.

8: That's smart. And it's this same kind of savvy that has served you quite well in your life. It has allowed you to make good decisions such that it has been quite seldom that you have been taken advantage of or taken for a fool. So this is good and useful. And this *being smart* only arises as a result of you correctly processing your uncertainty. You begin with the information presented. Then you weigh up the things you don't know or understand against what you do know. If you can resolve your uncertainty with what you already know, then fine. If you cannot resolve your uncertainty but it doesn't really matter (such as your example about your neighbour's breakfast menu this morning) then you shrug it off. But if it really matters – and our example of the cream that could make you rich would surely matter – then you find yourself doubting. And in our example, you used your doubt to drive a process of making sense of things such that you could come to a decision not to buy the magical cream.

What you did **not** do, is just believe. Just have faith. Just hand over the money.

So my question to you is this: why then do you expect yourself to behave differently when it comes to ideas and concepts shared with you by J-D and I?

Z: That's interesting. I'm not sure why.

8: Then I shall tell you why. In your mind you separate "real" stuff from "spiritual" stuff. And "real" stuff needs real proof whilst with "spiritual" stuff, you feel that you must just have faith and believe. And the reason for this is that you are suffering from one of the effects of religion. Most of the religions of your world work quite hard to propagate the notion that doubt is "bad". Well it isn't. It's just bad for business. Their business. If you belong to a religion, and then find yourself beginning to doubt, then what is happening is that you are finding that the answers that religion provides do not satisfy you. The things that they present to you that you do not know or do not understand cannot be resolved, in your mind, with the things you do know. And since the truth about God and your everlasting soul is quite an important thing, you find you can't shrug it off. You must know. So you doubt. The problem for the religions arises if you choose to pursue your doubts. Then you might very well find answers that **do** satisfy you elsewhere. And if you find better answers outside of that religion, you might very well leave that religion. Then you cease to do as it tells you. Cease to be controlled by the greater agenda of that religion's leaders. And, of course, cease to give them money. So it isn't odd that religious leaders are not too fond of people doubting and following their doubts to seek new and different answers from the ones they are providing. So they develop quite a cunning strategy: tell people that doubt is bad. Tell them that it is evidence of a wicked mind or of the devil in action. Make them feel really rotten about doubting. Then, when people do have uncertainty and questions, they will feel so bad about them that they won't go looking for answers to their questions. They will simply take the existence of their doubt as proof of their inherent sinfulness. And then they work extra hard to be "good". Mostly they will become fanatical about their faith as a means to cope with their doubt. Clever huh?

Z: Maybe. But it's not very nice, is it?

8: If you are of the opinion that religions propagate around your world by being "nice", then you are extremely unobservant. I don't say that the original teachings upon which the religions are founded do not contain any good, for clearly they do. And I don't say that there is not also some good done in the name of various religions, because clearly there is. But if you are ignoring the fact that religion's prime purpose is to be a tool of power and control of the masses, then you have your head in the sand.

But this chapter is not actually about religion. And I am not actually against religion *per se* because it has a role to play and no-one is actually a victim here. Right now all I actually wish to indicate is that religion has had a pervasive effect on shaping your planetary psyche. And given that it is very much contrary to the interests of religion that you question spiritual concepts, it is no surprise that you have a pre-programmed negative response to doubt.

"Do not doubt, just have faith!" they tell you. But in any other sphere of life, if you just believe what you are told, you end up getting cheated out of your possessions. And so, a little neurosis is born:

"I **must** just have faith in relation to spiritual matters, but I must keep my wits about me and trust my own experience everywhere else," you tell yourself.

But this is patently silly! Surely there should be nothing more **real** than your spirituality? Your own truest nature – your spirit self – should be the most real thing of all! So why should you not **always** simply trust your own truth and your own experience?

So now we have to undo some of this programming. We have to reconcile spirituality and real life. We have to dis-intermediate these clergymen and their doctrines from between you and your soul, between you and the ONE; the Source-God of which you are, in truth, an inseparable part. Because really, what silliness is this that you should have to go to some other person with ancient texts in order that you should know that which is within your heart; that which lies as close as your own breath?

Z: That does seem like an odd notion.

8: It is appropriate for those who seek to enter more deeply into duality to do so, for they are creating a victim state for themselves. They burrow ever deeper into duality by saying, "*I do not hold my own truth, someone else must hold it for me.*"

And so they always seek experts to tell them what is true: clergy, politicians, lawyers, doctors, scientists and so forth. These authorities must tell them what is in their own reality. But for those who seek to arise from this density, it is not so. Awakening ones might certainly take another being's perspective into account; you might share with them and learn from them. But your connection with God, Divinity and oneness can only occur directly and personally.

For the ascending ones it becomes appropriate to cease attempting to separate "spirituality" from "life". For the awakening being, all of life becomes "spiritual". For example, for us here in the upper densities of consciousness, there is no such concept as "spirituality" or "religion" because **everything** is "spiritual". And religion – being a set of doctrines and beliefs to which we must adhere – is utterly pointless to us. You see, everything is done in relationship with the ONE. It is **all** in service to God. We don't have to think about it, or try to be pious, or set aside some time for it. We can, quite simply, do no other.

So let me then complete my point here and say this: release your judgement of yourself for doubting. This judgement is unnecessary, counter-productive and causes you pain. You doubt, quite simply, because you do not know. Let me use your next Singularity Event as an example to illustrate the point. When Joy-Divine explained this to you and you understood that it was coming and what that meant, it was quite natural to feel excited and happy about the prospect. It is also quite natural to then think about it and to begin to wonder. To find that you "don't know about this". This is uncertainty.

Now, if you were to begin to fervently hope that it was true, perhaps even to believe that you needed it to be true for you to be okay, then you begin to focus on the uncertainty. You begin to attach yourself to it. It becomes a gnawing doubt. And if that's not bad enough, you now also decide that this doubt itself is bad.

In so doing you create a neurosis. You doubt, but you think doubt is bad, so you try to stop doubting, but you cannot create certainty, so you doubt even more. And so you find yourself spiralling into what I call "debilitating doubt".

Remember, one of the derived truths in the last chapter was, "*What you put out is what you get back*"?

Z: Yes. I remember.

8: And the corollary of that, is the equally true statement, "*What you resist, persists.*"

Z: Right.

8: So if you feel doubt, you can either do something about it, or you can focus on the doubt itself. If you focus on the doubt itself and wrestle with it, then it "persists". You get more of it. And, holding a judgement about your doubt that tells you that the doubt itself is wrong, is pretty much guaranteed to make you focus on the doubt. You are quite likely to get an attack of "debilitating doubt".

Round and round and round you go. You keep doubting and you keep feeling bad about it. All because somewhere inside of you there resides this originating thought that you may not doubt.

Perverse. Odd. And not very useful.

Z: Wow, huh? I see that. Okay. So then I'd like to let go of that judgement. Maybe it **is** okay for me to feel doubt about ever experiencing another Singularity Event...

8: Let's leave the specifics of your doubts aside for a moment. Let's look rather at what is going on behind the scenes.

Do you know the future?

Z: Well... No.

8: Do you have any certainty at all about what will happen in the future?

Z: No.

8: Do you feel like you have control over the future?

Z: No.

8: Do you have your own direct and personal knowledge of the material J-D and I are sharing with you in these conversations?

Z: No. If I did, I wouldn't need you to tell me about it.

8: So, there is no way for you to be certain within yourself about these things at this point?

Z: No.

8: Well, there you have it then. Uncertainty is what you have and uncertainty is completely reasonable under these circumstances. The problem comes in with your attachment. You want certainty about this information. But what you have not yet understood is that this cannot actually be. The things J-D and I tell you of, and perhaps even more especially the things Adamu will tell you of, are not meant to be taken as articles of faith that you must simply believe! These are the things that we, as a result of **our** experiences have come to know to be true. And, as these things are not in your experience, we share them with you knowing that you will respond with surprise, amazement and wonder. These are our gifts to you that you can test, and try and see if they are also good and right for you. As your journey unfolds, you can use these, our gifts, as tools for your own growth.

What I am saying is that, at the very heart of the matter, all we are doing is offering you our perspectives. It is up to you to decide if you will make use of these gifts to inform the ways in which you will create yourself and your reality. We cannot create for you. And we cannot take from you your right to create something other than what we have created for ourselves. This would be absurd. Joy-Divine, 8 and Adamu are not the creators of your world and are certainly not responsible for what you and everyone else on Earth will or will not create.

So, until you create an experience and, in so doing, **make it true** for yourself, all we have done here is shine the light on certain distinct possibilities for you. And so, until you have created something as true for yourself, your uncertainty is right and good and healthy.

What is unhealthy is for you to attach to the uncertain outcomes and, even worse, to stand in judgement of yourself for being uncertain. It isn't **wrong** if you choose to do that. It's just not taking you forward to where you want to be. And it hurts you. It is, as I say, unhealthy.

Z: I understand, 8. So I'd like to stop doing that then. I'd like to stop getting stuck in my attachments to that of which I am uncertain. And if I **do** feel doubt, to stop judging myself for it.

8: Excellent. And that is what I am going to help you with in this chapter. I am going to help you to gain a better understanding of uncertainty. I am going to teach you of its power and magnificence. The result of this will **not** be that you will have no more uncertainty or that you will never again doubt. The result will be that you will embrace your uncertainty and learn to use it in wonderful new ways. You will come to see it as an amazing gift.

Z: Really, 8? That sounds quite hard to believe.

8: Does it? Then I accept the challenge! (he laughs)

To start with, let us create a hypothetical situation:

Imagine you are sitting next to a camp-fire on a dark and moonless night. You can only see as far as the light of the fire penetrates the gloom and you have no other source of light.

What do you do? Do you huddle closer and closer to the fire and shiver with fear at every leaping shadow? Or do you respond to the dark, unknown landscape with curiosity?

If you feel fear, then you stay put. You probably won't even **look** out at the darkness because it makes you feel uneasy.

If, instead of fear, you feel playful curiosity then, without a second thought, you stand up and venture out into the darkness. You allow your eyes to adjust to the darkness and begin to explore and to open yourself to new discoveries. And, in so doing, you expand your knowledge of your environment. And, as you learn new things, so you actually expand yourself!

Now this is obviously just a hypothetical situation. I am not saying that one should be foolhardy and stumble around in the dark of night. I am simply illustrating a point, which is about the way you respond to the unknown. If you respond to it with joy, you experience expansion of the Self. If you respond to it in fear, you experience a contraction of the Self.

Now the thing you must understand is that there is, and always will be, a great amount of "unknown" in your experience of life. There will always and forever be a great deal to be uncertain about.

Z: Really, 8? **Always**? Even for someone like you?

8: (laughs) Oh my goodness, yes! Let me explain: the ONE is infinite, right?

Z: Right.

8: And within the ONE is an infinite multiplexity of manyness, right?

Z: Yes...

8: And, since change is the only constant, all of that manyness is eternally and infinitely changing, expanding and growing. Right?

Z: Right.

8: Do you understand what that means? It means that the ONE is infinite and yet is expanding at an infinitely fast rate! It is simply mind boggling to even attempt to comprehend it. And this of course means that there is an impossibly huge amount of stuff "out there" beyond the periphery of any one being's perceptual field. And what is "out there" just gets more and more! And no matter how fast you grow, learn, experience and understand, the "unknown" will always grow faster than you. Because the faster you "expand", the more you expand the ONE and the faster you help all other aspects of the ONE to grow. It's really awesomely beautiful. The mystery just deepens and expands.

So yes, assuredly, there is **always** more and more unknown, uncharted and unexplored territory. There is always newness. There is always mystery. And mystery, when viewed from the personal perspective, is uncertainty. The question is quite simply how you will choose to respond to it. Will you shrink back from it in fear or will you explore it with joy? That is up to you. And, as always, you will get exactly what you are creating and you will experience the results of your creation.

Do you follow?

Z: Yes. Thank you for the patient explanation. That makes sense.

8: So let's see how this has worked in your life. Let me ask you this: that boy who first sat down with a pebble in his hand and asked me if I was "out there".

(**Zingdad note:** see Chapter 1: An Introduction to Zingdad)

That boy who asked me if I loved him. That boy who sat there night after night asking his questions and laboriously finding a path out of his incomprehension with yes/no answers...

Was he venturing out into the darkness or was he sitting close to the fire?

Z: He was venturing out.

8: And how did that work out for him?

Z: Quite well, it seems.

8: You think?

I think it was one of your finest moments!

If you think about it, **The Ascension Papers** and all the other processes and questing that you have done, all flowed forth from that moment. Certainly, along the way you developed and refined your ability to listen. But it was in **that first moment** with that pebble in your hand that you stood up from your comfortable, safe spot at the fire. You turned to face the darkness of the unknown and you stepped forth boldly for the very first time. With no precedent, with no cause to believe that it would work, with no-one to show you the way, you chose joy over fear in the face of uncertainty.

It was a moment of your life that I will always treasure.

I had no intention, in this lifetime of yours, to have conversations like this with you. It was not a part of any plan that I was aware of that I'd reveal myself to you and that we'd converse as we now do. But how could I resist such courage, such a willingness to open yourself, to expand yourself and to explore the unknown? I could not! You made my heart beam. I was so proud to be a part of what you were trying to do. And so I could not help but play along.

And now, in continuing these conversations, you continue to broaden your search. You continue to expand yourself into the darkness. In fact you turn the areas of darkness you encounter into areas of light by the very act of exploring them. You bring **your** light to them.

And **this** is what you have done with uncertainty.

Do you not see? *The Ascension Papers* is entirely a product of your uncertainty. And you don't know it yet, but *The Ascension Papers* is just the beginning. This is really just the record of your first foray into the darkness of uncertainty. You have an eternity of discovery and creation ahead of you. You cannot now even begin to imagine the beauty and joy that will flow forth from your future creations as you bring your light to the darkness. As you expand into uncertainty.

Now, I ask you, do you wish for us to take away your uncertainty? Do you wish to cease to experience it?

Z: Good grief, 8, that is a very surprising perspective on all this. Wow. No, I guess I don't want to stop having uncertainty.

But how do I not get attached; how do I not slip into debilitating doubt?

8: Let's look at this. You started this conversation by telling me of your doubt. You admitted that you found that you could even doubt my independent existence. And yet, despite that, still you come to me for a conversation about this. Still you keep asking questions and exploring possible answers. Still you open yourself to the possibility of growth. Still you move out into the darkness in ever greater arcs, searching the unknown. And **that** is what I meant when I said to you previously that you had done enough work with fear and doubt to allow *The Ascension Papers* to come through. What I meant was that you had come far enough not to let it debilitate you. Not to bring you to a halt. Because that is what happens when you feel uncertainty and you respond to it with fear and then judge yourself for feeling the fear. This is what I was telling you when I spoke of "debilitating doubt".

It is quite okay to feel some fear of the unknown, but when, as a result of the fear or your judgements about it, you choose not to search the unknown, then you enter an area of difficulty. You then make it impossible for yourself to begin to find answers for your doubt. You shut down your own creative power. And so you remain in a state of doubt and you cannot get out of it. You find you are debilitated by it.

So, you have already passed that first hurdle. Though you still feel the pain of doubt, you do not any more allow it to stop your growth and progression. And that is as a result of your own choice to keep moving forward, irrespective of the doubt.

Now you wish to leap the next hurdle. You wish to cease causing yourself pain over your uncertainty.

Let's take a step back and look at the healthy way to deal with uncertainty:

The first thing to do is to make the choice to allow yourself to **look** at the unknown. If you feel a fear or a doubt or a question, don't shy away from it, don't fear it; go and **look** at it. Make a decision that you will seek to replace this uncertainty with insight, understanding, answers and wisdom. As soon as you do this, you will find that the "stuckness" of your doubt is replaced by the freedom of having options. When you have options, then you can choose. When you can choose, then you can create. And when you begin to create, then you re-connect once again with your God-Self. And of course, this is immediately a lot healthier. Even if you still have the same uncertainty and the same questions, just the fact of looking at your options allows the energy to flow again. And let me tell you something that is true – there are **always** options. If you can't see any, then you are simply choosing not to look.

If you do not have the answers you need then you must seek within, in your own inner truth, in your own heart, in your personal connection to the divine. This will often entail quite a bit of work. You will have to learn to listen to your inner voice. You will have to learn to trust yourself. To love yourself. But you will find, as you progress, that you begin to lose your fear of the unknown. You will venture out into those areas of unknown questions with greater and greater courage. You will begin to enjoy the process of searching your heart, your psyche and the whole universe for the deepest meaning.

Slowly your fear will transmute into love. And when you approach your uncertainty with true, open-hearted love, then you will discover a very magical thing – playful curiosity.

And this is when you leap your next hurdle. This is when you begin to play with uncertainty without causing yourself pain.

Playful curiosity allows you to enact your most creative self in the search for answers without attaching your ego to the outcome. You play. You have fun. You create. The most amazing and marvellous answers will come to you if you are able to reside in a state of playful curiosity. If you don't fear being wrong. Because "wrong" just means an answer that didn't work. And that, therefore, is another opportunity to **play again**!

You see?

And it all starts with uncertainty and how you choose to feel about it.

Z: That's awesome 8. I really like that. Because that is what happened when I got things wrong previously. I just found an answer that didn't work. It was internally inconsistent and it couldn't happen. It was tough going but I did begin to play again and now I have a much improved answer. And it is, as you say – it all starts with the willingness to explore my own uncertainty.

8: And there is more. Let's look at the opposite of uncertainty. Let's look at "certainty". Things that are certain are fixed. We say that we are certain about them precisely because we feel that they are unchangeable and immutable. We use these "certainties" and build our reality and our perceptions of ourselves upon them. They are our very deepest truths and, as such, they are the scaffolding upon which we create. And they are therefore very valuable to us. Without them we would have a hard time creating anything of any meaning or significance. I mean – how would we create realities such as the universe you are in and the planet you are on without the rules of physics being what they are? If there were no rules at all, there would be chaos, and life as you know it could not exist.

And how would you begin to understand yourself if nothing about you seemed to remain fixed for any length of time?

Z: Very difficult. I can see that.

8: So these truths of ours, these "certainties", have great value to us and we love them dearly. But they are, in fact, transitory. Given sufficient time, every single thing that we now hold to be true will come to be less true, and then eventually untrue. It is thus for you as an individual, it is thus for your spiritual monad, and it is thus for all of life, everywhere. The things you now believe about yourself and your reality will inevitably come to change and evolve. You will gain new beliefs as the old ones cease to serve you and you release them. That is the nature of "The Truth". Like everything else, it always changes. And so it is for all the things about which we are certain. In time we will come to be less certain of them and then, eventually, we may even come to be certain that they are **not** so!

Z: Everything, 8?

8: To the very best of my rather exhaustive effort to be able to discern, I will say that this is so of everything. Other than the one immutable truth, of course, which is...

Z: *"The ONE is."*

8: Correct. And this is only an immutable truth due to its innate capacity to contain infinite change. So, *"The ONE is,"* and as for the rest... *"Change is the only constant."*

And if there is only change then, given sufficient duration of experience, you will experience great change. Given infinite experience, you will change infinitely. Hardly sounds like there is much room there to hold onto small truths about your current reality, does it?

Z: No, I guess not. It sounds like uncertainty is a certainty.

8: (laughs) Exactly. And it is a very good thing that this is so. Because it is the areas of uncertainty that we can grow and change into. The areas we temporarily hold to be certain are the areas at which we stop looking and in which we stop growing. And so here is the important realisation:

> *"Without uncertainty there is nothing new and no creation.*
> *If you embrace uncertainty, you embrace creation."*

If you open your heart to uncertainty, then you allow your greatest, most divine self to play with it. You actually move into "genius". Uncertainty is the greatest muse of all!

> (**Zingdad note:** The ancient origin of the word genius referred to a state of consciousness in which a greater spirit, a genie, acted through the hands of a "mortal" being)

Cherish it. Seek it out. Explore it. Love it. And, most of all, **have fun** with it!

Z: 8, that is brilliant. I feel quite excited by this. It feels right to me. Thank you.

8: You are most welcome.

And yet... I can sense that you are still not completely done with this topic...

Z: Yes. You are right. Perhaps I just need to internalise what you have said. Or something. Because I still feel like I have some issue here.

8: Talk it out with me.

Z: Okay. Let's see. I think it goes like this. So, I have uncertainty. If I fear it enough, then I will get locked up and I won't move forward. So that's not healthy. If, on the other hand, I love it, then I begin to create. And I have fun creating. First I begin to define the questions inherent in my uncertainty and then I begin to find answers that seem to fit the questions. In so doing I find I'm beginning to really have fun. And then I begin to create some really amazing dialogues and have really astounding, awesome answers coming back at me and I find I am totally loving the process and it just feels so **right**.

8: But?

Z: Yeah. But!

But I **still** don't know if these answers are right or true. No matter how much better I am feeling about myself and my life, I still don't know if all this that I have been getting has any validity outside of the confines of my imagination.

Please don't get me wrong. I am astounded at the information I am getting. I am blown away at the internal consistency of the messages. I really, really don't believe it possible that I could – in the normal sense of it – have imagined all of this. It is so for me that there **must** be something "paranormal" going on here. But I **still** don't know if it is all true.

8: All right. I want to say a few things to you.

The first is an issue I have already addressed here, but I will state it a little differently. I want to say to you that it is **your job** to hold a degree of uncertainty – to "hold lightly" onto your view of reality. For it is in so doing that you are able to do the work that you are now doing. It allows you to write this book and do the many other creative tasks that will follow. You decided to create your path home in this way. That was your choice. In order to do that it is imperative then that you continue to hold some uncertainty. Otherwise you cannot create this path and will have to find another.

Secondly: how would it be if I waved a magic wand and you had complete certainty? If you **knew** with absolute conviction, and certainty and had not a shred of doubt in your soul, that all that is spoken of in *The Ascension Papers* is absolutely true? If you **knew** that each of your following Singularity Events were going to occur, and when and how they would occur? Then how would that be?

Z: Uhh... on the face of it that doesn't sound so bad. I mean I'd still be able to write all this down and tell folks about it, wouldn't I? I'd still be able to help everyone else to get Home!

8: Okay, wait a minute. Let's get something straight right now. You are not doing this for your readers. You are creating your own way Home. That is what you are doing. Because you can do no other. Yes, you are sharing the things that you discover on your path Home in case this is useful to others and, yes, there is some beautiful and magical co-creation happening as a result of this. That is all true. But you are **not** rescuing anyone. If you begin to see it that way, then I assure you, you are going to get hurt. You will develop a saviour complex instead of seeing this as your own path Home that is also being offered as a gift to others. Okay?

Z: Thanks 8. Phew! That's right and I appreciate the reminder. I have given up on rescuing.

8: I'm glad that's sorted out. Now, back to the issue at hand. Let me ask you again. How would it be if you had absolute certainty about your sequence of Singularity Events all the way Home?

Z: I'm thinking about this, 8. And it dawns on me that I would then find other things that would bother me in the same way; other things that I did not know that felt like areas of uncertainty. So then I'd be right back here where I am now, but with something else to nag you about.

8:... And if we then procured absolute certainty for you about **that**?

Z:... Then I'd just carry on some more until I hit my next uncertainty.

8: Right.

So, there are three versions of you. Two of these versions of you are standing on opposite sides of a wall called uncertainty. On the darkly shadowed side of the wall there is the version of you who is plagued by doubt, and on the bright, sunny side is the version of you who is joyfully, playfully creating his reality. There is nothing anyone at all can do for the version of you who is on the dark side in order to make him feel happy, safe or okay. Only he can help himself. And he helps himself by making the choice to stop fearing his own uncertainty. Every time you choose to trust yourself and to love the process, you climb the wall and cross over into the light. When you are on the bright side, then you are the version of self who is playing with creation. And the longer you spend on the bright side, the more you see that you are safe there and that you can trust yourself. As long as you stand in your own truth and follow your inner-most heart, you will always be safe and okay. Even as you traverse great change, such as the death of your physical body; even then you will be safe and okay.

And it is absolutely essential that you do learn to hear your God-Self speaking to you through the portal of your heart... and learn to trust this! You see, it will always be possible to bring uncertainty to your mind. Always. But when you cease fearing it and begin loving it instead then, obviously, it will not trouble you. And how you feel about it is very much your choice.

Initially you will have to work hard at the choice. In due course you will master it and there will be no more fear. But there will always be uncertainty. Always. And this is a wonderful thing because that means you will always have options. You will always be able to create. There will always be scope for growth and change.

Z: I see. And the third version?

8: Which "third version"? There is no third version.

Z: But... you said...

8: Okay (he laughs) I am just playing with you. The third version is the version of self who has no uncertainty whatsoever. But I meant it when I said that there is no third version. Because if you have no uncertainty at all, then you have no options and no choices. There is nothing to create. This means that this version is truly, utterly and completely dead. Which is another way of saying that he does not exist.

There is no-one and nothing that has no uncertainty. Uncertainty is life. It is growth. It is existence.

Z: It's taken me a while to really get this. I see I have actually gotten you to explain everything twice. I thank you for your patience and kindness. I think I do finally get it.

8: That is good.

And now I shall finish where I began. Now we shall make of you a mystic.

Are you ready?

Z: (laughs) I guess so. But how?

8: Do you agree with me when I say, "*You always get exactly what you create*"?

Z: I am seeing that to be more and more so in my life as I proceed. Yes. I agree that it must be true.

8: So then you'll agree that the more you focus on something, the more you will get of it?

Z: That is logically correct and also congruent with my own experience. Yes.

8: So what will happen if you **love** the uncertainty? Really love it with an open heart and so, focus on it and stare deeply into it?

Z: Uhh... you'll get more of it. A **lot** more of it.

8: Yes. Exactly. The mystery will deepen. It will enshroud you. You will come to touch and experience more and more of the great unfathomable mystery. And because you do not fear it, you do not feel you need to handle it, control it and manage it... you do not feel you need to have a comfortable explanation for it... you can allow the experience to be what it is and just **be** in it. You see?

Z: Yes...?

8: Okay. So then. Can you agree with me that the infinite Source-God is way, way, way beyond your capacity to even begin to comprehend in Its fullness? And is therefore, in greatest part, a profound mystery?

Z: Obviously. Yes.

8: Then you should be able to make the logical leap which is this: to embrace the mystery with an open heart is to bring yourself closer to experiencing direct union with the divine!

When you really open yourself to the mystery, you bring it forward into your experience. And you do so without the need to make it less than it is. You release your need to dissect and reductively understand that which you experience. You let it **be**. You let yourself **be**. You let God **be**. You allow yourself to experience the ONE with all of your being instead of trying to fit It into the tight little confines of your mind.

You experience the ONE with **all** your being.

And **this** is the beginning of the path to true ecstatic union with the ONE.

Z: Oh my God!

8: Yes! Exactly!

And so? Is that what you seek? Do you seek ecstatic union with the divine?

Z: With all my heart, I do! I have had hints and tastes of this in some very deep meditations and certainly in my Mountain Experience. But my heart yearns for more. I want to **know** God with all my being. I want to feel a more permanent sense of oneness with all beings and all things everywhere. I have been striving for this for quite some time now – trying to find a way to experience it deeply and fully.

8: I'll take that as a firm "yes" then (he smiles). And of course your spirit-family and I know of your striving and your yearning. It is a part of your ascension process that you feel this and that you desire it. And *The Ascension Papers* are our way of responding to that. You **are** going to experience the complete union with the divine that you desire. But first there is some work to do. And that is **exactly** what we are doing here. We are doing the work. And this particular chapter is about us working with doubt and uncertainty. And I am here to tell you that your uncertainty is not only where your areas of creativity lie, but it is also where you will find this experience that you so deeply desire. It is where you will, in a sense, find God.

Z: Wow, 8, that's gorgeous. I have never thought about it like that.

8: Such thinking is **not** encouraged in the system in which you live. It causes people to cease to be manipulable. Not only do you go cold-turkey on religion, but you also give up on things such as politics and war and hatred and violence and... all of that sadness. Such thinking takes you out of the system. It causes you to ascend. So it isn't taught or encouraged.

Some of the only places it was systematically taught in your reality were the mystery schools that you were wondering about. Thousands of years ago these schools were established to transmit the knowledge of the ancients. Information that came from the remnants of older civilisations. Individuals who sought profound spiritual training could go to these mystery schools. Different schools took different approaches, but one of the cornerstones of many of them was training in understanding fear; learning that fear is a tool that can be used, but that it is not to be the controlling principle. As the initiates in the mystery schools came to truly master their fear, they would be willing to approach the Great Mystery also without fear. They would be willing to experience the divine directly. But, of course, the mystery schools' initiates – or mystics – also lost all fear of the leaders of their world. Royalty and clergy found their mutual interests were being undermined by the teachings of these schools. After all, if you begin to experience the divine directly, would you think another mortal man is worthy of being bowed to? Would you find his petty dictates to be worth following? And what interest could all the folderol of religion hold for you if you have embraced the eternal mystery? Would you listen to a man making utterances about how God demands this thing and that thing from you when you have experienced the divine directly within your own heart?

And so it came to be that these mystery schools were driven underground for that very reason. Those in power identified the mystery schools as threatening to their status. They struck back with vigour. The mystery schools were either crushed and silenced or they became secret, hidden organisations. A number of them hid their true teachings behind layers of secrecy; the outermost layers appearing to be ordinary societies of guildsmen or groups of "spiritual enquiry" and the like. There would be tests and pledges and secret swearings-in that would indoctrinate members deeper and deeper into the organisation. Until, eventually, after greatly proving yourself, you might slowly become privy to their true secrets.

The problem with this is that the very act of hiding the mystery teachings and making them the sole property of the secret, select few, changed the nature of these teachings. The ones who held the knowledge in these now secret societies became enamoured of their own egos and they ceased trying to share what was known. They felt important and special for the fact that they had attained the lofty heights that allowed them access to this information. And of course this also became a means for personal enrichment and the wielding of power. So, instead of being instruments of shining the light, these organisations transformed into being instruments of the very darkness that they were created to resist. The great ancient teachings became secondary. The ranks and structures and vows and paraphernalia of the organisation became primary. And so it all contorted into near meaninglessness. And the ancient wisdoms were all but lost. The darkness seemed to have overwhelmed the light.

It is so that wisps of the great teachings of the mystery schools live on today, hidden in secret and arcane groups, but the process of unlocking them essentially invalidates them. Which is ironic and sad.

And so it is that the time now comes for these groups to see that everything has changed. It is now time for them to complete their journey and make available to all their treasure house of knowledge. In so doing they shall return to true service. This will be their final test – if they have the courage to do so.

But we shall not bait our breath for them. Whether they do or not will be of import to themselves only. Those who thirst for the essence of the knowledge will find it, irrespective of what the holders of the ancient mysteries do or don't do. The Light is rising and it is now possible to reach you and teach you what you need to know in many different ways. The awakening is happening and there is nothing anyone on your planet can do to stop it. We will touch your heart and help you to find your way without all the hocus-pocus of secret handshakes in the dark.

Z: Wow, what a story, 8. I had no idea! But I want to back-track a bit. The mystery schools were driven underground because they undermined the power of the religious authorities? But what I don't understand is how it came to be that we gave our power away to the religions in the first place.

8: That is a very long story. I'll get to it some time soon. For now, just observe in yourself how easy it is to fear the unknown. It is not strange to do so. Out there in the dark there might lurk a tiger to gobble you up! (he smiles) So the unknown can be scary. And it is easy to fear the unknown that lies beyond death. And so it is that you might be willing to have intermediaries tell you about God and about how life works and about what you should, and should not, be doing while you are alive in order to ensure your safety and happiness after death. You would then be willing to place religions and scriptures and clerics (who themselves are but confused and doubting men) between your own heart and the ONE.

You most certainly can do this if you wish, but then do not wonder why you cannot directly experience the ONE. You cannot because it is nearly impossible to see anything through all those thick, obfuscatory layers of demagoguery, doctrine and dogma.

Z: I understand.

8: And now, before I wrap this all up, there is a little gift I want to share with you.

Z: A gift? What is it?

8: To start with, let me ask you this: have you thought to ask yourself what would happen if you **didn**'t have another Singularity Event?

Z: What? Where did that come from? No. I haven't.

8: You see? Still you have fear! You don't even want to **look** at that possibility. And because you won't look at it, it has power over you. **Look at it**. What would happen?

Z: Okay. I'll look at it. Each Singularity Event is an amazing, happy experience of reconnecting with the divine that precipitates my ascension into the next dimension. If that didn't happen, then how would I...

Oh. Wait a minute. You have just been telling me about a union with the divine through embracing the mystery. Is this a "different" union with the divine?

8: No. There is only one ONE. And finding union with the ONE in your heart is just that. These Singularity Events are simply your experience of a phase shift in the way you relate to the ONE.

Z: But that means I don't actually **need** a Singularity Event to carry me forward. It's not the event that "makes it happen"; that's just an experience along the way!

8: Bingo! Every day you are raising your consciousness. Every day you are moving closer to oneness. You are already, right now, busy ascending. It is inevitable that you will get there.

Z: So then, there really is nothing to fear!

8: How's that for a gift? And the best part is, you gave it to yourself.

Z: That is simply fabulous, 8. But why didn't you just tell me that right at the beginning?

8: It is not the outcome that is important, my friend. It is the process. How much uncertainty have we played with and how much have we converted to wisdom, growth and learning from doing this? A great deal! The process is where the love lies.

But now I must wrap this all up. To do so, I am going to ask you a few questions.

Tell me again. Is it true that you seek direct, personal ecstatic union with the divine – that you seek to know God directly?

Z: Yes! That is certainly true.

8: And do you agree that you cannot accomplish this by following the teachings and doctrines of a religion and by subjugating your truth to the utterances of other men?

Z: Well, that certainly seems true for me. Perhaps others are on their right path if they follow a religion. But that is not right for me.

8: Discernment in action. Very good.

Then, can you see that, in order to accomplish this goal of direct knowing and experience of the ONE, you must be willing to approach It with your heart, and not with your mind? That you must be willing to plumb the mystery? To experience it as **it** is without demanding to understand it and contain all your experiences in your mind?

Z: Yes. I follow that. And I agree.

8: So you embrace the mystery?

Z: I do.

8: And you understand that this implies a willingness to release your fear of the unknown. It means that you actually **love** uncertainty and embrace it as a great gift.

Z: Yes. I understand it like that. I agree.

8: Then I declare you to be... a mystic!

Z: Ha ha! 8, that is fabulous!

8: It is. And see what you have just agreed to: that you embrace uncertainty as a gift. Remember the challenge right at the beginning of this chapter?

Z: Oh my goodness, yes! You have won!

8: No my friend. It is **you** who have won.

And with that, this chapter is done!

* * * * *

CHAPTER 10.
WHAT IS EVIL?

Zingdad: Hi 8.

8: Hello my dear friend. What are we going to talk about today?

Z: Gee, 8, I was going to ask you that.

8: Consider it open mic night at Club 8 (he smiles). You choose the subject.

Z: Well, there **is** something that has been on my mind a bit. It is the matter of "evil".

You and J-D have both stated that everyone creates their own reality. You have made the case that everyone, through their choices, creates all the things that have happened in their lives. Even the bad things. But that has got me wondering... does this mean there is no such thing as evil? And if there **is** such a thing... what exactly is it?

8: Ah, yes. A very interesting question. Do you want the short answer or the long answer?

Z: I guess shorter is probably better...

8: All right then. The short answer is:

"If there is such a thing as evil, then it is an opportunity to learn about love."

Z: That's it?!?

8: Yes. That's it.

Z: No no no no no no no no. You don't understand. I'm talking about **evil** here. I'm talking about things such as people who are willing to commit genocide – murdering whole populations of other people for the sake of power or wealth or political expediency. I'm talking about terrorists who have no regard for the sanctity of life. And people who would commit rape. People who would abuse children and babies. You know? That's what I'm asking about. Real evil. And what about demons? Are there really such beings? And is there really such a thing as demonic possession? I want to know all of it. And while we are at it, I want to know if there is such a being as Lucifer. You know... Satan... The Devil... him. Does he really exist? **That** is what I want to know about. Once and for all, I want to know about all that dark stuff so I can figure out what to do about it. And please, 8... you can't be wanting to tell me that it's all just an opportunity to "*learn about love*"! Surely? If you had incarnated on Earth you'd know that there is some really, really atrocious stuff going on down here!

8: Ah. I see. So apparently you want the long answer then.

Z: The long answer?

8: I just said that the short answer is, "*If there is such a thing as evil, then it is an opportunity to learn about love*". That doesn't seem to please you. So we'll do the long answer instead. It will be, by far, our longest conversation yet. It will wend its way past numerous fascinating points and then eventually arrive at the same end-point as the short answer: "*If there is such a thing as evil, then it is an opportunity to learn about love.*" And then, when we have arrived at that point, you will want to know more about love itself. And so that will be our next chapter: "What is Love?"

Z: You seem pretty sure about all this.

8: I've seen this discussion from many perspectives. I know what to expect.

So now. It seems to me that you want us to address two basic questions. First, "*What is evil?*" Second, "*How should one respond to the presence of evil?*" And, finally, you want to know about this little list of horrors that you have come up with. We will deal with that under the heading, "*Manifestations of evil.*"

How does that sound?

Z: Thank you, 8. That sounds right.

8: Okay then, let's get started. Question 1:

WHAT IS EVIL?

We need to agree on a definition for evil before we can properly discuss it. Otherwise we might have different things in mind and all manner of misapprehensions might creep in.

Z: I agree.

8: Good. Then how do you feel about this definition for evil:

"Evil is any action, which seems to take away a being's right to choose."

Z: Umm. Well... I don't know about that. That doesn't seem quite right. That seems... a bit... lame.

8: Lame? You clearly have not given this due consideration! I'll explain this to you, but in order to do so, I need you to name three actions that you would consider to be evil.

Z: Three evil actions? All right. How about rape, murder and theft?

8: That will do very well for the purposes of this example. Let's start with rape.

Let's say we have two people: Person A and Person B. They are both adults of sober mind and in full possession of all their faculties. They are also strangers to one another and have had no previous dealings whatsoever.

Z: Right.

8: Now, if Person A were to approach Person B, and say something like, "*I'd really like to have sex with you; would you like to have sex with me too?*" would that be evil?

Z: Err... no.

Somewhat forward.

And probably not the most successful strategy I've ever heard of.

But it's not evil.

8: Good. And then, if person B, said, "*No thank you,*" and the two of them went their separate ways, would that be evil?

Z: No, obviously not.

8: And what if person A said, "*Yes, sure,*" and they actually **did** have sex?

Z: Then they'd both be very, very easy (laughs).

8: I concede (he smiles). But still this isn't actually evil?

Z: Not in any way that I can see. Two consenting adults, who know what they want, agreeing to have sex? That's not evil. It's not **my** style to have sex with strangers and I personally can think of all kinds of reasons why it's a bad idea. But that's me. If there are two people out there agreeing to it, then that's their stuff. But it's certainly not evil.

8: Now let's see what happens when we remove the element of choice from one of the participants in the equation. Now Person A approaches person B and offers person B no choice whatsoever but simply coerces person B, by force or threat, into non-consensual sex. Is that evil?

Z: That's rape. And yes, I very much do think that's evil.

8: Well then, that is my point exactly. It isn't the **act** that is evil. It is the fact of someone feeling that their choices have been taken away. **That** is what is evil.

Z: Ah yes. I do see your point.

8: And the exact same case can be made with every single other act that you might try to define as evil. To further illustrate my point, let us look at another of the actions that you named: murder.

What if Person A approached Person B and said, "*Would you like me to terminate your connection with your body?*"

And Person B replies, "*Yes, please.*"

What then?

Z: Hmm. That would be weird.

I suppose, at a push, I can envisage a circumstance where this could happen. If Person B, for example, is terminally ill and suffering unbearable pain and Person A, out of a feeling of compassion, offers to help Person B to die. This sort of thing does happen sometimes. It's called assisted suicide.

8: In the culture you currently inhabit there are many taboos around death and dying which spring from the powerful illusion that death is final. That it is your end. There have been other cultures on your planet that have known that death is simply a transition. Like going to sleep before again waking up. Like breathing out before again breathing in. This view is the predominant view in more advanced cultures on other planets too. It is a more beneficial perspective, as it allows you to be less rigid and fearful around the notion of death. And in such cultures, if it happens that a being comes to a place where they feel that their path is best served by their departure from the mortal plane, then that being might find a way to leave on their own, or they might be assisted to go. Their passing might even be ritualised into a grand celebration where some "holy person" is responsible for the termination of the body connection. Such things would seem abominable to most in your culture but only because your context is mostly one of a desperate fear of death. From the context of such other civilisations it can be a beautiful and glorious thing.

Z: That's most interesting, 8. I can see how that might be.

8: But this is not how it is in your culture. Choosing to terminate your connection with your body is seldom seen as an acceptable choice in your culture, is it?

Z: No it really isn't. In fact suicide is actually considered to be a crime in many countries. I've always thought that to be odd. I mean how are you going to punish the "criminal" who has just killed himself? But anyhow, as a result of this taboo, assisted suicide is one of those legal and ethical morasses. In some countries it is legally permissible and in others it isn't. And there certainly are ethical considerations that need to be addressed.

8: Are there really? Well you go ahead and address them all you like. For myself, I am quite clear on what I hold to be right. In this regard, as in all others, my position is this:

YOUR RIGHT TO CHOOSE

Whoever you are, whatever the situation, I believe in your right to choose for yourself.

I believe it is your job to know best what is right for you. And no-one should therefore take from you your right to choose.

If you feel you need advice or guidance in making any choice, then those whom you hold to be the wisest and best informed may be asked to assist you in making your choice. And these ones have the right to agree to assist you, to refuse to assist you, or to ask for fair compensation for assisting you. If they agree to assist you, then they must take responsibility for their assistance.

If you are somehow incapacitated and are therefore not in a position to be able to choose, then those whom you love most must choose for you and must take responsibility for their choice.

If you are somehow incapacitated and you find that you cannot enact the choices you have made for yourself, then you have the right to ask someone whom you consider competent to assist you in enacting that choice. And that person has the right to agree to assist you, to refuse to assist you, or to ask for fair compensation for assisting you. And they must take responsibility for the assistance they have rendered.

And **that** is what is right for me. And I have no doubt that this is right for me because, quite simply, this is what I want for myself now and would want for myself if I were ever incarnated in a system such as yours. In every situation I would always want to be able to choose for myself. I would never want to be at the mercy of some system – legal or otherwise – to decide what is best for me. What does a legal system care about me? What does it know of my unique situation and my experiences? Nothing. Legal systems and the like should be the final fallback position for when all else fails, not the first point of reference.

Z: What you say seems right and valid to me. I agree with this. Thank you, 8.

8: I'm glad you find value here. But the original point of this intellectual perambulation was actually to address the issue of death when there is choice involved. If you are offered the choice to have someone terminate your life and you have the absolute right to accept the offer or to reject it... then...

Z:... then I agree, this is not evil. I stand with you on this one. And I also say that I would always want the right to choose for myself. And I would therefore want to grant others that same right to choose. This is not evil. This is moral and right. That is my position too.

8: And everyone else can decide for themselves?

Z: Yes. Of course they have their own choices to make. As long as their choices do not take from me my right to choose for myself.

8: Hmm... yes... choices. You see the beauty of it? If we are saying that taking away the right to choose is evil, then offering someone more and more choices is... what?

Z: Well, if taking someone's right to choose away is evil, then offering someone more choices would be the opposite of evil.

8: That is a good answer.

Z: But what is the opposite of evil? Love?

8: It is hard to answer this question because, from my perspective, evil is a temporary, illusory experience and Love is a very powerful, very real, eternally valid force. I'd say love is certainly the correct response to evil. Love is that which quenches evil. But is it the opposite of evil? No.

The closest thing I can name as the opposite of evil would have to be "choice" or perhaps "creation".

Z: Okay. It was just a point of curiosity anyway.

8: Let's move on then and finish this little section of the discussion with the final point. You named theft as the third evil act. So let's look at this.

How would it be if Person A were to ask Person B, "*May I have your television set and your hi-fi, please?*"

There is surely nothing evil about that?

Z: I wouldn't think so. If Person A agrees to Person B's request, then it is a gift that is given. That's not evil, that's just generosity. And if Person A said, "*No,*" and Person B accepted that and went on his way, then there is also no harm done.

8: That's right. And we can play this out with as many more examples of what you might call evil behaviours as you like. The bottom line will always be that evil is only perceived to be done when choice seems to be removed. Put the choice back in and there is no evil.

Z: I see that, thanks 8. And thanks for your patience with the explanation too. I can certainly see your perspective that evil is the removal of the right to choose. But I'm not sure that's the **whole** of the story. I mean... what about a different definition like, "evil is the desire to cause another great harm" or "evil is harm for its own sake" or something like that?

8: I understand your desire to frame evil in terms of something "wrong" like "causing harm" but the problem is that such a definition just doesn't stand up to scrutiny. If I desire to cause you harm but instead of just doing it to you, I first ask you and you agree to it then...

Z: Well then I guess, it's just like all of your examples above. If I agree to it, then it isn't evil. If I have the right to say "no", and you respect that, then obviously...

Okay. If there is a hole in your argument, then I really can't see it. I accept your definition, "evil is the removal of the other's right to choose."

8: Okay, good. Except you missed something. I said:

> *"Evil is any action, which **seems to** take away a being's right to choose."*

That part about "*seems to*" is very important. What it means is that I cannot **really** take your right to choose away. No one can do that. Not really. But you and I can agree to create the illusion thereof for ourselves.

Z: Ah, yes. By now I have had enough exposure to these concepts to see where this is going. It's the whole victim/perpetrator thing again, isn't it? I cannot truly be your victim. I can only have the illusion that I am.

8: Now you're getting it.

Z: And in the previous chapter you said that uncertainty was what presented us with choices. You said that these choices were creation and growth and life. You said that when there is absolute certainty then there are no more choices and therefore no more life. And since we are all a part of the ONE and none of us can be destroyed, that is not possible. So, in conclusion, if it is true that I cannot ever have absolute certainty then, in the same way, it must also be true that you cannot actually ever take away my right to choose!

8: Good! And so you see how all of the concepts tie in together – how they all interrelate and form one consistent, congruent whole?

Such is the nature of truth that you were asking me about in Chapter 8.

Z: I begin to *feel* that now.

8: Excellent. And that feeling is *your* truth. That feeling of *rightness* when everything adds up and is in balance and harmony in your being... that is your truth saying "yes". You stumbled on this one a few times. You previously confused your ego-desires and your excitement with your truth. And it was necessary that you did this. You needed to see that mistake and learn from it. And then you made a new choice to always find your heart's truth and to honour and respect that. And so, here we are now. Now you are really finding your own truth inside yourself. It is **that** feeling of everything being **right** within yourself.

Z: I've got it, 8. Thank you. But we've gotten a little off track.

8: Not really. We'll come back to this realisation about "your truth" in a little while. For now, we have just discovered that no-one can truly take away your right to choose. But we can, of course, share an illusion in which I can *seem to* take from you your right to choose.

Z: So then evil is an illusory thing?

8: This is my perspective, yes. It is something that you can, within this reality you currently inhabit, **seem** to experience. It can seem very real to you. But it is still just an illusion. Let me tell you a truth about good and evil. It goes like this:

"There is not a single thing that is either good or evil, but that you feel that way about it."

Z: You're saying that nothing is intrinsically evil. Nothing at all. But some things might still feel evil to me?

8: That is exactly what I'm saying. Or I can rephrase it like this: evil does not exist objectively but it might certainly be experienced subjectively.

Z: Uhh... That is another way of saying I can feel like I am experiencing evil, but that does not mean it really, truly exists?

8: Correct.

Z: Okay, wow. I don't really know what to do with this information. Because I can totally get this intellectually. I've seen the argument and even felt the truth of it in my heart but... I don't know if I am yet willing to accept that all the wickedness and vileness, all the atrocities that have ever been committed and that continue to be committed are... what? An agreed-upon co-created illusion?

8: I understand. And that is why we must have this conversation. Because you must come to see it this way before you can ascend to Unity Consciousness. So I present you with a choice: on the one hand you can choose to continue to label certain beings and their behaviours as evil and, in so doing, you can keep yourself distanced and divorced from them, so that you can remain in a state of judgement of them and so you can keep feeling superior to them. On the other hand you can choose to be willing to come to an understanding that no-one is truly "other" than you, that nothing is eternally unlovable or unforgivable.

Z: And that's the choice? If I am not willing to come to see it this way then I can't ascend to unity consciousness?

8: That is the truth of it. As with all things, you always have a choice. This time your choice is between unity consciousness and duality (or separation) consciousness. Understand that there is no right or wrong about what you choose and no judgement of you for the choices you make. But what you choose defines who you are and creates the reality that you will experience. And, quite simply, you cannot become a being of Unity Consciousness and you cannot reside in a unity reality without being willing to see all as **one**, without being willing to see the "other" as "self" and without being willing to let go of the mechanisms of separation, such as judgement and hatred.

You see, my dear friend, this is the choice offered to you by duality. You can accept the offer of duality and continue to see yourself as separate from all else and travel ever outwards on the path of separation with fear as your motivator. Or, on the other hand, you can choose love. If you adhere to a choice for love, then you step onto the path of unity. You begin to travel back Home to oneness. It is true that you can, for some while, travel the path of love whilst still clinging to the illusion of separation. This is what happens with those who choose either the "Service to Other" or the "Service to Self" modes of being. And that is fine if that is what you choose. But sooner or later these paths too will converge and these beings will realise that the concepts of Other and Self are not what they first thought. That indeed there is only oneness.

If you follow what I am saying, then you will understand that it might seem as if there are many possible options and choices on your path. But really, it is not so. There is really only one choice.

Either you accept **all** as being one, or you create more separation.

The choice is yours. And you cannot move towards being one with All That Is, whilst still at the same time holding onto the view that some beings are so despicable and unlovable that you can simply refuse to accept them as being part of the oneness. That you can label them "evil" and thereby damn them to eternal darkness.

All is one. Or it is not. Your choice.

Z: You have explained that very well, thank you 8. I get it now. I must choose between two ideas. On the one hand there is the idea of certain beings being beyond all possibility of ever being loveable. And so we label them and their activities as evil. On the other hand is the understanding that all of this is just a temporary illusory state. And that all beings are inherently worthy of love and are a part of God. That I am truly one with all beings and all things everywhere.

8: Yes. That is the choice.

Z: Well then, I choose oneness.

8: That is well. But if you make this choice half-heartedly, then it is of no value. You must make it completely and truly from the heart before it will result in a change in your experience of life.

Z: I understand and I am ready to make that choice. Will you help me to release the last vestiges of the beliefs and choices that keep me on the path of separation?

8: Yes. I will. And that is why I choose to have this conversation about evil today.

Z: Why **you** chose? This topic was **my** choice!

8: Yes. Exactly. You will still understand this eventually.

Z: (I smile and shake my head) Okay, so let me try to summarise what I have understood from you about evil:

It is when I feel that I have had my options taken away from me that I feel as if evil is being done to me. But these occasions when I might experience this are illusory. That is to say that I have actually chosen the experience of having my choices taken away from me and I can, in fact, always choose other. No matter how it might seem to me at the time.

8: Yes. And the fact that you are experiencing this evil means that you are probably working quite hard at believing that you have no other choice but to experience it. This is what you have chosen. You, as a creator, have created the illusion that you are not a creator. And you, as an inseparable part of the oneness, have created the experience that you are completely separate and alone.

Z: Whew! That's quite a paradox, isn't it, 8?

8: Yes, it is. But is this not consistent with the way the universe would be if you were in fact the creator of your own reality?

Z: It is.

8: And the opposite would also be true. If you were prepared to begin to choose that you were one with all, as you have now chosen, then something interesting would happen: as you make this choice and as it becomes more manifest in your reality, so it would come to be that, in time, you will cease to experience evil.

Z: Really? Choosing for oneness means I will cease to experience evil?

8: Yes. The degree to which you know it to be true that you are really one with All That Is, is the degree to which you will no longer experience evil. You can only experience the illusion of evil whilst you reside in a state of separation. Of duality. Once you remember your intrinsic oneness, then you cannot experience evil being done to you, nor can you contemplate doing it to another. It is only in the state of separation or duality that you can either experience the actions of another being as evil, or indeed contemplate enacting evil upon another being.

Z: Can you explain that to me, 8?

8: Certainly. At the level of oneness it is impossible for me to set out to do any harm to you whatsoever.

Z: Why 8?

8: Precisely because I know that you and I are one! You see, all beings who reside in a place of unity consciousness, directly experience everything that they do to another as being done to themselves. If I hurt you, then instantly, with that very action, I hurt myself in exactly equal measure also. In fact, the hurt I do to you **is** the hurt I do to myself also. That is what happens at the level of unity consciousness. And, as I don't desire to hurt myself, I won't try to hurt you.

You on Earth are residing within an illusion of duality, which means you have an illusion that this is not so. The instrument of "time" is used to separate you from your choices, so you do not see that it is so that everything you do to others you are doing exactly and precisely to yourself also. But we, outside of the illusion of duality, see it directly. We are **one**. We know this. We experience it. What I do to you, I do to myself. So a unity conscious being will never seek to cause harm because that harm **is** harm to self.

Z: Wait a minute, 8, are you saying that everything I do to another I also directly do to myself? Literally?

8: Yes. It is so. But you have a clever illusion of time and space that separates you from your creations so that you can believe that it is not so. But it **is** so. Hurt another and you hurt yourself. You might need to travel a bit of time and space to feel the hurt and so you might not realise that you did it to yourself. And you might be able to tell yourself when the hurt comes back to you that it was another being who did it to you. That is the power of the illusion. But it is none-the-less so; everything you do to another, you do to yourself. Therefore it would be very wise to, "*Do unto others exactly as you would have them do unto you.*" That is the best way to get treated as you wish to be treated.

Z: Okay, so if I walk up to a stranger and slap him through the face and run away then, after some time he will find me and hit me back?

8: Try not to be so simplistic in your thinking. Here is a better description:

What kind of a person would you be if you could just walk up to a stranger and slap him? Or perhaps a better way of asking this is, what kinds of beliefs are you expressing about yourself and about life, when you do this? Perhaps you are expressing a bratty child-like, "*I don't give a damn and I can get away with anything,*" kind of a feeling? So you take advantage of that stranger's unsuspecting, trusting nature. He is not defensive when you approach. So you slap him and run away. What you have actually done is shock him out of a feeling of trusting safety. You have stolen from him some of his innocence.

Now, it might seem to you that you selected this stranger at random, but you did not. You and he had a contract. This was agreed upon at higher levels. Quite simply, his soul needed this experience for reasons of its own. But we'll not overcomplicate matters. We'll let that soul's choices and motivations go. The point is that that soul **did** actually ask for it. And so, at the level of the incarnated personalities, you gave him the gift that he was asking for.

So now, time passes for you. You move on and have probably totally forgotten that incident. Now you are, perhaps, in a bar having a drink. You see a beautiful young lady and decide to go and chat her up. Things proceed well. As you talk to her she seems like everything you are looking for in a girl. And she seems to really like you too. A romantic entanglement begins. You see each other a few times more and then, just as you are totally falling in love with her, just as you are ready to give your heart to her... you find her in bed with your best friend.

Z: Slap!

8: Exactly. You have just experienced the return of your gift. With a little interest.

You have just felt what it is like to be shocked out of your feeling of trusting safety. You have had your innocence stolen.

And that's okay, because, on a soul-level you asked for it. You needed to know what it was like to feel this. Doing this to the other and having this done to you are two sides of the same coin. Two sides of the same experience. And, on a soul level, you created that. How you respond – what you will **do** with this – that will be up to you.

Do you make choices out of wisdom and compassion that lead you to wholeness and oneness? Or do you make choices out of ignorance and hatred that lead to pain and separation?

Choices, choices, choices.

You always get to choose and you always get the results of your choices.

Z: That was most instructive, thank you, 8. And so, if I apply that to my real-life situation, then I can see that when I previously chose to allow my ego-desires, fears and needs to push the story of the Singularity Event in the direction of a grand rescue for us all...

8: Same thing. In a number of different ways you experienced that being returned to you with interest. You caused others some distress. Those who had followed your works and read the previous version of this book. Some of them came to feel quite considerable pain when things did not transpire as had been promised in 2012. So they experienced feelings of loss, doubt, fear, distrust... You get the idea.

Z: And then I had that returned to me.

8: In a number of ways. You put yourself through the same kind of wringer when things did not transpire as had been written. But that was not sufficient. In order for your soul contract to be concluded, you needed to experience this being done to you.

Z: And now suddenly I understand it. This was why my home was burgled and my laptop stolen, wasn't it?

8: Let's see, shall we? Because you have, understandably, been struggling to make sense of that. So tell me, what were the feelings that this burglary evoked in you?

Z: Loss, doubt, fear, distrust... I get the idea.

8: And then? What did you decide to do with that?

Z: I went through hell, actually. I was so angry and I felt so violated. My home didn't feel safe any more. And I lost a lot of work that was not backed up that I'll never get back. There was stuff I was working on that I'll have to start again on and...

8: ... not to diminish your pain because I know it was acute for you. But that is not the question. What did you **do** with that?

Z: I... ah... well. Not much. I decided to try to understand how I had created that experience. I started to engage you in conversation. And I learnt a lot through it all about boundaries and about getting the results of our choices. But I didn't ever feel like I had closure. I didn't ever feel like I understood **why** it had happened. But now it all comes together. Now, in this conversation it has all landed for me. I finally get it.

8: So you can let go of that too?

Z: Yes. Now I can let go of it.

8: And your burglar?

Z: He was never found.

And at first I could not stop myself from wishing all kinds of evil upon him. I wanted him caught and then I wanted him to come to harm, for what he had done to me – and to Lisa too of course! But then... well... I don't need to take you through my whole long process, but really I came to realise that he is obviously just another human being dealing with his own fear and lack. He took from me because he felt that was the only way to get what he needed. I don't need to know his story. I can just let him go and hope that he makes better choices in future. For his own sake.

8: So you can let go of him also?

Z: Yes. I have let go of the whole situation now. It's over and I have learned and grown a great deal.

8: And so? Have you just made your choices out of ignorance and hatred? Or have you made choices out of wisdom and compassion?

Z: It took a while, but I definitely feel I got to wisdom and compassion in the end. In great part, thanks to your assistance.

8: Every step of the way, it was about what you were willing to choose. Don't diminish that. And since you chose from wisdom and compassion, what you get is wholeness and oneness.

You actually *felt* that happen, didn't you? As you made the choice to come to acceptance of the loss of your laptop, so you found the necessary insight arriving that allowed you to begin to move on. As you chose for that and opened yourself to greater wisdom and grace, so you came to additional new insights that allowed you re-write the Singularity Event story in its *rightness*. And as you concluded the re-telling of the Singularity Event, so you are now able to come to a complete understanding of the situation with the laptop. These two experiences were energetically entangled for you. They were resolved together for you.

And now you can see that all has unfolded in divine right order. All have gotten exactly what they asked for and needed, and all continue to choose as they see fit and get the results of their choices.

Balance and harmony.

Job done.

Z: Yes. Job done.

It's amazing how these seemingly completely unrelated things are actually *for me* energetically linked. And how they are now resolved and released together.

8: You are now slowly becoming aware of your own creator nature. You are now beginning to see the cause-and-effect nature of your experiences. When you see this clearly you cannot any more think of yourself as being a victim to random events.

Others can, of course, look at your life and think that you are ascribing meaning where there is none. That these two things are not related. But you can *feel* how they are related. You know this is true in a way that you cannot deny.

Z: It's true.

I really do arrive at the awareness that I absolutely do create my experiences with my choices and beliefs.

8: I'll tell you something interesting then. Your burglar has had his action repaid to him with interest too. It would not have been to the greater good if he had been "caught". The reasons for this are complicated and unnecessary to our dialogue, but the point is that "Earth justice" involving police and prison was not required or useful here. But do not doubt; your burglar has already had his energetic investment returned and with considerable interest. He took from you the tools of your trade, your means of expressing yourself, your sense of security... and he has experienced far greater loss in all of these same areas.

I am telling you this to re-emphasize this point you are making. It doesn't matter whether you are aware of your own creator nature or not. What you put out, will come back to you.

Z: *"Everyone always gets **exactly** what they have created."*

8: You did, and so did your burglar. There are no victims, only creators. And of course,

> *"What you do to another you do to yourself also."*

Z: I really do understand this now. So here in separation, we are inside the illusion. We experience ourselves as causing each other harm and taking from each other the right to choose. But this really is just an illusion. We are actually just doing all of this to ourselves. And you guys in the higher dimensions and in other realities and what-not, you don't have this illusion of time and space, so you can't believe you are separate from each other. You **know** that, whatever you do, you do to yourself. Is that right?

8: For those of us who are of unity consciousness, this is so. If your every experience shows you unambiguously that you are one with all other parts of reality, then you'd be pretty unobservant if you didn't accept it to be true. That is how it is for us and this is how it is now slowly becoming for you.

Z: So you guys would never consciously choose to hurt anyone else because that would immediately result in your hurting yourself.

8: That's what I am saying.

And the other thing, of course, is that a being of true unity consciousness cannot experience hurt in the same way you believe you can. We do not have mortal forms that can be harmed, so we cannot imagine that we can be physically damaged or killed. The hurt we can endure is what you might call emotional hurt, or possibly, psychological hurt. And these hurts are understood differently from the way you understand them. If we experience these, then we do not think that they have been inflicted upon us by another being or by some external experience. We understand, quite simply, that they are the results of our own choices. If I am hurt in an interaction with another being, then I understand that my own choices have caused me pain. The interaction with the "other self" is simply the catalyst. Indeed, if I am observant, I will see that this is all just a gift that shows me which of my choices and beliefs do not serve me.

A being of unity consciousness cannot experience evil being done to it, nor can it contemplate doing evil to another Self.

Z: I think I understand this now.

8: That's good. Then you will understand that it is only inside a duality reality, from the perspective of separation, when you do not know that you are ONE, that a being might wish to act in a way that is deeply hurtful and destructive to themselves and to others. Only in such a reality might they experience their inner turmoil in such a way that it can cause them to hate themselves so badly that they can be willing to do all manner of atrocious things to each other.

Z: I see.

8: And equally it is so that, it is only inside a duality reality, from the perspective of separation, when you do not know that you are ONE, that you might look at the actions of such a being and be able to say, "*You are evil.*"

Outside of duality you will know that you, and the being with whom you are interacting, are both being shown how the choices that you have previously made have resulted in some pain and confusion for yourselves. The miracle of the situation is the way in which this interaction has perfectly brought two disparate Selves together for an interaction that perfectly shows both of you exactly how those choices are not serving you. Before this interaction you might not have seen this. But now, as a result of the interaction, you can see it clearly. And now that you **have** seen it, you can choose differently. And when you have made a better choice, the previous choice and its results can be healed and loved and re-integrated.

It's a wondrous gift, you see.

But, inside of duality, you might very well experience this interaction as evil. It might be the victim's experience that they were innocently going about their life when they were horribly victimised by some evil-doer. And it might be the perpetrator's experience that they had a horrible, deprived life, which drove them to behave in this terrible way. And no-one can tell either of them that their experiences are not valid. It **is** their experience!

Every experience presents you with a choice. Almost everyone playing the duality game will, after every such interaction, make another victim-based choice. Which will serve to keep them in duality and invite more such interactions. But it is possible to escape this trap. It is possible, instead, to accept that the interaction is an experience that you have brought to yourself as a result of your choices. If you can do this, then you can begin to look to yourself to make new choices that better suit you. It might help to realise that all of these experiences play out within an illusion. And that there is a greater truth at hand, which is that, at another level, you and the other player both know that this is something you have chosen and agreed upon.

Z: That's very hard to do though, 8.

8: It is. But it was never meant to be easy. I'll explain this in a moment with, "The Monastic Order Parable".

Z: (laughs) The **what**!?!

8: (smiles) You'll see. But before we can get to that, I'd like to first offer you an illustration of how a victim relationship could originate.

Imagine now that you are no longer incarnated. You are here with me in spirit-space and we are planning a new lifetime. I come before you and say to you:

"You know me, I am 8. I have played the role of Spirit-Guide to you when you were lost in duality and helped you to find your way home. I am also your dearly beloved friend and on one level we are partners of long standing. On

another level we have found oneness together. You know me. And now I come to you with my need. In order for me to proceed as I desire, I really need to understand the experience of the victim state. I feel I have a need to incarnate and then experience what it is like to place myself utterly in another's power such that they might treat me very badly and then cruelly kill me. I need to play that out, see how it feels and see how I respond to that. Are you willing to incarnate into a duality system with me where we might Veil ourselves and play out that scenario? Will you play the role of perpetrator for me?"

So then, if you agreed to my proposal, we could have a situation where we both send a part of ourselves beyond the Veil and I get to experience being a powerless victim and you get to play the role of the evil perpetrator. We see what that is like and we learn something about ourselves and then we deal with what we have learned.

You see?

Z: I follow, yes.

8: And can you see that this doesn't actually make you evil? You have simply helped me to experience that which I desired.

Z: I get that, yes. Thank you for the explanation. But I very much hope that you never do come to me with such a request.

8: And why is that?

Z: Because then I'm afraid I would have to turn you down. I'm very sorry but I will not be your perpetrator. I will not ever seek to hurt you or treat you badly. I will never choose to act in any way towards you other than in love, respect and honour.

8: All right. But why? If I have asked this of you, why will you not do it for me?

Z: Because, my beloved 8, it is wrong for me. Because no matter how much you might need to experience such a role, I have no desire in my heart or in my being to play the opposite part.

8: Why?

Z: Because... I am not willing to do that to myself. Because being your cruel abuser would hurt me too much. In this life, and especially in my past lives, I have seen what it is to be a perpetrator.

> (**Zingdad Note:** see Chapter 1, *"The Wizard"*)

I know what this is and I have no need to know any more of it. I am not willing. I love myself too much to put myself through that and I love you too much to do it to you. That is how I feel in my heart. I'm sorry if I disappoint you.

8: My dear friend! Quite the contrary. Why would that disappoint me?

Z: Because, if I am not willing to be your perpetrator, then you can't have the experiences you feel you need. Isn't it?

8: No, it isn't. Is your world not full of people who are willing to enact some form of victimisation upon anyone who will but allow it?

Z: Yes. I guess so. So you are saying that you will always be able to find **someone** to play that role for you.

8: That's quite right. In actual fact, it's a lot simpler than that. The fact of my desiring some experience creates an imbalance in the field of consciousness. Remember there is actually only one of us here?

Z: Okay... so...

8: So if there is only one of us here, then an aspect of the ONE desiring to experience something, is the same as the ONE desiring it. This means that you can't have the desire without the means of the fulfilment. The ONE can, and will, only express that desire in me if there is also another Self who answers that desire by being willing to play the corresponding role. And when we are done playing our respective roles, we can heal any pain that we have by realising that we are actually ONE, actually the same greater being. And **that** is how it happens. When you are willing to see the horrible, evil, wicked, perpetrator as Self, then you become something greater than you were. Then, you ascend. And the same thing, of course, occurs when you are willing to see the sad, pathetic, weak, dismal victim as Self.

Z: Oh wow, 8. I feel you have just expressed something very important there. I feel it in my soul that this is something of profound importance to me.

8: Not just to you. To everyone who is ready to seek unity consciousness. This is an idea that we'll develop further as we go. But for now I want to turn your question back to you. Given our discussion, what do you now think will happen if I ask you to play perpetrator to me and you turn me down? What then?

Z: Well, in light of this new information, it would seem to me that I am either the right response to your need or I am not. If I am, then I will say "yes", if I am not, then I will say "no". And, as we have discovered, saying "yes" does not make me evil because then I am simply showing you something about yourself. And saying "no", is also okay because, assuredly, there will be *someone* for whom it is right that they should respond "yes".

8: So, where is the victim? Where is the evil?

Z: There is none! Because I always have a choice. We all do. And when we make our choices we are simply showing ourselves something about ourselves!

8: Right. And at the risk of belabouring the point, if you choose to agree to be my perpetrator, I might come to perceive you as being evil, but only inside the illusion of the game. And it will only be a temporary experience.

Z: Yes, I get that now.

8: And always **you** have the choice to respond in your own highest good. And if you go to your heart and make choices with your deepest truth, then your choices will be in harmony with what the unity conscious part of yourself is also choosing for you.

So you see, all there really is, is choice. You choose and then you experience the results of your choices.

Z: I see that, 8, thanks.

8: So! Let's recap. You now agree with me that beings feel as if evil has been done when they feel their choices have been removed?

Z: Yep. Got that one.

8: And do you also agree that you *actually* always have choices? You might have the illusion that you do not, but if you are willing to take responsibility for yourself and if you are willing to use your guidance and listen to your truth in your own heart, then you will also see through the illusion. Then you will know that you always have choices.

Z: Yes, I get that too. At the level of oneness there is no evil, only choices. And by connecting with my heart, I connect with that which exists at the level of oneness.

8: You are coming along very nicely. Yes. That is well said.

And now, before we move on, I want to briefly revisit my request of you to be my perpetrator. When you chose to turn my request down, what was it that motivated your choice?

Z: Love. I decided that I didn't want to hurt you because I made a choice for love.

8: That's right, you did. You chose to only express yourself in such a way that you would love your expressions. And that is a very fine choice indeed. You chose to let go of the need to create with pain and fear. Now you only create with love. Can you see why that choice would please me?

Z: Yes I can.

8: And when I pressed you for the reasons for your choices, you very nicely illustrated an important point; you expressed the realisation that being my perpetrator would hurt **you** very much. Right? So that means that the beings in your current reality who might be regarded as the great evil ones have apparently caused themselves considerable pain in playing that role for you.

Z: Yes. I can see that. But I still can't approve of what they did, and are still doing!

8: That's fine. This means that they offer you a gift, which costs them very dearly to give. It is the opportunity to choose whether or not you want to be their victim. If you decide you **do** want to be their victim, then there they are! Willing to play the role you want them to play. And if you choose not to play the victim, then you show yourself that you **really** have made that choice. You see, without their extremely well crafted offer, you would not be able to say that you have finally and completely chosen not to be a victim.

Z: I don't follow that exactly...?

8: Okay. I promised we'd get to it and here it is:

The Parable of the Monastic Order

There were once two men of similar ages who were both born into modest circumstances. The one had a very astute business mind, which he conscientiously applied to accumulating wealth. He had barely left his parents' home before he was already doing quite well for himself. By the time he was in his mid-thirties he was by far the richest man in town.

The other man did not pursue wealth and he was not very keen on hard work either. He was a poet and a musician and his favourite thing was to sit all day at the river catching fish and composing songs.

But, as disparate as these two men might have seemed, they both had a deep interest in spiritual matters. They both had a hunger for their own enlightenment. And so it was that they both came to the decision to dedicate themselves totally to their spiritual growth. They each decided that the appropriate way for them to do this was to join the monastery on the hill above their town.

Z: They wanted to be monks?

8: Exactly. And one of the requirements of this monastic order was that the monks take an oath of poverty, give up all their possessions and forswear all future attachment to material goods.

Z: Hah, the rich man would struggle with that!

8: And he did! Given that he had spent his life accumulating wealth, that he was very good at it and that it had come to be his measure of success and the basis of many others' high esteem of him... it was indeed very difficult for him to let go of it. The poor man, on the other hand, had no such difficulty. As he owned almost nothing, he gave up almost nothing!

Z: Yes, I see. But how does this illustrate the point you were making about choosing to stop being a victim?

8: Obliquely. Stay with me and I will get there. You see, as it happens, both of these men **did** take the oath of poverty and both were accepted into the monastery. Both were then brothers of the order and neither had a single physical possession to call their own.

Z: Okay...

8: So what do you think; which of them then knew, to the very depths of his soul, what it is to choose poverty over wealth?

Z: Ah, I see! It is the man who was rich who really knew the value of this decision. He would **really** know what it means to give up on all wealth and possessions.

8: Yes. And so it is for you in this duality-reality you inhabit. You are all very wealthy in opportunities for victimhood. You are invited in a million different ways every single day to be a victim all over again. Every time you turn on the television, open a newspaper or read a magazine, you are being bombarded with messages about your own victimhood, over and over again.

Your political, legal and financial systems exist upon the basis that you are all victims and they strive to keep you in that state.

Your employers need you to be victims so that you keep doing the jobs you hate for the money they offer you.

Everywhere, in every direction you look, you are surrounded by offerings of your own victimhood on a platter.

And it is all terribly compelling and deeply addictive. So you keep believing that it is the good, right and responsible thing to do to get that job, pay that mortgage, buy that insurance against every conceivable disaster, consult with those experts on everything from what is right and moral, to what is true for your soul, to what is good for your health, to what you should be eating, to how you should relate to your own life-partner and how you should treat your own children, to... well, you get the idea... you are addicted to being a victim.

And there are some pretty compelling pay-offs. You get to say, "*It's not my fault! I didn't do it! It's not fair!*" and my personal favourite, "*Why me?*" And you get to feel as if someone else is to blame for everything. "*They wronged me! I was cheated! They never gave me my chance!*" And so you let yourself off the hook from ever having to take responsibility.

Pretty addictive stuff.

And pretty childish too, don't you think?

Z: Yeah, when you put it like that, it sounds as if we're all just brats throwing tantrums.

8: It certainly can look that way sometimes. But that's okay. The point of childhood is that it is there to be experienced, and from those experiences we begin to discover ourselves and decide who we want to be when we grow up. It's a difficult place to be and a bit of tantrum throwing is, I suppose, par for the course. And, given a little time, everyone does indeed grow up. And the very hallmark of growing up is... taking responsibility. That is what a grown-up does. And a spiritually mature being is one who is willing to take absolute responsibility for all of its own experiences.

Z: And a spiritual child doesn't take responsibility? A spiritual child sees itself as a victim?

8: That's right.

Z: Hmmm. So I guess it's time to give up the victim addiction then.

8: Yes. And just like the rich man who gave up his attachment to wealth and temporal power, just like the junkie who gives up an addiction to a drug, so you will be one who knows **to the depths of your soul** that you are finally and completely done with victimhood. When you ascend out of this duality system into your own creator status, you will never again fall foul of believing that you are a victim. You will have seen victimhood in all of its most beguiling guises. You will have vanquished it in your own soul, in your own experience and with your own decisions. You will have created yourself as a creator. Which is, of course, the only legitimate way to become a creator-being.

Z: Ha ha! There's that paradox again. But this time we see it from the other side. If we are to be creators, then we must be willing to create that we are creators!

That's just so mind-bogglingly cool.

8: It is said that as a being first awakes to self-mastery, so that being begins to laugh and laugh and laugh. And very often it is so. The solutions to the problems and traps that previously bound you are discovered to be nothing more than great cosmic jokes.

Okay then, let's recap. Tell me what you think: is there really such a thing as evil?

Z: Given what I have come to understand, I would say the answer is both yes and no. It's an illusory thing. If you choose it, allow it and invite it, then you can experience it.

8: You mean,

> *"There is not a single thing that is either good or evil, but that you feel that way about it."*

Z: Ha! Right!

8: But what is the illusion that we are actually experiencing?

Z: We are experiencing the illusion of having our choices taken away.

8: So then you would agree that;

> *"Evil is any action, which seems to take away a being's right to choose."*

Z: Yes, I would agree.

8: Good. Then we are on the same page and we have, I believe, answered the first question, "*What is evil?*"

Z: Yes, we have, thank you.

8: And that sets us up perfectly to address the second question, which is:

HOW SHOULD ONE RESPOND TO THE PRESENCE OF EVIL?

And so? Do you want to take a shot at it? How do **you** feel you should respond to the experience of evil?

Z: It seems that such an experience calls for a transcendent moment. It asks of me that I choose to remember that I really am one with all others. That I choose, and act, from a place of great love.

8: That is very well answered. And it is also in keeping with the other thing I told you about evil which was,

"If there is such a thing as evil, then it is an opportunity to learn about love."

Z: I think I understand this pretty well but, I have to say I don't yet completely *feel* it. And, I'm almost embarrassed to say, there is still an objection to this in my mind.

I feel as if I should be beyond this because it all still comes back to the whole victim/perpetrator/rescuer triangle. And I should have that one sorted by now. We have discussed it so much!

8: Go easy on yourself. It takes a lot of work to release deeply ingrained ideas and beliefs. Allow yourself a little grace. You have one final round to go with this triangle and I have been expecting this conversation.

So... out with it... what is bothering you? Then I can help you to move these insights from your head where you **think** it to be true, to your heart where you **know** it to be true.

THE VICTIM TRIANGLE – ONE LAST TIME

Z: It's like this: I have come to see that evil is an illusion and that, by embracing the oneness, I can release myself from experiencing it. And that's just dandy for me. But what about everyone else who is still suffering with it?

8: Ah. Compassion.

Compassion is a wonderful, and yet terrible, double-edged sword. It allows you to really share in another's experience, which brings you closer to the oneness. But it also attaches you to this other's suffering, which pulls you back into duality.

Let me ask you something. Over the last few years you have been very actively letting go of your own victim consciousness, have you not? You have been moving out of the victim relationships you have had with your world and moving into a new situation where you will be in greater harmony with life, have you not?

Z: You're talking about my move from the city to the forest?

8: That is what happened on a physical level. But, of course, it is the movement that is happening on an emotional and spiritual level that I am more interested in. You have successfully concluded a radical transition in life choices, have you not?

Z: Yes I have, but...

8: So this is the outer-experience of someone who is seeking, and finding, his heart-connection.

If *The Ascension Papers* is the scaffolding, then your life is the structure you have built upon that scaffolding. You should find ways to keep telling your story, to keep sharing with others what you are doing. You will find that it brings you value to share it and others will find value in reading about what you are doing. And, more than that, you will find that doing so expands you. Telling your story will open you to giving even greater gifts.

Z: I can see how that is true. I have started a blog section on my website where I have been writing about my experiences with exiting my city lifestyle and moving to the forest and writing about this has been quite rewarding.

8: In unexpected ways, this will come to yield far greater rewards than you can now imagine.

But that is a side issue. The point is that you have been very active in making these changes to release yourself from your old victim relationships with the world. There has been massive movement in your psyche and this has been reflected in your external world. You have been letting go of victim and you are now discovering yourself to be a creator-being. Right?

Z: Every day more and more.

8: Okay. Well, here comes the question... Does the fact that you are doing this mean that you should insist and demand that everyone else in your world should also do this? Must everyone on the planet do what **you** are doing right now, just because you are doing it? Must every single person make the exact same choices you are making?

Z: No. That doesn't seem reasonable. Of course not.

8: And so, what then about all the many others who still wish to play the victim game? **Must** they stop, right now, just because you decided to stop?

Do you need to first force them to stop playing their victim game before you can go on and play another game? Or are you willing to let them do as they wish while you go and create a new game for yourself with those who share your vision of what constitutes a good game? A game that is more congruent with the kinder, more loving version of yourself that you discover yourself to be?

Z: When you put it like that, then I can see it. Obviously I must be willing to allow them to continue with their victim game if that is what they wish to do.

8: To take from them their right to choose, even if what they are choosing seems, to you, to be cruel and unkind, would be...

Z: Evil?

How odd. It would be evil to take from others their right to experience evil.

8: So then, the fact that there **is** the experience of evil to be had – and the fact that some are playing victim and perpetrator with each other – is this your problem?

Z: No, I guess not. I mean, I know it isn't my problem.

But then, why do I feel guilty for saying so?

8: It is really quite simply that you are experiencing one of your final objections to your decision to cease being a rescuer. You can see that you should be able to let people choose what they want to choose, but when their choices lead them into painful outcomes, that makes you feel uncomfortable. As if it were wrong of you to let them get on with what they have decided they want to do.

Of course you can do whatever you want to do. You can respond to every invitation to dance, exactly as you most desire. But what you should remember is that, with every choice you take, you create yourself. With each choice, you decide what your reality will be like. And if you are choosing to rescue someone, then you are creating yourself as the rescuer. And the rescuer is a part of the victim/perpetrator/rescuer triangle. And all three of those are actually, when properly understood, just victims. If you choose to rescue anyone, then you are still choosing to be a victim and giving up your divine right to be a creator-being. If you choose that, then you continue to reside inside this separation reality at the level of duality consciousness.

Z: It's disappointing to realise that I am **still** not done with this.

8: Rescuer is the final hurdle for the ascending soul. Of all the victim addictions, rescuer is by far the most difficult to kick, and it is also the last one to be released. In the analogy of the monastic order we used above, finally letting go of rescuer would be like a tycoon being able to choose poverty and enter the monastery.

Z: Why is rescuer so difficult to release?

8: Well, with rescuer you get to tell yourself a story about what a good and noble person you are being. You are **helping**! That is **good**! While victim is a weak person and perpetrator is a bad person, when you are in rescuer mode you get to tell yourself that you are being a good person.

The problem with this is that you inevitably find all of your good intentions going up in smoke. The victims you rescue become dependent upon you and start claiming more and more from you. Then you start to resent the victims and start to withhold help. Then the victims feels as if they are **your** victim because you aren't fulfilling your side of the bargain. And you feel like a victim because the victims are abusing your good nature. And the perpetrators hate you for meddling in their relationships with the victims. And soon, all of you need help. And **then,** who are you going to call?

Z: Err... Ghostbusters?

8: (laughs) Very funny.

Z: (smiles) I do see what you are saying, though – then all three of us will need a rescuer. And **then** what?

8: One way or another, it never ends. As long as you are holding onto the idea of yourself as a rescuer then, in truth, you are keeping yourself in victim. You will never be free of the triangle.

Z: Okay. So I have previously decided to be done with rescuer. I reaffirm that decision now.

8: Excellent.

This is exactly how you transform your consciousness. You make a decision to hold a new perspective and then, each time an objection to that new perspective arises, you deal with it by finding a way to make the same decision again, even in light of the objection. Then you return to that new perspective. You navigate the transition in your consciousness by overcoming the obstacles that the objections to it represent. In time you will have hurdled all of your objections and you will find yourself permanently residing in that new perspective. That's how it works and that is what we are doing here. That is how you are transforming yourself from a victim to a creator.

Z: I do see that and I thank you for being with me every step of the way.

I can do with a little more help, though. What would you suggest; how should I respond to a world in which I see people making choices which lead them to painful outcomes?

8: I have a strategy, which I can offer you. If you encounter someone who is clearly in need of help, then this strategy will allow you to offer them assistance without lapsing into rescuer.

Z: That sounds awesome, thanks 8.

8: And, while we are at it, we will look at the other two legs of the victim triangle too, namely victim and perpetrator. I will offer you strategies, which you may adapt to your own life if you find yourself in any of these modes. Together, these strategies will go some way towards answering the question of, "*How do I deal with the presence of evil?*"

FIRSTLY: WHERE YOU ARE THE PERPETRATOR

This occurs when you find yourself in a situation where you have, either intentionally or unintentionally, made another being feel as if their choices have been removed from them.

What should you do?

Start with courage in hand. Be brave and face what you have done. If at all possible, speak to the victim and seek first to understand very clearly from them how they have experienced the situation. What did they feel? How were they hurt? When you have asked all the questions you needed ask, such that you feel you have really understood their experience and that they have said everything they might have wanted to say to you, then you should feed back to them what you have heard and check with them that you have really understood their perspective correctly. When they agree that you have a really good understanding of how they felt then, **and only then**, is it time for you to give them your perspective. If you give your side before you have completely understood theirs, then you will be tempted to simply make excuses for yourself, to try to "get out of it". This is just being a cowardly. So have the courage first to truly and deeply see the experience from the victim's side. **Then** tell them why you did what you did. Tell them from your heart what it was that you intended and what motivated you. In all probability you never intended to do the harm that was done. In all probability it was an unintended side-effect of your trying to do something else entirely. Explain yourself as best you can and ask them then to feed back to you what they have heard from you. Work with them until you feel that they have correctly understood you and your motivations.

When this is done, then the healing can begin. Now you must undertake not to do this again. You have seen how it caused harm, so make the choice not to hurt yourself or any other like this again. It is very useful if you can try to find the very deepest core choice or belief that allowed this to happen. If you work with a surface choice, then you will have to address this again and again until you **do** find the core choice that does not serve you. Tell your victim about your new decision and tell them how it is that you believe this new decision will keep you from hurting them or anyone else in this manner ever again.

The next thing to do is to seek redress. Try to find something that you can do for the person whom you have harmed that will somehow balance the harm you have done. If it is possible to directly repair that which was damaged, then do that and more. If this is not possible, then try to do something else for them, which will benefit them in greater measure than the harm done to them. What I am suggesting is that you see if you can can give back more than you took. And make your redress as personal as possible and as directly related to the healing of the harm you did as possible.

When this is done, work to gain every iota of wisdom that you can from the experience. Bring to your consciousness everything that you have learned from this. Make a note also to be compassionate in future of others who misstep in ways similar to that which you have done.

After all this is concluded, you will have balanced and redressed the harm. You will have forgiveness from the other and from yourself. You will have gained the compassion and wisdom enfolded in the situation. You will be done here.

And **that** is what you do when you find yourself cast as the perpetrator.

Z: That is some good stuff, 8. I can see that this would really work to bring balance and healing.

8: If you are of sufficient consciousness that you would be willing and able to apply these principles, then you are quite seldom going to find yourself in the perpetrator role. But it certainly can still happen. As we have been discussing in the last few chapters, you yourself came to feel as if you were a perpetrator on quite a large scale. So this can happen, even to the ascending soul.

Z: So, 8, what about when you can't have that kind of a discussion with your victim. Like, if they are no longer incarnated or if they are not personally known to you.

8: Then life will have that conversation with you. Just as we have discussed. You will get the experience back from life so that you really and truly **do** understand. Until you **get** what you have done, you are not done. When you do, then you can say, "*I get it,*" and mean it. Then you can say, "*I am sorry,*" and mean it. And you can tell your story to whomsoever will have use of it so that they can understand it without it being you just making excuses. And then you can know what it is that you want to give back to Life by way of redress.

Z: Um. That brings me to a next point. I really do want to give a gift to life. It's odd. When I first became aware that I had to revise **The Ascension Papers** and release the 3rd edition, I didn't really know why but I had the strongest feeling that I wanted to make at least the e-book version available for free. Since there are no printing or postage costs, I can do that. And then I can give this book away to anybody and everybody who wants it. And that thought arrived at the same time as the thought that I needed to correctly explain the

Singularity Event. It was the same thought: *"Get it right **and** give it away for free."* And now it seems to me that **this** is my redress. On a deep, deep level I knew that making this text available for free to all who want it and have need of it will not just redress my previous harm but, being free, this book will then be able to get to many, many more people than otherwise. So then I am more than redressing the harm. And also this does seem to be as direct a response to my misstep as is possible.

8: There is a poetic harmony in this. So if that is what your heart calls you to do, then I support this idea entirely.

One word of caution, however. Don't overbalance so far in the opposite direction that you cause imbalance. Don't now block the energy flow. By all means do as you intend and make this work available for free but do not disallow others from giving something back, if they feel called to do so. What I am saying is that one must never block your ability to receive over a desire to give. That will just get you stuck at another, higher level of consciousness – in polarity rather than in duality.

Z: I'll give all of this some careful thought and come up with an answer from my heart, thank you, 8.

> (**Zingdad note:** Please see the *"Closing Thoughts"* section at the end of this book for this and so much more.)

8: You do that.

Now, let's move onto the next way in which you can perceive evil.

SECONDLY: WHEN YOU ARE THE VICTIM

If you can get the perpetrator to play ball and go through the same process outlined above, then that would be great. But ultimately, if your perpetrator was willing to go through such a process, then you wouldn't really see yourself as a victim. Just someone involved in an unhappy circumstance that eventually turned out okay. So, if you are really feeling like a victim, then it is because you feel that this other being will never right the wrong they have done to you.

What to do then?

The very first thing to do when you are feeling like a victim is to give yourself choices. When you have choices that you can take, then you are immediately a creator again. And you cannot be both a creator and a victim **unless** you are a creator who is creating the illusion that you are a victim. Which is exactly what you will be doing in this situation.

So that is the first thing you must do. Move your consciousness into creator mode. Recognise that you have choices. A very powerful thing you can do in this regard is to say to yourself:

"In every moment I create myself with my choices. What choices do I have now and how will I create myself with each of those choices?"

Then list your choices. Think of every possible thing you can conceive of that you could do in this situation. Write them down, if there are more than a handful. Then, next to each choice, write down what kind of a person you would be if you made that choice. Be honest and clear. **Then** write down what kind of person you really want to be. You might for example want to be, *"the most magnificent, loving version of myself,"* or possibly, *"the wisest, most creative person I can be,"* or something like that.

Now see if any of the choices you wrote down conform to a choice that would be taken by that most loving and magnificent version of yourself. Chances are none of them do. That is why you are experiencing yourself as a victim. Because you aren't choosing to be the highest version of Self that you can be. The victim experience is a gift. It is asking of you to choose again.

And now you are in a magical and wondrous moment. Some alchemy of the soul is about to happen, if you will only let it. Now you can ask yourself the very important question, *"What **would** the most magnificent, loving version of myself do in this situation?"* Does the answer come to mind immediately? Then write it down. Then do it! If you don't have an immediate answer to your question, you can simply allow yourself to "percolate". Hold the question in your heart and be willing to hear the answer. Perhaps you will wake up the next morning with the answer. Perhaps you will receive it indirectly from someone else or through inspiration. But let me tell you this, if you hold the question in your heart the answer will come.

And when it does come, you might feel resistant to it. It might feel like it is "unfair" to not try to punish your perpetrator. Or it might feel like you won't be able to rise above your feelings of anger and betrayal. Or whatever. The point is that this, right here, is your first objection. You know what to do, but you have an objection to doing it. So what will you choose?

And while you are working this choice out for yourself, it might be very useful to do some delving into your psyche. Go into your deepest beliefs and memories. Especially your childhood. Go and find the seed-thought which you hold that caused you to invite this experience of victimhood into your life. Realise that you are holding onto beliefs that are not bringing you closer to love, joy or peace. Work with it until you find the beliefs that you are holding onto that are inviting the victim experiences you are having. Work with them until you are ready to let them go.

And if you cannot? If you find yourself to be stuck? Then I would recommend that you seek a gifted counsellor or therapist to help with this. It might be that the deepest origin of your pain is beyond your reach – in another lifetime or at another level of existence altogether. In such an instance, it can be very beneficial to seek external assistance from someone capable of offering you input and guidance.

> (**Zingdad note:** When 8 first uttered these words to me, I had no idea that I would come to be one of those people; a healer who can offer assistance with exactly these kinds of processes. It is truly amazing how life proceeds, is it not? And so, certainly, if you need help to heal and release your own victim-pain, then assuredly that is something I am really very, very good at. For more information see my Soul Re-Integration page here: zingdad.com/healing-a-helping/soul-re-integration)

If you are willing to chose to rise above your victim situation and to do as your grandest version of Self would do then, one way or another, this will be possible for you. And if you stay with that choice long enough, you will see the wonderful outcomes that will flow forth from it. You will come to feel light and free. You will come to know yourself as the powerful creator being that you truly are.

You see?

Z: Yes. I do see.

8: But you must seek. And you must be willing to change.

When the soul is ready to progress, it will do so. If it struggles to do so, then help is available. If it is ready and willing to accept the help, then the path will open up.

Z: I see. I like that.

8: And then, in due course, you will find that you are no longer having victim experiences. You will find that you are making decisions which allow you to leave behind all those relationships which do not serve you. And then you will finally be ready to know that, indeed, you have created every single victim experience you have ever had.

And then you will be done with being a victim!

Z: Awesome! Thanks 8. And the third victim state is rescuer?

8: Correct.

THIRDLY: WHEN YOU ARE THE RESCUER

When someone in your life finds themselves feeling like a victim, you might find them reaching out to you for help. If you yourself are still of victim consciousness, then you are very likely to be pulled into playing rescuer to this other being. If, on the other hand, you are completely done with the victim triangle, then you will not have that difficulty. You will see their whole situation for what it is. You will see that they are creating their entire drama all for their own purposes, just as you used to do when you played the same victim game. And you will see that their pain is not of your making and that, in fact, you cannot be responsible for healing their pain. You cannot choose for them. You cannot fix them. You cannot change them. And you would know that, were you to try, then you would very soon embroil yourself in their pain, starting out as their rescuer and then moving swiftly to becoming both their perpetrator and their victim. You would not be willing to do that and you would be fully aware that, in fact, only they can heal themselves. They themselves first need to decide that their life is not as they would wish it to be. If they find that they cannot, by themselves, affect the change that they desire, then, of course, they can ask for help. For no help can come to anyone who is unwilling to be helped.

Now, it is possible that this person does not know **how** to do all of this. Perhaps they believe that something or someone outside of themselves must change before they can be happy. Perhaps they wish to see how they are responsible for their own choices but don't know how to come to that perspective. Perhaps they don't know how to find out which choices are harming them. Perhaps they don't know how to make better choices. And so it could be possible for you to help them to help themselves without moving into rescuer.

Z: And you are going to share with me a strategy for doing this?

8: I am. Let us formalise it into a three-step process:

BEING OF ASSISTANCE WITHOUT BECOMING A RESCUER: THE THREE-STEP PROCESS

Step 1: Raise your own consciousness to a higher vibration by saying to yourself:

"All is ONE and all is perfect. Both.............. (this other being's name) and I are perfect expressions of the ONE. I wish to serve the highest good for all by assisting.............. to heal him/herself. I am motivated only by love."

Step 2: Understand the position of this other being. You can do so by seeing yourself in their situation and also by talking to them and asking them questions about their experience until you really can understand their position. In this step you are **not** trying to fix anything, or change anything. This is not your opportunity to lecture them or tell them anything at all. In this step you are simply trying to understand, as well as you possibly can, what their situation is and what it is that ails them. You may ask questions. Questions are good. But ask the questions that lead you to deeper understanding of their situation and exactly how they feel. In so doing you give them the first gift. You give them the gift of your attention. If you can do this without any judgement or criticism, then you give them a very loving gift indeed. Keep going with this until you feel that you really understand their situation. And check with them that you do. Tell them what you have heard them say and ask if they agree that this is an accurate description of their experience. You will be amazed what a wonderful healing gift **just this** step will be.

Step 3: Once you have a really good grasp of the situation, you can ask yourself what is the very highest and best offering of assistance that you can give this other. What is it that you would want done for yourself if you were in their situation?

Z: Oh right:,"*Do unto others as you would that they should do unto you.*"

8: That's it.

But here comes the twist. And pay attention, because this is important.

Before you actually offer any assistance, remember, whatever you do to this other being, you do to yourself also. So be willing to experience for yourself whatever you are giving to this other being and then watch for it. It will find its way to you. If, for example, you rush in and take away this other being's choices, then you will come to find your choices being taken away too. If you treat the other being as if they are not actually capable of finding their own way, then you too will come to lose your way. If, on the other hand, you offer loving and respectful assistance, then this will be offered to you too when you need it. If you treat this being as part of the oneness, then you will find yourself feeling as if you are part of the oneness too.

You get the idea?

Not only, "*Do unto others that which you would have done to you,*" but, "*Do unto others, realising that you are doing exactly that to yourself.*" Be sure that you are ready to have this done to you also.

Z: I see. That is excellent advice, 8. I can see that this could really help without causing me to be pulled into rescuer.

8: I have something more that I would like to offer you in this regard.

Z: Please...

8: If you were stuck in victim, is it not true that what you would most like is to be helped out of victim? To be helped to see that you are actually the creator of your own reality? Would that not be the way you would want yourself to be helped in such a circumstance?

Z: Yes. That certainly would be what I would want for myself.

8: Well, if it should come to be that you wish to assist someone else who is in a victim state then, obviously, what you will wish to do for them is to help them to return to creator consciousness.

Z: "Do unto others" and all that...

8: Precisely.

Now, as with all things, there is a right way to do this and a wrong way. The wrong way is to tell this person who is sitting in their pain and confusion to, *"Pull yourself together because you just created all of this yourself anyway!"*

Z: (laugh) Oh my goodness, I can see how **that** wouldn't work!

8: No, indeed. The right way is far more gentle and loving than that. And **far** more effective. If you can help this being to see that they have options and choices, then they can immediately move out of victim.

Z: Oh, right... just the same as I would do for myself if I found myself in victim.

8: Isn't that what we are saying? Do to the other exactly as you would like to have done to yourself.

Z: Yes, I see.

8: So, just as you would go about showing yourself that you have choices, so you could help a friend who is in victim to realise that they always have choices. And if they are open to it, you might be able to help them to reach for a transcendent choice... a choice that not only shows them that they are not a victim but, in fact, a far greater version of themselves than they previously thought.

And that is the path of the unifier. That is the way of a being who is returning to oneness.

Z: That's brilliant, 8. Thank you. I will apply that to my life. I will make it my way.

8: Instead of simply accepting this as gospel, I would suggest to you that you try living this and then see how it works for you. In keeping with all that I have just said, I ask you to remember I am not here to impart instructions or doctrine or dogma. I am simply offering you choices. So if you choose to take this on board, then I recommend that you do so with an experimental mind-set. If you want to try it out, then of course you need to really *live it* in your every interaction, every day. Do this for a while until it feels natural. Then take stock of your life and see if you are happier with yourself when you live this way or not. See if your life brings you greater joy or not. See if you feel greater love for yourself and for others or not. Decide if this is right for you based upon your own experience, rather than based upon my say so.

Z: Got it. Thanks 8.

8: Good then. But before we can move on from here, I would like us to do a little practical work. Let's see how you would apply your new understandings, shall we?

Z: Okay...

8: All right, then let's create a scenario. Imagine you have a friend, let's call him Uther, who is quite badly stuck in victim consciousness. Uther is struggling a bit with his life and many aspects of it are just not working out for him. He expresses to you some ideas such as, "*I hate my job and my boss is an idiot,*" or, "*These stupid politicians are screwing up the whole country,*" or, "*My wife just doesn't understand me,*" or, "*Nothing ever goes my way,*" or, "*If I had just had different parents as a kid I wouldn't be so messed up today,*" or, *"If only my body wasn't such a mess, I'd be happy."* Such ideas. You can see that he is in pain. You can see that his life is not bringing him joy and that he clearly doesn't know how to improve matters.

Now that you know what you know, what would you do?

Z: Hmm... I can empathise. I have felt some of these things in my life and so I know what he is feeling. I'm not there any more – I now understand things differently. But I sure can understand that he is where he is.

8: So? What do you do?

Z: Well... let me apply the three steps.

First I recognise that all is ONE and all is perfect. Both Uther and I are perfect expressions of the ONE. I wish to serve the highest good for all by assisting Uther to heal himself. I am motivated only by love.

Second and third I state my intent to make a choice which not only does to Uther that which I would want done to myself, but does to Uther realising that I **am** doing exactly that to myself... that I am willing to make that exact choice for myself.

(I give a little thought to the situation and then...)

All right. This is what I have come up with. Uther has not actually asked me for help. He is simply expressing pain. So I don't know if he just wants to moan or if he actually wants to move out of victim. So I'll begin by deciding if I want to sit in commiseration with Uther or not. If I do, then I'll be right there with him where he is at. I'll let him tell me about his pain and confusion and give him a safe place to share without being judgemental and without criticising him or making him wrong. At most I will ask him questions that will allow him to better express what is going on in his life. I'll make sure that I am really hearing him and check my understanding with him to be sure that I have really got it. I will give him the gift of my full attention and my listening. I will bear witness. I will "be present" with Uther.

That is the choice I have come up with and I feel that it is a good one because it is congruent with the three steps. I myself would be very, very happy if someone should offer me such an attentive and loving ear if I had some pain that I was working through.

8: Excellent. You make me proud. And I can give you another reason why this is a good choice: if you were to apply this, you would be amazed at how much progress Uther would make towards solving his own problems. Just being in the presence of a loving, attentive listener like that will almost always bring great healing. Progress will follow. And after simply talking to you in this manner, Uther is most likely to say to you, "*You have helped me so much!*" or something similar. And you will tell him, "*No, my friend, I just listened. You helped yourself.*" And both of you will walk away feeling uplifted.

Quite different from the situation where you decide to rush in and rescue Uther, where you tell him exactly how he must pull himself together and what he should do to fix up his life. Such a path would result in you both feeling blocked, unheard and resentful.

Z: Hmm. Yes. I've been there. On both sides of that equation. It just doesn't work.

8: All right now, the next question. What will you do if Uther did actually ask you for help and advice? Perhaps he finds he is not making enough progress by just talking about his life. Or perhaps he sees that you are not struggling as he is and wants to tap into your learning and experience. What then?

Z: Again I will apply the three steps.

(I give it a little thought...)

What I have come up with is that it will be unhelpful if I tell Uther what he must do.

I think a really great way for me to tell him what I think, is by telling him some appropriate part of my story. Then he can hear for himself how similar (or otherwise) he thinks my experience was to his and he can hear what I did in that situation and how it turned out for me. Then he can decide for himself if he will do as I did, or do as I suggest (if that is different from what I actually did). I will make it clear to him that I do not expect of him that he should do what I say. I offer my thoughts with love and he is welcome to do with them as he sees fit.

This works for me because, again, it is congruent with the three steps. If I had a friend who had sorted something out that I was still struggling with, I would like it if I could ask his advice. I would want him to have the freedom to give me his advice. I would want it given in such a way as to allow me to see how he had applied it in his life and how it had worked for him, or why it was that he felt it would work for me. And finally, I wouldn't want him to get all attached to the outcome that I should do exactly as he said. If I wanted to hear his advice, and yet have the freedom not to apply it, that should be okay with him. Or else I wouldn't want his advice at all.

8: That is well said.

And I'd like to point something out to you.

Z: Yes?

8: if your friend Uther asked you for advice on how he could free himself from his victim consciousness... is it not possible that you could simply share *The Ascension Papers* with him?

Z: Oh, right. (laughs) That is exactly what I could have done! And it is exactly what I would have wanted. When I felt deeply lost in my own victim state, I would have wanted someone to give me exactly this book.

8: So truly, *The Ascension Papers* is you doing to others that which you would most like done to yourself.

Z: Hmm... yes... I see! This is quite perfect, isn't it?

8: Together all of us are providing the Self with a path out of a difficult position in a way that is both gentle and respectful. It is true that the Self who writes the book and the Self who reads this book may choose to accept the wisdom herein or reject it. Or to take the bits and pieces they might like. This is the way you would want it to be given to you, is it not? Sharing with no coercion?

Z: It is, yes.

8: And so you give away that which you most desire and, in so doing, you give it to yourself! That is the beauty of your sharing it.

And so we discover an important corollary to the idea that you should only give to another that which you are willing to receive for yourself. It is this: if there is something you feel you want or need, then you should find a way to give that which you need to another. Because indeed it is so that you always gain that which you first give away.

Z: That's lovely, 8. I understand that in a whole new way now. I will apply this and see how it works for me.

8: Good boy! And so you can reaffirm the decision to let go of the need to rescue anyone ever again, can't you?

Z: I certainly can. That objection is dealt with.

Because when I play rescuer, then I am giving away that which I actually **don't** want. I don't want someone else to make my decisions for me, to take my learning opportunities from me or to tell me what to do.

8: Good. So then don't do it to others.

Give only that which you would desire for yourself.

Z: That's great, thanks 8.

You know, it's strange that I felt embarrassed to **again** raise the subject of being a rescuer when I had felt like it had been dealt with many times already. I felt like I was being silly. But it is plain now that there was so much more for me to learn about this. So I am really pleased now that I did raise it again.

8: I wish you to understand that the work of re-creation of the Self (which is what you are doing here) is challenging indeed. Every single human being on planet Earth is already held in the very highest regard by those of the higher realms and other realities precisely because of the profundity of the task that you have, collectively and individually, willingly shouldered. And this work of the transformation of conscious is the very cutting edge of the miracle that is the experiment called "humanity". And dealing with your objections **is how** you work these transformations in your own consciousness.

This is why you find me to be patient in addressing these issues with you. If you were truly just wasting time and energy and "being silly" then, you know full well, I'd not entertain that.

Now. There is one last thing I would say to you about helping other beings who find themselves in victim. It is this: please remember that it is their perfect right to remain in victim, if that is what they wish. The fact that they are asking you for help does not mean you should attach yourself to the idea that they should change in the way you want them to change. You can offer your help but you cannot force them to take it. You cannot demand of them that they do what you expect them to do, simply because they have expressed a need to you. Almost everyone on this planet is still busy playing the victim game. Most people still need their victim dramas to continue to play out so that they can have the experiences they came here to have. Even if they ask you for help and even if they say they want to stop playing victim, **still** it might be that they actually want, and need, to continue with victim. It is not your place to coerce them to change.

Z: Yes, I can see that. I agree that I should either offer my help without expectation. Or not offer it at all.

8: Yes. Apply the three-step process with courage and an open heart. At the very least you will be creating yourself as a being of loving compassion who is not a victim. That is a good start. The degree to which the other being gains value and makes changes in their life is up to them.

Z: Thank you, 8. I will try all these strategies and see how they work in my life.

8: Good. If properly applied and adapted to each situation, you should find yourself releasing the direct experience of evil from your own situation.

Z: Thanks, 8.

But what about indirect experiences? Like... what about all the stuff that goes on "out there" in the world? There is a whole lot of bad stuff happening on this planet. While it doesn't necessarily impact my life directly, I am still very much aware of it. Can you help me to find a healthy perspective on that so that I can release it and let it go?

8: That sounds like the perfect cue for the third part of this conversation:

Manifestations of Evil

We aren't going to look at **all** the ways in which evil is manifest. A complete list would need many more pages than you would be able to type. What we are going to do is to confine ourselves to addressing the areas of concern that you asked about in the opening to this chapter. These were:

1. People willing to commit genocide for the sake of power, wealth or political expediency

2. Terrorists

3. People who would rape or abuse women and children

4. Demons and demonic possession

5. Lucifer, Satan and the Devil

I'm going to talk to you about each of these issues and then, when I am done, you will be able to release your concerns about them. And then you will also be willing to understand that it is truly so that...

"If there is such a thing as evil, then it is an opportunity to learn about love."

Irrespective of the context.

Are you amenable?

Z: Of course! Let's do it.

8: All right then.

The first manifestation of evil you wanted to know about was:

PEOPLE WILLING TO COMMIT GENOCIDE FOR THE SAKE OF POWER, WEALTH OR POLITICAL EXPEDIENCY

Let me begin telling you about these people by continuing where we just left off when we were talking about rescuer. Remember I was just saying that there are many people who are not done with their own victim dramas?

Z: Yes.

8: Well it is so that the greatest majority of people on your planet are indeed still deeply engaged in the victim state. And so it is that pretty much everyone you would meet from day to day is, to one extent or another, playing out a number of concurrent victim dramas in their lives.

This is right and appropriate because this is what they came to this planet for. On a soul level they chose to come here and they knew that they were going to have these experiences when they made these choices.

Z:... and so we shouldn't try to rescue them. I get that.

8: Steady on. I am making another point now. Not only should you not try to rescue them, but you should also allow that they actually need a perpetrator. If you are going to sit on the one side of a see-saw, then you need someone to sit on the other side. That's the only way to make the ride work. Well, in just this way, victim and perpetrator need each other. The one without the other has no movement. And until each being is ready to finally release the whole victim experience, they will still need perpetrators. Until they make this decision powerfully and finally on a soul level, they will not be able to leave this game behind and move on to another, perhaps kinder, more loving, game. Until each of you has mastered both the dark and the light of your own souls, you will not be your own master. And only masters ascend.

And so, the point I am making is that there is a need for perpetrators in order to allow victims to experience and explore their own beings. To provide them with the choices that they need so that they can create themselves again and again until they have mastered themselves.

Z: I see. But how does this pertain to those people who would commit genocide?

8: What I have just said pertains to all victim/perpetrator relationships. But, all right, let's get into the specifics of this question: those who commit genocide for the sake of expediency.

How about I use an example of something that is very much in your planetary consciousness right now? An issue that is highly emotive, thorny and hotly debated. How about I use the example of the 9-11 attack on the World Trade Centre?

> (**Zingdad Note:** when I was first writing this, the 9-11 attack was already a good few years behind us but, at this point it had become a very hotly debated issue. The "official story" as told by government agencies was being heavily called into question, all kinds of holes were being poked in the explanations given and attention was being called to the vast areas they had simply glossed over. Though, since then, time has passed and new "hot topic" issues have come and gone, the issues of what **really** happened during 9-11, how the three buildings came to fall and who was behind it all, have never been even nearly satisfactorily resolved. For this reason 8 and I decided to continue to use this example as is in this third edition.)

Z: Whew! That certainly is a very contentious issue for many here on Earth. But now we're talking about terrorism and I thought we were supposed to be talking about genocide.

8: I know. I am not in the habit of letting my attention wander. If **you** were paying attention you would recall that we were actually talking about the

people who would commit genocide. If you are to understand these people and how and why they act as they do, then you will need to understand that genocide itself is just one of the deeds that they get up to. It is really just one page in a much greater story. And if I am to tell you this story, then it is best that I begin telling it from a place to which you can relate.

THE STORY OF JOHN, THE CONSPIRACY THEORIST

I will begin by telling a story of a man – we shall call him John – who has lost a family member in what has been called "the 9-11 terrorist attack". This was quite possibly the most visible terrorist attack in the history of humanity. It was captured on film from every angle and shown over and over again on television around the world. Not only was John deeply aggrieved by his loss, but the way in which this vile act was presented to him over and over again resulted in his grief becoming inflamed to the point of profound rage.

"What kind of foul, evil demon would do this?" John wondered about these terrorists. And almost magically, in answer to his question, there appeared on his television screen an image of a bearded man in a turban. This, he was told, was the arch-villain. This was the evil mastermind behind the whole operation. There were even recordings in which this man claimed responsibility. And soon after that John saw further images on his television of other middle-eastern men. These dark-eyed foreigners with a foreign religion and an ideology of hatred, the talking heads on the television authoritatively informed him, were the perpetrators. Finally, John had a target for his rage. And the way all this was presented to him caused the target of his hatred to grow from a small handful of men to a whole culture... a whole religion. In fact John found he now hated the residents of a whole geographical region! And when the cowboy-hatted president of his nation talked war talk, John found his voice calling agreement: Yes, punishment! Yes, vengeance! Yes, retribution! John found the idea of going to war against the terrorists an idea that he could very easily support. If he wasn't too old, he told himself, he'd volunteer himself. He'd love to go and kill some of those "evil monsters," he told himself.

And of course John was not the only one in his country to feel this way. Or even the world. This was quite a popular sentiment for a while there.

And so there was war.

But it very quickly changed from a surgically clear operation to something muddy and complex. And John's fervour began to wane when he first read about "collateral damage". It's a term that means civilians being killed. You see, John is a bright enough fellow and his heart is actually in the right place. And this wasn't what he wanted. He wanted **terrorists** punished. Not simple, poor, innocent village folk in some far away country. But all the time there was this idea of catching the chief terrorist. And John was reminded again and again of the man in the turban who had made video recordings in which he had taken responsibility for the 9-11 attack. Bringing him to justice was an idea that John could still get behind. And, while John waited for the chief terrorist to be brought to justice, somehow this one war became two. John wasn't entirely sure how that happened. First they were hunting in the mountains for this arch-enemy and then they were looking for Weapons of Mass Destruction in a different country altogether. Which had links, the television told him, to the 9-11 terrorists. Traumatised, fearful and very angry, John was willing to keep supporting the war effort. "*Go kill them all,*" was his thought on the subject.

But the more these wars dragged on, the more young people came back in body bags and with missing limbs, the more fire left John's belly. And the more this began to look less and less like a good and righteous war to him too. First, there **were no** Weapons of Mass Destruction to be found. Then he read that there was no connection at all between the 9-11 terrorists and this second country. He began to suspect that there was another reason for this expansion of the war. He wondered if it wasn't just all about oil. Or possibly all about a vendetta between his country's leader and the leader of the other country. And then, a little later, John first encountered a conspiracy theory which claimed that *the whole 9-11 attack had been instigated by people inside his own country's government*!

The conspiracy theorist came with all kinds of evidence that supported the contention that it was not, after all, two airliners that brought the two skyscrapers down but, in fact, powerful high-explosives that must have been placed inside the buildings before the time. And then there was the video he saw showing a third building being demolished with no aeroplane hitting it at all. At first John rejected these ideas. They were too abhorrent to contemplate. But the ideas fascinated him because he had no answer for them. They taunted him in his mind. So he kept going back to the Internet to look for more. And he kept finding more. More and more evidence that, at the very least, a group of people in power in his government had worked quite hard to allow the aircraft attacks to happen. More and more evidence that the buildings were actually destroyed with explosives. Never any proof – but always more evidence.

Layer upon layer of cover-ups. Facts not fitting with the official story. Professionals in various industries such as engineers, architects, pilots and so forth all coming forward with more probing, unanswered questions. All saying that it was, quite literally, impossible for things to have transpired in accordance with the official story. All demanding the truth. All convinced that the official story was a whitewash. John read how, from every angle, the official story was debunked and then finally decided for himself that the conspiracy theories were true. And, as soon as he opened this door, John was hit by an avalanche. The deeper down the rabbit hole he went, the more information he found. More and more stories of deception and deceit that had played out across the face of the globe, going back into history. Shameful covert operations being conducted with, it seemed, the knowledge and blessing of his country's leaders. Murders and assassinations, wars instigated in foreign lands, arms and equipment supplied to despots and madmen to use against their own people, narcotics being traded for guns... on and on it went. Everywhere John looked he found stories detailing gross abuses of public trust by those in power, which were then hidden behind layers of lies and deception. And these conspiracy theories all tied together. The one leading to the other. All of them adding up in a way that, quite sickeningly, explained why the world was the way it was. It went a long way toward explaining why there was so much hatred in the world.

And that is where we leave John.

Z: Wow, 8. You paint quite a bleak picture. And is it all true – all this conspiracy theory stuff?

8: True?

Z: Yes, I mean, did it all happen the way the conspiracy theorists say?

8: (sighs) My dear young friend. I know this is hard for you to understand, but please try. There is no objective truth outside of yourself other than, *"The ONE is,"* remember?

Z: Oh yes. I do remember that. But surely this attack either happened one way or it did not?

8: No. You still don't really get it yet. There is **no** objective truth of this story that exists outside of yourself – or of any other story, for that matter. It doesn't exist. Things simply do not work that way. There are perspectives and probabilities which all of you, inside this game, are busy co-creating. But no single version is fixed. No single version is eternally valid.

This is why I was telling you about John's perspective, rather than about things that "actually happened". Because outside of you and John and everyone else on this planet... outside of yourselves there is nothing going on. Outside of the creators, there is no creation.

So the only thing you need to concern yourself with is your own subjective experience. And for each of you this is a little different. You each have a slightly different experience and story. So please pay attention when I say, it is not the "story" that is important. You believe it is, but it isn't. The story is just a mechanism, a device, a plot line, which you are using as a vehicle to understand yourself and to create yourself. And that is all that matters: your discovery, creation and re-creation of yourself.

So listen! It does not matter what did, or did not, happen. What matters is the way you feel about it. What you decide, choose and create as a result of this perceived external stimulus. What is important is your own inner-reality.

So there is the truth of you, and then there is the story that you are using to help you to get to the truth of you. The story is subordinate. It is only of importance whilst it serves the primary goal. Which is your self-discovery and self-creation.

You understand?

Z: I do, thanks 8. I mean, I understand what you are saying and it does make sense and I really appreciate it. But I don't understand yet how there is no one version of events. How can there be many, equally true stories?

8: You'll get there. In time you will certainly come to see that it is so and can only be so. For now, let us return to our discussion.

So, I say again... there is the **story** and then there is **the truth of you**. Now I want to get back to our friend John. I want to talk about his subjective experiences and I want to look at how he can now create himself as a result of them.

You see, ultimately, the question of the conspiracy theories being true or not is an irrelevant question. It is meaningless. But from John's direct, personal and subjective experience, it is an over-riding and vital question. And if John is willing to be really, deeply honest with himself, he will admit that there is no absolute proof of anything in any direction. No-one has been able to offer any kind of evidence that would make any particular version of the truth absolute and unarguable. All he has is a burgeoning collection of evidence from which he can reach his own conclusions. And if he is deeply honest and also incredibly observant, then he will realise that it is his own ideas, beliefs and preconceptions that led him to collect the evidence he has collected. You see? He **is** creating his reality without even being aware of it. John believes he is simply observing his outer reality. But he is not. He is going out into his world and carefully filtering what he observes and then creating a picture inside himself with the puzzle pieces he has hand-picked. Given a slightly different starting position, with a slightly different set of presuppositions, John would have gone about collecting entirely different bits of evidence and holding onto different ideas of what is true. He would end up with an entirely different belief about what was going on in his "story".

His story.

History.

It is all fiction. A selection of perspectives and views. Collect different perspectives and views and it all looks entirely different.

But it is not the story that matters; it is what you do with it. How you feel about it. Because **that** is when you are creating yourself and discovering yourself. Dis-covering. Removing the cover. Exposing yourself for what you really are.

Z: Fantastic stuff, 8! This is awesome. I am beginning to understand now. So how did John create himself?

8: Well, you see, John very much does believe in an external truth about events. And, as a result of his journey, he came to decide that the conspiracy theories were mostly true. They made sense to him. He found them to be an accurate reflection of his reality. And so? Given that, what was John to do? How was he to respond?

And the answer, of course, is that it depends entirely on what he really wants. He must decide what he wants, and he will create himself with his choices.

If he wants to do so, he can go on a crusade for "the truth" in which he seeks to force the government to loosen its steely grip on its secrets. To try to force those in power to tell the truth. To go and meet and interview those who were there at ground zero. Find and view new video footage of the event. Talk to experts. Try to "awaken" his fellow citizens to "the truth" (while they, on the whole, would really prefer to hit the snooze button one more time). He can do that. And there are many versions of John doing exactly that right now. And there is nothing wrong with that, if that is what they want to do.

Or he can let it go and give up. Decide the machine is far too big to battle and then he can walk away with a deep sense of distrust and disillusionment. In so doing he can replace a belief that "the authorities" are to be trusted with a belief that they are actually the enemies of humanity.

Or he can get active in politics and try to fix the system from within. Perhaps look for some lone voice inside the system who looks to be an honest broker of the truth to support. Get involved in trying to get more voters for this "person of truth" within the "system of lies".

And, of course, there are many, many other ways in which John might respond. You see, he is constantly being offered all kinds of choices all along the way. It seems as if there are a million different things he can choose at every point. Will he believe this theory or that one? Will he trust this politician or that one? Will he protest against this thing or support that thing? Will he go to that town hall meeting and raise his concerns? Will he lose faith enough to take his anger and distrust underground; to get guns and ammunition and have clandestine meetings with others of a like mind? And what about a legal challenge to force those who are in power to tell the truth? Or will he put his faith in the system once more and trust that it will repair itself? What about just voting for the "right" candidate this time?

So many, many choices.

But you see, that too is all an illusion. There is really only one choice: to go deeper into the victim game or to raise yourself out of it. And **all** of the choices outlined above for John are really just the same choice: to go deeper into the game. You see, the game itself never shows you the other option... it never shows you that you can raise yourself out of the game. Instead it dazzles you with stage-magician lights. You only see the choices that it wants you to see and **all** of those choices are about going deeper into the game. This is why it is such a successful system. It keeps everyone playing the same game. Exactly as it is meant to.

Z: So you are saying that the game is designed so as to keep the victims playing and believing?

8: Yes. The game is designed to show you only the choices that keep you playing the game... the victim choices. It is particularly good at offering you the kind of choices where you end up supporting the victimisation of other people. Those are the best kind of game-continuing choices. If you can be induced to cause another person to be victimised too, then the game is working twice as well.

And now I want to talk a little about the engine room of these choices. To do so, I want to leave John behind and introduce you to someone else. Let's call him Maximilian. Max for short. Max is what I call a "Super Powerful Individual" or SPI for short.

THE SUPER POWERFUL INDIVIDUALS

Z: What's an SPI? Like the president of a country, or the owner of a large corporation, or what?

8: No, a Super Powerful Individual would be one of a very small number of people who, despite having a great deal of power in your world, is largely invisible and unknown. So, Max would not see himself as a citizen of one country or another. Rather, he would see countries and their political leaders as a means to manage assets. He doesn't belong to a country; countries belong to him! He would also not think of himself as merely owning corporations; he would think of corporations as tools for his use. Max is one of a handful of people who, collectively, own everything on the planet that they would consider to be worth owning. In fact, most SPIs would probably believe that they own the people of the planet too. And, most especially, they would feel as if they own everyone whom you would normally count to be powerful: presidents, CEOs, kings and cardinals are all the SPI's special assets. Politicians come and go with election terms. Members of corporate boards can be unseated by the shareholders. But the SPI is there to stay. Behind the scenes. Unseen. Untouchable.

If you were one of these men, then you would hold some pretty impressive powers. If the democratically elected leader of a country doesn't behave in accordance with your will, you could have him deposed, foment a revolt and have him overthrown or have him assassinated - whatever would serve the bigger picture of a world conforming to your wishes.   And, as you control the flow of capital around the world, so you could dictate how one region would get richer and another poorer. You could bring on boom times and you could trigger a global financial bust. You could start wars on a regional or even global scale, or you could stop them. You have that kind of power.

Z: So then, are these SPIs the Illuminati?

8: I prefer not to use the term, "Illuminati", as this invites misunderstanding. There is a meme in your collective consciousness that there is such a hidden organisation, a cohesive shadowy underground unit that is running affairs on your planet. But that is an incorrect understanding. These ones, these Super Powerful Individuals, are very much not the kinds of beings who band together and work harmoniously towards a collective goal. There simply is no such organisation. The most cohesive unit of organisation these beings seem to be able to hold together is the family. Some families have extremely dominant, powerful beings at their head and these families prosper because their members are willing to align behind the head. Others are not so successful because they are racked with internal strife over who will lead. Often certain families will form allegiances and will work together for a while. Sometimes those allegiances become institutionalised over time. And there are many clubs and groups and gatherings to which the SPIs will belong and attend. But to imagine all the Super Powerful Individuals of the planet sitting together, plotting together, working as one, is to quite fundamentally misunderstand who and what they are. These are all incredibly strong individualists. Each one essentially looking after their own personal interests first. Strict hierarchies with harshly enforced discipline are the only way cohesion can be maintained. And even then the inner functioning of their organisations can be quite Byzantine, as there is endless intrigue, back-stabbing and double crossing. So you understand; this is not the planet-spanning unified organisation that you might have imagined it to be. Rather it is a number of families, each operating along roughly feudal lines, with a most senior "head" running the family. Even though there are, as I say, allegiances and compacts between some of the families.

Z: Hmm. Okay, I think I have a better understanding now.

8: You do? Well then, let me ask you a question: If you were Max, what would you want? What would you want to do, or to achieve, or experience, or have? What would you want?

Z: That's an interesting question. I guess I wouldn't actually **want** for anything. Not anything material anyway. I'd have everything I could possibly imagine I needed. I guess I'd probably decide to enjoy my wealth and power by finding ways to use it to help others.

8: You'd essentially begin to give it away?

Z: Yes. I think so.

8: Glad to hear it. And so would the other SPIs. That would mean that they would be able to swallow your empire whole, and in so doing, become even more wealthy and powerful. And I won't even bother getting into the details of how tough you'd actually find it to give your money away responsibly so that the giving did not cause more harm than it solved. That's a whole other discussion. The point I will make is that you would very soon become irrelevant in the world of the Super Powerful. You would very quickly no longer be very powerful at all. So I'm going to ask you to try to answer the question again. Try to shift your perspective. Try to imagine yourself as someone who **is** that powerful. You would not have become that powerful if you hadn't been honed and trained from birth to be the bearer of that power. And your family would not have placed you at the head of the empire if you had not shown every aptitude, capacity and determination to bear that mantle. Every moment of your upbringing, education and training would have been about pitting you in competition with other possible heirs to the throne. You would have had to have been a ruthless, brilliant player to ever get to the head of this empire. And it wouldn't just be dropped into your lap either. You would have been given incrementally increasing levels of power and responsibility and you would have had to have shown yourself to be the smartest and the best at every turn.

Z: Hmm. I see. I guess I would see myself in competition with everyone else in the power game. I'd have competed internally to get to being the head of my family's empire; now I'd see myself as being in competition with everyone else. I think I'd see it as a challenge to expand my family's empire and win the wealth and power game.

8: Yes. It **is** a sort of a game to them. Often a breathtakingly cruel and vicious game. A deadly serious game for those who get in their way. But a game none the less.

Z: Okay. I see. So if you ask what I would want if I were to try to imagine myself into Max's shoes, then my answer is that I would want to win the game. Even though I would have obscene wealth and power, I would want **more**. In fact, I would want **it all**. As does everyone else "at the top", I'm sure. So then my desire would be to be the very best at the game and to outmanoeuvre all the other SPIs and grab ever more power and control and to crush everyone in my way.

8: You intuitively can see that it would be so?

Z: Yes, easily. Some time ago I played a computer game called "Civilisation". In it you get to be the head of a tiny new-founded empire starting out at 6000BC. You manage all aspects of your empire's growth and development and nurture it and watch it grow. You found new cities and they grow. And then you begin to encounter other empires. You trade and make treaties. And all is well until resources start to run out. You can't expand any more because you become surrounded by neighbours. It becomes an inevitable part of the game that war will then break out. Instead of expanding through growth, you expand by conquest. It's just good strategy, after all. It's just the way you win the game!

Funny thing is, as I found myself winning the game because a sufficient percentage of the game world was under my control, I didn't want to stop. I had invested so much energy and attention in **my** civilisation that I didn't want to end with "good enough". I wanted to stay with the game until the whole world was mine – until all my enemies were crushed – until not a single corner of the globe was not under my control.

Oops. I guess I'm revealing quite a lot about myself, aren't I?

8: What you reveal is that you actually really **do** understand the problem of power. So you have compassion and can release judgement. This is very good.

Now, tell me, if you were Max, what would you want with regards to all the little folk "at the bottom"? All the regular folk who are factory workers, clerks, shop-assistants, office managers, soldiers and what-not?

Z: Umm... I guess I'd want them to keep working. To keep slaving away. And to do what I want them to do, when I want them to do it. And to not get noisy and disobedient along the way.

8: And what if they did get disobedient? What if some of them stopped serving your will? What if they began to realise what was going on? What if one day someone looked up from the factory floor and said, "*I don't like this job awfully much. I'm going to do something I love doing instead. I'm going to find my most blissful expression of Self and discover my true nature and then ascend from this system.*" What then?

Z: Well that would be bad news for me. Because obviously such a thing could catch on. If others saw this guy doing what he loved and being happy, then they might want to do it too. Soon all my minions would be off in tie-dyed clothing, making daisy chains and singing "Kumbaya" or whatever. They wouldn't be serving me. I'd start to lose at the game.

8: But it's okay, isn't it, because that isn't going to happen. I mean, think for a second. How many people who are slaving away in factories, shops and offices around the world can just give up and do what they want?

Z: Not very many at all.

8: And why is that?

Z: Well, mostly because they have debts to pay. And even if they have no debt, how will they pay for stuff like food and housing and so on? And even if they could pay for that, what about the future? What about their children's education?

8: Exactly. So that's the first point. Debt. Remember these Super Powerful Individuals run the show. They essentially own the world's economy. Certainly they own all the banks. So, the more folks are deeply in debt, the more they keep slaving away. In the factories, shops and businesses that are also owned by the Super Powerful.

Z: Wow. That's pretty shocking. Or really great strategy. Depending on your perspective.

8: And that's still nothing. There are many other ways to keep Joe, the factory worker's, eyes down on the factory floor. Debt is only one of them. Some of the others are even nastier. Remember the example above of the 9-11 attack?

Z: Oh no! You mean the 9-11 attack is nothing but a huge control mechanism to keep people manipulable?

8: What do **you** think?

Z: I... uh... Oh, but wait a minute, 8. What happened to all that stuff about, "*the story being less important than The Truth Of You*"? Are you now saying that the conspiracy theories are true?

8: No. I am telling you another story. Nothing more, nothing less. Or did you feel at some point that I was demanding of you that you must believe me?

Z: But 8! What's the point of this if it isn't true?

8: The point? It is the same as the point of the story that you are telling yourself by living your life. The point is that you are giving yourself experiences so that you can choose and create. Exactly as I told you before. I am telling you about this so that you can hit rock-bottom on the victim drug to which you are addicted so that you can decide to let it go and **create**! Take ownership! Wake up! Discover who you really are!

If **anything** I have said to you in all of our conversations was valid, do you think there would be a single story out there that was absolute? That was not actually a creation... a fiction... an elaborate stage play? **Your** stage play that **you** are co-creating!

Z: So then, what is the value of telling me about these SPIs? Why not tell me any old mother goose story?

8: I could. But it would not conform to your experience. It would not be of use to you. I'll say it again, so **please** pay attention this time round, okay? It really **is** the important bit and you really must try to take notice of this:

There is **no** objective truth to any story. There are only perspectives and probabilities, which all those playing each game co-create together. But even so, each co-creator has their own unique perspective, experience and story within the greater story. There is no one absolute story, which makes any other story untrue. Which is okay because it is not, after all, the story that is important. You simply need to pretend that the story is the most important thing in order for the game to work. But, as you are now leaving the game, you can come to the realisation that the story is simply the means by which you show yourself your inner being, as projected into an outer reality. You simply use the mechanism of the story to discover yourself and create yourself. Now, the story can be very compelling. It is meant to be. But you are now ready to realise that it is only of value in the context of **the truth of you**. Other than that, it is meaningless.

And so you can now understand the story for what it is. It is something that you can use to show yourself something about yourself and then, depending on how much you like what you see about yourself, you can make new choices about yourself.

Discover yourself and create yourself. That is the point of all of it.

So now you ask me why I tell you about these SPIs. Well here is the answer: I myself am now using story. I am using your story. Your co-created reality. And I am telling you something about your story. You can decide for yourself to what degree what I am telling you is valid. And then you can decide what this information tells you about yourself. And then you can decide how you will create yourself.

How's that?

Z: I'm actually struggling with this, 8. I think I only now get what you were saying about "story". And I don't know how to respond. It makes me feel as if there is no more point in hearing about these things. If it is all just made up... then what is the point in talking about it?

8: All right, let me help you with this.

Do you remember dreaming last night?

Z: Yes. As a matter of fact I had a very long and elaborate dream. And then I woke up and I was telling Lisa about my dream and she and I had a conversation about the dream. And then I woke up again! And I realised that **both** experiences had been a dream.

8: Many people will have these kinds of dream-within-a-dream experiences. If you are willing to pay attention to it, it is a very important message that you are imparting to yourself in such a dream. You are showing yourself how you can wake up from a dream and believe that you are awake, that the dream was all just a fiction, and yet you are **still** inside a dream. It is still all just a fiction. And then you wake up again and...

...and...

Z: I guess I can realise that I **am still** living inside a fiction.

8: Yes. And it is quite a compelling fiction. I mean, do you not really feel as if there is a character who has chosen the pseudonym Zingdad and who is choosing to write a book called *The Ascension Papers*?

Z: Yes. I do. I feel like that is me.

8: And there are many people around the world who are co-creating this fiction. They **also** believe that there is a character called Zingdad who is writing this book called *The Ascension Papers*. But they experience this fiction a little differently. They experience this character as being someone who lives far away who writes these words that they can read.

But what would happen if you all should wake up now and realise that this was just a great, elaborate dream that you dreamed together? If you realised that the Zingdad character was just your character in the dream and that you are something much more? Something much more creatively powerful and real. And **The Ascension Papers** was not actually a book that **you** were writing, but that it was actually one of a number of mutually agreed upon wake-up calls that you had all arranged for yourselves. A bit like setting an alarm clock before going to sleep.

What then?

Would you then wake up and say, "*Oh, those stories were just stories. And stories are unimportant and meaningless. It's all just rubbish. Let's forget it and go and do something real*"?

Or would you see the great beauty and truth that was shown to you in these magnificent epic stories spanning many lifetimes that each of you are telling yourselves? Would you come together and share your experiences and learnings? Would you show each other your stories? Would you love and cherish the tales you had told and the meaning and value you had extracted from them?

Z: Yes. Yes. I see it.

These lives we are living are our stories. And we, collectively, are telling ourselves these stories. We are the authors of the tale and we are the characters inside the tale. And, in living these stories, we are discovering some very powerful truths about ourselves. And that is why the stories are important.

Okay.

But then, why is it important to understand about these Super Powerful Individuals?

8: It works like this: your readers experience the reality of Zingdad in their lives because their lives are impacted by your works. They believe you exist, because they read this book. And, as a result of this, they are offered choices in this work and they can decide for themselves how they are going to respond and create themselves.

But how would it be if you experience an impact on your life, but its origin is very cleverly hidden from you? You see, there are these other beings who are experiencing themselves to be these SPIs. That is the fiction **they** are creating for themselves in this story. And their works are quite pervasive. You'd have to live very far from so-called civilisation in order to completely avoid being impacted by their works. But you struggle to make decisions about this impact because it is not obvious what is going on. And that is what I am doing: I am helping to make overt that which was hidden.

I said before that there is no one single story that is absolutely true. I also said that there are only probabilities and perspectives. What I should add now is this: the more energy that is put into a particular probability, the more that probability gains value. The less energy that is put into it, the more it fades away into non-existence.

Z: You mean, the more we believe in something, the more real it is?

8: Something like that. You make choices, and by your choices you focus your energies. When you focus your energy on something, you add to its creation. You make it more real for yourself. If many people join together and make something real for themselves, then this thing has a greater probability. That is how a co-created world works. And sometimes you are misdirected. You are collectively mesmerised into putting your energies into things which actually feed something hidden behind it. You feed an illusion and the creator of the illusion is fed as well.

And that is what is happening here. Even though very few of you know of the existence of the SPIs, still you are very vividly and powerfully bringing them into your reality by focusing your energies on that which they are presenting to you.

So, I wish to tell you what it is that they are doing and how. Then you will be aware. Then you can release your energies from that. Then you can cease to create this for yourself. Unless of course you like it, in which case... well that would be up to you.

Z: Ah.

Thank you again for your patience, 8. I appreciate that you are prepared to nurse-maid me to my own awakening. This really does begin to make sense to me.

I am ready to get back to the story of the SPIs. I want to know how they are featuring in my story so that I can make better choices in my life.

8: That's great. Well done.

Z: All right, so you were saying something about the 9-11 attack. You were suggesting that maybe the SPIs were actually behind this? Really?

8: Yes. I didn't use the example of 9-11 for nothing when I was telling you about John. I was showing you how it might be a story whose plotline is being directed by the SPIs. Such things have been going on all throughout your history. One of the best methods the SPIs have to keep their minions servile is to stoke a war. As long as people can be convinced that there is some evil other nation, evil other religion, evil other ideology, evil other **whatever** out there that wishes to destroy them, their family and their way of life... then sure as nuts they will be willing to put their shoulder to the wheel and do their bit. Perhaps they will even feel as if they must volunteer to go to fight in the war. And then, if they die in the war, there is just one more reason for everyone else in their family to get angry and full of hatred at the wicked enemy.

Anger and hatred... these are probably even better than debt at keeping people in duality and separateness.

And did you ever wonder about religions?

Z: Religions? What specifically?

8: Well isn't it really very, very peculiar that most religions seem to be founded upon the words and deeds of the most deeply peaceful humans who ever walked the Earth? I mean, all dogma and beliefs aside, if you go and have a look at what is at the core of these religions' teachings, then they are about a striving for peace amongst people and a desire to do right in the world. And yet you keep finding the most fervent adherents of one of these systems of peace being whipped up to go and kill the most fervent adherents of some other system of peace. It happens so often, it's not even thought of as strange. And sometimes the differences in faith are so minor as to be indistinguishable to outsiders.

Does this not seem really odd?

Z: Yes. I hadn't thought about it that way before.

8: And so now I have to ask you; how does it happen that a person who believes in one of these religions with all its beautiful thoughts about loving your brother and so forth... how does it happen that such a person is persuaded to kill his other brother from another faith?

Z: I don't know.

8: Well, I'll tell you. It happens by the simple expedient of some leader telling him that the person of the other faith is not, in fact, his brother. He gets told that the other faith is an abomination. It is evil. And that **his** faith actually permits the killing of people of another faith. Not only permits it, but **requires** it.

Mad, huh?

That a system of love, peace and tolerance could be the very reason why you should allow yourself to be so deeply bigoted that someone who believes something just a little different from what you do, should be killed.

No internal inconsistencies there then! (he laughs sadly)

Z: Wow. That's a very good point, 8. So why? Why would these religious leaders do that?

8: Well it's quite simple. It's those Super Powerful folk again. They noticed a good while ago that there were these spiritual teachings that were counter-productive to their interests. Every now and again a teacher would come around, spreading a message of love, peace, unity and tolerance that would cause a few of their minions to lose interest in the game they were creating. Sometimes there were even schools directly teaching ascension, which led to the minions exiting the game. So the Super Powerful ones devised a very cunning plan indeed. They found a way to turn these religions to their own use. Instead of allowing the religions to continue being simple sets of faith shared by people ministering to each other as brother and sister, they were politicised. Power structures were built into the religions. Dogmas were established. They were turned into **organisations**. Often religious leaders were more powerful than kings and emperors. And then it was decreed that the people of a certain area **had** to follow a particular faith. They were ordered, "*You **must** believe this.*" And if you believed differently from the dogma, you were punished. Usually very cruelly and violently and mostly ending in death. And now the people in charge of these wonderful systems of peace were suddenly men of great power. See how it works?

Z: That's pretty sickening.

8: I can see how it might feel that way to you. But remember...

> *"There is not a single thing that is good or evil, but that you feel that way about it."*

Z: Oh yes.

8: So that means it is your choice to be here in this system. The system is designed to keep you here. You keep getting every inducement to stay.

So these Super Powerful Individuals... are they evil?

Z: Well, it seems to me as if they are certainly capable of behaving in some pretty evil ways. That is to say, the incarnated aspects certainly do. And the incarnated aspects of us "minions" certainly could feel as if we were the victims of a great evil being perpetrated upon us.

But, if I understand this correctly, that is a lower-order perspective. And choosing that perspective will result in my staying here in duality. My anger and indignation will cause me to want to strike back. And so I will stay separate from the oneness.

8:... which means they win. Even if it is the Super Powerful that you decide to hate and fight against – it doesn't matter – the fact that you decide to hate and to fight means they win. Because you stay here. And you stay serving their agenda. See how it works? And if, for example, you decide to band together with other warriors and take up arms against them, if you decide to fight against them, guess what will happen next?

Z: I don't know.

8: Along will come someone who is a worthy and capable leader. Someone well versed in strategy and warfare. Someone who seems to hate "the evil sons-of-bitches" even more than you do! And then you'll be ready to follow him to battle, to do what he says, and... bingo!... You're back in the game serving them. Directly and indirectly. Directly, because they are masters of the strategy of managing any opposition. They do this by making it their business to **lead** that opposition. As you begin to organise a resistance group, so they will find ways to put their puppet in charge of your resistance group. You won't know it, but your leader will be one of their minions strategically positioned in your organisation by them to rule you!

And you serve them indirectly as well. From whom, for example, do you think you will buy your weapons? Where will you get all your other equipment and infrastructure from? Everything you will need to engage in resistance to the Super Powerful, will be bought from the Super Powerful. And every cent that changes hands in every transaction is also taxed and inflation-taxed to further enrich them. And so on and so on. And the same is true if you engage in more "peaceful resistance". If you congregate with others on Internet forums and discuss "the evils of The Powers That Be" and "spread the word" about the truth of what is really going on. You might think that you are helping to raise consciousness amongst the people of the world. You might think that you are doing something to crimp the activities of the Super Powerful by spreading the truth. And then, as you go, you'll find all kinds of "experts" who seem to be leading lights in the "truth movement". Surely it must have entered your mind that at least **some** of these "leading lights" are in the employ of the Super Powerful? Isn't that what you would do if **you** were Max? And if that **is** the case, how do you decide whom to trust? Who is telling you the **real** truth and who is selling you a version of the truth that is seeded with lies that are there to manipulate you? Suddenly things are not so simple, are they? You see, the Super Powerful didn't get to be the Super Powerful by being stupid. And they have seen and survived every kind of rebellion and insurrection there is. And each time they have become smarter, wilier and more powerful. And they have **long** memories and agendas. They think in terms of many generations, not in terms of what happens now, in this lifetime. That is how they succeed so amazingly at the game. And so it is that we arrive at the situation where they have a whole planet full of minions slaving away, doing their bidding and hardly a single one even begins to guess it! And even those who **do** discover this seem not to be able to do anything about it. In fact, in trying to do something about it, they just strengthen the hand of the Super Powerful.

And the final point about waging a war against "the evil Illuminati" or whatever you are calling them: who exactly will you strike against? Will you "stick it to the man" by bombing your local government offices? Do you actually think any of the Super Powerful will be found there? And if not there, then where will you find them? And I will tell you, you will not find them! The Super Powerful are so deeply hidden, so far behind the scenes, that you will nearly never see their names in the press and even less often see their faces. So, no matter who you bomb or shoot, you will just be hurting some proxy. Some puppet. Some poor sack who is also just trying to make his way in life as best he can. And so you have not hurt the SPIs at all, and all you have done is contribute to a bit more hatred in the world. Which, ironically, just makes them more powerful.

So you lose.

Then you lose.

And then you lose some more.

And when you have lost completely, then you just lose some more.

And **that** is what happens if you try to play against them in their game. And it **is** their game. You cannot beat them, or the system, by fighting it. The game is set up such that you have a handful of nothing and they hold all the aces. And, just in case, they have a selection of every other card they could possibly want up their sleeves. And if that isn't enough they can just change the rules any time they want.

Remember when I said it was all a game to them? Sometimes a vicious and cruel game, but still a game? The thing to remember about this is that they have a role to play. As long as they keep providing you with the very strongest inducements to stay in the game, then they are doing their job.

Z: That's their job?

8: On a soul-level, yes. Mostly their incarnated personalities don't know this. But essentially that is the soul-contract they have with everyone who enters this particular game. And I know you'll find it quite difficult to drum up much empathy for them right now but, you know, these beings carry a very heavy burden. And their lives, contrary to your popular imaginings, are not very happy at all. It is not just one glamorous party after another. Yes, there are compensations to being the richest and most powerful humans on the planet, but there are some grave costs to the personality as well. Allow me to give you a little summation:

The Super Powerful are completely hidden from you. If you know a name or have seen a picture in the tabloids or on the television, then this is, at best, a functionary of the truly powerful ones. The SPIs are **not** themselves involved in politics, nor are they chairmen of boards. They are hidden. They hold the reigns of power **through** other individuals who are their functionaries. If you can see the hands on the reigns of power then you are looking at a functionary.

The truly powerful are bred to it. Born, and not made, as they say. You do not get to join their ranks by being successful at business or by being wealthy. You cannot become one of them by joining some secret society and working your way up to the top-most ranks. You cannot join them by winning elections. At most you can become their servant. A conscious and willing vassal, perhaps. The Super Powerful are almost a breed apart. It is a vital part of their success strategy that they carefully protect the integrity of their family lines. Their genetic purity is something of an obsession with them. And with good reason. For one thing, their genetics are free from a great number of the afflictions that plague the rest of humanity.

From the very crib they are trained, conditioned and drilled to be what they are. Their upbringing is hard. Much harder than you could imagine. When other babies are being coddled and taught about love and sharing, these ones are being taught tough lessons involving self-discipline and self-reliance. They are taught unquestioning obedience, but only to their master. They are taught that all others are pawns; minions there for their use. Cunning, back-stabbing, deceit, lies and manipulation are all valuable tools of their trade. As long as your actions lead to a greater accumulation of power for your family, then you are serving the family's interests. And, if this means you personally rising to power over other SPIs through morally ambiguous means, then that too is acceptable. If not out-right respected.

And, whilst ludicrous levels of opulence are taken for granted, kindness, gentleness, patience, tenderness, and such manifestations of love are in pitiful short supply.

There is so much expectation placed upon the shoulders of these ones that there is no place whatsoever for failing to achieve excellently, always, at everything that is endeavoured. Any sign of weakness is derided. It is shameful. It is to be weeded out. Failure is not tolerated.

There is so much more that I could say here about their existence. But all I wish to do for now is to give you but a hint. I'm sure you begin to see that these beings have a very, very hard life. Right from the cradle to the grave. Love, in their eyes, is a luxury they cannot afford. Of course they misunderstand love. If they did not, they would not be able to think as they do. But all that too is part of the contract.

Z: But why, 8? Why? I don't understand it at all. If at least they were having a merry old time, living it up, then that would make sense to me. If they were doing this because they really liked having all the power and it really made them happy, then at least that would make sense. But if having the power is actually an almost unbearable burden, then why do it? I mean, if they are so unhappy, why don't they just get their flunkies to come out in the press and on TV and say, "*Sorry folks. There has been a bit of an error. We find we don't actually like running the show. It's not as much fun as it seemed. And we know you folk don't really like the ways things have turned out on your end either. So now we'll all just share our toys and play nice. The party is at our house. Everyone's invited!*" Sort of thing. Then everyone would be happy.

8: Happy? I'm not sure everyone would be happy. If the truth were to begin to come out in that sort of a fashion, then I rather suspect there would be a lot more rage than happiness. How happy would people be if they were told that the reason they have been at war with each other is, quite simply, because that was the best way to make a handful of people richer and more powerful? If you had lost a member of your family to such a war, would you accept an, *"Oh well, bygones,"* sort of a response? No. The depth of the deception is staggering. And if this began to come out, people would go into shock. There would be all kinds of responses such as denial, anger and rage. Very, very few would respond by deciding to just be happy. And anyway... what makes you think people **want** to be happy?

Z: I... uh...

8: Yes, of course that is what everyone **really** wants. But if that were your prime motivation – to just be happy – would you really have chosen to incarnate on planet Earth in this civilisation and at this time? No. There are places in All That Is that really are all about the finding of happiness. And we'll talk a lot more about that some time soon. But let me assure you, in case you are feeling confused on this point, that this planetary reality at this space/time nexus is not all about people trying to be happy. And **that** is how I can begin to answer your question. You ask me why the Super Powerful Individuals are doing this if it makes them unhappy. Well, I guess I can ask you the same question. Why have any of you come to this planet and incarnated here if it makes you unhappy? As you keep telling us you are, in your prayers and meditations. Why? Why any of this?

Z: I understand we come here to discover who we really are from a position of forgetting.

8: Yes, that is the prime motivation. To discover yourself. To create yourself anew. There are an infinite number of other subordinate reasons. Like healing some pain. Like finding oneness by exploring not-oneness. Like understanding what love really is by forgoing it for a while. And so forth. The reality you inhabit is a wonder. It is an unbelievable tool for creation and discovery. And so each of you, for reasons of your own, chose to go there. And each of you will find some wonderful, amazing prize as you leave there.

That is **why** you went there in the first place.

Now. Do you think it would be any different for the Super Powerful Individuals?

Z: I don't know. I suppose not.

8: It will not. Everyone who goes there plays a selection of roles. The Super Powerful play the role which helps to create a particular spiritual climate on your planet.

Z: Explain?

8: At the heart of every human being is a spark of the divine. You are all, therefore, essentially good, kind and loving. You each actually **want** to find your gift and give it. To do good, be kind and help each other. You want to find love, express love, **be** love. You want your bodies to be healthy and strong. You want your relationships to be good. And so on. So you see, if you all had what you really wanted, it would be a hop, skip and a jump and you'd be discovering your truth in your heart. You'd be bringing amazing quantities of light into your being and then you'd ascend out of the system. Every second person's grandpa or aunt would be the most wonderfully wise sage. There would be wisdom for the asking. Concepts like the oneness of all would be universally understood. There would be no division amongst nations or races or religions or any other grouping. Each individual would simply be following their own truest path home.

Z: Sounds wonderful!

8: And this is exactly what happens in many other realities. There are even many planets in your galaxy where this is the way it is. And it **is** wonderful when it is like this. And if that is what you, on a soul level, needed or desired, then that is where you'd be – on some other unity-conscious planet where there is peace, love and joy.

But you aren't there, are you?

Z: Apparently not.

So, if I understand you correctly, then I am here in this reality because this is what I, on a soul level, wanted to experience. And this means that I actually need these Super Powerful Individuals to do as they are doing. If they did not, the world would not be as it is. And if it was not as it is, I would not have **this** opportunity to experience and express myself.

8: Give the man a cigar!

Z: Jeepers, 8. I'm stunned. If I continue along this path you'll be asking me next to recognise the sacrifice of these individuals... the fact that they give up on a life of simple pleasures where there is love in abundance and joy in the moment so that they can play this hard, cruel role that the rest of us need them to play.

8: Don't be too quick to cry long tears for them. All have agreed to the roles they are playing.

I'd like to tell you something new now that will help you to understand why I say this. Did you know that, on a soul-level **you** were being groomed to be a part of the SPI club? That was the path you were on and that was the meaning of what you have called your "wizard lifetime".

(**Zingdad note:** See Chapter 1)

It was expected that you'd take the programming and follow the path and step into that role. Something went "wrong" with you though. You rejected the STS path that was laid out for you. Which caused some consternation in certain quarters and then I was called to figure out what was "to be done" with you.

Z: Oh my goodness, I didn't realise that! But now that you say it, it makes perfect sense!

8: The magic you wielded in that lifetime was not **your** magic. It was given to you, by others, to create a certain perspective within you. This should have had the consequence of making the STS path, and its concomitant ascendency to membership of the SPI club (albeit in a somewhat different reality than the one you are now in), an automatic choice for you. This was a part of your grooming and training. You should have developed a taste for having power over others. You should have taken to having abilities that others could only dream of. All of this **should** have seduced you. But it didn't. You found it to be unpalatable and you rejected the path. It's rare for this to happen, but not unheard of.

There is much, much more that I can tell you about this and I will, but it won't be of much interest to your readers. The only reason I raise this now in this very public way is that it is useful in bringing home the realisation that every single role is chosen. Everything is by agreement. And, just as each of you have agreed to enter into all kinds of loving relationships with friends and family in each incarnation, so have you also agreed to enter into the more antagonistic relationships you have experienced. And, in just the same way, the broader relationships have also been agreed upon. And so it is also true that collectively, all of you on Earth right now have, at the soul-level, entered into an agreement with the Super Powerful. They agreed to provide you with an environment that will make it as compelling as possible for you to stay so that you can play out the other dramas and relationships that you wish to experience. They get the experiences they have created for themselves in return; don't you fret about that. And the rule still applies: whatever they are doing to you as a planetary consciousness they are doing to themselves also. And this will continue until they too see that this doesn't serve them. Until they too are ready to awaken to their greater magnificence.

You see?

You are all in this together. You are **all** victims of your own making. Every one of you. Including the SPIs. And this will continue for each of you until you are finally ready to be done with the victim game in all of its many guises. And then, when you are quite done with all of this, then perhaps you will want to play another game. That is when you might decide to break free from the inducements to stay in this reality. If you do, then you will come to a place in your development where all the crazy things that are being instigated in this world will no longer entertain you. You will see through the illusions of this world.

War, religion, a swathe of manufactured diseases, food depleted of nutrients but pumped full of poisons, toxins added to your water supply, debt, inflation and other iniquitous financial ideas, politics, non-stop violence and aggression in entertainment, a ravaged and polluted world, fear-based news media and even things such as alcohol, nicotine and drugs, are all just some of the things which are used to keep you from finding love and peace within yourself. Which keep you from seeing every other as a brother or a sister. Which keep you from knowing that the greatest truth lies inside your own heart.

Z: It's pretty sickening to me that they are willing to do this to us, their fellow human beings, just to maintain power and control. How do they get to be so heartless? Or do they actually have a hatred for "the little people"?

8: Well, by now you might understand if I say to you that the Super Powerful look upon you, the citizens of the world, as their assets. Perhaps a bit in the way a farmer might think about his livestock. The farmer does, in his own way, love his livestock. He takes care of them, tends their needs, keeps them free from disease, protects them from predators and so on. The relationship shows many of the hallmarks of genuine loving concern. Except, of course, when it comes time to slaughter. When the farmer needs to get a return on his investment, the relationship begins to show some other characteristics. The livestock are loaded onto trucks, carted off to the abattoir and slaughtered.

If you were able to look at all of this with a disaffected eye, you might come to the conclusion that the farmer loves the **herd** but does not care about the **individuals** in the herd.

Z: And you are saying that the SPIs are like that?

8: One cannot speak for all of them – they are all individuals with individual thoughts and styles – but their behaviour certainly shows this approach. Many of them hold a belief that it is their duty and almost sacred trust to manage and look after the human race. The race as a whole. Like a farmer looks after a herd as a whole. But along the way he would happily have certain individuals slaughtered to pay his bills and, if they began to over-graze his land, he would consider it irresponsible not to do a bit of culling. You see, the individuals are just not considered to be important. And so they will use you in whatever way they see fit in the pursuance of their own goals.

The SPIs are, as I have said, the ultimate owners of anything big and important enough to be worth owning. And if the economy grows in such a way as to cause them to **not** own everything worth owning? Then they are not beyond trashing the economy so that they can then buy everything for a fraction of its previous worth. As the economy rights itself again, so it is that they are once again in possession of almost all of it. The fact that countless peoples' lives were ruined and that many starved and that others' hopes and dreams were dashed, does not concern them. It is not the individual who matters to them.

So we started this section of this chapter with your question about genocide for the sake of expediency. Well, the Super Powerful Individuals are not the only ones to have ever instigated genocide. But they are the ones who have done it most consistently throughout the whole of your recorded history. When history tells you it was this or that group or leader that was responsible, the chances are very strong that it played out in accordance with the wishes of the SPIs.

Z: I don't really know what to make of all this, 8. It is horrifying and chilling.

8: Maybe so. And now you have a number of choices. You can believe what I have said because it matches some of your observations of life. Or you can disbelieve it because it doesn't, or because you don't want it to. And if you do decide to believe this, then you can get angry and full of hate. You can try to hit back. And lose.

Or, if you are ready to stop being hurt by the game, you can awaken and discover who you really are and you can see it for what it is: a very big game. A serious and scary game. But a game, none the less. One that allowed you to undergo some of the most incredible experiences that can be had anywhere in All That Is. A wondrous, magnificent machine which outputs powerful choices allowing you to explore profound and amazing discoveries of who and what you really are.

This whole world, as it is, exists to show you who you are.

It reflects, with perfect precision and fidelity, your own ideas, beliefs, thoughts and choices back at you. And ultimately the Super Powerful Individuals are just one part of the machine. Without them it would not function.

And if you want to choose to see yourself as their victim, then it is apparent that you want to go for another spin around the inner workings of this particular machine. If, on the other hand, you come to the realisation that only you can create your reality and that you are no-one's victim, well then everything will begin to change for you. Then you will become the master of your own being, your own destiny and all of your own experiences.

And then? In that state of master consciousness, how then will you think of the Super Powerful Individuals? I tell you, you will not think of them as super powerful any more. You will see them as nothing other than role players in a great play. Ones who have had some quite interesting parts to play. You will see the difficulty, the pain and the complexity in their roles. And you will have understanding and compassion. Anger and vengeance will have left you.

And **that** is the story I will tell you of the Super Powerful Individuals. I tell it to you like this so that you will hear and understand that I am not trying to paint you a rosy picture. I am not trying to tell you that, *"Things are not as bad as you think."* No. Indeed things are probably a whole lot worse than you had thought. And yet... this is not a problem. Because, indeed, it does not matter how bad things are in your world, if those things are what is required for you to come to your own awakening.

You are all a bit like drug addicts who have been addicted too long to a very powerful narcotic called V. V is for victim. And you all take repeated doses of V, even though you sometimes have a bad trip, even though you sometimes over-dose, still your addiction drives you to keep taking it. And at some point you need to hit some kind of rock bottom experience, which will make you say, "*Enough!*" And then, and only then, will you decide to kick the habit.

So, the world you see around you, is as it is because you are as you are. And when you are done and done and **done** with victim, then, I promise you, your world will look entirely different to you. You will no longer encounter any victim experiences. You will see a new world through new eyes.

And now, to bring this question to a close; can you see that, without the Super Powerful Individuals playing the role they are playing, the game would not work at all? The planetary system would be quite different? Your experiences would be quite different? And you would not be offered the choices and opportunities for self-discovery and self-creation that you currently have?

Z: I can, yes.

8: And can you see that it is actually so that you agreed to this experience before you came here? And that you continue to agree to it every day? And that you can choose to release yourself from this agreement and come to choose something else if you like?

Z: Yes. I can speak from my own experience and say that I am right now finding out what it is to free myself from my own inner victim states. I am letting go of deeply limiting beliefs. And, as I do so, I am also moving to a place in my life and my world where I no longer feel as if I am the victim of anything. Not of other people or political systems or... anything. And since finding my "right place" in this world I really don't encounter much of the "negative" stuff that I used to see all around me just a few years ago. And if I contrast how I now feel with how badly victimised I felt as a young man... wow... it is quite amazing what a difference it has made to release myself from my own bondage.

8: Then that is my point exactly. Your outer world reflects your inner world. Most make the mistake, if they are unhappy, of expecting the outer world to change first before they believe they can find happiness. But this does not work. The outer world does not seem to be willing to change, so they stay unhappy. But then there are some who come to the realisation that the only way they will be able to make themselves happy is by changing their inner world. They do this and they find happiness. Perhaps they find it miraculous then to discover that their outer-world also follows suit and changes to fit with their state of happiness. Is this magic? A miracle? Maybe! Or perhaps this is just the way things would work if there were only one of us here experiencing itself in a fractal holographic expression of Itself. So perhaps we should not be surprised that it is so.

And this is one of the great lessons that this reality can teach you.

And so, tell me how you now perceive these Super Powerful Individuals? Are they evil? Are their actions evil?

Z: No, I really begin to understand what you have been saying all along. Because, yes, from the subjective standpoint they **are** evil. Without a second's thought they are willing to remove from billions of people their right to choose. But that is an illusion. Objectively, we all always have the right to choose. So then, they are not evil.

And, thanks to them, we have the most amazing opportunities for self-discovery. So then they are again not evil.

It all depends on your perspective, doesn't it?

8: Yes, it does. While you are still deep in the game and struggling to make sense of it, you see all kinds of beings around you as evil. As soon as you **do** make sense of it, you see it all for what it is. And then you leave the game and you see the perfection of the whole arrangement.

Z: Yeah, as a result of this conversation I am actually ready to know this to be true. Thanks, 8.

8: You are most welcome.

Let us move on to the next manifestation of evil you wanted to know about.

TERRORISTS

Do you really need me to talk about this one any more?

Z: No. I guess not. I think I can see this for what it is.

8: Good. Then can you give us a brief summation and we move on?

Z: I'll give it a bash...

I think there could be many underlying reasons why someone might be driven to commit acts of terror. But ultimately, it is the act of someone who is so deeply lost in his own powerlessness that he feels the only way to try to fix things is to commit some really horrendous act of violence. It is clear that this is a deeply traumatised soul lashing out at the world, which he feels has victimised him. This is a being who has chosen to experience the life he has and, as a result of his experiences, he chooses to respond to the world by expressing more fear, hate and anger into it. In so doing, he creates more of that which hurt him in the first place. And, in so doing, he also gives all of us the opportunity to choose how **we** are going to respond. We can see his solution isn't working. We can see how killing people and destroying the lives of the survivors doesn't result in a better world for anyone. So what are we going to do with **his** act of terrorism? Are we going to respond as he did with the desire to return the favour with interest? Are we going to try to kill him and his people and destroy lives over there where he lives? We can do that, but I'm not sure why we think it will help. It certainly didn't help when he did it over here where we are. Or are we going to make a new choice about ourselves to cease to be willing to kill each other. Or what?

And that is where I leave this. Terrorists are simply people who have responded to terrible circumstances with terrible choices, thereby creating more terrible circumstances. That is their story. The important bit is how we respond to this. What are our choices and how will we create ourselves in return?

8: I like how you handled that.

The next manifestation of evil you asked about was:

People Who Rape or Abuse Women, Children and Babies

What can I say about this one that hasn't already been said in previous discussions or, indirectly, in this one? It **is** a very tough issue to come to terms with and so it keeps coming up for you. I understand that. But the resolution of it remains the same. Before any violent or abusive interaction can take place between two beings it will be so that they, on some deep level, will be carrying within themselves a trauma. You see, one must have some considerable inner-pain to work out if one is going to choose to engage in such an interaction. To be willing to do such a thing to another **or** to be willing to allow this to be done to themselves... they must certainly have some difficulty within their psyche that needs to be addressed. The event itself then is really just the manifestation of the pre-existing inner-turmoil. As a result of the event, this pain is now made overt and is present in their reality. Now they can no longer deny the existence of the trauma. Now they must each make their way through their pain. The difference is that the perpetrator gets to be reviled by society. Gets to be told over and over how deeply wrong he is. He might end up spending time in prison and, even in prison, be treated like a pariah. It is a long, dark ride through the depths of the wretchedness of the soul to be on such a journey.

For the raped and abused the experience is no picnic either, of course. But at least one can hope that there might be loving support after the event. The victim might, depending on the circumstances, get psychological counselling and so forth.

Of course I'm not asking you to pity the perpetrator in such cases. That would probably be more than one can really ask. But I offer you this perspective. And I don't imply either that this is **always** how it proceeds, of course. It happens too that the rapist receives no censure from his society and that the victim is treated like a criminal. All manner of variations are possible but none of this detracts from the basic fact that, on a soul level, each chose and invited the interaction for their own purposes.

And so, is the perpetrator evil? Is the act evil? It is the self-same answer over and over again. It is the same answer as with the Super Powerful Individuals. And the answer is, of course, that it depends on your perspective. From the subjective experience of the victim and those who are close to the victim, the answer is almost certainly a resounding "yes". And who can say they are wrong to feel this way? Who can blame them for wishing untold harm and eternal torment upon the perpetrator? From the objective perspective though, he is of course not evil. He is a soul working out his deep-seated pain and confusion. And he has a contract with the soul that is expressed as the victim. And that contract is enacted. And so, from that perspective, not even the act can be labelled evil. It is what it is.

You, yourself have had another incarnation in which you were repeatedly abused as a child; both sexually and violently.

(**Zingdad Note:** see Chapter 1, "*Lost in my own dream world*")

And not just any child, but one who was mentally disabled. In your instance it was your soul's desire to understand the victim state quite deeply that led you to choose those experiences. And while that poor, dear boy was living though those experiences there can be no doubt that they were... words fail me... deeply, deeply traumatic. Yes, that is so. But I tell you now that you would not be here today engaged in your ascension path without having had, if not those experiences, then ones quite similar to them. They were the counter-balance to other experiences in which you played quite a malevolent perpetrator.

(**Zingdad Note:** see Chapter 1, "*The Wizard*")

If you remove from your soul the one experience, you must remove the other. You would not be able to leave here without knowing both sides. Your psyche would be in a state of imbalance. So you **could** have chosen not to experience either, but if you go down that road, you end up choosing not to do anything at all whilst incarnated here in this system. And then, what is the point? You would learn nothing at all about the Self. And coming to this reality would not hold any value for you. So you engage. You engage deeply. You fling yourself bravely into this system and you risk everything. You risk that, indeed, you might discover all manner of unendurably despicable things about yourself. And then you do! And then, when you are done with that, you begin to discover your true power, your eternal beauty and your magnificence. For it is so that you who have been here will know and understand love far more powerfully than another being who was not here. And this is so, of course, because you have truly been to where there was **no** love and then found your way back. You really, really will know what love is when you have done that!

So I ask you again: is the perpetrator evil? Is the act evil?

Z: I am really beginning to get this, 8. You have been kind enough to stay with me on this, looking at it over and over again from all kinds of perspectives. So now, as you ask me this, I can really see it. It really is only evil from the limited, subjective experience. Objectively, it is not evil. I actually get it.

8: I am pleased. As this becomes your truth, you will liberate yourself from all kinds of inner turmoil. You can expect to find yourself releasing your emotional pain and even symptoms of physical pain and discomfort, as you let go of your desire to hold all these other beings and their actions as "evil".

But let us get into an interesting one next. You asked me about...

DEMONS AND DEMONIC POSSESSION

Z: Yes. Are there such things as demons?

8: The word, "demon", means a great many different things to different people under different circumstances. It most certainly doesn't cover just one class of being! The first thing you should know is that the word demon started out in your ancient times meaning something quite different to what it now means to you. At its origin, the word meant something like "higher being"; essentially any being which existed between your "mortal realm" and the realm of "the gods". All such beings were called *daemons*. Any being that was of a finer density than that which humans perceived themselves to be, could be called a *daemon*. It was certainly not an inherently negative term. Daemons were very often kind and benevolent spirits. Though it is true that some of them might also have been indifferent or even malevolent too. But the point is that the word daemon had no inherent negative connotation. It was simply a catch-all word that meant something like "higher spirit being". Perhaps in your current parlance you might express this as "higher dimensional being."

Z: Interesting!

8: But over time the meaning of the word changed. And certainly it was expedient to the expansion of the monotheistic religions to characterise all such beings as evil and therefore not to be consorted with. Wherever you have people using religion as a tool to gain and maintain power, you will find them casting any path to spiritual truth and growth, other than the one they offer, as evil. But, be that as it may, it is so that, in your present reality, the word has come to be loaded with the most negative of connotations. It is now taken to mean exclusively a spirit being of a deeply malevolent nature.

Z: But such beings do exist?

8: Are you asking if there are beings that reside at densities other than your own who desire something other than your best interests?

Z: Yes.

8: Don't be naïve. Of course there are! A huge variety of spirit beings exist that have, for all kinds of reasons, come to feel the desire to manipulate and damage others. Just as there are such beings incarnated on your planet right now, so there are such beings in the discarnate state. Mostly these ones are of a very small amount of light. Lost ones. Sad, small energies that have hurt themselves badly and lost their way. And now they would steal a little light from you to sustain themselves if they could. They are really nothing more than small leeches.

There are ones who are a little more powerful than that too. Ones who have, with full intent and purpose, chosen a path of negative orientation. And then there are also the ones who are directly minions of The Adversary – which we shall talk about in a while.

So, yes, these all exist. But what of it? You are no more their victim than you are a victim of anyone else. You should be aware that they exist and then you should choose not to give them any of your energy. Create with love and they shall have no purchase upon you. And that is as simple as it is. There are some basic spiritual protection tools that I could teach you if you wish to formalise your own defence until such time as you know yourself to be above such concerns.

Z: Thank you, 8, that would be useful.

8: All right, we'll talk about that as a separate discussion.

For now I wish you to understand that these beings are not your problem if you are not willing to allow them access to your energy.

Z: Okay, but what about demonic possession? Does it, or does it not, happen?

8: It does. Those who are willing to create the opening for such any experience will probably get it. There are, as I have said, a fair number of spirit beings that are of a negative energy. If you offer access to your energy, you can be sure that there will be someone who is willing to take what you offer. How would it be if you left your home open and unlocked with all your possessions unguarded and then went off on holiday?

Z: I guess I'd come home to a pretty empty house.

8: If you were lucky! More than likely your house would first be stripped bare and then all kinds of undesirables would move in. And who could blame them? Here is a house full of stuff for them to steal and sell. And there are nice dry rooms for them to sleep in. And there is free water and free electricity to use. Wonderful!

Z: Until I return home?

8: Hmm. Yes. And then you must decide what you are going to do. If you do want to evict the squatters, then you can get help. If you own the house, then you can get law enforcement officials to kick them out. And then you have the mammoth task of setting things back to rights. Certainly it will take you some time and a great degree of effort to replace everything that was lost and to repair everything that was broken. But if you are determined, you will be able to accomplish this and will emerge from the experience a great deal wiser.

This is a good analogy for what occurs in the spirit realm. You have a physical body and a number of more subtle spirit bodies. These are your home and you must take responsibility for them. You must secure your walls and lock your gates and only give access to those whom you love and trust. But when you are new to this you won't know how and so you are given help. You might call those who help with this, your Spirit-Guide or guardian angel. It is often so that you might have a particular Spirit-Guide who is responsible for your spiritual protection. Such a one is called the Gate Keeper.

Z: Oh! Are...

8: ...yes, amongst many other roles, I am your Gate Keeper. But we are not talking about you and I now. We are talking about people on Earth in general. And for every incarnated soul it is so that your whole spiritual guidance team is appointed before you enter each incarnation to assist you with your psycho-spiritual protection. If you want to maximise your protection, you can make the conscious choice to allow them to protect you. And you can help them in their task too by listening to your intuition. And as you "grow up" spiritually, so you can also learn to take more and more responsibility for your own protection. And then the time will come when you will no longer need a guide for protection. And that is how it should be. But unfortunately it doesn't always work that way. Sometimes incarnated beings make some very strange choices. Sometimes they are led to believe that they can gain certain gifts, powers or tools with which to manipulate their reality by negotiating with negative beings. Sadly, the negative beings are not very reliable. They will tell any lie and make any promise to get what they want and will give nothing in return, if they can get away with it. A human being with their shields down and their spiritual guidance disabled is a very vulnerable thing. Such a path, therefore, never ends happily.

Sometimes, though, it is a matter of self-destructive urges that would lead beings to cease to care for their own protection and to disallow their Spirit-Guides from protecting them. They might open their defences and invite all and sundry in.

Whatever the motivation, for such beings it will not be long before the house of their being becomes a squat for all kinds of undesirables.

Just as the case is with evicting squatters from your house, so too cleaning your spiritual abode is a traumatic thing. I would most strongly advocate that you not allow yourself to wander down this path. Take charge of your own spiritual hygiene and, at the same time, avail yourself of the help that is offered to you by your guidance team. Trust your own heart and choose for love. Then you'll be fine. These squatters cannot invade your spiritual home if you do not actually open the door to it. They are not able to over-power you. You are not their victim. So, quite simply, do not choose this!

Z: And what if I know of someone, a friend, who has such a problem?

8: If your friend wants help and is willing to make different choices, then they may be helped. But you will need to get competent help for such an exercise. If you look, you will find a variety of people who are competent to assist. So help your friend to choose someone with whom they will feel comfortable. Then the journey towards a "clean home" begins. It might be a long journey. Parts of it might be quite distressing. Your task will be to make sure that you don't move into rescuer. Help this being to help themselves. Do not rescue them.

> (**Zingdad note:** Though it is, as 8 has said, not the most pleasant healing journey, since these words were first written, I have come to assist with a number of such "house cleanings". If you, or someone you know, is in need of such assistance, then there **are** people who can help. I am one such. To arrange a consultation to discuss healing, you may contact me via my website here: zingdad.com/contact-zingdad.)

The closing point I would like to make on this subject is this: as with any manifestation of evil, you certainly can choose to experience it. And choosing to experience it can make your life very uncomfortable. But the over-arching point is that it **is** your choice. You can always choose **not** to experience it. And for so long as that is the case, you are not actually victimised by it.

Z: Thanks, 8. I think I have an understanding of this situation.

8: And very soon you will be able to discover for yourself that, truly, these beings that would act in a "demonic" fashion are actually quite small, lost and powerless. Their stories are always very sad ones. They are actually in desperate need of help. Which they will get when they are ready to receive it. But that is not for this discussion.

Let's move on then to the three names that you have given, which seem to add up, in your society, to the very epitome of evil.

LUCIFER, SATAN AND THE DEVIL

Z: Oh, yes. This should be interesting...

8: Oh, it will be. But before we get started, I wish to briefly point something out. The words and names you use in your world are very imprecise things.

One of the many reasons for this is that people ascribe different meanings to words. Some words are more prone than others to having diverse meanings and these names, Lucifer, Satan and the Devil, more so than most. And when you consider that, on the whole, these words are an attempt by those behind the Veil to describe what is beyond it... well it is bound to lead to some confusion.

And this provides me with a challenge. In being willing to describe and discuss the beings that may be represented by these three names, I am going to have to exercise some editorial control. I am going to discuss the beings that I believe are the closest match for these names. That is the best I can do, so it will have to suffice.

Z: Okay. But I don't see the problem...

8: Please understand. There is no one single being anywhere who answers to any of these names. Where such beings might exist, the very concept of a **name** is meaningless. It is only in your very, very limited sphere of existence that these names exist at all.

Let's take Lucifer, for example. The name literally means something like, "that which carries light". So, should I try to find the greatest carrier of the light and describe **that** being to you?

Or should I instead look within the cultures that pre-date yours, from whom you inherited this concept, and see that this name refers, quite literally, to the planet Venus?

Or should I look deeper into those early cultures and see the allegorical value that they ascribed to Venus and see how this story corresponds somewhat to a greater story of your reality?

Or should I look at the babble of contrasting views offered by the many religions in your reality and somehow try to sift out to whom it is that they refer with this name? Because, I can tell you, there are a good number of different beings and principles that could all answer to the description thus provided!

Z: Ah. Now I begin to see the problem.

8: So, I am simply stating upfront that the understandings that follow are my best attempt to deal with this complexity and ambiguity in a way that is both useful and truthful.

Z: Thanks, 8. I understand and accept your offer to deal with this as you think best.

8: Thank you. Although I have already begun to talk about Lucifer, I find it would better serve our purposes if we first talked about the Devil and then I continue with Lucifer next. Are you amenable?

Z: Sure, no problem. But does that mean that these are different beings?

8: They sometimes get conflated together. But in my view they are indeed different beings.

So...

THE DEVIL

The Devil occurs in one guise or another in a number of your religions. But it is, quite simply, an entirely fictitious construct created by those religions themselves.

The sponsoring thought from which the Devil springs is that the religion in question's doctrine is perfect and flawless and therefore unarguable and undeniable. It is, after all, the "word of God", or at least the word of God as spoken by His very best representatives. Do you see the problem?

Z: No. I don't understand how **that** could be the sponsoring thought for the Devil.

8: It wouldn't be if everyone in the world who ever came into contact with this particular doctrine just immediately accepted it. I mean, surely, the word of God should brook no opposition? Surely all who encountered it should immediately have their hearts swayed and immediately fall in line and **believe**. So either the scriptures in question **are not** the word of God, or...

Z:... or there is some powerful supernatural agency interfering with things?

8: Exactly! And so, enter stage left, bearing horns and a trident, a certain goatish fellow of ill repute.

Z: (laughs) 8, you crack me up!

8: (laughs) I do. But this **is** a serious subject. Think, for example, of medieval Europe. This was a time when a small group of men had nearly absolute power, based upon the fact that they were religious leaders. Their word was law. And their authority came, they said, from God. They were, they said, God's agents on Earth. Power, wealth and status was theirs and there was no-one who could challenge them. Or was there? Occasionally there would arise various spiritual views, which diminished their power. Some of these ideas would gain popularity, as ordinary people found them to be preferable to the ideas espoused by the church. And then, what would happen? The church would come down on this heresy with a heavy hand. And of course, the justification was that these heretics were inspired by the Devil. So the church would send someone to persuade the heretics to change their minds and to again affirm that the church's line was the only correct one. And the fact that these confessions were extracted with torture and the fact that the end product was almost always death for the heretic, was seen as an acceptable price for the saving of the heretic's soul from the clutches of the Devil. At one point it got so bad that genocide was committed on the population of a whole region in the South of France, ostensibly for heresy. The Cathars were a distinct cultural group who were both prosperous and spiritually advanced. Greedy eyes desired their land and the church was easily swayed to declare heresy as a pretext for exterminating them to steal what was theirs. This mission to exterminate the Cathars was, in fact, the first crusade.

So the subject of the Devil is a deadly serious one. But not for the reasons you might have thought. It is serious because the Devil has been invoked as justification for some of the most egregiously vile acts ever committed in your history.

It has been the same in a great many of the wars that have raged upon your planet too. Each time one group wants to go out and slaughter another, some benighted soul will get it into his head to claim that God is on their side, that the opposite side are for the Devil and that it is their holy duty to kill as many of the "devil worshippers" as possible.

And, sad to say, this kind of thinking did not end in the dark ages. Still to this day each minuscule splinter of each religion everywhere claims some kind of special truth. Some kind of greater connection with God. And then they claim that every other splinter and every other religion has, to some degree or another, been lead astray by... you guessed it... the Devil. And each time someone leaves their religion or lapses it is, of course, the Devil who led them astray. And to them it would not matter in the least bit if the person in question found a greater sense of peace and harmony outside of their religion. Still they would be wrong and still it would be the work of the Devil.

And you can see the logic. As long as you require your specific and exclusive story to be **the only truth** and the only word of God, then you are going to have some considerable difficulty if something comes along that can powerfully argue against your doctrine. The creation of the notion of the Devil is a very powerful defence. It keeps you "right" and it makes the opposing story even more wrong without you even needing to examine the ideas you are holding to be true. In fact, the more powerful the opposing ideas are, the greater the evidence that they are "inspired by the Devil". Because such a powerful and cunning argument can only come from the Devil. Right?

Z: Whew! I see the argument. But how do you deal with that?

8: You don't. It is **not** your job to win converts. If someone so badly needs to hold onto their specific belief that they need to believe that all other beliefs are inspired by the Devil, then you should let them do just that. Don't try to change their mind. If you go out to persuade people that their beliefs and ideas are wrong, then you are committing spiritual violence. Don't do it. Remember – what you do to others, you do to yourself also. And, as you don't wish to have others trying to change your beliefs for you, so you should not do this to others.

Find what is right and true for you. Live that. And, just as you love to be able to learn from others, so you may share your truth as a gift; offer it, but offer it openly and lovingly. Allow others to take from your truth if they so desire, but do not attach yourself to the need that they should agree with you or be changed by what you say.

If you do this, then the Devil will cease to matter to you. You will not come into contact with those who are creating this construct.

Z: This is a very interesting thought, 8. I had not previously considered it possible that the Devil is actually created by those who claim to hate him.

8: It is a very important realisation. Remember that you create with your attention. Whatever you focus on, you bring into being. Not only the things you like, but the things you dislike too. And the more powerful the emotions, the more powerful the creation. So, yes, hate creates! It certainly does. Less powerfully than love, but it still creates.

So what you should take from this is the realisation that it would serve you well to release all hatred from your own being. These powerful negative emotions simply bring to your life that which you **don't** want. Focus your attention and thoughts and creations on that which you love, and you shall get that which you **do** want.

Do you see?

Z: I do. Thank you, 8.

So, if the Devil is created by those who claim to be in opposition to him, does that mean the Devil is not real?

8: Ah ha! I am **so** glad that you asked that question! Because the answer to this is both interesting and important.

No. I am **not** saying that the Devil is not real. In fact, quite the opposite. He **is** real. If he were not real, then you would not be creator-beings! So many of you have focused so much attention and emotional energy on this construct that it has taken on an independent validity. A great many people, over a good deal of time, have externalised into this being all that they have found to be unacceptable and repugnant within themselves and their world. Everything that is vile and disgusting and unlovable has been divorced from the Self and the world and embedded in the Devil. That's a whole lot of energy, life and creative force! So, yes, creators, you have created. You have created many wondrous and magnificent things and you have created some very sad and painful things too. The Devil is not one of your happier creations.

Z: I am at a loss for words. Wow. So what now? What do we do about this?

8: You grow up. I have said it before in this conversation and I say it again. The mark of an adult is one who takes responsibility for his or her life. The mark of a spiritually mature being is one that takes responsibility for its creations. And this is what you must do. If you take responsibility for everything in your life and your experience, if you take responsibility for everything you have ever done or said, if you take ownership of who and what you are, then there is no place for the Devil in your life. There is no need, value or desire in your being for some other who is responsible for the "wrong", so that you can be "right". If you take total, absolute and ultimate responsibility for all that you are, then this little creation shows itself to be a fable. You release it from yourself and your life.

Z: But what about others who are still holding onto it?

8: Not your problem. Or are you their rescuer?

Z: Ah! No, I am not.

8: So?

Z: So then I am fine. If there is such a thing as the Devil, then it is simply me showing myself that I have not taken responsibility for myself. I should respond by growing up and taking ownership of my experiences and my creations. Then it has no further bearing on my life.

8: That is a good response. Shall we move on?

Z: Okay thanks.

8: Next you wanted to know about...

LUCIFER

Z: Yes, please. Is this also a fictitious being that we have created? Or is it a real being and truly the source of all evil?

8: That which would be the best fit for the name, Lucifer, very much does exist. And he might well be called the "inventor of evil" but probably not the "source of all evil".

Z: A surprising answer!

8: There is more to come. A good deal more. What follows now is a very important story. If you understand the story of Lucifer, then you understand much. But to tell the story correctly, I need to step back a bit and tell you of the creation of your reality and proceed from there to tell the tale of Lucifer.

Z: Okay. Let's hear it!

8: It goes like this:

In the beginning was the ONE and the ONE was all and all was balance and harmony. Then, from within the great stillness, the perfect peace of the ONE, arose awareness of Self. "*Here I am,*" said the ONE. And with that awareness, arose curiosity: "*Here I am... **but what am I?**"* And so it was that the ONE desired to discover Itself and that desire was curiosity and curiosity's expression was pure creativity. And out of creativity arose different parts to the ONE, which were all explored.

And All That Is, in every reality that ever has, and ever will be, created, is all just the ONE answering this same, basic ancient question: "*What am I?*"

And since the ONE is truly infinite, this is a question that will never be answered to its completeness. The answering is a process that will continue to unfold for all of eternity. And it is the *process* of the answering, not the answer, that is the purpose of every mote of consciousness in All That Is.

And so it is that every single mote of consciousness everywhere always begins its journey with a similar dawning of its consciousness. As it first gains self-awareness, so it begins to discover itself: "*Here I am. But what am I?*" It is really and truly so that this is the way every single beingness has begun. It is so because it is the way the ONE began. From what is, self-awareness dawns and self-discovery and curiosity, is the means by which self-awareness is expressed. And so it is that the first act of consciousness is always this curiosity about Self. "*Here I am. But what am I?*"

Indeed, at every level of your being, from the very highest right down to the very smallest particle of Self engaged here in the deepest density, it is true that the only function and purpose you really and truly have... is to discover yourself. To find out who and what you really are. This is the purpose you began with, and this will continue to be your purpose for all eternity.

Discover yourself. Know yourself. Express yourself. **Be** what you are, to the fullest possible extent.

And, when you understand that **this** is what drives the ONE, this very desire for discovery of the Self, then you understand that every time you discover yourself a little more, you are contributing to the ONE. Then **you** are an aspect of the ONE that is being "successful". Then **you** are contributing to the ONE's greater self-knowledge. And the more grandly you discover yourself, the more grandly you are contributing. And so, it should be obvious, that if you can procure a situation in which you could catalyse other Selves, other aspects of the ONE, to quickly and very powerfully attain a greater degree of self-knowledge, then you would be doing a very great service to the ONE indeed.

Z: And what happens at the journey's end, 8? What happens when I have finally and completely discovered myself?

8: We are digressing, but it is an interesting question. So I shall answer. You can never cease discovering yourself. You see, you can **always**, if you try, create more. And, in so doing, you can realise that there is more that you did not know about yourself. But, that said, there can be an end to the journey. Any time you really and truly wish the journey to end, you simply return yourself wholly and completely to the ONE. You cease your separation, your creation, your expression and your discovery and then you gift all that you are to the oneness. When you do this, then your consciousness merges completely with the ONE until there is no separation within you. Until there is only ONE. In so doing, you make the ultimate discovery about yourself: you discover that you are so utterly and completely one with the ONE that you realize that you are all there ever was and all there ever will be. That all the journeying and adventuring and discovering and creating was all just you discovering yourself. That it's only ever been you. You, and all your many other aspects of Self, playing out every single role and creating every single creation in All That Is.

That is what lies at the end of the journey, should you so choose it. And even if, and when, you **do** choose it, in choosing it you will discover that there is **still** an on-going, never-ending process of self-creation and self-discovery. And still it is you doing this. Now it's just you, as the ONE.

And that is the story. In fact I would say it is **the only** story. It is your story, my story and the story of every other particle of consciousness that ever was. You get permutations and variations in the story as beings strive to discover themselves in different ways, but that too is all just a part of the story of self-discovery.

Z: I feel such a quiet, comfortable resonance with this. I understand and know what you have told me to be true. Thank you for telling me this.

8: It is my pleasure. But now, to get back to Lucifer's story, we need to backtrack to a point before this universe and the whole separation reality existed. So we return our narrative to the ONE.

In the mind of the ONE there was an on-going exploration into Its own nature and beingness. And it came to be that many themes and variations of what the ONE is had been explored by the many parts of the ONE and the many parts of the ONE had grown adept at interacting with each other in their joyful quest for expansion and discovery. And so things proceeded until a new question dawned upon the ONE: "*What if I were **not** one? What if I were **many**?*" And this thought created a ripple of disturbance amongst the other parts of the ONE. It was a troubling thought. Troubling to contemplate. It felt dangerous. It opened the door to, "*What if I am not the only one?*" and, "*Am I alone?*" and, "*Are there others such as I?*" and, "*If there are others, how shall I find them?*" All of these, and many more troubling questions, lay on the other side of the door that had now been opened and most of the parts of the ONE were troubled and shied away from this question.

But the thoughts of the ONE are not as the thoughts of a man. The thoughts of the ONE are alive. Each thought is, itself, an angelic being of unimaginable creative power. And **this** thought was a Bright One who was vast, and terrible in its beauty. Such a being as could comprehend in its mind the impossibility of separation and manyness within the oneness. This thought of the ONE **was** Lucifer and Lucifer was the thought. And the thought took form and began its mighty journey of discovery: "*Here I am now. But what am I?*"

And as Lucifer began to explore, discover and create itself, so this Bright One drew itself from the rest of the ONE; it drew a cloak made from the stuff of its own consciousness around itself that it might be made **alone**.

Alone.

Alone.

Alone.

All one unto itself and apart from all others. Separate. Apart. Removed. And so, cloaked within its own mind, Lucifer was the first of the ONE's creations ever to conceive of not-oneness. Lucifer's thoughts were his own. And for the first time in All That Is, one being uttered the word, "I", and it was not the ONE speaking. One being conceptualised, "me" and "self" as a truth that was independent of the other creations of the ONE. And ego was born.

And as Lucifer sank deeper into his forgetting of the ONE, so he found only that which he created in his own mind to be real and true.

And all the angels of the ONE stood in awe for they could see that truly it had been accomplished: a part of the ONE had made Itself separate. Though it was illusory and untrue, for the Bright One was still there in their company and held forever in the heart of the ONE, still it was also true that Lucifer had lost himself deep within his own cloak of forgetting. The Bright One had turned his sight inwards and sealed his perspective such that he could not see the glory and magnificence of the ONE in whose heart forever he was cradled.

And so it was that the first part of the question was being answered. The ONE had asked, *"What if I were not one?"* and Lucifer knew not-oneness and so he, himself, was the answer. But such an answer is not a simple thing. The answer exists in its unfoldment, in its process. And so, for a veritable eternity, Lucifer would busy himself with the exploration of every possible variation to this answer until it is complete. Until it is answered. And then his creation will be **done** and he will return his creation to the ONE and himself to wholeness and oneness.

And as Lucifer worked on his creations, so too was there still a desire to know, *"What if I were many?"* and that desire was the motivation for some of those angels of the ONE who were most adept at creation and discovery, who were most sure of their inherent beingness, to drew nearer to Lucifer that they too might pass a part of their consciousnesses through the cloak that he had cast about himself. And, as they did, they found themselves entering the mind-scape of Lucifer. And they entered also into the deep forgetting that is separation from the ONE.

Some of this angelic host retained a great deal of their self-possession. Even though they passed through the cloak of forgetting, they managed to remember that they were, indeed, all part of the ONE. And so they entered very shallowly into the vast and expanding realm that the Bright One was creating within Its own mind. A mind-scape that would exponentially expand to always encompass all that any mind can imagine or comprehend of in separation. These angels that remembered themselves, that retained the awareness of the divine connection between all things, began to play and explore and create. And together they created glorious and rich interplays of their light. Like children creating sand castles, they played. And they sang songs of love to one another and gave their gifts freely and such was the beauty and splendour of their creations together that it rang through the mind of Lucifer and touched his heart. And he was reminded and he knew: *"Yes, I am, I am, I am. And I am one with the ONE, I am,"* and so Lucifer awoke from his slumber and returned to the host with love in his heart.

Z: He what? No he didn't. That's not how the story goes!

8: Isn't it?

Z: No. It can't be. I mean, I was following the story and all kinds of things were making sense to me. Such as that the Veil that J-D introduced me to is Lucifer's cloak. I felt an amazing dawning of realisation with that. So I liked the story. Except the ending. As nice as it is, it can't be true. Because here we are now. Here is the universe and the world and human civilisation and all of this pain and separation stuff. So that's not it.

8: You aren't wrong. But what you haven't understood is that there are many iterations to this story. This first version is true enough... as far as any such stories can be. But this is very difficult to explain to you because you insist on your linear view of things. If you can simply understand that there are many, many iterations of this story and that all of them happened, not one-after-the-other, not even "all at once" but just that all are true and all happened, then I can tell you of another iteration.

Z: Okay. I think I can cope with that. Because, of course, the level at which these things occur is outside of time, is it not?

8: In ways that you will simply not be able to comprehend, this is so, yes.

Z: Okay, so these other iterations?

8: With each version of this story, a new variation was tried; a new permutation of the game of separation. With each variation, the angels became more and more adventurous as regards their choices and what they would be willing to do and try beyond the Veil. You see, the great consciousnesses experience their imaginings with creation. When such beings wonder, "*What if?*", then they actually create a reality where it **is** so. They can then see, within themselves and their own experiences, how that would be. And so it was that the angels created new realms and realities beyond number. And each overflowed with light and life and beauty. Each reality was the love that flowed naturally and easily from the hearts and minds of the angels. And so, as beautiful as this all was, the outcome was always the same: in short order all parts of the ONE that were beyond the Veil would find such high expressions of love together that they would be returned, together with Lucifer, to oneness.

And then it came to the mind of Lucifer that the problem was one of creating a mechanism that would counter the drive to oneness; a wedge that would allow the angels themselves to create more and more separateness between themselves so that their expressions could multiply. So that their expressions could create new expressions of their own. And, with great excitement, Lucifer drew his cloak once more with a new thought in his mind.

And as it is with the ONE, so too it is with the angels. Their thoughts are life and that life will be manifest. And this time, into the mind of Lucifer, beyond the cloak of separation was born this new thought: The Adversary. And this being's very nature and purpose was to be dissent. To be an agent of eternal separation. To provide the most powerful inducement to all other particles of consciousness to remain beyond the Veil. That was Lucifer's new thought and it was the gift he gave to the angelic host in their latest iteration of the game.

And this brings me to the last name on our list.

SATAN

At its origin, the root of the word, "Satan," means something very like, "The Adversary".

And so, as the angels entered also into forgetting and began again the game of rediscovering and remembering Self, so they found amongst their number a dark one. The very shadow of the light of Lucifer. One could very well say that Lucifer was Satan's Inner-Self.

And, as this new one began to discover Itself, it discovered that It was not love and not kindness. The opposite of that. For Lucifer invented, for the purposes of the deepening of the creations beyond the Veil, the very soul of antagonism. Hatred. Wilful destructiveness. Aggression. Manipulation. Malevolence. Yes... evil. That which takes from you your right to choose. Squeeze a being into believing that it has no options and force it to your will and you will have stung quite badly that being's sense of what is fair and right. That being will go to quite some effort to repay the favour. And bingo... suddenly those beyond the Veil became embroiled in a whole new game. The angels found themselves reacting with shock and rage to this new interloper in their games of loving creation. Their rage caused a fragmentation: on the one side a being that **is** love and oneness... and on the other, a being that wishes to strike back and enact justice and revenge. And so trust was broken in the hearts of the hurt parts of the ONE. And in such a state, when they encountered one another, they reacted to each other with fear and their fear led them to create pain and harm for each other. And truly, they too became adversarial. They began to act more and more as The Adversary did. And so it came to be that deeper and deeper layers were created by ever greater acts of separation and fragmentation of the souls of the parts of the ONE.

And so it was.

The tale that flows from this becomes far too complex to do justice to in a linear fashion. You'd really need to see it with a multidimensional mind to understand it correctly; as you eventually will when you are done with incarnation. But at least you have the beginnings of the story and of how things came to be as they are.

But if we can skip forward in the story, then we can find beings becoming so hurt by their interactions with each other than they can no longer believe that they are creating themselves or their experiences. And so they tumble another step deeper into separation... into a state called duality. Such beings believe, of course, that they are weak little creations and that the creator is "someone else". And this belief allows for a vastly more complex reality to come into being. There is scope for far greater manyness when all the parts involved do not believe that they are creating their experiences. Much richer creation can play out. And it does.

Your whole universe, as you experience it, exists well within this level of consciousness.

In due course, Adamu will tell you some amazing stories. Stories of creation where whole civilisations tumbled down from high consciousness to low. Stories of life and love and stories of war and chaos.

These are the stories of separation in its fullest expression.

And your world, life on planet Earth, is a very important part of this great story. You will enjoy very much, I am sure, to hear from Adamu how it all knits together.

But behind all of the great stories, there are individuals. Sentient, living, conscious beings. Such as you are – the human beings of planet Earth. Across the whole universe and beyond, these are the stories of your lives, your struggles and your triumphs, all in the face of the impossible odds provided by The Adversary and his willing minions; those who gave their will over to Satan. Those who chose to bear his standard and fight his fight. Those who served only greater separation and division.

But throughout that fight, right from the loftiest levels of consciousness, right down to the deepest and densest depths, as a result of our interactions with Satan and his minions, those who were beyond the Veil felt things like fear and hatred. We separated ourselves more and more from each other. We broke our sense of oneness. We fell down deeper into the lower densities. We built up layer upon layer of darkness upon our own souls. We lost faith in ourselves and trust in one another. We learned to expect the worst of each other. We learned to treat each other like objects to use and abuse for our own ends. And this was how our own creator-nature responded to our experiences. That is to say, as soon as we began to see evil around us, so we began to create more evil from within ourselves. To one degree or another we became the agents of separation. We **ourselves** became the adversary. Every time we chose fear, hate, anger, and separation over love, kindness, joy and unity, we served the interests of The Adversary.

And **all** of us have done this. All of us. Some of us have done this powerfully enough to fall down into the depths of separation. If you are incarnated on planet Earth, then you are one such. And some of us have used these incarnations to even more powerfully create separation. Some of us have used our God-Light, even inside incarnated lives, to sow greater fear, pain and anguish. As all do, to some extent, in each lifetime. And this is how the deepest game in separation continues. Because, when in separation, this is what parts of the ONE do.

This is what God does when God meets The Adversary.

And this is the source of your inner pain and hidden shame. It is that which drives you to psychologists and anti-depressant drugs. It is that which causes your self-loathing, which is at the heart of your addictions and self-destructive habits. It is the cause of all the violence and psycho-emotional pathology, which is rampant upon planet Earth and on a vast number of other planets besides. A great many of your physical illnesses also spring forth from the deep seated feeling that you are, at your core "ill". Inside yourself, you feel yourself to be wrong and broken, but you do not know why, so you manifest these experiences of being ill, wrong and broken into your bodies.

All of us have played The Adversary. **All** are guilty of this.

Z: Oh my God, 8! I suddenly feel as if I'm fighting back tears. I know I have done this! What must I do with this knowledge? What do I do now?

8: You smile and say, "*Mission accomplished*"!

Z: Mission accomplished?!?

8: Yes. But now try to say it with less horror in your voice. And without the question marks. And with a smile.

Z: How? I don't understand?

8: Well, let's go back to first principles. The point of all this was to create a reality where you could lose yourself completely in separation and duality. That is the first objective of the experiment. The second part is when you turn around and begin to remember who you really are.

And so? Is the first part of the experiment not well and truly served by you becoming The Adversary yourself? By you acting out your separation and duality? By you treating yourself and all other Selves as abominably as you can?

Z: Why, yes, I suppose it is. I suppose in those moments, I was as deeply in separation as I could be.

8: Right. So you can now see it for what it was and say...

Z: Mission accomplished.

8: Yes.

But it is a painful mission and I can see why you wouldn't be feeling very enthusiastic about accomplishing it.

The second part is a lot more fun, though. The second part is when you begin to remember who you are. You begin to discover that you are a being of pure radiant light. That your truest nature is Love. That you are really ONE with All That Is. That you are a powerful, magnificent, creator being. That you exist to discover yourself and create yourself exactly as you most deeply desire yourself to be.

And isn't it nice to know that you are quite firmly on that part of the journey now?

Z: Yes. It is. But what do I do with the stuff that I did while I was on the first part of the journey?

8: It is your gift to yourself and to the ONE. It is how you expressed yourself in your deepest forgetting in response to The Adversary. It is how you expressed yourself as The Adversary. Now you know. Now you can make other choices. And now, when you encounter The Adversary in another being, you can understand this is them, as they are, while they are still on the outward journey. They are still in the first part of their journey. And that is all. Now you can release your judgement of them.

Z: Yes. I see.

8: And you can release your anger at those who make the world as it is. Those who are in power and seemingly making very poor choices for the rest of humanity. Those who plot and plan and create evil. Like fomenting war between nations with trickery and deception. Like manufacturing diseases that blight humanity. Like suppressing technology that is clean, in favour of technology that pollutes the planet. Like creating systems of money that enslave the masses. Like creating systems of economy that keep the majority in crushing poverty. Like allowing death, disease and famine to rage when all of this could be eradicated instantly. And on and on. You can release your anger towards them because you have done the same. To some small degree in this lifetime and to a far greater degree in lifetimes past... you were a part of all this. And now you can see that those who are behaving in this way are simply the same as you, but on a different part of their journey. They are doing the tough stuff. They have yet to begin to forgive themselves and to love themselves. And when they do, then they too will begin to return Home.

And the ones who will have it the very hardest of all? The ones with the greatest burden and the most pain to resolve? These ones are the minions of Satan. The particles of consciousness who have consciously chosen the role, here beyond the Veil, of keeping the duality system alive. The ones who have accepted the mantle of being the bearers of separation. The ones who have, lifetime-after-lifetime, fed the system by playing roles that have kept all others from finding love and oneness. These are the most separate of all. The most alone. The most individuated. And trust me when I say to you that theirs is a deeply painful place to be. And their journey home is going to bring them even more pain. Because, you see, for them it is not a simple matter of releasing the falsenesses about themselves. They have been true to their purpose and nature in their actions. So ahead of them lies a particularly difficult journey. But they will be helped. It is not expected to be easy, but they will be helped.

Z: Wow. I almost feel... compassion.

8: Yes. Compassion is appropriate.

Z: And these ones, these minions of Satan. Are they the Super Powerful Individuals you spoke of previously?

8: There are different particles, which have played different roles in different ways. Some have, for example, been violently aggressive and in this way torn whole planetary civilisations apart. Others have used subtler means. And yes, perhaps the subtlest game is the one being played by some of Satan's minions upon Planet Earth. They are supplied with certain gifts and abilities in exchange for their service. So yes, I would say that the SPIs are the mortal expressions of these souls that are the minions of Satan.

Z: Some things are beginning to fall into place for me now. But let's just get this straight then; Is Lucifer the cause of all evil, or is he not?

8: As usual, this too is a perspective issue. It depends on how you look at it. Perhaps I could express it like this. Do you remember in the movie called Forest Gump, the main character had a saying that went something like, "*My momma always told me that life is like a box of chocolates.*"

Z: (laughs) Yes, I remember.

8: Well, if life is like a box of chocolates, then I would say that Lucifer invented "The Adversary flavour" chocolate. And seeing as The Adversary is really all about appearing to take from others their right to choose, one could also call it "evil flavour" chocolate.

It's there in the box along with all kinds of other flavours. In your various lifetimes you get to try all of the flavours to see if you like them. But, in each case, it is up to you to decide how long you are going to keep each of these chocolates in your mouth. How long you chew and savour the flavour. And whether you spit it out or whether you take it into your being by swallowing it. All of that is up to you. And if you do take it into your being, do you go back again and again for more "evil flavour" chocolates, or do you instead find a way to let it pass through your body so that you can release it from your being and decide not to choose that flavour again?

You see? It **is** there. You can choose to experience it, if you want to. And once you have sampled it, you can decide what you want to do with that experience. Nobody forces you to do anything. You are the creator of your own reality. The fact that evil exists as a possible experience does not mean that you have to choose to experience it. And even if you do, **still** you are not its victim, because now you know something about yourself. You know, whether you like it or not, whether it serves your path or not. You have profoundly increased your self-knowledge for having had this experience.

Z: All right. I can accept from your story that Lucifer invented evil, but is not actually evil. But then it seems to me that his invention, The Adversary, **is** evil. Or am I wrong?

8: In order for you to understand this, I am going to need to explain to you about Consciousness Construct Holders now, even though you haven't yet done quite enough work to get the whole message. But we will have to do our best.

Z: What does that mean, 8? That I have not done enough work to get this message?

8: Quite simply that you must be readied to understand things. Because of the manner in which you are receiving this material, it is not possible for me to place ideas in your mind if the building blocks of that idea are not already there. And so it is that each chapter not only addresses the issues it seeks to address, but it also plants many seeds and lays much groundwork for the following chapters. And, as has often happened, if you are not ready to receive a chapter, then you find yourself unable to get down to writing. This is by design. You are needing to be still for a while so that you can undergo a little internal metamorphosis to bring yourself to readiness to receive the next chapter.

Z: And now you want to tell me about these Consciousness Construct Holders, but you feel there is not sufficient groundwork?

8: There is insufficient to tell the **whole** story. But we will get by.

Let me start by explaining that your experience of your reality is a deeply illusory one. You understand that by now. You live in a world that is predicated on layer upon layer of illusion. Nothing that you think is real is actually real. And the things that you think are not real, are. It is both a wonder and a miracle. And your reality is created thus very specifically for a very important purpose: the search for Self-knowledge of the ONE in all Its endless magnificence. This reality of yours is an unbelievable powerful tool of self-discovery. But in order for it to *work*, the illusions must work. These illusions are like the cogs of the machine – if they do not function, then the whole machine does not function. And there is a set of cogs – possibly some of the most important of all the cogs – which are what I call the Consciousness Construct Holders.

By now you and your readers are quite familiar with one of these Consciousness Construct Holders.

Z: We are?

8: Oh indeed! Does it surprise you to know that your very own Inner-Self, Joy-Divine, is in fact one such Consciousness Construct Holder?

Z: I... umm... I don't know. I am not sure what to think about that. Tell me more about what a Consciousness Construct Holder is and then maybe I'll be able to tell you how I feel about that.

8: Certainly.

As I have explained, in order for your reality to work, you need certain powerful illusions. One of the most powerful of all the illusions is your experience that your emotions are somewhat alien to your own being, that these are just things that you happen to feel, and that these feelings happen to you as a result of outside stimuli. One could imagine that your feeling of happiness is analogous to, for example, a piece of chocolate cake. You believe you need to either bake the cake or buy it from somewhere if you wish to be able to have the sensation of eating chocolate cake. Well, this is the thing that your reality seems to show you; that you must achieve a particular goal or buy a particular thing or win the love of a particular person or lose a number of kilograms or whatever other silliness you are telling yourself, before you can feel happy. And if you were observant, you would see that this never works. Hitting the target, at best allows you only a momentary feeling of happiness and then you return to your normal, not-so-happy state. And so you decide that you must just keep chasing ever greater targets in the hope that some day you'll be really lastingly happy.

And so you come to believe yourself to be a victim to your emotions and **that** is one of the very powerful inducements you have to stay trapped inside this reality. And so it is that, here at the level of deep separation and duality, you believe you are not in control of your own emotions. A great many people actually come to decide that their emotions are the enemy and they try to divorce themselves from their own feelings. This is a tragically poor decision. It takes them exactly opposite to the direction in which they really want to go. If you desire mastery of your Self, your life, your experience and your reality then, ironically, you should completely embrace your feelings and emotions and work to come to the realisation that they are absolutely under your control. When you own and control your emotions, then you are a small step from being the master of your reality. When you are in perfect control of your emotions, then you use them as powerful tools of creation. You give them full reign, but always in the direction that you want them to go. You do not get blown around by them, as a leaf in the storm. And neither do you try to shut them down and silence them. And when you are in that heightened state of Self-possession and Self-creation, then you are approaching your true sense of oneness with All That Is. Then you have learned much of what this system of reality has to teach, and you will be ready to leave here in triumph.

But the point is that you should only leave once you have discovered this, and created it to be so for yourself. Or else the system would have failed to work for you as it should.

So, eventually I can tell you about Joy-Divine. This being has the role of holding the frequency, the energetic framework, that is the very essence of pure **joy**. The very truest nature of the thing that you would call joy is held steady, sure and true by this dear brother-soul of mine; your Inner-Self. And **that** is where the name Joy-Divine comes from. It is a name that is appropriate in this reality. But it holds no significance in other realities, you understand. It is really more of a job title than a name.

Z: Well, of course this is all fascinating to me! Given that this is my Inner-Self we are talking about I would love to talk a **lot** more about this and find out more. But I think that would just be a selfish hogging of this conversation. We probably need to get back to the topic itself?

8: (gently smiles) This **is** the topic itself. You see, I need you to understand the notion of a Consciousness Construct Holder in order to paint a bigger picture. These are beings who hold within themselves a particular resonant frequency of consciousness. They hold these for you, who live inside this reality, so that you can have the illusion that those things are outside of yourselves. And so it is possible for you to walk around all day feeling emotionally empty. It is possible for you to believe that you can never make yourself happy again. It is possible for you to believe that only something outside of yourself can bring you happiness. Typically then, when you do hit whatever target you feel should result in your happiness, then your energy is momentarily brought into resonance with the energy – the consciousness construct – held by Joy-Divine. And, for that moment, you suddenly feel uplifted and happy. And then you can go on believing that happiness lies outside of yourself. The illusion is maintained and you can carry on playing the game you-as-you-really-are wished to play.

This illusion is vital to the continuation of the victim-based game almost everyone on Earth is very intent upon playing. If you realise that you can self-emote then you realise that you can decide to create how you will feel about things. Then you are no longer a victim to your external experiences. Soon after this discovery you will begin to see through other illusions. And as you see through the illusions, so you leave the victim game. And the corollary of this should be quite obvious: if you wish to leave the victim game, then it is necessary that you begin to see through the illusion. You will, and must, come to realise that you are able to decide for yourself **exactly** how you want to feel at any particular moment. You are the one who controls your own feelings and emotions. It will take time and practise for you to show yourself this. You have, after all, spent a great deal of energy, across many lifetimes, teaching yourself that it is not so. So you should be willing to work at remembering that this is an illusion. But, as you do awaken to the truth, so you will realise the power of it. Once you understand that your feelings and emotions are completely and utterly your own to command, then you are a very short step from being able to create your entire reality and experience as you desire.

But we'll talk about this at much greater length when we discuss how you can learn to create your own reality. And now **that** seed is planted.

Z: Okay! Fabulous. I am beginning to understand more and more. Lights are going on for me about all kinds of stuff now.

8: That's good.

But for now, back to the story about the Consciousness Construct Holders. These are all sovereign beings of high consciousness who use their own very being to hold these frequencies for you. It is their nature, their duty, their privilege and their pleasure to do this for you. There are, for example, two beings who hold the true archetype for what is male and what is female in this reality. These two are twin souls who are the original "god and goddess" or, perhaps more correctly, "divine masculine and divine feminine". And then there is the office of the great unifier, the great energy that is responsible for holding the resonance, which is the energy of bringing all the separate parts back home to wholeness and oneness. This has been called the Christ energy. And there are many, many others. All absolutely important to the functioning of the game. Without any one of them, the game would simply not work. Like a machine that suddenly loses a vital cog.

Z: And so to Satan...

8: Yes. You see, I needed to preamble it like this because your very natural and normal feeling would be to see Satan as the unforgiven and unforgivable. As that which you must shun and revile. And that is a normal reaction to your conditioning. Nothing wrong with that. Or rather, there is nothing wrong with that **unless** you desire to return to oneness. Then it is time to grow up a little. Time to let go of the *scary-boogieman-that-comes-to-fetch-naughty-children-in-the-night* syndrome. Time to see this being for what it is and then make some appropriate decisions.

This is a being that holds a consciousness construct, nothing more and nothing less. And the consciousness construct it holds just happens to be The Adversary. And so, just as we can feel it acceptable to name Joy-Divine for his function, for the office that he holds, so it is acceptable that we can call this being, The Adversary. Or we can, if we like, use the modern derivative of a more ancient name, which means exactly the same thing, and call him Satan.

Z: So then, if I feel happiness, if I get into energetic resonance with Joy-Divine, what happens if I allow myself to get into energetic resonance with The Adversary?

8: Unpleasant things happen. You easily get very angry, or even fly into a rage. Resentment simmers towards all who you feel have wronged you. You hold grudges. You desire to hurt or damage others around you. You get all wound up around your own rightness and the wrongness of the people around you. You get unreasonable. You use verbal weapons to cause emotional harm and physical weapons to cause physical harm. You lead those "like you" to war against those "unlike you". In short, **you** become The Adversary. And there are few faster ways for you to drill yourself down, as deep as you can possibly go, into the victim game than this. This **is** the ultimate tool for keeping you inside the game. The Adversary is by far the single most effective cog in this particular machine.

And there we are! I think we have done a very good job of explaining the concept, given the minimal groundwork we had to work with.

Z: Maybe. But there is something I don't understand.

8: Of course there is. (smiles) Go ahead and ask.

Z: Well what you have described as the experience of coming into resonance with The Adversary – it really doesn't sound very nice.

8: Nice?!? No, of course it isn't **nice**! It was never meant to be nice. It was meant to drive you into a deep state of separation. Which, in itself, is the most painful thing imaginable – to be violently ripped from a feeling of belonging, of oneness, of rightness with All That Is. It is very, very un-nice!

Z: So I really don't want to experience that ever again. I reject that. It is just not me any more ever again!

8: Ah. Yes. We need to be very careful here. You would do well to remember that you create your own reality, and that you do it with your focus and attention. And saying "never again" is resistance. And, "*What you resist persists,*" remember? You do not want to be saying that anything is not part of yourself, not part of the oneness. Everything is part of the ONE. That includes you, just as much as it includes The Adversary.

Z: But 8! That makes it impossible! How then am I to proceed? I don't want to come into resonance with The Adversary and now you tell me I can't reject him either! So what am I then to do?

8: Please realise that the only reason you can experience The Adversary energy is because it already exists inside of the ONE. It already exists inside of you. It is an entirely illusory creation that you have put this energy outside of yourself. This is what you did to enter into this victim-game. You see? That is what I was telling you about the Consciousness Construct Holders. Did you not follow that? That all of the emotions and feelings and archetypes are all from within the oneness and are all ultimately from within you. But you need to experience them as being external to you if you are going to experience separation. You wanted to see what it would be like if these things seemed to be created from outside of you. **That** is how you experience duality. There is you, and then **outside of you** is the creator. That is duality. Right?

Z: Okay I get that.

8: But it is an illusion. All is truly ONE. All of this is really within you. And every time that you reject something, divorce it from yourself and place it outside of yourself, then you push yourself back into duality.

Z: Ohhhhhhhh. Sloooooowly I begin to get it. The Adversary is a fiendishly clever device. If you move into resonance with it, then you create duality, and if you reject it and push it away... then you create duality! Whatever you do with it, you create duality. Wow. That is... brilliant.

8: It is. The Adversary is the key to duality. And coming to understand this correctly is also the key to your release from duality. If you wish to find oneness with All That Is, then you will need to unpick this lock.

As you have quite aptly said, it is *fiendishly* clever.

Z: Okay. Good then. I am willing to do this. I am willing to try to unpick this fiendish lock. Will you help me?

8: I am here. But I want you to do it for yourself. You have been equipped with all the lock-picks you need and you have been shown how to use them. It would be far better for you if you could do it yourself. And, in so doing, I am going to show you a formula that you can use for finding your own solutions to such problems that cannot be solved from the head. You solve it from the heart. Here is how.

FINDING YOUR OWN SOLUTIONS FROM THE HEART
THE FOUR PART PROCESS

You are now going to do the first part. Which is to relax, ground yourself and move into your heart. So go and have a cup of tea. Go sit outside in the sun. Relax and release this issue from your mind. Then move into your heart. And **then** come back to your laptop. I will be waiting for you to take this conversation forward.

Z: Okay. This is exciting. And a bit daunting because I don't know how it will turn out. But I'll play along.

(I come back about an hour later)

Z: So instead of having tea and sitting in the sunshine I had a whole meal and a long soak in the bath. (smiles) Sorry.

8: (laughs) Excellent. The point really was for you to just take a step back and relax. To approach this from the heart rather than from the mind. If you work from the mind, then you work analytically. You reduce problems to their constituent bits and can only come up with variations on solutions that you have seen before. When you come from the heart, you see problems holistically and can make intuitive leaps to entirely new solutions. And that was the point of asking you to go and relax and move into your heart. Eating and drinking also has a "grounding" effect. And so this was part one of the four part process.

For part two, you have to state the problem. So now please tell me, as clearly and succinctly as you can, what is the problem, as you see it?

Z: Okay. The issue here is that I am caught between a desire to cease resonating with the energy of The Adversary and a need to not reject this being as the unlovable other.

8: That is a good first attempt at defining the problem. You have talked about the **symptoms** of the problem. You don't want to feel this resonance with The Adversary and you don't want to divorce yourself from another aspect of the ONE. That is fine. But it isn't the **actual** problem. What is the cause of the problem? What is at the root of this issue?

Now is the moment you must go to your heart. You heart knows. You mind wrestles with the obvious and tries to reframe the same old shapes into new pictures. Your heart sees the whole picture. Become aware of your heart now. Feel it in your chest. Feel how it feels. What **is** that feeling? Allow your heart to talk to you. And tell me what you get. What is the problem?

Z: Oneness. Unity. The problem is that I don't want to continue to create ever more duality for myself. I want to come to know myself as being ONE with everything. I want to experience divine union with God. And, dancing with The Adversary takes me in the wrong direction. And, rejecting anyone and standing in judgement of them **also** takes me in the wrong direction. So I can't choose either of these things. I can't resonate with The Adversary and I can also not reject him in any of his guises.

So what should I do?

8: Part two was to state the problem from the heart. You have done that. Part three, you might be surprised to know, is **not** to find the answer. Answers are just temporary, illusory stories. They are not all that interesting. Far more important than finding the answer to some little puzzle, is taking the opportunity to define yourself. And **that** is part three. Instead of telling me the answer to this problem, why not instead, tell me who **you** are. Or rather who you really want to be. Who you will be when you have remembered who you **really** are?

Z: I don't understand.

8: If you did, then I wouldn't be needed to show you this. Are you willing to play along and see where this goes?

Z: Of course. Yes. Okay, so the question you are asking me is: who do I say I am? Who do I say I will discover myself to be when I have woken up. Who is the ascended version of me? Is that the question?

8: Yes. Now again go to your heart... and answer...

Z: I am a creator being of infinite power. I am love. I am ONE with the oneness. I bring enlightenment and delight. I am joy. I am my most magical, magnificent Self.

8: Bold. And true. Good going. And now, part four: stand in that place of oneness and tell me the solution to your previous problem. How do you, the creator being of infinite power and love who is one with the oneness, proceed without either dancing with the Devil or declaring anyone to be beyond redemption?

Z: Hmm. I see something now: both of those are the same thing – dancing with the devil **is** declaring the other to be beyond redemption. The answer for me is to realise that all is indeed already ONE. And that all these experiences exist within myself. It is an illusion that they are outside of me. There is truly nothing "outside" of me. That is the illusion. It is all "inside" of me. So if I experience The Adversary, then I have created that experience. I chose to feel as if the experience was outside of me and outside of my control so that I could have the illusory experience of being in a game called victim. If I want to stop playing that game, then I simply realise that I am ONE with All That Is and that the experience comes from within. I take responsibility.

8: That is very well done. In this moment you have entirely changed the game for yourself. You have moved your own consciousness into Gnosis. Which is the full realisation that you are both the actor and the playwright of your own stage-play. This is a great day.

It's a radical thought, but once you have truly understood that all is ONE, then this is a logical inevitability. The reason you do not get to it very easily yourself is because it is so at odds with your experience. But what you must understand is this:

There is no "out there" out there.

Z: Explain?

8: It is not just your feelings that are inside of yourself. **Everything** you perceive is inside you. There is, quite literally, nothing outside of yourself. What is outside of you is an illusion. The world you perceive is merely your own projection. It comes from what is real, which is what is inside of you.

Hard to grasp?

Z: Yeah, quite.

8: You'll get there. You are ready for this. I want you to think for a moment about who you **really** are. Do you not have the perception sometimes that you are just a point of consciousness, which is observing your life?

Z: Yes, I do. Sometimes when I meditate or when I try to become hyper-aware, then I get this feeling that I am a point of no dimensions inside my own head. Then I am aware that I am not my body, not my thoughts, not my choices, not my emotions, not my ideas nor my experiences. I become aware that I am simply the observer of all this.

8: Yes. This is correct from one perspective. But the reason this experience can be quite unattractive to you is because you then come to feel that you are nothing but the observer. It feels a bit as if you are negating yourself. And the reason for that is the Veil. When you are in this place of awareness, you are right up against the Veil. On the one hand you are aware that the illusory stuff is just that: illusory. But on the other hand you are unable to become aware of what is actually real. Because the Veil is shielding you from seeing the truth of your own Self. So it is quite a stark place.

Z: Yes. But I don't mind. It can be quite peaceful. And on a very few occasions I have had the experience of suddenly being aware that "I" am not only that point of consciousness, not only my body, but everything that I perceive. Every sound I hear, everything I see. It is all me. I have somehow known this to be true, in a very few meditations.

8: It is the same thing actually. If you come to see yourself as the observer, then you are one small step from realising that you are creating that which you are observing. You come to the realisation that you are the film projector showing yourself the movie of your own experiences.

Z: But 8, if this is true, then it has some pretty profound implications. It means that I really am the creator of my own reality.

8: You don't say!

Z: (laughs) Yes, I **know** this is what you have been telling me all along, but I didn't realise you meant it quite this literally.

8: Ah. And when I have I ever not meant **exactly** what I said? Do I not tend towards the deliberate and the precise?

Z: Yes, (laughs) that is so. I suppose it's just a bit of an adjustment to realise that the truth has been right in front of my face all along.

Okay, so what do I do with this info now?

8: We were talking about the problem of what to do about The Adversary. Given what you now know, what will you decide to do?

Z: I guess there isn't actually all that much to do. I simply come to the realisation that all my experiences are my own projections. I have worked very hard to forget that fact. Once that was completely forgotten, I got to experience myself as "what I am not". And now I am busy remembering it. As I remember it, so I will stop needing to believe there are others "outside of me" who are doing things in my life. I now come to realise that there are parts of this illusory construct that are unbelievably beautiful and loveable. I really love this planet. I love to experience life here. So I now find a way to keep creating the stuff I love, and then I release the need to create stuff that I don't like.

8: May I offer you my take on it? Can I tell you what this all means to me?

Z: Oh yes, please!

8: First: your outer world is a projection of your inner reality. It is your story.

Second: the illusion you have had is that the outer world is what is really real and important and the inner world is either unreal or unimportant.

Third: this led you to try to change things in your outer world to make them more like you wanted them.

Fourth: this was the cause of a lot of pain and confusion because, the harder you tried to fix the things external to yourself, the more you failed and hurt yourself.

Fifth: the more you hurt yourself, the more your outer-world reflected your pain back at you. The more messed up, troubled and confused your reality became.

Sixth: at some point, finally, everyone hits a terminus. At some point you come to the decision to stop trying to fix your outer-world and to try to heal your Inner-Self instead.

Seventh: as you begin to succeed at healing your own inner world, so you may notice your outer-world becoming happier and more harmonious.

Eighth: so, wake up! Become observant! See what works! See the obvious thing that is being presented to you. If there is something in your outer-world that troubles you, you should look **inside**. Find what it is inside you that troubles you. Find your own inner pain or confusion. Find a way to love it and heal it. If, and when, you do, then the problem in your outer-world will miraculously cease to hurt you. It will heal. It will do so in beautiful and surprising ways. And this is because you will cease to project a damaged and broken reality outwards.

Z: Yes.

Yes, I get it.

Click!

8: It is a game-changing realisation, isn't it? We have been playing around in the shallows up till now. We have been preparing the soil and planting the seeds. And now! Now we see the first shoots of new green life. Now you can begin to re-imagine everything. Now everything changes for you. Now you must learn how to create effectively and powerfully, knowing full well that you **do** create. And very soon you will be ready to change the state of your game completely.

Z: But 8; I have to ask about the idea of "others". I mean, sure, I am projecting my reality. But what about my beloved soul-mate, Lisa? She seems to exist in my outer-reality. And what about my readers? Are these other beings in my world not real?

8: They are all absolutely real. Just not in the way you have imagined them to be. They are all just as you are. They are beautiful and divine aspects of the ONE; facets of the same great jewel shining in the light that they themselves are casting.

The trick is to understand that each and every aspect of the ONE projects its own reality. Every single reality is different. But here is the thing: you may decide to allow your reality to be influenced by the projections of another, if you choose. You might decide to agree to experience certain parts of your reality the same as someone else does. This agreement is a *consensus*. And so you have a *consensus reality*. You create it together, so it is *co-created*. And that is how you come to feel that you and others all inhabit the same reality. Actually you have simply come to an agreement with a number of other aspects of the ONE to experience similar things in a similar way. And that is how a game is played. A group gets together and arrives at consensus on the rules of the reality and then they enter the game.

But now we need to get back to the main thread of this discussion. We were, after all, talking about the issue of what to do about The Adversary.

Z: Yes. But I think I get it now. I project my reality. I am telling myself a story. By living myself into the story I get to experience myself in amazing new ways. This allows me to decide for myself whether the things I believe about myself and choose for myself are good. I get to see if they are working for me and making me happy in all kinds of different scenarios. If they do, then I keep them. If they don't, then I make a new choice. This is the beauty and the value of the story that I am in.

So what happens if I encounter The Adversary? Well then, I decide if I like the encounter or not. Does it take me forward to where I have said I want to be, or does it not? If it does, then I have no problems. If it doesn't, then I make a new decision about myself so that I no longer invite this interaction.

And if I think about it... it seems to me that an interaction with The Adversary is really just me, showing myself some place within myself where I don't love myself. This is me, showing myself something that I reject and find unacceptable. That is why I set it apart as the enemy; as The Adversary. So, it very much seems to me that the answer would be to find that unloved part of myself and love it. If I could do that consistently each time I experienced The Adversary, then I think I'd probably come to cease experiencing The Adversary at all.

8: Bravo.

There are two important conversations that we need to have quite soon that you are now ready for. The first is about "Negative Consciousness Constructs". It will form an integral part of the conversation about the nature of love. In it you will come to a new understanding of things such as pain, fear, anger and jealousy. You will see that these things are only a problem when they are "outside of you" - when you remove them from yourself and make them unlovable. When you reintegrate these things into your heart and make yourself whole again, then they not only lose their power over you but, in fact, become great and powerful tools, which you can use to the greater good of all.

And then I need to do a little more work with you so that you can correctly understand Shadow. Each and every part of the ONE that has encountered The Adversary has created a bit of The Adversary within themselves. This self-created inner-adversary is called Shadow, and for very good reason. It is your Shadow-Self. Though we have come to great understanding here about how to respond to The Adversary, there is a great deal of very important work that you will still come to do on this topic. And it is an essential topic. As long as anyone is under the influence of their own Shadow, they will lead themselves astray. They will use their creative power to self-harm. So this is a very important area where we need to do additional work so that you can step back into the power of your divine eternal self without risk of ever again causing yourself (or others) any harm.

> (**Zingdad note:** Some years and much work later, I am extremely pleased to offer "Shining the Light on Shadow" as Part 2 of Dreamer Awake! For more information please go to: zingdad.com/dreamer-awake)

Z: I look forward to both of those very much!

8: Good. But for now, can we agree to leave the issue of The Adversary behind us?

Z: Oh, yes. This has been resolved for me in quite an unexpected way. I understand this issue now and it certainly doesn't trouble me any more.

8: Good, but before we move on, I must ask you the usual question. Given what you now know... is Satan evil?

Z: (laughs) I have to laugh because I would have thought that is like asking, "*Is the pope Catholic?*" And yet, here I am, discovering that the answer to this is not as unambiguous as I had thought. It would seem to me that it is possible to experience Satan as evil. But it is also possible to see that this is just the role he plays here in this reality. And without him playing that role, this particular reality would not work as it does. And finally, it is also possible to see that I am allowing, choosing and creating all that I experience and so I am never actually victimised. There actually is no such thing as "evil", after all!

You know, 8, I've just had a thought.

8: And that is...

Z: Well, it strikes me that it must be a pretty miserable and lonely job being The Adversary.

8: I believe it is a role that carries substantial challenges. There is going to have to be a great deal of love and healing given before this being will be able to find its way home when this reality is collapsed. But this too was chosen.

Z: Hmm... I am amazed to find myself again feeling some empathy here.

8: That is well.

And now it is time to bring this conversation to a conclusion.

> *"If there is such a thing as evil, then it is an opportunity to learn about love."*

This is true because, as you have discovered, evil is an illusory experience. And it is an illusion that you are only able to have when you believe that you are in a state of separation from the ONE. So that is the answer. Return your consciousness to the oneness and you will no longer be able to experience evil. You will no longer be able to feel your choices can be taken from you. You will no longer be able to feel that you are the victim of another. The whole experience of evil in all its guises will be left behind you.

Z: That works for me. Thank you, 8.

Now the only question is, **how** do I return my consciousness to the oneness?

8: That's right, that **is** the question. But you see, we first had to remove this obstacle from your path. As long as you were holding onto the idea that there are others out there who are so unacceptable that they cannot be a part of the ONE, then you yourself would not be able to return. It is like a blockage that you had placed inside your own heart. But that is shifted now and so we may proceed. And the way we proceed is... **Love**. Love is the one and only way to move back to a state of oneness.

Z: And that is what we're talking about in the next chapter! Just as you said it would be.

8: That's right. See you in the next chapter.

* * * * *

Chapter 11.
What is Love?

Zingdad: Hi, 8.

8: Hello, my dear friend. It is good to be talking to you again.

Z: It is! And although we talk all the time, it's been several months since we wrote the previous chapter together.

8: And you have been quite busy in that time, have you not?

Z: I certainly have. After the sale went through on our land, things became quite frenetic for Lisa and I. We had a building site to prepare and then we had a construction company come in to do the structural work on our new house while we cleared vast tracts of invasive vegetation from our land. This took them four months to complete and then the construction company left us with, basically, just a timber frame on stilts. Since then, Lisa and I have been working with a handyman completing our house. The three of us have been working on site every hour that God gives. And now, after four months of exhausting labour, we have at last moved in. The house is **very** far from done and, to some extent, we'll be living on a building site for a few months still. But we have all the basics and we are here now, in our own home.

8: And you built it yourself.

Z: One of the most rewarding things I've ever done.

8: And now you are ready to record another chapter together?

Z: Yes, indeed. While my hands have been kept busy with the building of the house, I have felt as if my soul has been pupating. So I am very keen to continue the journey of *The Ascension Papers* with you. And I do believe we are now going to have a conversation about Love, are we not?

8: What is about to unfold is so much more than just a conversation.

Do you recall, in your discussions of your Mountain Experience with Joy-Divine, you came to the understanding that you brought that experience to yourself by choosing to follow your heart? And that your Mountain Experience was the moment of the transition of your soul from one level of consciousness to another?

Z: I recall, yes.

8: Well, what I'd like to add to what Joy-Divine said is that the reason this was the moment when you moved from third density consciousness to fourth density consciousness was because this is when you moved your ego into your heart. You see, by deciding to "follow your heart" you are aligning the separate part of self that resides in duality (which is your ego) with the part of yourself that is connected to the oneness and resides outside of duality (which is your soul). **That** is what it means to follow your heart.

And when you become a heart-centred being, you are of the fourth density of consciousness.

And, of course, since your Mountain Experience you have done a great deal more work. The preceding chapters of **The Ascension Papers** have since then been written and there is a great deal of additional work that you have done too that has not necessarily been recorded in these conversations. And so you are ready now. It is time for the next transition in your consciousness.

Z: My second Singularity Event?

8: Yes.

Z: Really, 8? But how? How will that happen? I've been on countless hikes since my first and, well, none of them have...

8: Don't be simplistic. It was not "hiking" that brought you your first Singularity Event. It was your consistent and repeated choices to follow your heart. As it happened, that hike was simply the perfect place at the perfect time for you and Lisa to reach a moment of perfect stillness. It all came together in divine-right fashion for you to touch the heart of oneness and to feel your own eternal connection with All That Is. But it's not about the details of what was going on in the environment outside of you! It's about what happens inside of you...

And *inside of you*, since your first Singularity Event, as recorded in the preceding chapters, you have willingly opened yourself to the notion of oneness. You have embraced the mystery and accepted the position of the mystic: that you can have a direct experience of, and relationship with, the divine. You have also been willing to face your fears head-on and deal with the very concept of fear itself. And you have been willing to take responsibility for yourself and for your creation of your reality. So you are ready for the next transition.

What is needed now is another moment of true stillness. You clutter your mind with so much noise and your life with so much activity that it becomes very difficult to allow for these great transitions of your soul. Perhaps it is counter-intuitive to you, but indeed it is so that your greatest transformation will always happen when you are at your most still.

Z: Can you help me to understand that?

8: Let me use a very simple example. Throw a stone up into the air, as hard and as high as you can. It accelerates out of your hand in the skyward direction. This is its outward flight. Then, as gravity begins to tug upon it, the stone begins to slow. Finally, at its apogee, the stone comes to a halt. And only then, in this moment of perfect stillness, can it change direction and begin its homeward flight back to you. The flight home features an ever-increasing acceleration, it is true. But the moment of change of direction is right in the middle of the stone's moment of greatest stillness. And you are, right now, again at a point where you can have a great change of direction in your soul. You **should** have come to this transition already but for the fact that you have not come to stillness. Quite simply, you don't know how. Noise and activity is such an habitual thing for you that you actually know no other. But you really **must** come to stillness now. Without this stillness, you will not change direction.

If you do not come to stillness, then we can have a long and interesting conversation about love. I can tell you many interesting things about it and we will go off on all those curious tangents that we both enjoy so much and it will all be fine and fascinating, but it will not actually take you where you need to go. You will attain some intellectual understanding about love. But you will gain no **knowing** in your heart. And the discussion we need to have here must be built upon that sure **knowing**. Without it, the conversation we both really desire to have, will not occur. We will talk around the heart of the matter and never really get to its essence.

And you will not have the transformation of the soul that such a deep knowing will bring.

Z: So I must... what... meditate? And then?

8: Something more than your normal meditation is required of you. You meditate fairly regularly and that is good. But your meditations are not actually the stillness of being that you think they are. Every meditation chases after one purpose or another. There is no fault with that, but something else is required now. You see, it is now time for you to change your mode of being entirely. Like the stone that has rushed away from the home of the hand, so you too must come to perfect stillness before you can change direction. And, from within that stillness, you must listen only to your heart. It might take you some time to get this right. You are so used to filling every corner of your consciousness with noise and movement that you might need to practice being still quite a bit before you achieve the goal, and are able to really hear your heart.

But I understand that all this is just so much theory to you. What you are asking of me is that I should give you something practical to **do**.

Z: Yes, please.

8: It is a beautiful irony: until you know how to truly **be**, you will still need something to **do** to enable **be**ing. (He smiles) This is similar to saying that until you know silence, you need to find something to say to permit your silence. What a marvellous cosmic joke.

But I am able to help you with this. Here is what you should do:

Pick a day in which you have no appointments. Set that day aside. It is to be your day of stillness and listening. Tell everyone that you will be non-contactable on that day. Tell those who share your home with you that you will not speak to them on that day and that they are not to speak to you either. It is your day of silence.

The night before your day of silence, you must switch off your mobile telephone and all such devices that might intrude upon you. You must switch off your computer, your television and your radio. All devices, which you use to input information into your consciousness, must be silent for your day of silence.

On the morning of the day of silence you must allow yourself to awaken without input. In other words, no alarm-clock or similar device. Awaken naturally. Stay in bed and **be still**. Listen to your heart.

Z: What does that mean, 8? What does it mean to listen to my heart?

8: In due course this will become second nature to you – much more normal and natural even than listening to a sound with your ears. But for now, I do understand that you need some guidance.

You should know that your heart is a portal. It is your connection to the Divine. It can be said that your Inner-Self resides within your heart. It can even be said that the oneness is within your heart. All wisdom and truth and creativity are instantly available and accessible to you through your heart. But you need to learn to listen, truly **listen**, to your heart. Because it speaks to you quietly and gently in the language of love. But believe me when I say, it speaks very eloquently when it needs to.

Z: Okay. But **how** do I listen?

8: For a start, make sure there is nothing else taking up residence in your consciousness, making a noise. Your heart will not compete for your attention! This is why you need to ask your family not to speak to you. It is why you must not engage with reading matter, not check your email, not speak to anyone. No external input at all. But you must also not busy yourself with work or chores or other activities. All of these things create thoughts and *noise* inside your mind. You must come to total stillness within your mind. And the maximum possible stillness of your hands, your body and your ears will assist this greatly.

That is the start.

Then, when you are still, you must listen to your heart. You can, if you need something to do, just listen to your physical heart beating. That will help you because it is a literal listening to your heart. But then you should seek to still your consciousness and see what you receive.

And this is how you should spend your day. Be still. Listen. Wait upon your heart.

Your heart might speak to you more in "feelings" than in words. But, if you pay attention, you will know exactly what those feelings mean.

Z: And then?

8: Then you see what it has to say!

Z: What if it has nothing to say?

8: Don't be obtuse child, all of the oneness is in there! All of life is in there! And life will express itself if you will but pay attention! Look around you at the universe, teeming with vigorous activity. Look at the world outside your window. Look at a drop of water under a microscope. Look at the nucleus of an atom. Where, anywhere, is the oneness saying nothing? The oneness is speaking with passionate eloquence all the time. The only problem is that you are sitting with your fingers in your ears, shouting nonsense doggerel, drowning out the truth and beauty that is flooding in at you all the time from all directions. For just one moment, do you think you can **shut up** and **listen**?

Or, to put this in slightly gentler terms: can you let go of your fears and your excuses and just go and see what is there?

Z: I am duly chastised (I smile sheepishly). Yes. I'll do this. Tomorrow is Sunday. I'll make that my day of silence and I'll see what I get.

8: Good.

It might be that tomorrow is just a practice run and that you actually need to do it again at some point. You might even need to spend a few days in silence. Be prepared for that.

Z: Okay, 8.

8: But if you manage, for even a single moment, to get out of the way, to be really still and to truly **listen** to your heart then, I assure you, you will gain wondrous insights. And it will come to you in your heart such that you **know** it to be true. Which is quite a different thing from the ideas that you can hold in your head and think about. **Knowing** and thinking are very different things. And when it arrives, you will have no doubt that it did arrive. It will be a powerful experience. And what arrives will be the basis upon which we will be able to build this chapter.

Will you do this?

Z: I am a bit daunted. It feels like there is so much riding on this and I have no idea if I'll be even get anything out of this. But I'll certainly try!

8: Good then, I shall speak to you again after Sunday...

(Sunday passed and, as intended, I had a day of silence. It is now a week later)

Z: Okay, 8, I had my day of silence. And it was pretty amazing!

8: Very good! And I am so pleased that it went so well for you. Tell us how the day proceeded.

Z: Sure. This is what happened...

My Day of Silence

On Sunday morning I awoke to the sounds of birds calling outside. As I awoke, I remembered that this was to be my day of silence, so I stayed in bed, quietly listening. Well, truth be told, mostly I was thinking about listening. I was actually filling my thoughts with all kinds of ideas about what listening to my heart should be like and how it should feel if I listened to my heart and what my heart should be saying to me and... well... I soon realised that I wasn't really being very still. So I began to meditate, which went a bit better. I relaxed my body entirely and cleared my mind of all thoughts. Which was great until I realised that I **had** released all thoughts, and began to think about that. And then I wondered how it would be to listen to my heart without thinking any thoughts. And then I realised I was filling my mind with babble again!

This was when it became apparent to me just how much harder this was going to be than I had initially thought.

I won't bore you with the details of my day, but I will tell you that I was quite often frustrated with myself. "Being still" sounds easy. You just stop thinking, and then you listen, right? I can tell you, it is quite a challenge to break the noise addiction. At least, I found it to be so.

By late afternoon, I was done wrestling with myself. I was done **trying** to be quiet. I had had enough of attempting to find the right way towards stillness. I was through with trying to listen. So, I decided the day was a waste and that, instead of trying to listen to my heart I should just enjoy the rest of the day. I looked for Lisa to tell her that I was throwing in the towel, that I'd try again some other time. But she was out for a walk with the dogs. So instead I made a snack and went and sat on the deck to watch a truly breath-taking sunset. It was magnificent. As I sat and marvelled with wonderment at the beauty of the spectacle, a deep peace settled over me. And in that quietude something came to me. A thought sidled in through the back-door of my mind. A thought about love. A beautiful thought. And as it arrived in my mind it touched me very deeply, bringing tears to my eyes. I didn't so much think this thought, as feel it. And I felt it to be true.

And then I knew; **this** was what I had been waiting for! Here it was. Finally, when I stopped trying and wresting... it was simply there in my mind as if it had always been!

I came inside and sat down at my laptop and, before I could think about how I was going to structure this, or what approach I would take, I found myself typing. It flowed out of me in one go, non-stop from my heart through my hands on the keyboard. It barely even nodded at my mind as it passed through. And so here is what I wrote...

I listened to my heart and this is what it said:

In the beginning of every particle of consciousness, right from the ONE, all the way down to the smallest, newest particle of life, there is a moment when that being gains self-awareness. In *The Ascension Papers* we have paraphrased that moment as that being saying, "*Here I am.*" But self-awareness is always curious. And therefore the next utterance can be paraphrased as, "*What am I?*"

The journey, it seems, always begins with, "*Here I am, but what am I?*" Then, the journey itself consists of, "*I might be **this**. No wait, maybe I am **that**. Or, what if I am **this**.*" On and on and on and on. Always searching for the answer.

Each time something new is tried, there is a fragmentation of the consciousness. New beings are sent out on a foray of self-discovery from within the consciousness of the parent being. Variations are tried. Multiples of possibilities explored. Whole clouds of consciousness are expressed. Multiplying and complexifying and then specialising and trying again. Always seeking, yet never finding, that moment of bliss and peace that comes from having found the answer to the question, "*What am I?*"

And, in every instance, with every answer we have tried, we have pushed away from each other and the ONE. Further and further, we have pushed out. Like a tidal wave that burst forth from but a teacup, we have surged out. Becoming a tsunami of consciousness, we have pushed off from one another – outwards, outwards, ever seeking **the truth**. Ever seeking the answer...

What

Am

I

?

And here we find ourselves now, living our lives on planet Earth, way down in the densest place of consciousness. You could say that this is about as far out as the wave would ever push because this is about the deepest forgetfulness of the point of origin that could ever be achieved. Thanks to the Veil of Unknowing and the choices we have all collectively taken; this is **it**. Perhaps it is possible to head out further? Perhaps someone wants to try? I don't. I am ready to be a part of the returning. Like all waves that have pushed up from the greatest depths of the ocean and found themselves crashing to the shore, this wave is going to return. It is going to go surging back with ever-increasing speed and exuberance to its source. To the ONE. We are returning!

And **how** are we to return?

It begins with the correct answer to the question, "*What am I?*"

And the correct answer for me, from the depths of my heart, is... Love.

Every other answer I have found only causes me further complexity. Every other answer pushes me outwards and away. Because every other answer implies something else that I am **not**.

For example. If I am (as I have discovered myself to be) a being called delight, the expression of joy-divine, then I am **not** all kinds of other things. I am **not** fear, pain, sadness, loss, anger, hatred or misery.

Obviously.

But I am also not stillness, peace, harmony, order, or patience. I am not even kindness, honesty, justice, valour, dignity, steadfastness, dependability, righteousness or any other such worthy thing.

Do you see? If I choose any thing at all and say, "*I am that,*" then I am, in that very self-same moment, saying, "*I am not that,*" to a whole host of other things. So anything that I would claim myself to be causes separation, division and a pushing away from the oneness.

The only exception to that rule that I can find is the statement, "*I am love*". Not passion. Not lust. Not need. Not any of these silly, temporary little feelings that we usually refer to when we say the word, love. No. I am Love with a capital L. I mean the kind of Love that looks at another being and sees God in their eyes. Sees the wonder and the perfection inside the heart of that being, irrespective of the exterior they are currently wearing. Love is that which is given to everything and everyone, everywhere, unconditionally, always. That is the Love I am talking about.

I am talking about the kind of Love that puts you down on your knees in gratitude that you are alive. That threatens to crush your heart with the beauty of the world around you. That makes you yearn to find the greatest and best and most magnificent gift that you can find within yourself, simply so that you have something that you can give back to life in gratitude for all that it has given to you.

That is my answer to the question. And so I find that I can declare with surety, steadfastness and conviction, "*I am Love!*"

And so, for my soul, I am an answer-bearer. I am a particle of life that is going back home. I can feel it! In the very moment of this declaration, the tide has turned. I am in the wave that is done rushing up the shore... and is now pulling back to sea.

And as I go back, so I will collect other particles of Self. I will see everything that I have ever been and done in this lifetime and I will say, "*I am love **and** I am **that.**" And so, yes, I am love **and** I am Arn who is Zingdad.

And then, as I proceed back home, so I will see particles of Self from my other incarnations and I will say, "*I am love and I am this too, and **that,** and that one, and that one also.*" And so, yes, I am love and I am Arn, and the wizard, and the autistic boy, and the space soldier, and the Lyran boy... and all that I have thought myself to be. I will declare, "*I am love and I am **all** of these beings!*" And all of these beings will get carried home with me in the tide of my Love.

And then I will meet my Inner-Self. I will see it for its amazing and beautiful Self. I will fall in love with this being. And I will see too its wounds and its pain. And I will soothe them all with my capacity for love. "*I am love,*" I will say, "*and I **am** that!*" So I am love and I am Delight and Joy-Divine and all that I have created myself to be, all the way into separation from the oneness.

I am love and I am all of that!

And so, whoever you are. Wherever you are. However you got to being where you are. There will come a time in your journey home, and in my journey home, where we will both be looking at the same great being and we will both say, "*I am love and I am **that.**" And then you and I shall be ONE. And indeed, in due course, all beings everywhere, in All That Is, will look to the ONE. And we shall **all** declare, "*I am love and I am **that!**"

But for now, I can only look forward to that moment when I will know that I am you, and you are me. But because I know that time is an illusion and that all time is really now, I can already look out at you from across the divide of this bit of text. I can see you reading this. I can look at you and say, "*I am love and I am **that!**"

* * * * *

... and that is what I got, 8.

8: Bravo, my friend.

I am well pleased, and so very proud of you. This is beyond beautiful.

And to think that you were worried that your heart might have nothing to say...

Z: Silly, huh?

8: Perhaps. But fortunately you know better now. The only time your heart would ever be still is if you yourself were in such a perfect state of blissful oneness and perfect balance that there would be nothing for it to add.

You see, anything that you do that causes imbalance will result in your heart speaking to you. And the song of returning to balance is the heart-song.

But you must not misunderstand; "imbalance" is not a bad thing! Not at all. If there were no imbalance, there would be no universe, no life, no "you" and no "me". Nothing would exist without imbalance. And Love itself is the returning to balance. So where anything exists, there is love returning that existence to oneness. Love is, therefore, the most powerful force in the universe. It is the pull of oneness itself.

Z: I have so many questions about all this, 8. I don't know where to begin...

8: You have done the work of being silent and listening to your heart and you have thereby attained the basic understanding that you need for us to be able to share this chapter. So I'm going to help you. I'm going to tell you a story that will go a long way towards helping you to clarify your understanding of the way life works and what love is. And then, when you have a better understanding, you'll know with greater clarity what it is that you wish to ask of me.

Z: That sounds great. Thank you, 8. I'd love to hear the story.

8: Here it is then...

THE STORY OF PUSH AND STAY AND THE INFINITE ELASTIC BALL

Z: I have to say, that is the most imaginative story title you have come up with yet!

8: You like it?

Z: I do. And I wonder what kind of a story could have a title like that?

8: It's a good one. But it's a bit different from most stories you would hear. This one requires of you that you not only listen to the story, but that you do some work to imagine the ideas I am going to express. If you do so, then you will receive the wisdom inherent in the story.

You are, of course, familiar with elastic bands. Well, I'm going to ask you to imagine something which is a little like a rubber band. But instead of being a band, it is a ball. The most curious attribute of this elastic ball is that it is infinite. Infinity is not something that you will easily understand, though, so I am going to take some time to explain this properly.

So the first attribute of the Infinite Elastic Ball is that it can be stretched out an infinite amount in any direction. It never snaps or breaks and it never runs out of stretch.

Secondly, it can be stretched in an infinite number of different directions. And here you are going to have to work with me to imagine this. A rubber band can only be stretched in two directions, right? Either end can be pulled outwards. But the infinite elastic ball can be stretched in **every** direction. Left, right, up, down, yesterday, next year, green, cinnamon, happy, vibrant, quartz...

Z: Whoa! Are those things directions?

8: For something that is infinite they are. They are directions in consciousness. You live in a narrowly confined, three-dimensional world. You imagine that the cardinal directions in space are the only directions you can move in. Some on your planet have become a little more imaginative and have come to the conclusion that "time" is also a direction. They are right. The next step is to realise that all things are of consciousness and that all consciousness can be traversed. But let's not get stuck here; in due course this will make better sense to you.

Back to the Infinite Elastic Ball. If you take these two properties: that it can be stretched out infinitely and in an infinite number of directions, then it follows that this ball includes everything. Nothing is outside of it, and everything is inside of it.

Z: I'm not sure I understand that. But I always have a bit of difficulty understanding the concept of infinity. Are you saying that anything that is infinite **must** include absolutely everything that exists?

8: Yes.

The word "Infinity" originally comes from the Latin word, *infinitas,* which means "unboundedness". If something has a boundary, then it is finite. And specifying that anything at all is **not** inside this ball, is to specify a boundary. But this ball is not finite, it is **in**-finite. Infinite. So there can be nothing that it does not include.

Z: That's a crazy thought. All things that are infinite, include all other things!

8: Exactly. This is actually a very interesting point that we might want to spend some time talking about in due course. But for now you can simply understand that all-inclusiveness is a property of the infinite.

Z: Okay, got it.

8: The third attribute of the Infinite Elastic Ball is the fact that, when it is not stretched out in any direction at all, it collapses down to nothingness and ceases to exist. Can you imagine that?

Z: Not really. If we are all inside the ball – if **everything** is inside of the ball – how can it cease to exist if we stop stretching it out?

8: This is a good question that you ask. It allows me to tell you something very important about the nature of All That Is. You struggle to imagine that the ball can snap back to nothingness because your experience of your reality is that "things" are real. You don't yet truly understand that all things are transitory illusions created by you, out of your collective consciousness.

You, at your core, are pure consciousness. This is your true nature. And pure consciousness, when it ceases all function, has no form. There is a dictum in the world of architecture and design which goes, "*form follows function,*" and in that context it means something like, "*purpose should dictate shape*". Now, I want to reuse that phrase in a different context. You see, in the most universal sense, it really is true that form **does** follow function. In fact, it is function that brings form into being. It is **do**ing and creating that causes all form to come into existence. If you cease all function, then you will lose all form. You will return to pure consciousness and simply be at one with the oneness. If all parts of the oneness were to cease all function, were to cease pushing out at the Infinite Elastic Ball, then yes, all would collapse to formlessness or no-thing-ness.

The fourth attribute of The Infinite Elastic Ball is called *Infinite Variation*. Understand, time does not act on the Infinite Elastic Ball – time is just one of the things **inside** the Infinite Elastic Ball. So there can be no past or future for the Infinite Elastic Ball. This means that this ball is always in all of its possible states. It is, right now, pulled out in every single direction it ever was pulled in **and** every single direction it ever will be pulled in. And it is also **not** pulled in any of those directions. It is right now expanded infinitely in infinite directions and also collapsed into nothingness. It is right now busy expanding **and** busy contracting. And every other permutation that we can imagine **and** a great many more that we cannot. The Infinite Elastic Ball is in all of these states, all at the same time. If it is to be truly infinite, it must be so that all possibilities exist at the same time. At no point is any possibility excluded. Otherwise there would again be a boundary, you see.

This really means that everything that is created always exists, and it all exists at the same time. All of it is **right now**. Because that is what "infinite" means.

Can you imagine that?

Z: That's a bit of a stretch for me. (laughs) But okay, I can imagine it. What does this all really mean?

8: Everything I have told you up to now was necessary background. But to get to the real meaning of this I am going to add some personalities to the story to whom you can relate. Allow me to introduce you to the two characters of our story: Push and Stay are their names.

As I have said, the oneness is creative and Self-creative. In its quest for Self-discovery, one of the things It has done is to imagine that there are different parts to Itself. And then, because It imagines it to be so, it **is** so. So, in the beginning, one part of the oneness says, "*I am going to push outwards so that I can look back and see what I am.*" It does so... and It sees Itself for the first time! And looking upon Itself, love is born. When any part of the oneness looks at any other part of the oneness, It sees the beauty, wonder and perfection of the oneness – of Itself – and It feels love. I can paraphrase it like this, *"The God in me sees the God in you."* It is truly love! It causes those parts to draw together in wonder and amazement at each other. They see that they are both of the oneness. They move towards each other and merge back with each other and then they are, once again, ONE.

It is love that draws them back together.

Z: That's beautiful.

8: It is. And what it means is that any part of the oneness, anywhere, only really needs to pay attention and really **see** any other part of the oneness, and this will happen. If you have eyes to really look and **see**, you will see God in every other around you. In every animal, every plant, every sunset. You'll see God in the insects, in the waves of the ocean and in the stars that shine. You'll see God in your own body and you will most certainly see God in the eyes of other people around you.

Z: But this doesn't often happen, does it 8? I don't know many people who experience their world like that. And much as I'd like to, I have only had glimpses of that. I'd really love to be able to see things like that all the time. Is that possible?

8: Oh, yes. You will, of course, have to undergo significant changes in your beliefs about yourself before you could be there **all** the time. But you are on your way there. It will just take a little time and bit of journeying. And the next step few steps on that journey are precisely what we are doing in this chapter.

And so I'd like to finish our story, as there is much that you can learn from Push and Stay.

A little earlier I mentioned that nothing would exist without imbalance. Now I will explain this in more detail.

IMBALANCE IN THE FIELD OF CONSCIOUSNESS

Everything that exists – including you, me, the chair you are sitting on, the universe you dwell in and every reality that has ever existed, in short, **everything** – is created with imbalances in the field of consciousness of the oneness. You see, if all is in perfect balance, then there is only consciousness.

No forms, no individuals, no personalities, no creations, no realities and no variation. Just a perfectly, blissfully still consciousness in silent repose. That is, one could say, the ONE at rest. But in order for the ONE to **do** anything, there must arise some imbalance. But there can only ever be **local** imbalance. All local imbalance **must** be re-balanced elsewhere in the ONE. So locally there is imbalance, but across the whole of the ONE there is always perfect balance. Not even for an instant can the whole of the ONE be thrown out of balance.

Z: I think I understand, 8. But perhaps you could help me to imagine this?

8: Oh, certainly. This phenomenon happens constantly on your planet with the tides in the oceans. When there is a high tide on one part of the globe, it is balanced by a low tide elsewhere. When a wave rises up from the ocean, it is balanced by a trough of equal size beside it. In all these instances, there are local increases and decreases in the ocean depth and volume, but across the whole of the ocean, there is no increase or decrease.

Do you follow?

Z: That helps a great deal, thank you.

8: So, with that understanding in place, you are ready to see that, in order for Push to come into being in one part of the ONE, there would, at the same time, **have** to be a counter-balance to Push that would immediately also come into being.

You cannot create Push without creating "not-Push". For the purposes of our story, we shall call "not-Push", Stay.

So, can you see that the creation of Push **is** the creation of Stay? And that the creation of Stay **is** the creation of Push? They are created together and are perfectly balanced, equal-but-opposite, expressions of the ONE.

These counter-balancing beings can seem, from a very localised perspective, to be two different beings that are acting differently and independently of each other. But this is only a temporary illusion. There is a greater truth, which is that they are actually the same one being who is also conscious of itself and who is simply acting *through* them.

Z: How can that be, 8? I can't really imagine that.

8: This is again quite an important understanding, so I shall take a moment to help you to understand:

Last night you slept soundly and barely moved your body for hours on end. Then, this morning you went out to your farmland and worked hard physically and were very active with your body. Right now you are writing *The Ascension Papers* and your mind and intuitive centres are very active. Inside of the flow of time, you might think that you are one person who sequentially goes through these three different states of being. But from outside of time, it might seem as if you are one being who also holds three other coexistent beings inside his consciousness. Possibly we would call these other three beings, Sleepingman, Hardworkingman and Writingman.

Z: Or maybe Snoozy, Sweaty and Smarty.

8: (laughs) Yes, perhaps.

But you can see, of course, that Snoozy, Sweaty and Smarty are each just aspects of you. And, in just that same way, the ONE is one being, but has within Its beingness an infinite number of different aspects. And for the purposes of this story, two of those aspects are Push and Stay.

Does that help you to understand?

Z: It does, thank you!

8: And as we have seen, Push pushes out, sees itself and comes charging back, full of excitement and wonder, and reunites with Stay.

Z: And then what happens to Push and Stay?

8: Well, through their little game of self-discovery, Push and Stay have enabled the ONE to experience Itself in a new and wonderful way. The ONE caught a glimpse of Itself and It discovered Love. As a result, It decides to try this experience again. So Push and Stay arise once again and decide that they loved the experience so much that they want to do it again, exactly the same. And so they try. But, here comes the part I like: even though they want to repeat the exact same experience, they cannot. Because, you see, you can never do the same thing twice.

Z: You can't?

8: No. Remember chapter 8? *"Change is the only constant"*.

Well I can prove that statement once again, using the story of Push and Stay, and at the same time I can tell you why they could not do the same thing again.

The first time Push pushed out, it **was** the first time. He can never push out *for the first time* again. The next time he pushes out, it will be the second time. So it is different. Now he has some experience of pushing out. He has some idea of what to expect. And the fact that he knows what to expect, changes the whole experience. He is not quite so surprised to see Stay. And when he returns to tell Stay what she looks like from "out there", she is not nearly so excited. They do not implode into each other with nearly the same force. The whole exercise is not nearly as ecstatic.

Z: Sounds like things are going to get less and less exciting for Push and Stay. Is their relationship doomed to failure? Do they need a marriage counsellor? (laughs)

8: (laughs) No. Fortunately not. Because, you see, they will only try to repeat the exercise once or twice before they will see the obvious and then they will change the game. Push and Stay are parts of the oneness. And, as such, they share in the attributes of the oneness. They are creative and self-creative. And they are curious and questing. So they change the rules and the game becomes new and exciting again.

Z: How? How do they change the rules, 8?

8: Well, what if this time Push decided to see how far he could push out? What if he decided to push out **so far** that he managed to forget that he was pushing out in the first place? That would be different! Because then, returning to Stay would be like the first time for him, even though it wouldn't be for her. And then something magical would happen. Because Push would push out for a whole long while, pushing and pushing until he was so far away from Stay that there was no way for him to see her. And because Push doesn't have the facility of memory, out-of-sight really is out-of-mind. So then he will have forgotten Stay. And if he has forgotten Stay, then he has also forgotten that he is Push. In that instant Push brings forth from his own consciousness a new being, whom we shall call Forget.

But you'll remember that I told you that all imbalance is always only local imbalance, because it is always perfectly balanced by another imbalance elsewhere in the infinite field of consciousness of the oneness. So when Push creates Forget he also, at the same time, creates "not-Forget". Whom we shall henceforth call, Remember. And so, memory is created. Remember is the first being in All That Is, who can hold within her mind something that she is not directly experiencing. Remember can see a simulacrum of Stay in her mind without actually being near to Stay.

Z: And Forget?

8: Well he has forgotten! So he is wandering around the outer extremities of The Infinite Elastic Ball. Let's focus our attention on him for a while, as he has much to teach us about ourselves.

Forget's lot in life is somewhat confusing. He has no knowledge of who he is, or how he came to be where he is, or what the point of his existence is. He simply **is**. But in his heart he knows that he is incomplete. In his heart, he feels a yearning for that which he has forgotten. But he doesn't know that. All he knows is that he feels a loss and that he feels disconnected. Forget is alone, without knowing how he came to be so, or why.

So? What does Forget do?

He does the only thing he can do. He pushes out in a new direction in consciousness. He does this by asking himself basic questions such as, "*Why am I here?*" or, "*What is my purpose?*"

Forget might decide to answer his question with, "*I am here because I am seeking to understand; to know the truth,*" and, in so doing, he creates within his consciousness a new being called Truth. Or he might say, "*I am doing whatever I do for the pure simple joy of it, because it is **fun**!*" and so he creates within himself, Joy. Or he might say, "*I do this to serve others; I am here for the good of all,*" and so he creates himself as Service. And those are just three possible options. There are an infinite number of options and alterations and variations as to why Forget might decide he exists and who he therefore decides that he is... and in which direction he therefore pushes out.

And, as he declares himself to be, so he is! For Forget, though he doesn't know it, is inseparably and eternally part of the oneness. He is God-like. He is creative and self-creative. And he has the power to create himself in any form he might choose. And, as he creates himself, so he **is**. But he does so within the confines of The Infinite Elastic ball which has, remember, the amazing property of Infinite Variation. You remember what that means?

Z: Yes. It means that everything that is created always exists, and it all exists at the same time. All of it is **right now**.

8: Good. Yes.

Z: I cheated – I scanned back to look. (laughs) I think I am a child of Forget...

8: (smiles)

So then, what do we realise if we apply the idea of Infinite Variation to the story? We understand that Forget created a number of different beings but, because of Infinite Variation, all these beings co-exist in the Now. That means they can play together, work together, create together. And they do!

Together, these beings begin to try to make sense of their existence. And so they create from their own essence and energy a reality in which to play. They seek to resolve their sense of disconnection and separation by playing out their thoughts about themselves in the realities, which they create. Again and again they try. Each time a reality is created, something is learned and understood and the reality is collapsed and returned to them. And then they do it all over again. Each new reality is more complex and amazing than the one before it. Each time populated by more and more variations and combinations of themselves. And each time, as it expends its usefulness, it is rolled up, collapsed and returned to them before they begin again.

And so we find them now, in our story: a huge group of diverse beings of phenomenal creative talent. And between them, they have created some pretty complex and amazing consciousness constructs such as space, time and dimensions, so that they can really spread their creations apart and separately experience all the various causes and effects of their creations on different parts of their own being. And within each dimension they have created many different realities, as were appropriate to that dimension. In the third dimension, for example, they have created that which would come to be called "the universe" by some of the parts of Self that went to play in it. It contains trillions of galaxies, each with billions of solar systems. Each solar system with a variable number of planets. And each planet teeming with many life-forms. Your science doesn't yet acknowledge this and you haven't a broad enough perspective to see it, but it is true: there is not a single planet anywhere that does not, at some point in time, harbour many forms of life. This construct called "the universe" is itself a living entity, which is densely populated with an infinite variation and complexity of life. It is one of the brightest jewels created by the children of Forget. But, beautiful as it is, for almost all of its creation it was just another experiment. Though it brought these beings a great deal of insight into themselves as they played out their games of creating and populating the universe, it did not bring them that for which they most yearned: connection, true belonging, blissful oneness, completion... a return Home.

It is a sad and confusing irony; they yearned for healing and wholeness. And the harder they worked to try to find it, the more they fragmented themselves and created separation. The more they sought to understand themselves, the more they diversified, separated and disintegrated themselves and the less they found of their own true nature.

Z: Oh, 8, this is too sad! Is there no hope for us?

8: Wait a minute there. I am telling you a story. A story about Push and Stay and the Infinite Elastic Ball. I didn't say this was about **you**!

Z: So it's only a story then?

8: Of course it is only a story! How could you think it was anything other than a story? It is even called **the story** of Push and Stay and the Infinite Elastic Ball. How did you get confused?

Z: It started to sound like the truth.

8: Ah! It sounded like that **to you** did it?

Remember your whole life is nothing but a story. A fiction. A wholly invented play that you are putting on for yourself to show yourself something about yourself. It is not real.

But story is a very powerful thing. We can learn a great deal about ourselves from stories. And if I tell you a story that really captures your imagination, then it might cause you to begin to tell your own story in a different way.

Clearly, my story about Push and Stay started to do this for you. You began to see yourself in this story. But then you made the very normal mistake: you began to demand that it should be something other than what it is. You began to demand that it should be **true**. But it cannot be **true**. Because there is only one truth.

Z: "*The ONE is.*"

8: That's right! Everything else is just story. Nothing more, nothing less.

And, if you take a moment to consider the Infinite Elastic Ball, then you will remember that one of its characteristics is Infinite Variation. That means that everything that can be created, is created. And all of it co-exists in the eternal now. This means that any story that you can come up with, can seem to be true from a particular perspective. But it also means that, from another perspective, it can also be untrue. Or partly true. Or fishcakes.

Z: Fishcakes? (laughs) Okay I get it; you mean that anything is possible and I shouldn't confine myself to needing a story to be true or false or... anything else that I might be able to define in my mind.

8: Correct. Stories are what they are – they are stories. You can decide if a story has value for you or is about you. You can decide what story you want to tell and then you can decide how you are going to tell it. You can decide if you want your story to play out within another bigger story and, notably, you can decide if you are going to co-create a story with other beings. There is a great deal you can do with your story, both in how you go about telling the story and in the content of the story. But there is one thing you can never do with any story: you cannot make it **true**. Not in the ultimate sense. You cannot create a true story that is not also false, from some other perspective.

So, struggling with this concept of true and false is not really a very productive way to spend your energy. Nothing is ultimately true other than, "*The ONE Is.*" All else is just a matter of temporary, local imbalance. And Infinite Variation tells us that all things that can be created co-exist and are equally true. All things are, and all things are not. That is the nature of the Infinite Elastic Ball.

Z: But, 8, you have just used the Infinite Elastic Ball to prove something to me while, at the same time, saying that the Infinite Elastic Ball is just a story! And

I don't know if it's true or not and now I don't even know if that matters. Ugh! I am frustrated and confused! I feel even **more** like a child of Forget right now. I feel like I am never going to figure this out.

8: Is that so? Well then, how about I tell you more about the children of Forget? In fact, how about I tell you about the great saving grace, which they could use to find their way Home?

Z: Home?

8: To Remember, remember.

Z: Oh yes. I remember. (laughs) So you are saying there is hope for the children of Forget? That they can go home after all?

8: Yes. There is always the one great saving grace. But before I can tell you about that, I first have to tell you more about **why** the children of Forget kept finding their way into ever deeper forgetting and, no matter how hard they try, they never seem to be able to remember.

It has to do with identification; who you are declaring yourself to be. You see, all parts of the ONE have the attributes of the ONE. They are creative and self-creative. This means that you are able to create yourself as you desire. I can put it this way:

*"You are who **you** say you are."*

So what happens if you declare yourself to be **your function**? Then you are declaring yourself to **be** that which you **do**. And this is something that almost everyone on Earth does – they declare themselves to be what they do. Go to a social event and meet someone new and they, almost invariably, will open the conversation by asking you what you do. What is your job, your function. There is an implicit belief that, if they know what you do, then they will know who you are. But the problem, of course, is that this idea is so pervasive that you come to agree with it and believe it yourself. You come to say, *"I am what I do,"* and then, because you say it is so, it **is**! Then you **are** what you do.

Now, I want to introduce a word to you. It is a word you know very well. But it is also a word you have so misunderstood that you actually need a formal introduction to it so that you can meet it anew and discover what that word really means. You must understand it correctly and use it correctly. Because it is a very useful word for a very useful concept.

The word is **ego**.

Ego is the part of the self that "does". It is the part that strives, that achieves, that gets up, gets out and gets going. In our little story, ego is exemplified by Push. It is the part of the Self that says, "*I am going to go and do this or that,*" and then does it. Ego says, "*I do.*"

Now, I ask you, does that sound like a bad thing?

Z: No. It certainly doesn't. By that definition, ego is required for, well, everything. I mean I couldn't get out of bed in the morning without ego. I certainly wouldn't be sitting here typing on this keyboard without ego.

8: You're right. Without ego you would **do** nothing. A mother would not hug her child. Lovers would not stare into each other's eyes. You would not make nourishing food for your body. Nothing that you would consider a good and loving thing to do would ever be done. Nothing at all would ever be done.

I'll take it further: without ego, your universe would never have come into being. The creator-beings, who came together to create this universe, did so by making decisions and choices and then enacting them. The very first, most basic decision of the ONE to seek to discover itself, the impetus to create, is ego. Push is ego.

Z: But so is war and destruction and killing and all that other stuff.

8: Yes, indeed, so it is! All activity is undertaken by ego. Whether it is good activity or bad activity is just your judgement of it. Ego is simply a tool. It is the part of you that **does**. We have spoken a lot in *The Ascension Papers* about **do**ing and **be**ing. The part of your consciousness that is involved with **do**ing is your ego.

You cannot honestly think that there is something inherently wrong or bad about that, can you?

Z: No. From what you are saying, I can see that ego is neither good nor bad. It's like a tool that you can use to build either a hospital or a bomb. Like a knife that can be used to cut food or to kill. It is just a tool. I get it.

But why then is there this idea, especially in spiritual circles, that the ego is bad? You often hear it said that the ego is the enemy – that it must be vanquished or overcome or even destroyed before one can grow spiritually. I've even heard it said by some people that I quite respect, that ego can be said to stand for, "*Edging God Out.*"

Is this all so much nonsense?

8: It is a misunderstanding. And quite an understandable one at that.

Z: An understandable misunderstanding? (laughs)

8: (smiles) Language can be fun sometimes, can it not?

But let me tell you why it is a misunderstanding and why it is understandable that it occurs.

Firstly there is, as I have said, nothing at all wrong with ego.

But if you identify yourself with your ego, then you are, absolutely guaranteed, to be heading away from oneness. You are heading towards separation.

Z: Ah! And that's a bad thing so...

8: Not so fast, Sparky! I didn't say that was a "bad" thing. If you **want** to be heading towards separation, like Push did, then it's a good thing. But if you want to be heading towards oneness, then it is an inappropriate thing. If you want to go home, then you must face home when you walk. Identifying with ego is facing away from home. Because you are, in fact, **not** what you **do**. What you **do** is just a transitory game you are playing with illusions. It is a part that you are play-acting. With this doing, you create your form. But your form is your expression. It is not what you **are**. If you made a sculpture, you wouldn't suddenly think that you **were** that sculpture!

And, as surely as if you were a sculptor, you are creating your form with your doing. And here I mean "form" in the greater sense **and** in the normal sense – your spiritual form and your physical form are created by your function. But this function is simply something that you are choosing to do for a while. This, you might say, is your purpose. It is, you might say, **why** you exist. And it is so, for so long as you say it is so. But believe me, if you ceased to do this thing, you would not cease to exist! So it is not really **why** you exist. At best it is a function to which you are well suited and which you enjoy fulfilling. And there is nothing at all wrong with that! But you need to understand that your purpose is chosen by you. And that, in due course, you will modify it and choose a new purpose. Please understand me; you are not defined by your purpose. Your purpose is defined by you. You are not what you do.

And it is important that you understand this, because if you define yourself by what you do, then you are heading towards separation.

When you declare yourself to be your creations, you limit yourself radically. The sum total of your creations is a very little thing compared to all the rest of infinity. So you choose to see yourself as very small, finite, limited, mortal and very much separated from everyone else. The only way to find some modicum of safety is to vigorously defend your creations and to seek to aggressively increase the extent of your creations. And this is why beings who are deeply ego-centric always take their creations **very seriously**. If you **are** your creations, then suddenly your creations become **very important**. Do they not? Have you ever seen people who are very deeply involved in their egos sitting around discussing their creations? They are always Very Important People and they are always engaged in Very Important Business. Lots of frowns and seriousness is called for. It doesn't matter if it's the board of directors of some company or members of parliament of a country or delegates to the United Nations; when people of ego gather, it is serious business. Love, laughter and kindness are never on the agenda.

And this is quite unsurprising. If you are saying, "*I* **am** *this doing*," then you will throw yourself with all that you are into the doing of that thing. You measure your value by how well you do that thing. You will seek affirmation for doing it well. You'll expect a great deal of stroking for all the doing that you have done well. In this world, that often means lots of money. But there are other ego strokes that you might seek, such as peer-approval or a fancy job-title or the corner office or whatever. If you are what you do, then you crave those kinds of rewards. And the flip-side, of course, is that you live in the shadow of constant dread that you will make some mistake and that your doing will be seen to be defective. Because this will mean to you that **you** are defective, you see. So ego-strokes on the one hand, counter-balanced by a desperately hidden, unacknowledged panic on the other, is how these beings proceed. When a machine part is overloaded in a way that threatens to break it, we say it is stressed. Stressed materials eventually fail. When you live the life of an ego-centred being, you reside in a permanent state of stress. It is even commonly acknowledged in your society. Work stress. Executive stress. It, quite literally, ages you at an accelerated rate, it harms your body and your psyche. All due to misidentification.

But that is not the worst of it. When someone, in any way, threatens what the ego-centric being is doing then, naturally, they take it very personally. Because they believe that what they do **is** what they are. So it **is** personal for them. And they will be willing to defend what they do with their very life because, after all, it is who they are. It **is** their life.

And **this** is where a great many societal dysfunctions spring up.

War, for example, is a function of ego identification. Politicians identify themselves with their function and, when someone else threatens that function, they will send any number of their own populace off to slaughter in order to defend that function.

It is all a kind of insanity.

But you see, you are all children of Push. It is understandable and natural that you should therefore keep seeking to understand yourselves with more and more **do**ing. You think you will find answers to the great questions of life by **do**ing. You think science or philosophy or religion might bring you back home. But they won't. Because all these things are **do**ing. They are ego functions. You will never know oneness using your mind. You will never comprehend God with thoughts. You will never feel love in your ego centre. These things are impossible.

But that does not mean that the tools of thought, mind and ego are not useful! You'll notice that the whole of *The Ascension Papers* has all been ideas and thoughts and philosophies. It has all been ego-stuff. And this is not wrong! We have used ego-stuff to resolve other ego-stuff. So, if you are trying to ascend, then this is a useful application of ego-stuff. But we went about as far as we could go using ego stuff. Before we could proceed further, you needed to take even the smallest step without ego. That was what your day of silence was about. On that day, for the first time, you willingly and intentionally disengaged your ego completely for just a moment and, in that moment, you listened to your heart. For but an instant, you stopped **do**ing and found yourself in a state of **be**ing. And that changed everything.

You see – you are not your ego. You are, in fact, an indivisible part of the oneness. You are pure consciousness. And for so long as you experience yourself as separate from the rest of the oneness, then you shall be pulled back to oneness with Love. In fact, the more separate you are, the more Love will tug on you to return to oneness – the harder you will have to work to remain separate. Love is the elastic in the Infinite Elastic Ball. You see, your true nature is to be ONE with the oneness. So, the more you push away, the more balance seeks to assert itself. So you are pulled back ever more forcefully.

There are a number of ways for you to counter this pull so that you can keep pushing out. Identifying yourself with your form is a great way to accomplish just that. Releasing that identification will cause you to slow down your pushing away and even come to a halt. If you wish to return home, you can then simply identify yourself with that which you truly **are**.

And how do you do that? How do you find out what you truly **are**?

You go to the very centre of your being. You go to your heart. Buried deep inside your heart is a portal to the oneness. Indeed, you contain the whole of the oneness within you. It is but an illusion that there is anything at all outside of you. Everything you experience outside of you is a projection of your own psyche – it is the light of the ONE shining though the lens of your own consciousness that you are experiencing. You literally create your whole experience. You project it from within. So, if you go to your heart, you can find who you really **are**. And who you are is... the oneness!

All the forms you have created are just your creations, and you, of course, are their creator. And as the creator, you are not limited to the forms you have created, as you can create an endless number of other, different forms if you desire. And, by looking within, you can find every single other form that has ever been created is also right there inside your heart; all wisdom, knowledge and learning is yours. All ability is your ability. You become boundless. You discover your own God-like nature. You know everything you need to know and you can do everything you need to do.

And **this** is the one great saving grace that is always available to all the children of Forget. Any time they decide to cease identifying themselves with their ego and move into their heart, then they discover the saving grace. They discover Remember within themselves.

Z: And then? What will they do then?

8: What would **you** do then? Would you take this knowledge of yours and go rushing home to Stay, or would there be some others to whom you would want to gift the knowledge?

Z: The latter. I would want to gift what I had found.

8: Yes. Of course you would. Because that is what Love would do. So you move one step closer to home, but you do not rush all the way home. And from that position, one step closer, you help as you can. You remind those whom you can. And then, when you have done what you think you can do, you take another step closer to home. And from there you discover more God-like powers. You realise that there is **more** that you can do. And so you do more. Because that is what Love would do. And so you go, step by step, remembering and loving and healing and helping and reminding... all the way home. And then, finally, when you are just one minuscule step from home, when you stand at the very doorstep, before rushing into the waiting arms of Stay, you will realise that you do not arrive home on your own. You will realise that you are all of Push, because you have gathered up all the rest of Push. All of Push will arrive home to all of Stay. And the ecstatic implosion of Love will be wondrous indeed!

Z: I **do** love a happy ending!

8: All endings are happy. If you are not happy, then it is not the end. It's just some misunderstood pause somewhere in the middle.

Z: So that is the story of Push and Stay and the Infinite Elastic Ball?

8: It is. Did you like it?

Z: I liked it a lot. And it makes me realise that, really, what I need to discover is how to find my one saving grace. I want to find Remember within myself. I want to move completely into my heart and be one with all that I truly am.

Yes, I want to gift what I find as I do, but I want to be on that path and stay on that path all the way Home to Stay. To oneness.

8: That is well, my beloved friend. For that is what I wish for myself also.

Assuredly, you **are** on that path. And it will be my pleasure and privilege to assist you, as best as I am able, to remain on the path.

Really, your journey proceeds with your expanding your capacity to love. To "Love with a capital L" as you so eloquently described what you received on your day of silence.

So, what I'd like to do next is to engage you in a discussion about love with the objective that you begin learn how to **be** love.

We'll begin by talking about what love actually is. To the degree that this is possible, we will seek to comprehend love.

Then we shall move on to an understanding of why you should seek to do as I propose. Why should one learn to be love?

Then we can begin to deal with your blockages that keep you from being love.

And that done, you will be ready to begin living at the whole new level of consciousness that has just dawned for you.

Z: Okay, excellent.

8: I'm pleased you approve. So then, let's get to it.

1. EXACTLY WHAT IS LOVE?

I have told you that the oneness exists in a state of perfect balance. That the ONE is pure, infinite consciousness and that It is, therefore, everything and nothing. You are an indivisible part of the oneness and you exist as a differentiated being with various attributes because you are created out of various imbalances. These imbalances arise as you or your Inner-Self come to hold different ideas about yourself. You identify strongly with certain attributes of the oneness (I am this and I am that) and very weakly with other attributes (I am not these other things). So you are in a state of imbalance and will remain so until you identify equally with all attributes of the oneness, and therefore also with none. Well, Love is the force that is pulling you back to balance. It is that which returns you to oneness. Love makes whole that which is fragmented. Love returns all the pieces of the puzzle to their rightful places. It is Love that allows you to see through the illusions of separation and to see, even for a moment, the divine in the eyes of another. Love is the drawing together of that which is set apart. When true, pure, unconditional love plays in your consciousness, then you will really **see** oneness wherever you look. And because there is nothing that is not of the oneness, you shall see to the truest nature of everything. You see through all illusions and all lies. You see that everything and everyone is a part of you, as you are a part of the All. It means knowing from your heart that everything is divine and that there is nothing that is not divine. That everything is perfect. That nothing is wrong. That all is worthy of your love and that there is no need for fear or other negative emotions. **That** is love.

And if you should come to feel **that** kind of love, then everything for you will be magically altered. You shall understand anew all the things that you previously thought to be bad or unacceptable. You will see light and love and glory wherever you cast your eye. And not because you are fooled – quite the opposite – precisely because you are no longer fooled... because you cease believing the false evidence of illusions.

And because you know the light and glory to be true, so it will be true and so your world will be altered. You have always created your reality in every detail, from the very smallest to the very greatest, but now you will **know** that you do. Now you will move into conscious creation. And you will create with love. Love will be your motivation and love will be the tool of your creation.

There is much else I could say about love. I could try for more compelling and eloquent words. But they would always fail the grace and glory of what love really is. Love cannot be understood. Love is much greater than the mind that would seek to understand it. Love can only be experienced. And once you have had even a small taste of truly limitless, unconditional love, then you will be forever altered. Your life's quest will be to return to that state of love. In that moment you will know that there can be nothing even remotely as important to you as existing in that state of union with the divine that **is** love.

Z: Thank you very much for that, 8. In hearing your description I know it to be true because there have been two occasions in my life when I have known myself to be touched by true, unconditional love. The first was my "mountain experience" in which, as I have already related, my heart was opened and my life-path radically altered. The second such experience was described in the opening to this chapter, my "day of silence" in which I came to really feel the truth of what was happening to me.

On both of these occasions, each in very different ways, I came closer to an awareness of the divine perfection of all of life. Each time I came to perceive a little more clearly the oneness of all. And both of these were truly wonderful, blissful experiences that I could absolutely not have "invented" out of my mind or ego, with all the will in the world. Both were great gifts of grace.

So what you have to say about this makes perfect sense to me. And I **do** have a deep desire to return to that state of love and, eventually, when I am ready, to reside there permanently.

The other stuff about Love being that which pulls everything back to balance and oneness is new and interesting to me. I didn't know that. But it makes sense. Thank you.

8: You are welcome. We'll talk some more about these experiences in a moment. For now, let's move on to the next point:

2. WHY SHOULD ONE LEARN TO BE LOVE?

I can state this as clearly and succinctly as this: If you truly learn to love limitlessly and unconditionally, then the kingdom of heaven will be yours.

It is as simple as that.

But maybe you don't know what that means, so perhaps I should paint you a more descriptive picture.

For starters, you will know absolutely that you are part of the oneness and that everyone you meet, and everything you see, are also part of the oneness. You will see others in a very different way to that which you now do. You will see their light. This means that, at a glance, you will see who they really are. Sure, you will also see whatever metaphor and illusion they might temporarily be clothing themselves with, but this will not fool your eye. Like a beloved friend who wears a fancy-dress outfit, you will know the being for who they really are, rather than for the body they are inhabiting or the game they are playing. You will see to the truth of them. And they will see you too! You know that a great deal of the pain expressed by beings in your world is really just a deep desire to be **seen**. To be seen for who they really are. To be recognised. To be understood. To be loved as they are. Well, this is something that will be instantaneous and automatic. Each will **see** the other. All will be understood. All will be loved.

And so, of course, there will also be no more misunderstandings. And, not that you would want to lie ever again, for that would be counter-productive to your own goals, but it is true that you could not then lie or be lied to. You will, quite simply, see the truth of this other being. Their "words" or whatever other metaphorical and creative representations they might present to you, would really only be additional input. Primarily, you will know this being and their true nature and intent by their light.

Telepathy will not only be possible, but will actually become a normal mode of communication for you. If you know that you are, at core, the same ONE great being, then you'll have no trouble understanding that different parts of the oneness can share the same thought with Itself. If you think of another being, then you can bring them to your mind and instantly let them know what you are thinking. If you wish it, it can be so: instant mind-to-mind sharing of thoughts, feelings, experiences and ideas across any separation of distance and time.

And, of course, if you wish privacy for your thoughts, that too is yours.

And you will come to know yourself as a creator being of limitless power. Time, space, energy and matter are all illusions created to make certain types of games work. When you know that you are a part of the oneness, then the illusions only work when you want them to work. So these things become pliable. You can be taught (if you so choose) how to manipulate time, space, energy and matter. It is not very difficult to do. Once you see though the illusion, it becomes quite easy. Then you see that time and space are the same thing. They are simply an illusory separation of things. Energy is created by this separation and flows between two or more points that were separated by the illusion of time and space. Matter is simply the result of holding patterns of consciousness in the flow of the energy. Up till now, you have believed yourself to be **inside** the illusion. You have looked at the forms that result and, not only have you believed these things to be real, but you have actually believed yourselves to **be** these forms. But it is not so. These forms, which result from the patterns, are not you. They are just your temporary creations. You will see that. You will see that you are the creator of your form. And then you will learn how to alter the forms that you create, to your will. I mean, you will be able to consciously create (or at least co-create) your world, your body and anything around you, as you wish.

And then you will learn instant teleportation. You will be able to simply let go of a form here, where you are, and your body will simply disappear into nothingness, only to reappear from the nothingness elsewhere on the planet. Or, indeed on another planet, if you wish. All you need to do is hold your form's patterns in energy there and then you shall be there. Or, at least the form you are using to represent yourself shall be there. Teleportation is the favoured mode of transport for high-order unity-conscious beings throughout the universe. Neither space nor time will be an obstacle for you!

And, of course, you will never again feel the need to die. Death, as you know it, is a very important and valuable tool for beings on the outward journey. It is quite normal for beings heading outwards to get lost in their games and illusions and to lose sight of the greater purpose and goal of their journey. Not only do such beings get a little lost and confused, but they also begin to create a great deal of pain, fear and confusion for themselves. So, death was created to allow these beings to interrupt their passage so that they could, with some regularity, be brought back to their intended path. Death allows a means for the being to bring their journey to a halt and return to a higher consciousness for guidance and help. Without its merciful release, beings on the outward journey would become very weary and traumatised. But, as you move into a state of being pure, radiant love, such release becomes utterly superfluous. There will be nothing you will need release from. If you ever require rest and succour, you may simply still your ego-being and put down your burden and you will instantly find yourself in that state of blissful, balanced, harmonious oneness that is your truest nature. And for you this will be as normal as a night's sleep currently is.

And these are some of the general attributes of a life in true unity consciousness. And being of unity consciousness **is** the same thing as being love. Perfect, unconditional love for All That Is, **is** the same thing as recognising that you are one with All That Is.

But attaining such awareness and being of such high consciousness is not a limitation. You will not find yourself confined to a life such as I have just outlined. You might, for example, choose to reside in unity consciousness and, from there, make sojourns into the lower realms of separation and duality on missions of discovery or adventures of service. Or you could move through the portal of the oneness and go and visit other realities entirely. I don't simply mean other places in this universe or other universes, no, I mean other entirely different frames of creation. Creations, which do not operate at all like this one does. As you move from a place of oneness, you can enter any other realm that is within the oneness. And you may go and create there if you desire. This is all open to you to choose.

And you shall realise very quickly too that you no longer need a unidimensional perspective. You will realise that you can operate from outside of time. This means that you might want to maintain a life in one reality and, at the same time, explore and create in a thousand others. There are no limitations on you, save those which you place upon yourself.

These are some of the general traits of the life of a being who creates its world entirely with love and who lives in a unity-conscious reality. It is what you can expect for yourself if you open your heart to love, and then stay the course on your journey to oneness. But they are only general traits and you will be free, of course, to choose other experiences if you wish them.

As to the specifics of your life – where you will live, how you will live, what you will do – these, of course, are questions you will answer for yourself. I cannot tell you what you will decide. But I can tell you that you will be able, if you wish it, to live a truly sublime life. If you decide to surround yourself with others who are also of unity consciousness, then you shall feel nothing but soul-connection on all sides. You shall be held in the soft embrace of love all the days of your existence. You shall trust all whom you meet and your trust shall be well warranted. You shall seek always to give your greatest gift and you shall be loved, respected and rewarded for your giving. And whatever your greatest gift is, it shall indeed be something worthy of your time and attention. And you will give your gift away with open-hearted generosity. You shall never need to ask, "*But what is in it for me?*" because all those around you will be likewise giving their greatest gift. And in an infinite universe, there is guaranteed to be someone, somewhere whose greatest bliss it is to create exactly the thing that you might think you want or need. Taking your need to them will be a gift to them! The fact that you have need of their greatest gift will bless them. And **that** will be the new economy of the new world in which you shall dwell if you choose to live amongst others who are of unity consciousness: you will give and give and give. And when someone takes of your gift, it will bring you joy. And if there is something you want or need, you shall simply have to accept it, as it will be offered to you. And your accepting it will bring the giver joy. Love shall be the currency of the new world of the unity conscious, but the result of every transaction will be joy for all concerned.

Does any of this sound a little attractive to you?

Z: (laughs) Are you kidding? I feel like a kid who has just been offered the keys to the universal candy store!

8: The universal candy store. (smiles) Yes, and then some!

Z: But, I have to admit that it sounds very far off from where I am at now...

8: I understand that. But I did not desire to tell you of the next small step in your progression on your path back Home. I told you of your destination. The eventual outcome. Or certainly that which **could** be your eventual outcome, if you choose it. And if you do choose it then, as you begin the adventure of getting yourself to that outcome, so your life incrementally becomes more and more like that.

Why think small and aim low when you can expand your consciousness, think infinitely large and aim for All That Is?

Z: I like it. Okay, I'm in. Where do I sign up?

8: If you are ready for this... if you are ready for the New Earth populated by New Humans in a new Golden Age... If you are ready to be a creator being amongst creator beings... If you are ready to see God in the eyes of everyone you meet and to see the true beauty of Life in every vista you look upon... Then you are ready to really learn to be love.

Now, there are, of course, some obstacles to your loving like that. I am not oblivious to these challenges. You have expended a great deal of effort to be here in this reality, as it is. You have worked very, very hard to forget that you are ONE. And you have grown quite attached to your separation. It has become like an addiction to you. Even when it hurts you or seems to threaten to destroy you, still you cling to it. So, suggesting the direct path home is not really a viable solution.

Z: The direct path?

8: Yes. As it is true that you are creating your separation with a great degree of effort and will, so it is equally true that you would be able to return directly to oneness by the simple expedient of ceasing all effort and will. All you need to do to return to oneness is to cease all **do**ing. Release. Let go. Become perfectly still. I don't mean the momentary semi-stillness of meditation or even the slightly deeper stillness of your day of silence. I mean something orders of magnitude more still than that. I mean a complete cessation of all activity. Releasing your whole life-stream, releasing all ideas and beliefs you have about yourself and your world. Releasing **everything**. As you move towards perfect stillness, you will move towards oneness, until you merge once again with the oneness.

But this direct path is not something that you will wish to entertain. You are very attached to a whole host of ideas about yourself and you won't want to just let everything go. For example: you fear dying. You fear losing your individuality and even your identity. You fear losing the life that you have built. You fear for your loved ones if you should "go away".

And then you have all kinds of positive attachments too – you love what you are doing. You have a gift that you are beginning to discover, expand and give. You are in the middle of a process of expressing yourself and do not feel ready to simply abandon that. You are busy with a journey that captivates you. And you feel a loving attachment to those around you. You feel a connection to the land you live upon and the home you have built there. There are many such reasons that the direct path would be inappropriate for you. I understand this, and this is right and good. I mention the direct path simply to bring to your attention the realisation that it is not difficult to return Home to oneness. The hard work is **not** returning – retaining the illusion of separation is what is difficult. Returning home is easy. The "elastic" in the Infinite Elastic Ball is love. And it pulls on you all the time. If you simply ceased pushing out, then you would be returned home to oneness without needing to try.

But you don't want to just stop all doing, do you? You don't want to simply let go of this life of yours, this journey that you are on, and all that it entails. Do you?

Z: I sometimes think I do. I sometimes fantasize about just letting go of this life and drifting back home. Firstly to you, wherever you actually are, and then out of separation and then... I don't know where. Just home, I guess. But you are right. Those are just fantasies. I am not ready to let go yet. I am, quite simply, not done here yet.

8: And neither am I! So we remain here. But the good news is that this doesn't mean we cannot experience oneness! It just means that we have to find another way to do so. We don't just let go and go home – what we do instead is to bring home here. We engage in the shared, co-created work of bringing the kingdom of heaven to Earth, so to speak. One could say that we are not so much ascending ourselves, as ascending all of life! But doing it this way takes firm intention, commitment and more than a little effort. It is, perforce, the slower path home, but I very much do believe that you will enjoy the journey!

To travel this path, you will need to learn to release all the blockages and obstacles that you are creating between yourself and limitless Love. You will need to allow love to flow though you without hindrance. You will need to **be** Love.

Z: Is this really something I can learn?

8: Oh yes! Very much so. In fact, you don't really need to learn how to do this. It is your true nature. All you need to do is to release all the illusory programming you have taken on board. And then you might need a few pointers to get over some old habits. Then it should come naturally.

But, seeing as you are willing to do this, let's get on to...

3. How to Learn to Be Love

I am willing to teach you all that you need to know in order to open your heart to Love. But – and I cannot stress this enough – you will have to do the doing yourself. Love is an experiential thing. You will find your way there by **constantly** releasing the blockages that you have towards it and by **constantly** opening yourself to it. It will require of you that you set your intent and then stick to that intent; that you be conscious of your thoughts and feelings, and that you trust yourself and your heart. The road might seem tough at first, as you overcome stubborn programming but, as you go, it will get easier. As you begin to move into a truly open-hearted state of love, your life will, without a doubt, become more joyful, more abundant and easier. And as you see these rewards begin to unfold in your life, it will be easier to trust your heart. And so the path will become easier and your progression will accelerate. So there is much to look forward to. And I will give you the information that you need to help you to choose. But you must choose. And you must steadfastly keep choosing. Only you can create your reality for yourself.

Now there are three parts to the path that I am going to talk about; each of them with sub-headings. The three main parts are:

3.1 Removing the blockages you have to Love

3.2 The energy cycle of Love

3.3 **Be**ing love.

3.1 Removing the Blockages to Love

There are a number of ways you might be blocking your heart from opening to Love. I will address the three main ways. I do suggest that, if you resolve these three issues, you will almost certainly be able to overcome any others that might lurk in your psyche. You really just need to move with firm intent and consistency in the direction of removing these blockages, and they will begin to tumble.

3.1.1 JUDGEMENT

Judgement is when you feel the need to make another being, idea or thing wrong, in order for you to feel right. This rejection and divorce of the other is quite probably the biggest block in most peoples' hearts. For most it is such a normal and habitual thing that they are probably often not even aware that they are doing it. So the first thing to do is to become conscious of your own judgements of others. So, watch your thoughts. Then you will want to release your judgements so that you can begin to open your heart to others.

Judgement results from an incorrect understanding of what is. You are identifying yourself with your behaviour (which you are not) and then you are identifying others around you with their behaviour (which they are not). And then you are finding them *wrong* for that which they do, so that you can feel right about that which you are doing.

Let me help you to understand this in a new, more useful way.

Obviously, if you are not your behaviour and they are not their behaviour, then all of this is just unnecessary. But perhaps that won't help you quite yet. Because perhaps you are not quite ready to cease identifying yourself with your creations. So let's go a step further...

Can you remember that earlier on I told you about the property of the Infinite Elastic Ball called Infinite Variation?

Z: I do.

8: Well, what it means is that every possible thing that could be, is. Right now, it is. Every wonderful loving world that could exist, does. And every painful place of evil and torment too. All the possibilities exist. Infinity would not be infinity if they did not exist. The fact of their existence is not at question. The question that you should ask yourself is quite simply, **what do you want to experience**? Or, put another way, what do you wish to create for yourself?

And while you are asking that question, you should release others to experience anything and everything they might want and need to experience for themselves. Because you cannot create for yourself this freedom to experience exactly the world you want to experience if you are not willing to grant this to everyone else. What you do to others, you do to yourself also, remember? So give to others the right to create what they want. Release completely and lovingly everything you do not want for yourself. Cease any and all judgement of it, or of those who wish to experience it. And then choose what you want, and move towards that.

This is a very important understanding, so I am going to tell you about it again in a different way:

You'll recall I told you that everything that exists is created with imbalance and that nothing exists without imbalance. This means that everything that is created also immediately creates its "opposite" to counter balance it.

Z: I remember.

8: So think on this: you **cannot** create something without having someone else create the opposite.

This logically means that you should be grateful to every other being who is choosing every other thing that you are not choosing. You should be especially grateful to those who are choosing what seems to you to be the opposite of what you are choosing. All these beings are, in a way, making it possible for you to choose as you are. You could say that you are all counter-balancing each other, enabling them, making it possible for them to be as they are. You are, in fact, a particle of life that is in a dance with every other particle of life, everywhere. You are the soul-mate of every other being, everywhere. You are all intimately connected to all of life.

Do you see the short-sighted silliness of judgement? You cannot ask a single other being to stop doing what they are doing, without at the same time also stopping doing what you are doing. And the corollary is true – if you change yourself, then you change the whole universe. Can you see the power of the dictum that you should become the change you desire? For indeed, by changing yourself, you **do** change your whole world and your whole experience. You bring to yourself a whole universe of experience that is a direct reflection of who you are.

Indeed you **are** a creator being.

You have always been.

You have simply created without purpose and without direction in your ignorance.

So judgement is counter-productive. And a waste of your time and energy. And, most importantly, it places a huge block in your heart and stops the light of Love from channelling though you. It gets in the way of your creating for yourself a new world of Love.

Let it go!

If you encounter someone making a choice that is not right for you, then be thankful. Now **you** don't have to make that choice. Send them love. The more difficult their path is, the more love they need. Send them abundant love. And then think upon your choices. If you like the outcome of your choices, then you need to be especially grateful to all those others. Without their contribution, your choices would not be available to you. They would not be "counterbalanced" in the field of consciousness of the oneness.

Gratitude is the answer. Be grateful. Send thanks. Send love.

I made the statement earlier:

*"You are who **you** say you are."*

This statement was slipped in earlier in the context of telling you about ego. But it is a very important understanding. It has many uses. The first is, of course, that you should become very clear about who you think you **really** are, and then you should say so. I don't mean you should "say so" only in words. I mean you should express who you really believe yourself to be in your every thought and word and deed. You should say so from your heart. And then it will be so. But be clear! If you say contradictory things about yourself, then you will have a confused and incongruous experience of yourself and your life. This is never pleasant.

So how **do** you find who you really are and how do you express that?

You go to your heart! When you follow your heart and choose what is right for you, then that is discernment in action. This is your divine-right navigation of your own creator nature. It is you, quite simply, choosing and creating what is right for you. Quite a different thing from you standing on the outside, looking in to someone else's life and residing in judgement of them. We shall talk more about listening to your heart in a moment.

But for now, the point I wish to bring to the fore is this: you are who **you** say you are. If others stand in judgement of you, then these judgements of theirs do not tell you who you are.

> *"Other's judgements of you do not show you who **you** are, they show you who **they** are!"*

And this can be very useful. When you know who others are, then you can decide if their being resonates with yours. You can enact your discernment and decide if engaging with them is "right for you" or not. Surely you should draw yourself towards that which is "right for you" and away from that which is "wrong for you"? So it is useful to get a clear picture of who others are. And a great way to do this is to watch what they say of you!

But have a mind! Your judgements of others are just the same.

> *"Your judgements of others do not tell you anything about **them**. They tell you something about **yourself**!"*

So your judgements and ideas of others **are** useful – if you know how to use them! Watch those judgements and opinions rise to the surface and ask yourself, *"What am I telling myself about myself right now?"* Somewhere in your judgement there hides a deep desire that is denied. Or possibly a deep hurt that is unexpressed. There is something deep within yourself that you are hiding from yourself. It finds expression by rising to the surface when someone else, in some way, is doing this thing that you are denying yourself or rejecting from yourself.

So watch those judgements! They are **most** instructive. And if you process them correctly, they will dissolve, because the underlying rejection or denial in your own psyche is healed. Each judgement you dissolve is a step closer to Love.

3.1.2 NEGATIVE EMOTIONS

The second blockage to your heart that I wish to address is negative emotions. These are things such as fear, pain, anger, hatred, jealously, envy and greed. These emotions are both the result, and the cause, of blockages in the heart. Since they limit your capacity to find and express love I wish to address them with you now so that you might better understand them and learn to process them correctly so that they do not close your heart.

In order to explain this to you I am going to need to take a small tangent. Firstly I will need to make sure that you have an accurate understanding of the term, "duality", that you understand the role of Consciousness Construct Holders and emotions generally and then we can correctly understand negative emotions.

DUALITY

"Duality" is a much-used word in spiritual circles and we have used it here in *The Ascension Papers* quite a bit too. But what does it mean, do you think?

Z: I think I know. What I have gleaned from the our conversations is that there seems, first of all, to be an illusion of separation. Parts of the ONE have created separate identities for themselves by moving beyond the Veil. And from there, some of those in separation sank even deeper into the illusion by creating that they are even separate from the creator. I think that is what the word "duality" implies: the "two-ness" of creation and the creator. Of God and the universe.

8: Or of the ONE and yourself.

Z: Exactly what I mean, yes.

8: That's a good understanding. Later, when we get into a discussion of densities of consciousness, I'll explain all this to you in much greater detail but for now all I wish you to understand is that there are levels of separation:

Everything begins with oneness.
Then there is the very earliest level of separation called "individuation".
Deeper separation becomes "polarity".
The deepest separation is "duality".

This is an extremely cursory explanation, though, and lacks detail. So please don't attach too much to this until we have had an opportunity to discuss this thoroughly in a later chapter.

The point is, quite simply, that duality is the deepest level of separation. So much so that deeply duality-conscious beings do not even know that they are in duality. They are too deep in the illusion to even think in such terms. They believe that **all** beings are separate. If they choose to be religious, then they believe in a God or gods who are also separate from themselves. God is "over there", somewhere else, doing things that they have no power to influence.

Pure materialism – which is the theory that nothing but matter exists – is an example of a non-spiritual view from within the duality perspective. Those who ascribe to that view think that their own consciousness, mind, emotions, and being are all simply a function of their body and their brain. And they obviously also think that they are absolutely separate from all other beings.

There are probably an infinite number of things that you could believe to be true whilst being of duality consciousness.

Ironically, it is only once you begin to raise your consciousness out of duality and awaken to the realisation that all is ONE, that you actually become aware of duality at all. It is only then that you might be likely to even use the word, "duality". You first become aware that there **is** oneness but you also feel as if you yourself are separate from it. Such beings are what I call the "awakened duality-conscious". And then, as you proceed with your awakening, you come to release your fears and limitations and **know** that you too are one with the oneness. And then, at last, you begin to return to unity consciousness.

But for those who are firmly of duality consciousness, there is no possibility that they might accept that all is ONE or that they are actually ONE with the creator or that they can indeed create their own reality. And this brings me to the "two-ness" you were talking about. There is an unbridgeable separation, in the mind and belief system of the duality conscious, between the creator, on the one side and its creation on the other.

The consequence of this perspective is that there are two separate classes of things, as follows:

The Creator (or creators)	Creations
God (or gods)	Humans
Divine	Profane
Infinite, eternal, infallible	Limited, mortal, fallible
Spirit, ethereal, ineffable	Flesh, material, explicable

I could keep on putting more descriptors into the two boxes, but you get the idea, I am sure. The point about the essential "two-ness" of the world-view of those of duality consciousness has been made. And Joy-Divine has already addressed with you, at some length, how the duality conscious position is a very limited perspective and how the unity conscious perspective is a greater truth, and I have already explained at length that, "*The ONE is,*" so I won't rehash that here.

Z: So then how do we bring all of this duality consciousness to an end?

8: End it?

What you really need to understand is that duality consciousness (which is the same thing as victim consciousness) is not *wrong*. It is, quite simply, a level of existence deep inside this separation reality. Duality is one of the places you can go to when you visit Separation. And it's not *bad* to visit this place either. It's just a choice... one possible set of experiences out of many.

What you also need to understand is that there is much about duality and victimhood that is wonderful. When you are outside of it, you will actually think back on many aspects of it with great fondness.

Z: I find that hard to believe!

8: That is because you are only focussing on the negative. But think for a moment of how it feels to be totally, hopelessly, head-over-heels in love.

Z: It's wonderful. It's like being high on an impossibly amazing, intoxicating drug.

8: And it's also an utterly victim-consciousness experience.

In order to be in love, you need to believe that there is someone else who is so wonderful and perfect and that their presence *makes you feel* that way.

And when they express similar feelings of love and wonderment at you, this *makes you feel* even more, even stronger feelings of being in love.

But this is all victim-consciousness stuff. If you **knew** that you were the creator of your experiences and therefore **knew** that you had actually invited this whole interaction with this other person and also **knew** exactly how it would all turn out because it was all agreed upon beforehand and, crucially, if you **knew** that you were creating these "in love" feelings all by yourself... then what?

Z: I... don't know. It would all be a lot less exciting, I guess.

8: Exactly. Duality is a roller-coaster ride, for sure. It feels insanely dangerous and you feel like you are out of control and at risk. And that is exactly why souls line up to get in. And why they keep coming back, over and over again, lifetime after lifetime, for more. Excitement.

Z: Not me. After this one, I'm done.

8: Yes, I do believe you are. When you are ready to be done with duality, then you begin to awaken to your creator nature. That is you saying, "*I am ready to leave the fun-fair now,*" because creator consciousness and duality consciousness cannot co-exist in the same being at the same time. And since this is what you are doing, I'd be highly surprised if you decided to try to go back for another go-round.

But my point remains; even as you are getting ready to leave the ride and planning to exit the park, still, if you are honest, you must admit that there were wonderful experiences to be had. Falling in love is just one. The whole material world in which you could eat wonderful food, look at sunsets, listen to music... all the things you love... these are all effects of duality. And how much have you not actually loved the process of "not knowing" and then engaging Joy-Divine and I in conversation to receive wisdom and insight? None of these things would be possible without the illusion of duality.

Z: That's a useful and interesting perspective: there is nothing wrong with duality. It's just one kind of experience. It has its ups and its downs and it certainly can be very exciting. And when we are done with it, we can leave.

Thank you, 8, I think I have a far better understanding now of what duality really is.

8: So then, can you see, from what I have been saying, that duality conscious beings very much do not believe that they can, or do, create their experiences?

Z: By definition, they would not, no.

8: And this is exactly why there is a need, in a duality reality, for Consciousness Construct Holders.

Consciousness Construct Holders

I have, in the previous chapter, told you about Consciousness Construct Holders. These are beings who carry one consciousness construct or another into this reality. Your very own Inner-Self, for example, carries the consciousness construct of the energy which is "Joy". There are many, many other such Consciousness Construct Holders, each responsible for bringing a different energy into this reality.

And the reason this is necessary and desirable is to make it possible for this duality reality to work. If you do not believe that you can create joy within yourself, then how will you ever feel joy? Without Joy-Divine holding this frequency for duality-conscious beings, this would simply not be possible. And, in just the same way, every other feeling, emotion and experience is held for those who are not themselves of creator-consciousness so that they can experience it outside of themselves. If you do not believe you can create it, then it must be created for you. Consciousness Construct Holders are those beings that reside in the higher densities of this reality where they do exactly that: they create and hold for you those things that you do not know you can create for yourself.

I suppose a reasonable analogy would be that the Consciousness Construct Holders are each shining a light into this whole reality and the light that shines is the energy of their particular consciousness construct. This is the gift they give.

Which is all very nice but, of course, if you do not know that you can create these things, then you certainly can feel as if you are a victim to them.

Z: I've heard it said, particularity by macho-type guys, that emotions are a weakness to be overcome.

8: Indeed! For the deeply duality conscious, emotions are at best just strange feelings that happen to you at inopportune times and, at worst, real impediments in your life. And so it is that emotions are a distracting, troublesome and confusing thing for those of duality consciousness.

As you become aware of your own creator nature, however, you become aware that you can, and do, create your own experiences. And one of the first things you learn, as you discover your ability to create, is how to self-emote. What this term means is the ability to create your own emotions from within yourself. If you can sit quietly and, without changing anything at all in your outer environment, without finding things to be happy about, just create joy for its own sake inside your own heart... then you will have self-emoted joy.

What will have happened here is that you will have felt it strongly enough and often enough as you journeyed through duality that you **know** how it feels. But now, as you awaken to your creator nature, now you are able to create it yourself. You no longer need a Consciousness Construct Holder to do this for you. Instead of waiting to feel that light shine upon you, you can now choose to light your own lamp inside yourself and shine that light.

You have moved, in this regard, from victim to creator.

And this is another of the wonderful things that can be gained from coming to duality. This might be hard for you to understand right now but, until a part of the ONE comes here, it only knows its own energy. Coming here allows you to forget your own energy and to experience all the many, many other energies on offer. And then, when you have re-awakened to your own true creator nature, you can then create each, any, or all of those energies for yourself from within yourself. Do you have any idea at all how powerfully this evolves your soul? It's truly a wonder!

To reuse the analogy of the Infinite Elastic Ball, you yourself might previously have only known how to push out in the direction of joy but now, having been here, you know, directly and from within yourself, how to push out in a truly vast array of directions.

But I don't wish to digress too far in that direction. What I wish to bring to your attention is that there comes a point in each soul's journey through duality when it dawns upon that soul that it can indeed self-emote. That it is no longer the victim to its experiences for how it feels. When that soul is ready to take the next step, then there is a grand leap awaiting: the discovery of the awesome creative power of all the emotions that have been experienced and that can now be mastered.

The world of illusion has taught you that "what is true and real" is outside of yourself and that, as these "real" things change, so your emotions follow. You get happy when good things happen to you. But this is a lower-order reality. There is a greater truth that runs exactly the other way round: with your emotions you gravitate experiences to yourself. If you create joy and hold that frequency, then you will bring joyful experiences to yourself.

Z: I think that if you had told me this a few years ago, I would never have been able to believe you. But this is not a new concept for me and I have really tried it out. Or rather, I have begun to **live** this concept and I can say, unambiguously, that I know this to be true.

8: You raise an important point. The only way to turn such a concept from "strange theory" into "personal truth" is to experience it yourself, first-hand.

> (**Zingdad note:** I have created a 30-day experiential guide that takes you on a journey to discover the simple, yet amazing power of exactly this. It is called, Create Yourself, Create Your Life. This guide teaches you to cleanly and clearly hold an emotion and then see that emotion in action, transforming your life. If you are ready to know the power of emotions and to change your whole world, then check it out here: http://zingdad.com/books/create-yourself-create-your-life)

Z: So, emotions are very powerful tools of creation. When we first enter separation we are limited to being able to create only with our own energy because that is all we know. But, as a result of being here in separation, we each gain a whole rich palette with which we can create.

8: Precisely.

Z: So what about the negative emotions?

8: A valid question. And what I'd like to share with you in this regard now is the understanding that "negative" and "positive" is just a matter of perspective.

Z: *"There is not a single thing that is either good or evil but that you feel that way about it."*

8: Exactly.

Z: But you said we needed to correctly understand negative emotions so that they don't close our hearts.

8: That's right. So the negative emotions are energies that are carefully held by certain Consciousness Construct Holders and those energies are offered into this separation reality so that beings can use them and create with them.

If you wish to create separation, then you can use the negative emotions.

If you wish to create oneness, then you can use the positive emotions.

Some parts of the ONE wish to create separation, polarity and duality. These are wonderful creations that catalyse spectacular growth and evolution for all who visit them. The negative emotions are those emotions that make it possible for these separation realities to come into being and remain stable long enough for all the souls that wish to explore them to do so to their satiation.

All parts of the ONE that have explored separation, polarity and duality will eventually come to a point where they will have gained all that they needed from these realities and will wish to extricate themselves. The positive emotions are what make it possible for beings to return themselves to wholeness and then also to return themselves to oneness.

And here comes the crux: the degree to which you, yourself, are of duality consciousness is the degree to which you will feel as if you are a victim of these emotions. It is the degree to which you will feel as if they are something that *happens to you,* rather than something that you can choose and create for yourself.

Z: So... let me see if I've got this right.

Negative emotions create separation, positive emotions create oneness...

8: I must interrupt. Emotions do not create anything. **You** create.

Z: Ah. So then we create separation with negative emotions and we create oneness with positive emotions.

If I create enough separation, then I find myself in duality where I believe that I do not create my emotions. In that state I just experience a mixture of all kinds of emotions, depending on what I am creating, even though I am unaware that I am creating. And this is where I will stay until I am ready to leave separation. Then I will have to take ownership of my own creative faculties and create with positive emotions. This will cause me to create wholeness within myself so that I find myself moving out of duality, through polarity and back to oneness.

8: Yes. That is a good summation of the situation.

Z: Hmm. Before we move on from the topic of negative emotions, if I may, I'd like to work through some objections with you.

8: Naturally.

Z: Okay, so I do get all of this – I understand that I create my own emotions. But what to do about the fact that, for most of us down here on Earth, for most of the time, it doesn't feel like that. It feels as if *stuff happens* and then the emotions arise as a result of that. Not the other way round.

8: In other words, you feel as if you are a victim of your emotions?

Z: No. I'd say we feel as if we are victims of our circumstances. The emotions just follow. Let me give you some examples. If I was walking in the forest and a venomous snake suddenly rose up to strike me, I'd feel plenty of fear. And if Lisa decided that she wanted to leave me, I'd feel plenty of heartache. And when I read about the gross maladministration that the planet's politicians are inflicting upon us all, then I feel plenty angry.

In these kinds of experiences, I feel as if things are happening to me, and the emotions are following.

8: And **still** you are asking me about this? After all that has been discussed? Really?

Z: (sheepishly) No, I suppose I don't need you to answer that.

8: But then you know the rule. If you raise a question that has been thoroughly dealt with, then you must answer it yourself before we move on. So, you tell me – what do you do about the feeling that you are a victim to your experiences?

Z: It's a matter of shifting my perspective to the realisation that everything I am experiencing is, in some way, invited by me. Either by me, Zingdad, or by the me that I am outside of incarnation, my Inner-Self. Either I am consciously creating it or unconsciously inviting or allowing it.

I invite experiences so that I can make choices about them. When I have firmly made a choice about something, then I can let it go and it won't arise for me to look at again.

8: So, the snake?

Z: Would not really be a random event. I mean, I know that, in my experience here on the farm. Snakes don't hang around randomly waiting to bite humans. They clear off if they hear you coming. But I had a visitor who kept saying over and over, *"I hope we don't see a snake, I am petrified of snakes!"* and then, on a walk in the forest, sure as nuts, there was a huge puffadder lying across the road. It was the only one I'd seen in many, many months.

8: And you have never yet seen one on your own land.

You see? This is not your problem and you are not bringing it to yourself for it to become a problem. So...

Z: So, no need to fear.

8: And Lisa leaving you?

Z: Well, that was just a silly example. I know that what I have with Lisa is a sacred soul-contract. Our Inner-Selves are dancing together through our interaction. And yet, for all that, I also know that eternity is a very long time. And from that perspective, this here is a place where her Inner-Self and mine are co-creating and, equally there are many, many other places in eternity where we are not. What I mean is that I know and understand that our association does, from one perspective, come to an end. But, from another perspective, we will both be forever changed by this interaction between two mortal beings on planet Earth.

8: That is true and also quite beautifully put. But it doesn't answer your own question. Will you or will you not be heartbroken if Lisa leaves you? And are you then not a victim to that experience?

Z: Okay. So here's how I see it. If Lisa and I are both following our hearts, and so remaining in resonance with our Inner-Selves, then we are both doing our highest good. If it is in either her or my highest good that we terminate our relationship, then that will, on the one hand, be sad. It is sad when something wonderful ends. But, of course, it will also be right. And so, I won't feel a victim to that experience.

8: That's very well said.

And so, finally (he gives a little sigh) what about the politicians?

Z: Yeah. This is old hat already, isn't it?

The way I see it is that politicians are just a part of the furniture of a duality conscious world. People give their power to politicians by voting for them. Then the politicians become corrupted by that power, they abuse it and the people get angry. They then vote someone else into power, who does the same thing. And the politicians, as we have already discovered, are themselves just the pawns of the Super Powerful Individuals. They are actually just dancing the line between "following orders" and keeping their image polished.

As long as I am giving this my attention and getting angry and engaging in the whole political circus, then I am actually feeding the system.

8: That's quite correct.

Z: But that does lead me to wonder... How can we do things differently? How **can** we really make things work for us? All of us? There must be a better way... but what is it?

8: Now you are asking the right questions!

In due course you'll be talking to Adamu again.

> (**Zingdad Note:** See Book 3 of *The Ascension Papers* here
> zingdad.com/books/the-ascension-papers-book-3)

Ask him these kinds of questions. Ask him about what has worked in other civilisations across the galaxy. Ask him how other civilisations transitioned from primitive power-imbalances to highly-advanced love-based systems. And then see if what he has to say is not applicable to your situation.

But that is not what we are talking about now. What we are talking about is negative emotions and how you have allowed them to block your heart.

Now that you have heard my perspective on all of this, how do you think you can process them so that they no longer block your heart?

Z: I think I get the theory. It is to understand that I am the creator of my own emotions. To know that I choose how I feel. And then to be conscious of what I am choosing and to make choices that do not limit my ability to love. So that's the theory, but I can tell the practice will be quite challenging.

8: That's a very good start. If you have the theory straight in your mind, then at least you know where you are going. But you will not be done with turning this into practice for quite some time. For truly, when you master your emotions, then you will also be ready to master your creations. And when you arrive at that point, you will be ready to exit duality altogether.

Perhaps the greatest difficulty with negative emotions is that most of them are relegated to your Shadow. This is a part of your psyche that is hidden from the light of your own awareness. It is that part of yourself that is unclaimed by you. And since you are largely unaware of this part of yourself, it can enact all kinds of negative emotions upon you without you being able to understand how or why any of this is happening to you. So this is a vital topic that you will, in due course come to address in detail.

> (**Zingdad note:** Part 2 of ***Dreamer Awake!*** Is called "Shining the Light on Shadow" and it is exactly what 8 is talking about here: an in-depth journey into healing Shadow. Find our more here: zingdad.com/dreamer-awake)

But at least you have the concepts; you have understanding, and you are on your path towards a truly open heart.

Z: Thank you, 8! I think you said that the next point was about identifying ourselves with who we really are?

8: Correct. We have already addressed this when I spoke about ego, so I will be brief.

3.1.3 IDENTIFYING WITH YOUR CREATIONS RATHER THAN WITH WHO YOU REALLY ARE

As long as you think that you are your creations, then you will be creating separation.

There are a number of ways to realise that you are not your creations, which will also help you to begin awakening to your true nature. Meditation is a good way. But there are many different practices that are all termed meditation. I would recommend meditations that assist you to become present to the **now** moment. Release all your thoughts and ideas about what came before and what will come later. Be present in the **now**. Do this consistently and you will begin to realise that you are not your body; you are not your thoughts; you are not your beliefs; you are not your relationships; you are very much not the things you do or your job. And you are **certainly** not the money you earn or the possessions you own.

It can be quite difficult to move into the **now** moment if you are not used to being there. Most beings who are incarnated on your planet, especially in western societies such as your own, are totally conditioned to living alternately in the past and in the future with no stop in-between for the **now**. On the menu for your thought processes are things such as:

Worries and concerns about the future

Wishes and dreams about the future

Reminiscences and reveries about the past

Recriminations and bitterness about the past.

But, if you truly spent a moment in the **now**, you'd be able to release all of these things and see them for the illusory constructs of your mind that they really are. Your past and your future are not fixed. They are your creations and the truth of it is that you are actually creating them **now**. And they can be recreated any way you want and need. But you must first cease trying to live in the past and future. To do so is to try to live in these illusory creations. To attach to a single, limited perspective on your creations. And this takes you away from who you really are and away from your connection with the divine. Doing so identifies you with your creations, not with who you really are.

The antidote is to become truly present to the **now**. Make time every single day to be still. Make time often to listen to your heart. Break the habit of not-**now** consciousness. Move into the **now** more and more often until, eventually, you can reside there permanently.

Z: 8, I have also created a number of other Guided Meditation recordings that might be useful to readers in finding such a space. My Guided Journey called "open your heart" is my way of sharing with others the path I discovered that led to my own awakened and opened heart chakra.

> (**Zingdad note:** And a more recent Guided Meditation recording called, "Journey to the 6th dimension, might also be especially useful for those who are really ready for a massive release of not-now consciousness. Find the whole collection here: zingdad.com/healing-a-helping/guided-meditation-recordings)

8: Yes, indeed! There are many aids to this journey available to the seeker. From books on the subject to personal instruction at the hands of an experienced meditation instructor. What you offer in your Guided Meditation recordings is that which has been co-created with you, J-D, Adamu and I. And so really, this is the best that anyone can do: find what works for the Self and share that with others. As you have already discovered, many have found value in what you have created and many others still will. But, whatever the case, each will have to find their own path to stillness and to heart-connection in the way that works for them, and to each will be offered the assistance they need if they will but seek it. And for many these meditations of yours will be a very valuable ally in their journey.

And that brings us to the end of this rather lengthy discourse on blockages to your heart. If the seeker experiences any blockage and is willing to remove it and proceed to love, then the path will be opened. Help will be given. It takes commitment, a clear resolve and a little effort. But anyone who desires to get there, certainly will be able to do so. And the rewards for doing so are immense. Removing the blockages to Love means being able to open yourself to experiencing Love.

Which is what I will be addressing in the remaining two points.

3.2 THE ENERGY CYCLE OF LOVE

I have said before that you get what you create. But you reside in a time-bound system. This means that you are right now experiencing that which you have created in your past. If you understand cause and effect, then you can understand that your experiences today are the *effect*. Your choices and beliefs from your past are the *cause*. If you decide right now to radically change perspective and you instantly come to hold new ideas and beliefs, then it will take some amount of time for your reality to change. Over the next while you will experience less and less of the world built upon your old beliefs and more and more of the world built upon your new beliefs. This is the essential value of the consciousness construct called Time. It is that which separates cause from effect. So, if the cause occurs in your own consciousness right now, the effect will not occur in your reality for some time. Exactly how long it takes will depend upon how fundamental the change is and how firm you are in your resolve and intent. But what you should understand is that the process of changing your reality does take time. It is a matter of changing your own beliefs and choices and then holding to that inner-change, whilst allowing your outer-reality to transform over whatever period is required to conform to your inner-change.

With that background I wish to tell you this: if you wish to live in heaven tomorrow, then you should begin by being a citizen of heaven today. Begin by striving constantly to love yourself ever more magnificently. In so doing, your capacity to love others will expand. Then you should seek to be the most loving being that you can be. When you yourself are a citizen of heaven by your thoughts, your words and your deeds, then indeed, you will come to find your world slowly becoming more and more heavenly. And no death to this world will be required of you. Be the change you desire and the change **will** follow suit.

The advice I offer is to be patient with your life, be patient with yourself and give yourself a good deal of grace. But make a start right now! Your tomorrows are being created by the consciousness and energy that you express today. So you can, and will, have a tomorrow that is love-filled if you create with only love today. Every time you find it hard going and every time you falter, simply return to the path of love. So, begin again by being kind to yourself and by loving yourself. That you have faltered is proof that you are trying. Simply make a choice anew to engage with life using the energy of love.

And that brings me right to the heart of the matter. Love is an energy. It is the only **true** energy. All other energy is a derivative of love. The more love you give away, the more you have. The more you have, the more you can give. Love is the only thing that is like this. It is inexhaustible once you begin to express it. Imagine money was like that – imagine that the more you spent, the larger your bank balance would be. Everyone would be out on the streets buying and spending and giving it away! And this is how it should be with love. Give it away!

And not just to others. Give it to yourself **first**. Seek to love yourself limitlessly, exactly as you are. And the doorway to such self-love is self-acceptance. Make the choice to accept yourself, no matter what. Then seek to love what you do and do what you love. Then love those around you and surround yourself with those you love.

I have said that you are the light of awareness that shines from the Source through the lens of your consciousness. I have said that your consciousness is shaped by your thoughts, ideas, beliefs and choices. Well, if your choices are all about love, then your lens will grow very large and very clear indeed. It will let through vast amounts of light. You will see clearly and what you will see will be full of light.

And this is the essence of the process. The more love you allow to shine through you, the more you are creating with love. The more you create with love, the more you will experience love. And, of course, the more love you experience, the more you will have to give. And so a wonderful new cycle is begun in your life and it can continue cycling up like this until you are a radiant point of pure love. Like a sun, you shall shine brilliant love light upon all around you.

And when this is the state of your consciousness, then it will be impossible for you to experience anything but that which you are directly creating. It will be impossible to experience anything at all that is dark or negative because you, yourself, will be shining too much light for there to be any shadow anywhere around you.

And that is as simple as it is. In theory.

You might need a little more guidance to actually put this into practice.

Z: I certainly do. I mean – giving love in great abundance to all and sundry sounds like a great idea, but how do I actually do that? I mean, walking up to strangers and asking them if they want some love might not yield the desired result!

8: (laughs) Yes, I can certainly see that.

Your planetary culture has so badly messed up the concept of love that this might seem quite problematic indeed. (still laughing)

Z: And also, it is actually quite hard, I must admit, to feel loving feelings towards some people.

8: I can see that too. There is so much diversity of consciousness on your planet that you will actually find it very, very difficult to simply express love to **all** around you, **all** of the time. And that is why this is a process. You take it slowly. You do not start by demanding that the world should change and that the people around you should change. No. You look to yourself for change. And as you change yourself, so your world changes in response. In small increments, you open your heart. In small increments, your world becomes more loveable to you. The outcome eventually is that you become pure, radiant Love. And then your whole reality can do no other but reflect that back at you.

But it **is** a process. It takes time. And I can help you with it.

Z: Okay. So where do I start?

8: There are many ways to achieve the goal of further opening your heart. One that I can recommend is to begin by doing service. If you do service, then your heart opens and the energy of love begins to flow from you towards the being for whom you are doing the service. So this is how you begin. By doing service.

Z: Just for clarity, 8, may I ask what you mean when you say "service".

8: Ah good! You are quite right in asking me to define this word. It is quite often used, but also not often defined. Service is any action that you do to the benefit of another. It is generally thought of as "being of assistance", but I would say that there is much more to it than that. If you should cultivate, for example, the ability to really **listen** to another, without needing to interject your ideas and opinions, to only ask questions that might allow them to better tell **their** story, then you will be equipped to do great service. Many will feel profoundly helped for the fact that there was someone to whom they could really talk. Simple kindness can be service as well. Talking can be a service, if you are able to give the gift of your own wisdom without it also becoming a burden to others. Giving others the space to give what they have to give is a great service. If you can find ways of helping others to discover themselves and their gift, then you are probably doing one of the greatest services of all. What is not often realised is that the greatest services are often not particularly active. For example, assuming the best of someone or even **expecting** the best of them, such that you create a space for them to rise to the highest and best that they can be, is a wonderful service.

Here is a list of words that can be related to service. Go though them slowly, one by one, thinking upon each of them. With each word, think about someone who did this service to you and someone to whom you have done this service:

The first word is nurturing. Who has nurtured you? How? How did it feel? Who have you nurtured? How did that feel?

Now ask yourself the same questions about these words: healing, inspiring, supporting, enabling, empowering, sharing, energising, feeding, listening, helping, protecting, guiding...

Service is that which leads to the benefit of the other. And that "other" might be anyone. It might be your own body, a beloved friend, a total stranger, a community, an animal, a piece of land or the Earth as a whole.

Service is love in action.

And this is why it is appropriate that you do service to open your heart. Any service will do, but a small service will allow the flow of a small amount of energy and a big service will allow for the flow of a large amount of energy. The more energy you are permitting to flow, the more your heart is opened.

As you do service, bring your discernment to bear. See what part of this service feels "right for you" to do. And what part does not feel right. Give some thought (and open yourself to inspiration) to see if there is not another service that you can do that is a greater gift-giving for you. That is to say; is there not another service that you would feel greater joy in giving and that would be even more beneficial to life?

At some point on this journey of giving service you will begin to discover that you are not so much doing for the other, as you are doing it for yourself. Or perhaps doing it simply because it is the very "rightest" thing you can do. Doing it because this is what flows from your heart.

When you cease to feel like you are "doing service" and more like you are simply expressing your heart's gift, then you are in a very open-hearted state indeed. Then, in all likelihood, you are giving your great gift.

If you find your great gift and begin to give it, then you will be permitting a vast amount of energy to flow. So that is, obviously, a good idea. If you are seeking to move yourself to a higher level of consciousness, then it would be a good idea to discover your great gift and to give it.

So, follow your heart to find and express your great gift. Constantly listening to your heart and constantly doing what it tells you will lead you forward. And doing that which brings the most love will move you forward. Your great gift is your heart song. Singing your heart song **is** giving your great gift. These two things are the same thing. And your heart song is what your heart sings to you when it inspires you to find your way back to oneness.

So... you start by opening your heart. You always start there. And the easiest, quickest and surest way to open your heart is to do an act of pure service. Then see how that feels. That "seeing how it feels" is your opportunity to listen to your heart. It will talk to you in feelings. It will tell you, "more of this and less of that". Assuredly not everyone is well-suited to all types of service! Do an act of service and see what your heart has to say about it. What aspect of this doing did you enjoy? What aspect did you not enjoy? Where is there a service that you can do that brings you more joy and less displeasure? Follow your greatest joy to a place where you are giving your greatest gift and are residing only in a state of bliss. It will seem as if you are doing that which you were **made** to do. It will seem to you as if you are uniquely, perfectly suited to this task; as if everything you had ever done up to this point was all just training for this task. It will feel like your truest, greatest purpose. It will give you an amazing feeling of wonderful "rightness" to fulfil this service. And, by doing this task, you will be creating and catalysing love in the world around you. You will cause a return to oneness for yourself and inspire it in others around you. And you will be a part of the creation of heaven on Earth. You will be making your life sacred and thereby making your world sacred. You will change others around you for the better – not by demanding of them that they must change – no, by changing yourself and by giving your gift.

But it all starts with giving service. Give your great gift if you can. If you cannot, then give the greatest service you are able. And if you cannot give great service, then give many small services. Give service.

It is very important, however, that you realise that you are not supposed to give all gifts. You are not supposed to be the font of all love in the whole world. You are not supposed to serve every need that the world presents to you. You are only supposed to give the gift that you are best suited to giving. If you give gifts that you are **not** best suited to giving, then you do two things:

Firstly, you are squandering the energy available to you on lesser expressions. I could put it another way and say that you are wasting your time and resources doing something that you are not well suited to doing.

Secondly, you are doing someone else's job, which is actually doing them a disservice. You see, there is someone out there who is ideally suited to doing this job. Not only are you **not** doing what you are best suited to do, but you are also getting in the way of this other being doing what they **are** best suited to do.

And this is a very important understanding. You are not alone. You are not the only giver of gifts. You are a vital and irreplaceable part in the infinite dance of life, and it's not a one-man show! And the flow of energy should also not be a one-way stream! I have called it the energy cycle of love and the word cycle implies a rotation; a giving **and** a receiving.

The ego being believes that it is separate and alone. Individual. But the heart-centred creator being realises it is ONE with all other beings, everywhere. The heart-centred creator being realises that it exists only with, and through, other beings... only as a part of the great oneness.

So you cannot give your gift without having others give their gifts to you too. There must be "flow". If there is no flow, then there is no energy cycle. When it is static, it is lifeless. You cannot hoard love – it must pass though you. So you must give this energy away to others. The more you give, the more you open yourself to receive. But you **must** also be willing to receive! If you do not, you create a blockage. Blockages are the root cause of harm to the psyche, which results in emotional, spiritual and physical illnesses. So be willing to give first, but then also be willing to receive in equal measure in return.

And when you receive, make sure you honour both the gift and the giver. Be gracious. Say, "*Thank you.*" Give them something back. Keep the energy moving. Keep it alive. Keep it "alove". (he smiles). Let it flow.

And pass it on too! If you have received something that you have found to be of value, then find a way to give that same gift to another. This too keeps it alive. This too opens your heart. This too tells you something about your own great gift.

And this is the way the currency of the new Earth will flow: each being will find and express their ever-unfolding great gift. And because each being is unique, so too will their great gift be unique. There will never be "too much" of that which you will provide, because your expression will be unique. And anything and everything that you need, but are unable to provide for yourself; you will find some other being who desires to offer this as their great gift.

And that is the new economy. Not a single soul is asking, "*But what is in it for me?*" Not a single soul has need or want. All have abundance. And no one is trying to greedily grab more than they want or need because no one fears not having. There is always abundance because everyone knows that they are ONE.

And as you engage more and more with the energy cycle of love and less and less with the negative energies, so your tomorrows will become brighter and brighter. And then you will find yourself doing ever greater and greater service. Eventually you will only be creating with the light. You will find no more blockages in your heart. You will realise that you **are** the light.

Z: But what about things like money, 8? You say love is the new currency and that sounds fantastic. But how do I pay for a loaf of bread at the shop with love? If I offer the cashier a big wet kiss, I don't think that'll do. And in the real world people need at least the basic stuff like a roof over their heads, a meal on the table and so on. This takes money. And if I don't have money, then I might very soon find myself without a roof over my head or food on my table. So what about that?

8: So you think you need money?

You do not.

Money is, at best, bits of paper with printing on it and, at worst, numbers on a computer somewhere. You can do little with those bits of paper and even less with the computer numbers. These things are, in and of themselves, useless. But because people have agreed to it, they are a vehicle to exchange their energy and so you suddenly think that the vehicle is important.

But you are once again falling for the illusion that has been presented to you. You believe you need money. But you don't. You want food and shelter and clothing and so forth. And there are many ways to procure these things. Money is one way, yes. It is the way that the system encourages you to use because, when you **do** use money, you make others richer. Every time a cent changes hands, some unseen beings get a cut. It is inevitable and unavoidable. You use their system – they get their share!

But there are many, many other ways to do things. And if you are a creator being, then you will have no difficulty creating everything that you need. You will always have abundance. So the question really is not about money. It is whether you are a victim or a creator.

Z: (big sigh). 8, I don't know what to say.

I say that I am a creator. And I mostly believe that I am. I want to believe that I am. I think I am moving towards believing that I am. But... something like this comes along and it shows me that I am right back at square one and I don't believe that I am a creator after all. What to do?

8: (he smiles more kindly) I told you, did I not, that you would have to be patient with yourself? Well, here is where the patience comes in. You **are** still creating with fear. Your reality shows you this. There is no surprise here and this is exactly the way it should look, given where you are at in your progression. But now it is time for you to take an active hand in changing this. Now it is time to create that you are a creator. Now it is time for you to choose what energy you will be using in your creations.

So lighten up on yourself. Allow that you are still using money and that you still believe you need this external form of energy exchange in your life. Allow that you still fear being without money. That is, quite simply, where you are at, right now. It's okay. Let yourself off the hook. Let it be. Do what you think you need to do to make some money. But don't focus all your attention on this. Make sure you focus **more** of your attention on doing service and giving your gift – as I have described above. Give yourself grace and allow yourself to change as fast as you can without causing yourself distress. So, take care of this money business while you think you need it, and then get on with creating yourself anew as a creator being of pure Love.

Can you do that?

Z: Yes. Of course I can. And I will.

8: Good. Because then the energy cycle of love will begin to flow. And then you will begin to discover the magnificence and beauty of the fact that you are not alone. You are not the only gift giver. There are others around you who are finding their way to their own great gift and, as they discover it, so they too are giving it. And, right here in your previous question to me, you have expressed a need. You have said that you don't know how to create energy exchange without money. Right? Well, what if I told you that there are others who do! There are other planetary realities where beings have created whole civilisations of glorious abundance and they have engaged in energy exchanges of wonderful complexity, without ever even having **heard** of money. If you told them about your money system here on planet Earth, they would be mystified that anyone would want to use such a life-negative thing. So, the knowledge of how to build these life-positive exchange systems is out there. And not only is it "out there", but it is also available to you right here on planet Earth. Just as you are finding your way to your great gift through the writing of *The Ascension Papers*, so there are others who are busy giving their great gift by working out how to bring those life-positive exchange systems to your planetary consciousness. Usually these would be beings who have had incarnational experiences in these other realms where these life-positive systems of exchange are used. These beings would, by virtue of their past-life experiences and their training and experience in this life, be perfectly suited to working out systems and economies. But they would be beings of love. They would be seeking to give their gift, just as you are. They would be of unity-consciousness, just as you are. And the systems they will devise will empower and enrich all, not leach and steal from all, as the current system does.

So give your gift. Give it with great abundance. Give it to all who wish it. Give it until you realise that you have a greater gift yet to give. Then give **that**! Move always towards a greater version of yourself, giving an ever-greater gift of Love.

Z: So, 8, would you not say that perhaps *The Ascension Papers* is my great gift?

8: Is this the thing that you can find to do that causes the most Love?

Z: Um... yes, I think it is. I am engaged in a process of transmuting all that was painful and fearful in my own consciousness into something that is beautiful and love-filled. Writing *The Ascension Papers* **is** that process. It is the record of my own change, but also the means of that transformation. I guess I am, from my own perspective, retelling the story of what is, in a way that is full of Love, in a way that releases fear. I am retelling the story in a way that is congruent with all being ONE. Yes, I would say that *The Ascension Papers* is the greatest love story I could conceive of. And this plot mechanism of me being the one who "doesn't know" and asks the questions, and you and J-D being the ones who "do know" and who answer the questions, and the readers being the ones who read the words on the page... well... I slowly begin to realise that this too is just a fabrication, isn't it? We are the same being telling ourselves this story. We are ONE. We told ourselves many different tales of separation previously and now we are telling ourselves a tale of unity that causes those tales of separation to make sense in a new and wondrous way.

(smiles) I guess I got carried away with the answer to your question. The answer is yes, I **do** think that this is the thing I can do that causes the most love.

8: Do you feel, when you are doing this, that this is what you were born to do? That this is the thing you are best suited to be doing? That there is unlikely to be someone else who is better suited to doing this?

Z: Yes I do! I mean there are other people who are better suited to telling the stories they are telling and, thank God for them! I wouldn't want to live in a world without all the other wonderful heart-centred, spirit-filled, love-inspired books that are out there. But this story is uniquely mine to tell. Being the Zingdad who asks the questions and then being the vehicle though which these answers arrive, is my unique gift and privilege. No one else could do exactly this.

8: Well then, you have answered your own question. For so long as this is true, then *The Ascension Papers* is your great gift. In due course, you will find far greater gifts to give. But this is it, for you, for now.

How do you like it?

Z: I love it! I really do.

8: And how do you find your life has changed as a result of your giving this gift?

Z: (laughs) Oh wow! Radically. Every part of my life has changed. And every single change has been for the better. Miraculously and unbelievably so.

Oh – I begin to see what you are saying! Yes, I see it... following my heart is a process. And the life that I live and the world around me **is** changing. But, it is a process.

8: How much love is there in your life now, compared with, say, five year ago?

Z: I can't even compare. What I had then was deep poverty compared to now. Which is strange because then I was earning a fat income and now I'm not. But my life then was just sad compared to now. My life now is... the only word I can think of is, blessed. Full of light and happiness. Every single thing I do, from when I awake in the morning to when I go to bed at night, is congruent with my soul and with who I really am. I never feel pushed to do anything that I feel wrong about. The world around me is beautiful. And, amazingly, I only ever seem to deal with people who are kind and helpful. It's strange, but it's true. Everyone I meet is just wonderful. I hadn't really thought about that until now.

8: There you are. And you have only just begun the journey. And it will be the same for all who engage on such a journey. Open your heart and give your gift, and the world will change for you. It will take time, because you will take time to change. But it **will** unfold for you like a flower that slowly opens. As you open your heart, as you release your blockages, as you allow the Love to flow though you, as you give your gift, so your world will be your mirror. So it will shine Love back at you, so it will give gifts back to you, so it will show its open and abundant heart to you. The world is nothing more and nothing less than a mirror for your soul. You will only ever see shining back at you that which you really are. So shine your light of love. You will need patience and commitment. But the rewards will amaze you.

Give.

...and...

Receive.

Just as "breathe out" and "breathe in" are the cycle of breath, so are "give" and "receive" the cycle of love.

The gift that you are giving is a wonderful, delightful surprise to many. You know this. Many have expressed to you how they found themselves deeply touched by what you are doing. They find light and joy and truth here. It heals them and transforms them. They find that they can tell themselves a new story, for the fact that you are telling yours. You know this. They tell you it is so. So your gift is a good one. Now, can you find in yourself a willingness to receive also? Are you willing to unblock the blockage and receive in like measure to your gift? There are those who have gifts to give that you need to receive. They are perfectly suited to the giving of **their** gift and it is to the greatest service of love that they do. It is their great gift to give.

Are you willing to receive?

Z: I am, 8. I have had issues with receiving, I know. But now I understand it differently. I am now willing to receive. I am willing to engage directly with the energy cycle of Love.

8: Wonderful, my beloved friend!

In that case, I can move on to the next step. The first step was removing the blockages to love, the second step was engaging in the **do**ing of love. The third step is, **be**ing love.

3.3 BE LOVE

I trust that you are now ready to accept that oneness is your truest state and that love is your truest expression. I have made it clear to you that it is only as a result of a lot of hard work that you have been able to obtain for yourself this illusion of separation that is the duality experience. And it is only by looking deeply into life's shadows and creating with what you found there, that you have been able to experience your life as being full of fear, sadness, pain and confusion. And the fact that you can see this to be so is evidence that you are now seeing through that illusion. Seeing through an illusion is the step that comes right before releasing that very illusion. So this is good news.

The path forward involves you first releasing the negative energies, as detailed above in our discussion about energy blockages. Then you should begin to create ever more with the light energy of love. More light and less darkness and shadow is the process here. In due course, the whole negative-emotion experience will be but a memory. It is within you now, so you shall always have the right to create with these negative emotions if you choose, but I am saying you shall in due course release your belief that you **must** create with them. These illusions that you could be hurt or killed, that someone could take from you what is yours, that you could go without and be left needing and wanting and that you do not get what you create, will become very obvious for what they are... illusions. You will stand up in your own light and own your creations. And none shall be able to take from you without your explicit permission.

And, as you engage with this process, so something else will happen. Service and the giving of your great gift is, you see, the **do**ing of love. It is therefore an ego function. But it is what I would call right-doing because it is the doing that aligns you with your greatest good. It aligns your ego with your heart. And when you are truly perfectly aligned with your highest nature, then you **are** your highest nature. Then **you** are your inner-self, walking here on Earth.

Do you follow?

Because this is a very important point.

When you are in every way thinking, acting and being like your God-Self, then you will **be** your God-Self.

You see, it is only through constant hard and painful labour that you are able to maintain your separation from who and what you truly are. If you cease doing all this objectionable work then you will, and must, return to what is true and right – what is natural and normal.

The elasticity of the Infinite Elastic Ball will pull you homewards.

You will feel the movement in your being and it will feel **blissful**.

It won't happen all in one go, though. That would be the "direct route" that I spoke of previously. You are not choosing that. You are choosing the slower "scenic route". So, for you, it will happen in a series of steps. As you slowly learn to cease all the "pushing away" that has become habitual second nature to you – as the Infinite Elastic Ball pulls you back home another step – you will feel your consciousness changing. You will have transformative, blissful experiences and you will come to new ideas about yourself, your life, your goals, who you are, what you wish to do. And your world will change. In each of these steps, in a moment, everything will become more beautiful and life-filled. Everything will become illuminated. Full of light. And the light, of course, will actually be shining out from your own heart. It will be the light of love that shines from you that will illuminate the world for you!

And this will happen to everyone who chooses to follow their heart, to engage with the cycle of love, to give their gift – to all such beings it is a guaranteed certainty that you will have a series of such moments when you shall, quite simply, **be** love. With each step this shall be ever more true. And in those moments you will **see** ever more clearly. You will see with your heart what it is that you are moving towards. And because you have free will always, you will have the right to move towards it faster or to reject it.

None, it must be said, have ever rejected it!

But you will have the choice. And so, if this has happened to you, if you have experienced the light of the divine, then you now know what it was. And if you have not? Then you will know what it is when you do!

Z: And this is what happened to me during my Mountain Experience, 8?

8: Yes it was. That is when you felt your whole energy shift from one level of consciousness to another. You moved your self-identification from the separate self to the connected self. To put it another way, you shifted your centre from ego to heart. And that was your first Singularity Event.

You had another with your day of silence. On that day you purposefully stilled yourself so that you could engage the next shift in your consciousness. You became aware of your own true nature and that this was love. You became *consciously aware* of your own essential oneness with all.

Z: Right. So my Day of Silence was my second Singularity Event?

8: Well... did you or did you not have an experience in which you felt your consciousness shift? Did you not, in a moment, attain a new level of awareness? Did you not suddenly understand yourself to be more "one with the oneness"?

Z: Yes. That is all true. But my day of silence was quite unlike the mountain experience in so many ways.

8: This is good to note. Because otherwise your readers might be under the impression that *their* Singularity Events will have to be out in nature, or whilst exercising, or in some other way similar to your Mountain Experience.

Your Singularity Events will be utterly personal to you and they will not be about your external circumstances; they will be about the shift in consciousness that goes on within you. You will feel the change in your soul. What you will see, feel, know or experience will simply be whatever accompanies your inner leap of consciousness.

You see, each must experience these blissful moments first-hand. You cannot change the direction of your soul with thoughts and ideas. You change it with the deep knowing that comes from *feeling* your connection to the oneness.

Earlier in this chapter, I said the following to you:

*"Love cannot be understood, as it is much greater than the mind that would seek to understand it. Love can only be experienced. And once you have had even a small taste of true limitless, unconditional love, then you will be forever altered. Your life's quest will be to return to that state of Love. In that moment, you will know that there can be nothing even remotely as important to you as existing in that state of union with the divine that **is** love."*

And it is so. This is the one great saving grace. If you stop working so hard to be Forget, then you will have a series of awakenings. You will realise that Remember is right there inside your heart. As near as your own heartbeat. And speaking to you all the time. Constantly calling you to wake up. Constantly telling you about who you really are. Ever present, ever loving, gently reminding. All you have to do is to stop trying so hard to be Forget.

Z: And then we will have such wonderful, amazing blissful experiences?

8: Yes. And as you continue to engage with the process of being love, so you will have more. Each one is a step-up though the levels of consciousness. With each one, your psyche is moving up though one of the dimensional levels. You are spiritually ascending. And this will happen to you exactly three times as you become ready to leave duality behind.

Z: Three times? Why three times? Why not less? Why not more?

8: You will understand this properly when we have that much anticipated conversation about spiritual densities. But briefly then: the world you are living in right now exists at the third density. In order to be born into that world, you needed to be of 3rd density consciousness. With each Singularity Event, you step "up" one density and move closer to being permanently of unity consciousness. If you have had one such experience, then you are of 4th density consciousness, even though you still reside in a 3rd density world and inhabit a 3rd density body. After three Singularity Events, you reach the 6th density of consciousness, then you attain the lowest level of unity consciousness. That is to say, at the 6th density of consciousness you will still feel that there is value in holding the illusion of separation, but you know absolutely that it **is** an illusion. So you will be a unity conscious being, irrespective of the level of consciousness of those around you and of the world you inhabit.

But you are just one of many beings who are engaged on this journey home. As you each transform yourselves, so you transform your world. So the planet illuminates. It rises to the light. You are the agents of transformation. You are the saviours of yourselves. You are the ones you have been waiting for.

Z: Whoa, 8! That's a whole lot of amazing in one short paragraph! Can I unpack it slowly?

You are saying that by us engaging in our journeys of following our hearts and being love, so we are changing the world. Literally?

8: Well? Is this not your experience?

You are changed and so your perspective is changed. How you look at the world is changed. How you feel about what you perceive about you is changed. And you choose new experiences and different interactions. And then you express a different energy to the world. What you put out changes. And so what you get back changes. And then you begin to find your gift which impacts the world and causes changes. On and on I could go. In small ways and big, in subtle ways and profound... when you change, your world changes. And most assuredly, yes, a Singularity Event is a moment of life-alteration. It is the moment when all of your choices for change become realised.

Is this not true for you?

Were these two occasions not the culmination of many, many choices for you?

And with both of these events did you not feel your world change?

Did you not experience the light entering your life and lifting you up to a higher perspective?

Did you not feel yourself moving closer to your true nature?

Did you not see your path with greater clarity?

Z: Yes. All of that is true.

8: But it did not force or coerce or take your right to choose from you.

Z: No it didn't. Which is interesting because the mistake I made was to think that the Singularity Event would be somehow...

8: You expected it to be something from "outside of you" that would somehow come and save you from yourself. You thought that the Unity-Conscious Moment would be a light that would shine from outside of your being that would fix everything. This is what you wanted and expected and you were not ready to know that it will never be so. You cannot be saved by an outside agency, without at the same time being a victim. Without at the same time having your right to choose and create for yourself taken from you. But this cannot happen. No light-being or Christ light or God or angel or whatever you wish to think of, **could** take from you your right to create for yourself, if that being is itself of unity consciousness. What you do to another you do to yourself also, remember? And if some external being declared by its actions that you are broken and in need of rescuing, then that being would create itself thus also. If that other being removed from you your absolute right to create your own reality as you desire, then it would immediately also take that right from itself and it would cease to be a creator being. It would fall to low consciousness. And then it would no longer be able to save you.

You cannot be saved from outside of yourself.

It is as simple as that.

It cannot happen.

But there is **always** the one great saving grace. It is the fact that the light of the ONE shines always from within you. If you are willing to let it shine, then you suddenly see the grand cosmic joke: you were never lost! You never were anything other than a creator being of magnificent power creating your whole reality. You were always immortal. You were always indestructible. There never was anything to fear.

So yes. Those were the first two of the three unity-conscious moments that you'll experience while in duality. Now you know. Now you can go about letting go of the remaining vestiges of separation that you are still creating for yourself and be prepared... the next one will still happen. And then you will be of unity consciousness. Then this body of work will have served its purpose. And then a whole other level of creation will begin.

Z: So I am now of 5th density consciousness? What does that mean?

8: For almost all of this book you have repeatedly been promised a chapter dealing with, "Space, Time, Densities and Dimensions". We have touched on some of the salient points, as we have proceeded, but now it is time for you to get the whole picture. So that is what we shall do in the next chapter.

Z: Excellent!

And that means this chapter is done?

8: No. This chapter is actually only about to begin. It begins when all these words and ideas and mental constructs about Love stop. It begins when you stop talking about Love and start experiencing it. So take what we have said about love to heart.

Go now.

Go **be** love.

* * * * *

CLOSING THOUGHTS

My dear reader,

As you have read, this book has been many years in the writing to get to this 3rd edition (and I very much do believe this to be the final and definitive edition). Across these three versions, this book has been the very crucible of my soul, in which I have transformed my own victim-consciousness into creator-consciousness... where I turned fear into love. It is, therefore, my very greatest joy to have had the privilege of your time and attention as you have travelled this journey with me through the pages that now lie behind us. Your journey is your responsibility, of course, but I cannot help but hope that what you have read here has been as spiritually transformative and growthful for you as it was for me. If you give a gift, I suppose, you do wish for that gift to be loved and enjoyed as much as possible by the recipient, not so?

WHAT'S NEXT?

As you have also discovered, this journey doesn't end at the ending of this book! At the time of writing, I have completed almost all of the chapters of book 2 of *The Ascension Papers* and, as is my custom, made them available to read-as-I-write, for free on my website. I have gathered a great deal of the material for book 3 but that is not yet in a format that I can make available. The first part of *Dreamer Awake!* (which is, in a very real sense, the final part of *The Ascension Papers*) has been published and in the upcoming months I will be producing the following parts of that work. This is where I currently am. What will be the state of play as you read this, I wonder? Perhaps all of these things will already have been published? Perhaps many years ago already! Whatever the case, if you wish to journey onwards with me, then I will be delighted to share these continuing spiritual adventures with you. If you can believe it, the ride becomes even more amazing as we go!

Stay Connected!

If you'd like to stay in touch with me, then I have a number of vehicles for exactly this purpose. The first (and the one I most prefer) would be for you to sign up for my monthly newsletter here: zingdad.com/register. There's no downside to this and loads of upside. It's free, I don't overload your in-box, I am very respectful of your privacy and won't ever share your contact details with anyone else and, if you ever decide to unsubscribe, that's just one click away. With this newsletter I can let you know when I make new chapters (or even new books!) available and also inform you when I have new blog posts up or any other such news to share. And I can (and very often do) offer my newsletter members special discounts on my offerings. I think of my newsletter members as my extended spiritual family here on Earth!

You can also find me on various social media websites where I like to regularly share quotes from my books or new insights and whatever other news I have. But times change and these kinds of social media tools will come and go. So, when in doubt, please find me on my website, zingdad.com.

Gift Back

As you have just read, 8 makes it very clear that we should all get into the energy cycle of love. Give and receive. Whilst this "receiving" thing has been quite hard for me to come to terms with, since writing the above chapter, I have learned a great deal more about this subject. I have been taught that we should offer our gifts with an open heart and then give others the opportunity to give back by making clear what it is that we would like, want or need. And then they can decide how they wish to respond (if at all).

So, here it is!

If you have enjoyed this book and found it useful, then there are a number of ways in which you can express your gratitude back to me (and to J-D and 8).

The first is to help me to share this book as far and as wide as possible. This book is available for free in all the major e-book formats on my website (and elsewhere on the web). You would be assisting me and also helping the transition of the planetary consciousness if you told as many people as possible about the free e-book. Perhaps even download it from my website and forward it on. Since it is free, you can take a risk: send it on to anyone who might (even just the slightest possibility maybe) be interested in it. Share it. Give it away. Get it out there. As per the e-book licence notes, you are free to share it with anyone and everyone in any way you like. Email it to all of your contacts, re-host it on your website, put it on a file-sharing service... whatever you like. There are only two provisos: you may not, in any way, alter the e-book content or its digital file and you may not offer it for sale or as any part of anything that you are selling. It must be offered exactly as I offer it and it must be for free. Other than that: **give it away!**

If you help me to distribute the e-book in this manner, then that will already be a huge "thank you" for me!

If you'd like to say a more personal "thank you" then there are certainly some tangible ways in which you can do so.

Since the paperback version you are holding in your hand was sold at a small premium, this has already provided me with a small profit. That, in and of itself, is already a thank you.

Secondly, there are numerous other products and services that I offer; from the follow-up books to *The Ascension Papers* to guided meditation recordings and spiritual healing modalities. You'll find all of these on my website at zingdad.com. Offering these, and receiving payment in return, is the way in which I am able to afford to continue to live upon planet Earth. Your patronage and support will, therefore, not only be greatly appreciated but you will assuredly gain back (in terms of healing or books or whatever) far more than you will have spent. The energy cycle of love, indeed!

And finally, it is always wonderful to hear from those whose lives have been touched by my work. If you'd like to leave a short review of your experiences with this book on my website (or wherever you downloaded it from) then that that would be wonderful! And if you'd like to pen a few words to me personally, you are very welcome to do so via the contact form on my website, here: zingdad.com/contact-zingdad. I'd love to hear from you!

REALLY, REALLY CLOSING THOUGHTS. REALLY!

Can you imagine living in a world in which everyone you ever met was of Unity Consciousness? Can you imagine what a wonderful paradise it would be if everyone treated each other as self. If everyone was as loving, kind, trustworthy, giving and forgiving as they would want others to be towards them?

Let's make a pact to create that world. Let's create that world by being those people. Let's begin right now, with you and I.

Yes?

Yes!

With so much love,

Zingdad

Arn "Zingdad" Allingham
Knysna, South Africa
July 2014

* * * * *

CPSIA information can be obtained
at www.ICGtesting.com
Printed in the USA
LVHW080330070921
697174LV00003B/3